THE MAFIA'S BROKEN VOWS

An Off-Limits Dark Mafia Romance

Judy Hale

Copyright © 2024 by Judy Hale

All rights reserved.

No portion of this book may be reproduced, distributed, or transmitted in any form or by any means including photocopying, recording, copy-pasting, screenshots, or other electronic or mechanical methods without prior written permission of the copyright owner listed above, except in brief quotations embodied in critical reviews and certain other non-commercial uses as permitted by copyright law.

This is a work of fiction. Any resemblance to specific persons, brands, and actual events is either purely coincidental or a product of the author's vivid imagination.

CONTENTS

Trigger Warnings   VI
Playlist   VII
    VIII
Chapter One   1
Chapter Two   17
Chapter Three   28
Chapter Four   43
Chapter Five   57
Chapter Six   72
Chapter Seven   81
Chapter Eight   95
Chapter Nine   107
Chapter Ten   116
Chapter Eleven   131

Chapter Twelve	145
Chapter Thirteen	154
Chapter Fourteen	168
Chapter Fifteen	183
Chapter Sixteen	189
Chapter Seventeen	205
Chapter Eighteen	215
Chapter Nineteen	221
Chapter Twenty	224
Chapter Twenty-One	227
Chapter Twenty-Two	236
Chapter Twenty-Three	248
Chapter Twenty-Four	256
Chapter Twenty-Five	269
Chapter Twenty-Six	280
Chapter Twenty-Seven	289
Chapter Twenty-Eight	297
Chapter Twenty-Nine	308
Chapter Thirty	317
Chapter Thirty-One	328
Chapter Thirty-Two	339
Chapter Thirty-Three	347
Chapter Thirty-Four	360
Chapter Thirty-Five	370

Chapter Thirty-Six	382
Chapter Thirty-Seven	396
Chapter Thirty-Eight	411
Chapter Thirty-Nine	419
Chapter Forty	431
Chapter Forty-One	439
Chapter Forty-Two	448
Chapter Forty-Three	462
Chapter Forty-Four	468
Chapter Forty-Five	477
Chapter Forty-Six	487
Chapter Forty-Seven	503
Chapter Forty-Eight	516
Chapter Forty-Nine	528
Chapter Fifty	539
Epilogue	555
Also by Judy Hale	576
Chapter	578

TRIGGER WARNINGS

While telling this story is aimed at creating an immersive reading experience, it also involves exploring intense themes and situations.

There are elements in this story that some readers may find distressing or triggering.

To ensure you can make an informed decision about reading this book, I've prepared a detailed list of potential triggers Here

PLAYLIST

Back To Black—Amy Winehouse

Deja Vu—Lucidious
Bad Things—mgk, Camila Cabello
Gangsta's Paradise—Coolio, L.V.
Killer—Valerie Broussard

Trouble—Iggy Azalea, Jennifer Hudson
Power Rangers—Teni

Pillowtalk—Zayn

To the queens who dance in the dark, and the mortals who lead them.

CHAPTER ONE

Adele

TWO YEARS AGO

"So, Addy, what do you think of Chicago?" My boyfriend's deep, almost musical baritone washes over me.

Dante gestures at the city skyline visible through the restaurant's floor-to-ceiling windows, then rakes his fingers through his jaw-length hair—a simple yet distractingly sexy move.

A knot tightens in my belly as I follow Dante's gaze to the bustling city beyond the plate glass. Something about Chicago calls to me like a siren song, as if offering secrets I was born to uncover.

Which makes absolutely no sense because I've never been here before. Before today, I'd never left Boston.

Chalking the strange feeling up to my persistent tendency to wax poetic, I say instead, "It's a little . . . overwhelming."

The glint in his steel-gray eyes sharpens as if he knows exactly what I mean. I'm not just talking about the city. Dante overwhelms me sometimes. Most of the time, if I'm being completely honest.

We've been dating for three months, mostly over the phone, because I wasn't prepared to leave my comfort zone, and Dante doesn't like to come to Boston. Except for the few times he'd suddenly appear outside my dorm, waiting for me in his tinted black Escalade.

And then last week, he suggested I spend the weekend with him.

I've always sensed there's more to Dante than meets the eye. More than just being a hot, twenty-nine-year-old billionaire. It's in the shadows shifting in his gray eyes, a familiar darkness under his polished exterior—a void that echoes my own hidden depths.

And something else. Restraint.

Dante speaks to me and touches me with exaggerated gentleness—as if afraid I might run if he unleashed the full force of his passion on me. So, when he practically ordered me to come to Chicago, I thought I glimpsed the real Dante Vitelli. Like a moth to flame, I was hooked. It didn't matter that I'd never been on a plane or left Boston. I had to come.

And so, without telling my dad or my best friend and roommate Kira, I packed a bag and hopped on Dante's jet.

"But just remember that you're always in charge." Dante's voice brings me back to the present.

I release a nervous chuckle. "Somehow, that makes me feel even less in charge, Dante."

His grin reveals a flash of white teeth and deep grooves in his cheeks. "Do you trust me though?" He reaches for my hand, turns my palm up, and starts to trace along the outer edge with his index finger. Instantly, my nerves settle, replaced by a more primal feeling.

I may not know Dante as much as I would like, but I trust him to keep me safe and look out for me, so I nod. "I trust you."

Heat flares in his eyes. Something about those three words pleases him immensely. His gaze slowly dips to my cleavage, and I suppress a smile of feminine triumph. But I know what is driving him crazy is not so much the creamy orbs swelling over the neckline of my dress.

It's the thin red scar running between my breasts, the top just visible in my dress.

"How's your work going? You haven't posted much recently," Dante deliberately changes the subject.

By "work," he's not asking about my upcoming Forensics finals or dissertation. He's referring to my weekly blog. A passion project where I dig into unsolved murders from the 1900s and brainstorm on how today's detectives would solve them. Most people find my hobby weird or even slightly disturbing, but not Dante. He gets it.

Then again, Dante isn't like most people.

I pick up my glass of red wine, savoring the burst of flavor on my tongue. "It's going slow. I have more material than I know what to do with, but it's been so hard with college deadlines. Hopefully, I'll post something in the coming week." I pause, feeling a little self-conscious. "I still can't believe you read my blog, Dante."

"Oh, we're avid followers," comes his cryptic reply.

"Who's we?"

"My friends. You'll get to meet them tomorrow. My brother too."

"I will?" A thrill of excitement shoots through me at the thought of meeting his friends and getting to unravel more of the enigma that he is.

Dante's smile turns almost predatory. He traces his index finger around the hair tie on my wrist—his hair tie. The arousal that had been simmering under my skin since we arrived blooms again, leaving a rosy flush on my skin, and I feel my nipples grow tight.

Has it only been an hour since he had me screaming in pleasure in his lap? He'd sent a jet to get me and was waiting for me on the tarmac when I arrived. I felt his eyes on me the moment I appeared at the top of the aircraft steps and all the way to the black SUV idling on the tarmac.

As soon as my butt hit the cool leather of the passenger seat, Dante dragged me across the console.

I bite my lip, feeling myself growing slick again. It must be the long-distance thing. Although Dante makes me come every single night we speak on the phone, it's still nothing compared to seeing him in the flesh.

My reaction to Dante isn't something I fully understand. I wasn't even interested in dating until I met him. Now I can't seem to think straight when he speaks to me, much less touches me. And I can't get over his looks.

The restaurant's dim lighting bathes Dante in a warm, amber glow, accentuating the chiseled lines of his jaw. His light gray eyes smolder with an intensity that makes my breath catch every time. A thick five o'clock shadow adds a rugged edge to his features, contrasting with his enticing, full lips.

Earlier, his hair was neatly tied back, but now—thanks to my eager fingers—the inky locks fall freely, brushing against the crisp collar of his shirt.

Dante leans in, his voice a low, hypnotic rumble. "You're in for quite a weekend, Addy. You'll see and do things you've never done before." His lips curl into a provocative smile. "Starting now. Come here."

Before I can process his words, he tugs at my hand, and I'm once again on his lap.

"Wait," I whisper, my eyes widening as my heart starts to race. "What are you doing?"

In response, Dante pulls me flush against him, his large hands splaying possessively across my lower belly. I can't help but squirm as I feel the thick outline of his arousal pressing against my backside.

I steal a glance around the empty restaurant, a blush creeping up my neck. It's oddly quiet for a five-star Italian place in such a busy part of town.

Dante notices my nervousness and chuckles softly, his breath warm against my ear. "Don't worry, *bella*. It's just us tonight."

"But what about the staff?" I whisper, scanning the room. The *maître d'* who welcomed us and the waiters who served our main course have since vanished. I manage to suppress a moan as Dante suckles on the sensitive skin below my ear, but it escapes when his large palm strokes upward and cups my breast.

"I'm sure they're around somewhere," he murmurs against my skin. His thumb and index finger find my nipple, rolling it, then pinching it hard. I jerk and moan louder, helplessly grinding against him.

"Dante," I gasp, the sound both a plea and warning.

His hand leaves my breast, trailing higher until his fingers spear into my curly red hair—a nod to my Irish roots. He gathers the mass over one shoulder, fully baring my neck and jaw to his wicked mouth. Keeping his hand tangled in my hair, he takes complete control, dropping kisses from my exposed shoulder to the corner of my lips and back.

I'm panting, straining to meet his mouth, desperate to feel his breath, his lips, and the smooth glide of his tongue against mine. But his firm grip holds me steady as he continues his teasing.

He rasps against my skin. "I hope you're not too attached to this dress, because I plan to tear it off you."

A shiver of excitement runs down my spine, yet I can't help my smug smile. It's a simple white curve-hugging dress with a ruched bodice, off-the-shoulder sleeves, and a plunging neckline. I almost feel bad for the man. Almost.

I get why Dante reacted so strongly when he first saw me at the airstrip today, and his struggle since then to keep his eyes above my neckline; before now, he has never seen me in a dress. Even I don't remember the last time I wore a dress.

"I take it you hate it then?" I tease, my voice husky with desire.

"It's obscene. Downright revolting," Dante growls, his eyes darkening. His hand glides up my thigh, fingers teasing the hem of my dress before tracing tantalizing circles on the sensitive skin inside.

I giggle nervously. "I agree it's bad. You have my permission to rip it to shreds. When can we leave?" My breath hitches as his fingers inch dangerously close to my core.

"Leave?" Dante's lips curve into a wicked smile. "We're not leaving yet, *bella*. We're staying for dessert."

A gasp escapes me as he hooks his finger into the crotch of my panties, dragging the fabric away from my slick folds. "Dante," I whisper, "we'll get kicked out."

He chuckles darkly. "No, we won't. But I'll stop if you want me to."

Stop? Hell no. I shake my head, too aroused and intrigued to even consider it.

"In that case . . ." He adjusts the tablecloth, ensuring we're completely covered. "Be quiet. Keep a straight face." He disentangles his other hand from my hair and links it with mine. "Squeeze my hand if you need to, but don't make a sound, *capisci?*"

Before I can respond, he slides a long, thick finger inside me. I bite back a groan, my head falling back against his shoulder. Staying quiet is going to be a monumental challenge.

"Shh, Addy," he whispers, his breath fanning against my neck. "Look, the waiter is heading our way to see if we want dessert." He adds a second finger, pumping faster, the heel of his hand sliding against my clit. "Be a good girl and tell him what we want."

My eyes fly open as a rush of my arousal coats Dante's hand. Rather than feeling horrified, the thought of doing something as decadent as ordering dessert while he touches me beneath the table sends a thrill through me.

I brace myself as the waiter approaches us, squeezing Dante's hand hard. My eyes threaten to roll back as Dante simultaneously hits sensitive spots, but I force my lids to remain open and my eyes focused, sinking my teeth into my bottom lip even as my thighs shake with an impending release.

Suddenly, the restaurant doors burst open with a resounding thud. Both Dante and the waiter freeze, and I want to scream in frustration at how close I was before realizing that we have company.

I whip my head toward the entrance to see two burly men stride in, their guttural conversation in Gaelic filling the previously quiet space.

They're dressed similarly to Dante—expensive suits sans ties, revealing tattooed chests adorned with gleaming silver necklaces. They move with an air of entitled ownership, one sporting a shock of blond hair, the other bald with a star tattoo etched on the side of his face.

Dante tenses around me, and a chill of foreboding slithers down my back as he slowly withdraws his fingers from me. I watch, still dazed with arousal, as he meticulously wipes his hand on a napkin. His lips brush my temple in a soft kiss, but his whisper carries an unfamiliar edge. "I'm truly sorry, baby." His voice is tight, laced with an emotion I can't quite decipher.

"Um. It's okay," I mumble, mildly confused.

Just moments ago, Dante was ready to bring me to climax in front of a waiter, and now two strangers who haven't even glanced our way have completely transformed him. I steal a puzzled glance at Dante, watching his playful demeanor evaporate like mist and replaced by a cold, calculating look I've never witnessed before.

Dante's eyes lock onto the waiter, giving him an imperceptible nod. The waiter instantly changes course and approaches the newcomers with a smile that doesn't quite reach his eyes.

The two Irishmen boldly saunter deeper into the room. I have a feeling they would have made a beeline for us if not for the waiter's interception.

Dante suddenly pulls a nearby chair close, and the legs scrape harshly against the marble floor. I jump at the sound, my nerves already on edge. With smooth, controlled movements, he transfers me onto the seat, then drops another quick kiss on my temple.

"You'll be fine, Addy, I promise," he murmurs absently, then leans back in his chair, picks up his wine glass, and takes a casual sip, as if he's settling in to watch some anticipated drama unfold. He does all this without sparing me a glance; if he had, he would have seen my eyes wide with confusion and growing alarm.

What is happening right now?

"Good evening, gentlemen," the waiter greets, his tone carefully neutral. "I'm afraid the restaurant is closed to the public tonight."

The blond man smirks, his gaze sweeping the near-empty restaurant. "Really? Ah, that's a bloody shame right there. We was also thinking of bringin' our sluts here tonight, y'see. But we'll have to come back another time, eh?"

Dante's hand tightens around his wine glass, his knuckles turning white with the force of his grip. I can almost hear the crystal straining under the pressure.

"Of course, sir," the waiter replies, though his voice wavers slightly. "If you'll follow me, I can arrange a reservation for you." He gestures toward the entrance, attempting to guide them, but the men continue to look around, blatantly ignoring us.

"It's an old-time classic isn't it? Thirsty Irish bitch panting after some Italian dog," the tattooed one spits in Gaelic, his voice a low, guttural rumble while his companion barks out a derisive laugh.

I flinch at the crude words, but what shocks me more is Dante's reaction. His eyes flash with unmistakable recognition, and a cold, predatory snarl curls his lips, transforming his handsome features into something dangerous and alien.

The men turn to follow the waiter, oblivious to the storm brewing in Dante.

My stomach churns with unease. How does Dante understand Gaelic? Before I can voice my question, Dante suddenly rises from his seat with a fluid grace that belies the tension simmering beneath the surface.

"You know, my woman and I were just leaving," he says icily in English, but he deliberately thickens his Italian accent. "Perhaps you'd like to take our place?"

The men's gazes dart between Dante and each other, their expressions hardening. They take a few steps closer, still conversing in guttural Gaelic. The atmosphere crackles with palpable animosity.

Without warning, Dante yanks my chair backward. He positions himself between me and the table, and a sinking feeling settles in my gut as I realize Dante fully intends to fight these burly men.

"Dante, please, don't!" I hiss, but he ignores me. His hand grips my shoulder, firm but not painful.

"Just stay behind me, Addy," he says curtly, his voice low and tight.

In a blur of motion, Dante overturns our table. The crash of shattering plates and glasses is deafening. My eyes widen in horror as a gun materializes in his hand. The other two men draw their weapons, and suddenly the air explodes with gunshots.

I scream as my body moves on autopilot, scrambling away, darting from under one table to the next. Finally, far enough from the chaos, I grab onto the polished wood of the table leg, eyes screwed shut as the acrid smell of gunpowder mingles with the rich aroma of Italian cuisine, creating a nauseating contrast that makes my stomach roil.

And then it's over. Blessed silence descends on the restaurant once more. I hazard a peek from my hiding place, my heart pounding so hard I can feel it in my throat. I see Dante standing in the middle of the chaos, his stance wide. He cracks his neck from side to side as if releasing pent-up tension.

The two Irish men lie sprawled on the floor, their bodies eerily still, dark blood pooling around their heads. Their eyes vacant, while neat holes decorate their foreheads and their chests.

My gaze flicks between the bodies and Dante. His expression is bland, almost bored—disappointment etched in the slight downturn of his mouth, as if the confrontation ended too soon for his liking.

I close my eyes and pinch myself hard, telling myself it can't be real. It's a grotesque replay of my childhood nightmare.

The ringing in my ears,

The acrid smell of gunpowder and blood—too much blood,

The musty scent of old books mingling with the stench of violence,

The dark figure looming behind the smoking gun,

My mother's screams . . .

When I open my eyes, nothing has changed. It's not a dream. This is reality. And the tall, broad-shouldered figure standing over the bodies, his dark hair falling around his hauntingly beautiful face is Dante.

My playful, intensely passionate boyfriend—is gone, replaced by this barely controlled, graceful predator.

The man I thought I knew for the past three months was an illusion. This is the real Dante Vitelli, the one I've caught glimpses of. A man capable of taking a life without batting an eye. He's a cold-blooded killer, and from the looks of it, he's very good at it.

I shove a fist in my mouth to stifle the sob threatening to escape, wishing desperately that I'd never agreed to come to Chicago.

Is this what he wanted to show me? Who he really is?

It must be my karma. When I'd promised my Dad I'd never leave Boston without telling him, I fully intended to keep the promise at the time.

But then Dante happened to me, and I found myself weaving an intricate web of lies: telling my Dad about a non-existent birthday party at school, and spinning Kira, my best friend, a tale about a special father-daughter getaway.

Guilt gnaws at me as I recall how I gleefully left my two favorite people in the world, cocooned in deception, while I boarded Dante's jet for what I thought would be a weekend of passion.

Wish they could see me now.

Outside, the muffled sounds of traffic and rhythmic flashes of headlights through the windows mock the mayhem within. The world beyond these walls remains oblivious to the fact that a significant part of my life is screeching to a halt.

This is so far from how I envisioned my twenty-first birthday dinner going.

"Baby?" Dante's unnervingly calm voice cuts through my panicked thoughts, freezing me in place. I shrink back into my hiding place, terrified of him.

"Addy," he calls, softer now. The moment he spots me under the table, he squats down to his haunches. A smile spreads across his face, those once-beloved grooves deepening in his cheeks. "There you are!"

I gape in disbelief. The man is smiling! After everything he just did!

"It's over, Addy," he says, as if soothing a frightened child.

Oh, he's right about one thing—it damn well is over. I just need to get the hell out of Chicago and never lay eyes on him again.

His gaze locks on something far away and suddenly he tenses up again. It's the same unnatural stillness that came over him just before he shot those men.

What now?

I follow his line of vision to a movement in the corner. It's one of the waiters, holding a wall phone to his ear. If I thought I was in a nightmare before, what happens next shatters any remaining illusion.

Dante tut-tuts, the sound incongruously casual. He straightens to his full height then raises his arm, and another shot cracks through the air.

The waiter's head snaps back comically as a flash of red blossoms from his ear. The phone receiver flies from his hand, shattering into pieces, its coiled wire swinging uselessly from the wall.

The man crumples to the ground, his agonized screams filling the room. He clutches his ear, blood seeping between his fingers. My disbelieving gaze swings back to Dante. Not only did he shoot a phone out of someone's hand from clear across the room, but his response is a nonchalant shrug.

My stomach lurches, bile rising in my throat. This can't be happening. But the metallic scent of blood tells me it's all too real.

"That was stupid, Rocco. And by the way, you're fired." Dante says flatly, as if dismissing an incompetent employee rather than a man he just shot.

A new chill settles in my spine. Dear Lord, does he own this place? Was that why he could rent it out at short notice? Boldly touch me in front of the staff? My cheeks burn with embarrassment at the memory of what we were doing before the Irishmen arrived. It almost feels like a lifetime ago.

Dante's eyes scan the room, finally settling on a thin man cowering a few tables away. "You over there, Johnny, is it?" he calls out.

The man raises his head, his face as pale as the tablecloths. *"S-sì, signore,"* he stammers.

"Go and help Rocco," Dante orders, balling up a napkin and tossing it across the room. "Pressure and ice."

Johnny scrambles to comply, fear etched into his features. Dante crouches down again, his demeanor shifting once more, becoming almost gentle.

"Baby, come on," he coaxes, extending a large palm toward me.

Oh, hell no.

I recoil in horror, staring at his hand as if it might transform into a venomous snake. "You—you just killed those men," I croak.

Dante's smile is almost indulgent. "Addy, you heard them yourself. They were clearly suicidal. I was merely a means to help them along the path they desperately needed to take."

I nod mechanically, as if he's making perfect sense. "Of course. I heard them." My mind latches onto a detail, eager for anything to make sense of this madness. "So . . . you speak Gaelic?"

He shrugs. "A little. In this line of work, I have to."

"The line of work being . . .?" The words barely escape my dry throat.

He says nothing, but I hear him loud and clear. I'm not sure if it's the muscle ticking in his jaw or the way his eyes quickly flicker to the dead men on the floor, but suddenly, I get it.

It's official. I'm in hell. And Dante is the devil.

CHAPTER TWO

Adele

PRESENT DAY

The elevator slides open with a soft ding, ushering me onto the Forensics Floor of the Boston DA's office. Flickering fluorescent lights cast a harsh glow on the empty corridor.

Outside, rain pelts heavily against the windows, transforming the cityscape into a gray, watery blur. I'd cycled to work this morning, so there was no avoiding the deluge.

I quickly shed my raincoat, hang it in the cloakroom, then undo my ponytail and shake out my thick red curls to dry. Then I start heading down the corridor and toward the glass double doors.

Halfway through, my sneakers slip on a wet patch on the polished blue linoleum. Flailing wildly, I catch myself at the last second and manage to remain upright, but I end up landing awkwardly on my right foot.

My stiff right hip protests with a sharp twinge, and I wince.

"Shit," I mutter, eyeing the puddle someone tracked in. I slip a hand inside the waistband of my boot-cut jeans and quickly rub the knot of tense muscle beneath the jagged scar on my right hip.

I blame the stupid dream for this. It's the same nightmare I've had since I was five. The one with the masked gunman, the acrid smoke, the coppery taste of blood, and my mother's screams fading to silence.

Having the dream meant I overslept. Oversleeping meant missing my morning walk. Not walking meant my hip would stiffen up, making me more clumsy and likely to stumble.

Thinking I might need an exorcist to get rid of that particular nightmare for good, I adjust my messenger bag strap and carefully navigate the treacherous floor, making a mental note to inform housekeeping that the newest way to die is currently gathering on the corridor of the Forensics floor.

The quiet hum of equipment and a faint chemical smell greet me as I push open the heavy glass double doors, take a deep breath, and steel myself for another day of office politics and ethical tightropes. The pressure to make evidence fit into a certain narrative is sometimes simply too great not to cave under.

As I reach up to take my lab coat from the rack by the door, I hear the familiar drawl of Tim Carter, my coworker.

"You're late for our coffee date, darling. It's already cold."

Without turning around from the dual monitors on his desk, Tim hands me a cardboard cup of coffee. He must have seen my reflection through his screens.

I give my usual noncommittal thanks. Every day for the past six months, Tim has had a cup of coffee waiting for me as soon as I step into the office. I've taken it, politely said 'thank you', and never once told him that I don't drink coffee.

Tim finally turns around on his ergonomic chair, his striking blue eyes crinkling at the corners as he smiles. "Anytime. Are you alright, Addy?" He eyes my damp clothes, and unease settles in my stomach as his gaze lingers on me.

I nod. "Yeah, I'm good, thanks Tim." Tim has since stopped asking me out, after I turned him down a few dozen times, but his blatant hopeful interest is always written all over him.

"Doug is asking for you," Tim gives me a meaningful look.

I groan. My pain-in-the-ass boss and Monday mornings never seem to get along. It's like he waits for the start of the week to unload some bullshit on me, setting a nice tone for a shitty week.

"Of course he is," I smile sweetly. Doug Harrison may be the head of forensics, but Tim and I typically run the show. We're both up for promotion, something that should make us rivals, but Tim obviously wants me more than he wants the position, so I don't think he'd mind if I got the promotion.

"He's in a meeting with one of the prosecutors of the Martelli case, but I'm sure he'll find you soon enough since your office is right next to his."

Inconveniently so, I think to myself, bracing for whatever Monday morning surprise Doug has in store for me.

"Thanks, Tim," I force a smile and take the office sludge, knowing it's going down the drain. But it's easier than explaining and letting Tim see another piece of me. Only Dante knows how coffee drags me back to those endless nights of pain, the aroma of caffeine almost as strong as the antiseptic on floors and surfaces.

I didn't realize just how much coffee was consumed in hospitals.

Coffee meant pain. A wound dressing, another surgery, another round of physio. Even now, years later, my leg throbs at the memory.

I feel Tim's eyes on me as I walk away, more conscious than ever of my slight limp. Tim is brilliant, kind, supportive, and from a solid home. He's easy on the eyes as well with his blond surfer good looks and lean muscled frame.

He was an avid follower of my anonymous blog before I confessed to being the author. Although he ended up ratting me out to everyone else in the office, I forgave him, chalking it up to overexcitement.

The bottom line is, on paper, he's the type of guy I should date. A dependable friend who respects me and is interested in more than my looks.

So why can't I give him the answer he wants?

Because I know there's no point in trying. He's nothing like Dante, who hit me like a potent drug. Dark, dangerous, toxic. And so fucking exciting, I'm still withdrawing after two years.

As I weave through the maze of desks and equipment, I notice some of my coworkers huddled around the compact electron microscope, appearing to be brainstorming a difficult case, but their hushed chatter stops as soon as I'm within earshot.

Typical. They're probably talking about my blog again and the few million reasons why it's in bad taste to be running it. Nothing I haven't heard before. Although I think my dissection of the 1947 Black Dahlia murder might have been a little too intense, even for people who analyze blood spatters for a living.

"You'll get over it guys," I mutter under my breath.

I'd started an anonymous blog in my college sophomore year on a whim. It was my way to explore the darkness that fascinated me, to give voice to the thoughts I couldn't share with anyone else. And now it's exciting to share them with five thousand followers twice a month.

I reach my office at the far end of the room and drop my bag onto my desk, accidentally jostling the huge pile of papers, which then knocks over the small photo frame tucked face-down behind them, sending it clattering to the floor.

My breath huffs with annoyance as I snatch up the photo frame and throw it straight into the bin Then I march to the break room to dump the cold coffee down the sink. I'm feeling more settled when I return to my desk and power on my computer.

In less than a minute, however, I find myself diving into the trash and fishing out the frame. I carefully replace it on its usual corner on my desk, my throat tightening as I glance at the photo.

It's one of Dad and me at my college graduation, six weeks after my twenty-first birthday.

Six weeks after the night I went to Chicago.

I examine Dad's rare-toothed smile and the pride gleaming in his eyes as he hugs me tightly to his side. No one looking at the photo would ever guess that my father hadn't said one word to me in six weeks.

And now I haven't spoken to him in two.

Hot, angry tears spring to my eyes, but I shake them off, determined not to dwell this morning.

As my computer whirs to life, I glance furtively around the lab to see my colleagues still huddled around the same spot. Perfect.

I open an incognito browser window and quickly navigate to my blog. The familiar black background with crimson text fills my screen, and I feel a small thrill of excitement.

"The Scarlett Holmes Blog," the header proclaims. Not the most original title, but it's become my sanctuary. I scroll through, checking for new comments. A notification catches my eye—someone's left a detailed response to my latest post. I make a mental note to read it thoroughly during my lunch break, then close the page and begin my work for the day.

I'm deep into scrutinizing a particularly puzzling fiber analysis when the door to my boss's office opens, allowing the voices of my boss and Jim Pearson, one of the prosecuting attorneys, to cut through my concentration.

"We need that fiber sample yesterday, Doug," Jim hisses, his nasal voice sharp with frustration. "This entire case hinges on it."

"I know that," Doug replies, his tone tight. "But it was an honest mistake. A human error. However, what you're asking us to do is a deliberate breach of the rules. Jim, we can't just—"

"Can't just what? Do your job? Clean up your mess?" Jim cuts him off harshly. "Tommy Martelli's defense team are dirty, slimy bastards. We need to meet them on the mat for this. Otherwise, we'll lose the case, and you know that motherfucker deserves to rot in prison."

My boss's tone gets testy. "Okay, Jim. I really can't get involved here. We're neutral—"

"Spare me the sanctimonious bullshit, Doug, and clean up your fucking mess. I've already spoken to my contact in Chicago. They'll hand over the sample once we give them a positive ID. There'll be no memos, no paper trail. We do this under the radar. I want to see that smug defense team choke on their latest ruse."

Chicago. The word hits me like a sucker punch, and suddenly I'm not in the lab anymore. I'm back in that restaurant, the smell of gunpowder in my nostrils, Dante's eyes cold and predatory as he stood over the bodies. My stomach lurches, and I grip the edge of my desk, willing the memory away.

Doug's sigh of resignation comes through again. "Tim Carter is a Boy Scout. He can't pull this off."

"No, but the woman will. What's her name . . ." he trails off as if trying to recall. "O'Shea. Let O'Shea do it. I hear she's the brains around this place, yet she's hardly seen." Jim's parting jibe as he walks off roots me to the chair.

What the hell?

They're planning something shady, and my name has just come up as the prime candidate to carry out the operation. I'm not sure whether to be pleased or insulted by it.

I try to go back to work, but I'm too distracted, and I find myself counting down the seconds until—

Right on schedule, Doug's moon-like face pokes through my office door. "O'Shea. Nice of you to finally turn up to work. My office, right now." He leaves, fully expecting me to follow.

Shit. Shit. Shit. I already know what's coming, but still, my hands shake with dread. I stand, square my shoulders, and ignore the twinge in my hip.

Doug's small, cluttered office smells of stale coffee and cheap cologne. He's seated behind his desk, a steaming mug in his hand. To my surprise, he gestures to an identical mug on the corner of his desk.

"Have a seat. Coffee?"

I eye the mug suspiciously. Doug Harrison offering me coffee? This can't be good. "No, thanks," I say cautiously, settling into the chair across from him.

Doug leans back, his chair creaking under his weight. "You're one of our best analysts, Addy. Sharp, thorough, discreet." He pauses, his gaze boring into me. "That's why I need you for a . . . delicate situation."

My stomach tightens. "Doug, if this is about what I overheard—"

"Then you know you're going to Chicago," he interrupts, his tone leaving no room for argument.

The words hang in the air between us, heavy and suffocating. Chicago. The city I swore I'd never return to. I swallow hard, fighting to keep my voice steady. "But I'm in the middle of the Oscar case. Surely someone else can—"

"This takes priority," Harrison cuts me off again. "Jim Pearson has us by the throat. Apparently, some fool in Chicago mixed things up, and we didn't realize until too late. We need that fiber sample, or our jobs are on the line."

I open my mouth to protest again, but Harrison's next words stop me cold. "You're in line for team leader, and this move could be a big shove in that direction, O'Shea."

The implication is clear. Do this, or kiss my promotion goodbye. I'm being backed into a corner, and we both know it.

As he outlines the details, my mind races. An off-the-books evidence retrieval? The ethical implications alone are staggering. But beneath my professional concerns, a more personal dread is building. Chicago means the possibility of encountering Dante.

But what are the odds of running into him on a same-day return trip to Chicago? It's not as if he's the city's gatekeeper or something.

I take a deep breath, then ask, "When do I leave?" I hate how defeated my voice sounds.

A smile spreads across Harrison's face, smug and satisfied. "ASAP. The lab in Chicago is expecting you as of noon today."

Today. The word echoes in my head, panic rising in my chest. It's too soon. I'm not prepared—not for the trip, not for Chicago, and not for the possibility of . . .

"Doug," I try one last time, "the procedural issues alone—"

"Have been taken care of," Doug interrupts smoothly. "As you overheard, this comes from the top. It's already been arranged."

And just like that, I'm trapped. The weight of inevitability settles on my shoulders, heavy and suffocating. I nod, not trusting myself to speak.

"Excellent," Harrison says, leaning back in his chair. "I'll have Sarah book your flights. You'll be back tonight."

I stand on shaky legs, my hip protesting the sudden movement. As I turn to leave, Harrison calls out, "Oh, and Addy? Discretion is key here. I'm sure I don't need to remind you of the sensitive nature of this assignment."

I meet his gaze, the thinly veiled threat in his words not lost on me. "Of course not," I reply, my voice steadier than I feel.

As I walk back to my desk, the lab blurs around me. The hum of equipment, the chatter of my colleagues—it all fades into background noise. All I can hear is the pounding of my own heart, a desperate rhythm that seems to echo one word over and over:

Dante.

Dante.

Dante.

CHAPTER THREE

Adele

I secure my bike in my designated parking spot and glance at the skyscraper before me. Two weeks of living here, and I still can't believe this is home now. My best friend Kira's penthouse suite towers above, a world apart from the sprawling mansion I grew up in.

My phone buzzes as I push through the revolving door into the cool, polished lobby. I check and see that it's a message from my boss:

> **O'Shea. I heard you rescheduled your flight from 10 to 1 and went home instead of heading straight to the airport. Do I really need to remind you how crucial this assignment is?**

I roll my eyes. Big deal. Doug Harrison can suck it up. I need time to change into something more presentable before heading to Chicago.

Surely, it'd be in everyone's interest if I didn't turn up in my baggy jeans and rock band T-shirt?

Doug's hissy fit forgotten, I step into the private elevator. As it ascends, a familiar wave of guilt washes over me. The same guilt that's been gnawing at me since I moved out of the house and stopped taking my dad's calls. The mansion I grew up in suddenly feels hundreds of miles away, despite being only a fifteen-minute drive from here.

I firmly push the guilt aside as I've done countless times over the past two weeks since I moved out.

No, I made the right choice.

At twenty-three, moving out was long overdue, but considering Dad and I are all the family we each have left in the world, we'd stuck together for much longer than necessary. But his betrayal had tipped the scales and made me question if I wasn't better off alone than living with a man I no longer knew.

Kira's offer to move in with her couldn't have come at a better time. She'd recently moved back to Boston and into this penthouse and kept complaining that the walls didn't 'echo right' and she needed to hear another human being to 'keep things balanced.' I finally caved and moved in with her after Dad and I had that massive row.

The elevator comes to a smooth stop, and I step out onto our floor. I shake off my conflicted thoughts and open the penthouse door. The aroma of fresh basil and sizzling bacon wafts through the air, making my stomach rumble. I'd been in too much of a rush this morning to have breakfast, and right now is one of the reasons I'm so glad I moved in with Kira.

"Thank God," I mutter as I cross the cool marble floors of the large, brightly lit living room toward the open-plan kitchen, the sounds of my uneven footsteps muted in my work sneakers.

I spot Kira standing by the induction stove, her sleek black ponytail swishing as she works. Although she doesn't turn to acknowledge my nearly soundless approach, I know she heard me from the moment I came in.

Heck, she probably even heard the elevator doors swish open from outside the penthouse—her sense of hearing is that keen. Not that she needs it—Kira has every inch of this place mapped out.

She moves with the kind of ease and confidence that comes from familiarity, thanks to the subtle vibrations from her wristband—a device that helps her navigate the space around her.

"Everything okay, Addy? You left less than a couple of hours ago, and you're already back," Kira notes in her distinctive dulcet voice as she flips a pancake with a precision and grace that belies someone who has been without sight since the age of four.

Ever since I stumbled into my dorm room in my second year of college and found Kira, a performing arts major and a part-time DJ, with her headphones on, hands flying over a tactile mixing board, I've been in awe of her. And she only got better over the years.

By the time we graduated, Kira had become a sought-after DJ. She may not see her audience, but she sure knows how to make them move.

I slide onto one of the four white leather barstools arranged along the shiny black breakfast bar. "Doug needs me to go pick up a sample . . ."

I pause as if delaying saying it out loud would change my reality before finally finishing with a sigh, ". . . in Chicago."

Kira tilts her head slightly, the corners of her lips twitching upward as if she's caught onto something I haven't said. "Oh really!"

She turns toward my voice, her eyes wide with excitement and fixed at a point just over my shoulder. She has these striking hazel eyes that would make anyone do a double-take, and her eye movements are so coordinated they leave people oblivious to the fact that she can't see.

"Yeah, Chicago," I confirm.

"Oh my God, Addy," Kira gushes, "you'll finally get to see the city! I just know you're going to love it."

Er, no, I don't think so.

I shudder even as a pang of guilt hits me. Kira still has no idea that I've already been to Chicago. She knows nothing of my relationship with Dante or the disastrous birthday dinner two and a half years ago.

Kira continues, oblivious to my conflicted mood, gesturing wildly as if trying to capture the essence of the city. "Chicago is . . . vibrant, gritty. It's like a full-bodied experience. It also has a dark vibe to it. It's so you, Addy."

"What do you mean it's so me?"

She smirks, "I mean, your morbid fascination for the darker, more complex sides of things. Of people. Of life in general." Kira returns to her pancakes, her hand hovering over the pan to gauge the heat by the rising steam completely unaware of how my heart lurches and my gut tightens with unease.

Kira is much too perceptive. She doesn't even know I'm a crime junkie or about my blog, yet she's calling me out. But really, what did I expect being roomies with a girl who can hear subtle changes in people's breathing? Before I can open my mouth to deny that logic, she continues,

"And don't even get me started on the men."

"The men," I repeat, chuckling because I already know what she'll say next. I could even mime her next words.

"You know . . . the Italians. And no, don't roll your eyes at me," Kira scolds, just as I do exactly that.

"Come on, Kira. Chicago doesn't have a monopoly on hot Italian men. You can find them pretty much anywhere."

"Nope." She pops the p with emphasis. "Not the likes of which they've got in Chicago."

"Riiight," I drawl, shaking my head with a smile.

Kira and her mom moved here from Turkey when she was little, and except for attending Loyola Boston University and recently moving back here, she's lived in Chicago all her life. It's no surprise that to her, everywhere else pales in comparison.

I often tell myself that's part of the reason I didn't tell her about Dante, the man who just about ticks every box on Kira's perfect man list. That Kira's bias would cloud my judgment, but that's not the truth.

Dante is my secret—the one thing I should never have tried and that ended badly. Like that dangerous game you sneaked out to play and then got hurt and had to hide the injury from your parents.

"So, how long are you going to be there for? I could recommend some really cool places to visit." Kira leans forward, her fingers drumming eagerly on the countertop.

I force a laugh, but it comes out more like a strangled cough. "It's not that type of trip. I'm only going to collect something, so I'll probably be there for an hour, maximum. And then it's straight back to the airport."

I feel another twinge of guilt as I watch Kira's enthusiasm deflate slightly. If only she knew the real reason I'm dreading this trip. But some secrets are better left buried, even from your best friend.

Pushing aside my unease, I focus on Kira's puzzled look. "Someone in Ecolab forgot to do their job and send the correct samples to us."

"So why not get Ecolab to send it over then?"

"Right?" I throw my hands up. "You'd think that'd be the obvious solution, but Jim Pearson came and tore my boss a new one, and suddenly I'm being thrown on a plane to fetch."

I rub my arms, mimicking a shudder. "You know, I wouldn't want to be on the other side of the likes of Jim Pearson in a courtroom, Kira. He's like a snapping turtle."

Kira's lips quirk upward in a knowing smile. "Oh, I would be more wary of Martelli's defense team if I were you."

"Who said anything about the Martelli case?" I straighten in my chair, wondering if I've let anything slip about the upcoming trial of the mafia boss. I never talk about the cases at work.

Kira's shoulders drop slightly as she shakes her head. "You really think I don't know about Tommy Martelli's upcoming trial?" Her fingertips dance across the raised buttons along the edges of the overhead cupboards, quickly finding and pressing the right one to pop open the door.

"Addy," Kira begins, reaching in to grab the plates. "Tommy Martelli was part of the crime syndicate in Chicago. It's called 'The Outfit.'"

"He was?"

She nods. "He was exiled for doing stupid shit. So he went to New York, and instead of laying low, he did even more stupid shit that eventually got him arrested."

"By stupid shit, you mean . . . ?"

"Believe it or not, criminals have a code of conduct too, and Martelli broke it repeatedly. Anyway, both the New York Don—a super sexy guy, by the way, and the Chicago Don are teaming up to get him off the hook, hence the kickass defense team."

Kira takes a breath. "I hate to break it to you, Addy, but your so-called snapping turtle will be having his ragged ass handed back to him after the courtroom floor has been thoroughly wiped."

I gape at Kira, shocked by her seemingly vast knowledge. "How do you even know all this?"

She shrugs, smirking. "Just check any of the legit vlogs dedicated to Tommy and the trial. Besides, I told you, I like Italian men."

I see. It's a load of fan base crap, then, which goes to show how the world loves their antiheroes. Still, I'll take Kira's juicy conspiracy theories over the boring facts I glean from work.

I lean forward, lowering my voice. "Okay, so if Martelli offended both Dons, why are they trying to save him from going down?"

Kira's face lights up, her smile stretching from ear to ear as she pushes a plate of pancakes and bacon with strawberries and cream toward me. The savory scent makes my stomach growl but I find myself hungrier for Martelli's story.

"Addy, they need him off the authorities' hook so they can deal with him the mafia way. And I bet Martelli is on board with it too. At least this way he can, you know, negotiate for the life of his wife and kids."

"Why wouldn't Martelli negotiate for his own life?"

"Because he's a dead man whether he goes to prison or not and he knows it. At least with the mafia way, he can strike a deal to save his family from the bloodbath awaiting them."

"Oh, wow." I blink rapidly, my jaw working soundlessly as I process it all. "And you got all this from your Italian mafia fan club website or vlog—whatever?"

"We like to think of it as a support group. Anyway, your dad called again," Kira says, changing the subject.

I groan as my intrigue, as well as appetite, vanishes. "Of course he did."

Kira leans against the counter, her unseeing eyes somehow locking with mine. "Addy, I know you're angry with him, but he's your father. You can't just cut him out of your life."

"Yes, I can." I stab at the pancake with my fork, feeling my frustration mount.

"Adele . . ." Kira calls me gently. The Italian way. Probably something else she learned from her so-called 'support group'. It makes my heart skip a beat because there's only one other person who says my name like that.

Three syllables that make goosebumps prickle on my skin. It's been well over two years since I heard him say it.

Whisper it . . .

Groan it . . .

I snap myself out of the fog of lust gathering in my core and focus on my strained relationship with my dad. "Look, I don't know if I can forgive him, Kira."

How can I reconcile that the stern man who raised me to always tell the truth and respect the law is the same man involved in fraud and counterfeit currency?

She reaches out, her fingers brushing against my arm. The touch is gentle and comforting. "People make mistakes, Addy. It doesn't mean they don't love you."

That's the problem. I'm not so sure it was a mistake. It looks like my discovery of his double life was the mistake. "You don't even know what he did," I say to Kira.

"I would if you'd tell me."

I remain silent, unsure how to explain to her.

Kira nods as if understanding that I'm not ready to talk about it. "Is it worth losing your only relative for, though?"

I bite my lip. "I don't know. Probably not."

"That settles it then. You don't have to forgive him outright, but you should hear him out, Addy."

I look at Kira, marveling how so wise and confident she is. It strikes me how much strength resides in this woman who navigates the world without sight yet sees more than most people ever will.

"Maybe you're right," I concede with a sigh and take a bite of the pancake, the flavors exploding on my tongue.

"Of course I am," Kira smiles and returns to her own food, munching on the strawberries. "You'll feel better once you talk to him."

We fall into a comfortable silence; the only sounds are the clinking of silverware and the distant hum of the city.

***

After our meal, I head to my room to change out of my top, bootleg jeans, and sneakers. I instead choose a button-down white shirt tucked into a black pencil skirt that stops just above my knees and kitten-heeled boots then I pull my hair into a bun.

Next, I grab my work bag and empty it of sheaves of paper to make room for the small metallic evidence box.

This is so wrong, I muse, looking at the fingerprint-activated box. It should have been sent through secure post, or at least transported by a security personnel. *Well, who better to bend rules than bad-tempered lawyers?*

Shouldering the wide strap, I start to leave my room when my phone rings. It's my dad.

The phone suddenly feels like a deadweight in my hand, as Kira's words ring in my ears. I hesitate, my thumb hovering over the screen. Then I take a deep breath and swipe to connect.

"Adele." His voice comes through, flat and cold.

"Daddy," I reply, forcing some steel into the tremor in my voice.

"You've been ignoring my calls." His Irish twang, usually more pronounced when he's upset, is oddly muted.

"I've been busy with work," I say, tugging at a loose thread on my sleeve as I begin to pace, fully expecting to be guilt-tripped for ignoring my father, but I'm surprised when all I get is a noncommittal grunt.

"When are you coming back home?" He may as well be asking me what time it is. Over the past couple of years—ever since he started talking to me again after *Chicagogate,* that is—I've noticed my dad has been decidedly . . . more detached. He still hasn't forgiven me.

Well, I haven't forgiven him for being a liar and fraud, either.

A flash of irritation replaces my unease. "I'm not coming back, Daddy. I've moved out. I'm looking for my own place now. And it's about time, too, wouldn't you say?"

"Adele," he says, and for a moment, I think I hear a flicker of something in his voice. Warmth? Concern? But it's gone as quickly as it appeared. "You don't need to do that. There's more than enough room at the house. I know you're shocked and disappointed, but if you'd just let me explain some things about my job . . . about our family."

My free hand clenches into a fist. "Explain what exactly? How you turned ripping people off into an art form? Even if you could spin some story for that, nothing could ever make it right."

There's a long pause, then he says in a stern, eerily calm tone. "There is something you really need to calm down and hear. Something I couldn't tell you before now."

Instinctively, I know that whatever he has to say will change everything. And that's exactly what I don't want to happen. A familiar buzzing begins in my ear, but I ignore it. "Alright," I snap, suddenly needing the call to end.

"Good. So shall I expect you later today, then?"

I scoff, glancing at my watch. "No, you shan't. It'll have to wait a few days." I hesitate, debating on saying more, but in the end, I just blurt it out. "Because I'm going to Chicago."

There's a pause on the other end of the line, so long that I wonder if he's trying to set a world record for awkward silences.

I'm unsure why I felt the need to tell him that. I could say it's because I promised to keep him in the loop, but to be honest, that ship sailed the moment I realized he didn't deserve my honesty.

No, it's because I wanted to rattle him the way he did to me with that eerie pronouncement just now.

Finally, he speaks, and I can't stop my smirk as I hear his Irish twang. "Chicago? Do ye mean that?"

"Yep," I confirm, letting the satisfaction curl in my gut like a lazy cat. These days, getting a rise out of my dad is the only way I can tap into the well of emotions he used to spill more freely before.

I've apologized a million times for what happened that night of my twenty-first birthday, yet he continues to punish me with his icy detachment.

It's been two and a half fucking years, I often want to scream at him, but I know doing that would only push him away further.

His voice comes out sharp, almost shaky. "No. Adele, ye can't go there."

I chuckle, "Too late, Daddy. I'm already heading to the airport. Besides, it's for a crucial case at work. I can't not go."

Another pause, loaded with unspoken words, and I imagine him silently melting down.

While I understand my dad's overprotectiveness, it can be unsettling, a foreboding that clings like cobwebs in the corners of my mind.

And then I hear him say with a forced casualness, "Is it for the Martelli case?"

My breath catches. How did he guess? "I can't discuss it, Daddy," I remind him sharply. "Look, I'll be back tonight if that makes you feel any better."

"It bloody doesn't, Adele," he snaps, his voice completely devoid of emotion once again.

And then it's the dial tone.

Wow, how long did that flicker of emotion last there? Two minutes?

Why the fuck do I even still bother with this guy?

Because you know how much he's suffering. How much he's lost. You're all he has in this world.

And, like it or not, he's all you have.

I think back to that night in Chicago. As if sensing that my world was falling apart, my dad's call had come in moments after I ran out of Dante's restaurant. Shaken and scared, I immediately confessed to him where I was.

Of course he'd lost it. I'd fully expected him to, just not to the degree that he did. He stopped speaking to me, and if he could have grounded me for months, he would have done so.

But there was no need. I'd seen enough of Chicago anyway. Enough of the world, in fact, to tearfully promise myself and him that I'd never go there again. That I'd never leave Boston without telling him.

Yet here I am, leaving Boston and heading back there.

I grab my coat and shout to let Kira know I'm leaving. My reflection in the elevator mirrors brings me up short. The woman who stares back at me looks flushed. Terrified, even.

I take a deep breath to settle the flutters in my belly and say to her. "Chicago is a huge city, and your assignment is simple. Pick up the sample and come straight home. I promise you, the odds of running into him are one to three million. Practically zilch."

If only I could get my heart to believe me and stop racing like a horse going into battle.

CHAPTER FOUR

Dante

I lean back against the cool leather of the SUV seat, drumming my fingers on my thigh, a heavy metal track blaring in one ear, drowning out the eerie silence in the car.

On my other side, the tinted window is rolled halfway down to let in Chicago's pulse. I welcome the sounds of wailing sirens in the distance, screeching tires, honking trucks, and shouting people—the city's chaotic symphony, finding it oddly calming.

But what I really need is a release of this coiled tension inside. The gym calls to me, weights and punching bags, but duty anchors me here, in the backseat, waiting for Salvatore, my right-hand man, to emerge from the tall white building across the street.

After what feels like hours but is, in fact, only five or ten minutes, Sal pulls open the door and slips into the driver's seat with a restless energy about him. He shakes off the cold like a wet dog and cranks up the heating to replace the warmth lost from my partially rolled-down window. Unlike me, Sal hates the cold.

"What do we know?" I ask in a flat voice.

He flashes me his signature boyish grin through the rearview mirror. "Can you believe that Boston has just sent someone to collect that sample?"

I shake my head in disgust and grumble, "That's too fucking close for comfort, Sal."

Someone must have tipped Boston off about my plan to get rid of that sample. The evidence being used to nail Martelli for murder—a piece of fiber lifted off the victim—was found to match the custom-made carpet in Martelli's Rolls-Royce.

We tried getting Ecolab to mix things up to buy time until we were able to get rid of the damning evidence for good. The operation was planned for tomorrow, but on a hunch, I decided to move things up and get it done today. Sal and the rest of my men thought I was crazy, as usual, but since no one had any real objection, here we are.

"True, it's close," Sal replies, "but thanks to you, we're still a step ahead of the prosecution."

That offers little comfort, knowing there are too many informants everywhere, turning this trial into a fucking game of spies. "As long as you're sure they haven't yet collected the sample."

Sal taps his thumb against the steering wheel in a rapid, three-beat rhythm—a nervous tic he hasn't managed to shake. "No, but they will be in due course."

Which, to Sal, probably means they're on their way right now.

I smirk at his precise vagueness. "Then give Pietro the clear to move."

"*Sì,* Dante." Sal settles back into the driver's seat, his eyes glinting with excitement. He clicks on his earbud and gives the order to Pietro. "We're all set. Go."

The tension in my shoulders eases slightly, though the weight of everything else remains, pressing down on me like a heavy cloak. One wrong move and this could all come crashing down on me.

Three years ago, two Capos, Tommy Martelli and Orlando De Luca, were on the verge of rebelling against the Outfit. Nico, the Don, and also my older brother, chose to eliminate only one of them: Martelli.

He offered me no explanation except for his gut instinct, which I respect, but I typically need more than a hunch to kill a man. So I insisted they both face the same justice—live or die. In one of his rare conciliatory moods, Nico relented and let them both live.

Now, it turns out Nico's initial instinct was spot on. Three years later, Martelli is in the feds' clutches, while I'm about to marry De Luca's daughter. And I now feel personally responsible for bringing Tommy Martelli to the justice he should have had from the very beginning.

Starting with getting his charges dropped.

"By the way, Dante," Sal says with a teasing grin, breaking the sudden tense silence, "I hear your future mother-in-law has been picking out china patterns and all. I dare say she is even more excited than the bride to get hitched to your family."

The thought of my impending marriage leaves a sour taste on my tongue and an unpleasant twisting in my gut. "Yeah? Well, I sincerely hope for her sake she lives to see the day." The words come out harsher than intended, but I don't give a fuck.

"Killing your future mother-in-law won't stop the alliance, *fratello*."

"I have no intention of hurting her," I shrug. But if the woman's track record is anything to go by, the very things she's most desperate for have a way of eluding her.

I suspect Bianca De Luca is the major driving force behind this alliance. Years ago, she was supposed to marry my father, but she somehow missed out on that. And now her daughter is on the way to becoming a Vitelli.

If my wife-to-be didn't constantly torture my eyes with dirty texts, I would otherwise be inclined to think the woman was just as uninterested as me. But no, it appears the girl wants to marry me. As if the universe didn't hate me enough.

Fuck.

The very idea of marrying Alina to keep her mother happy and her father loyal to the Outfit makes my suit feel about three sizes too small, which is why I've moved the date back.

Twice.

Nico is pissed off, but there's not much he can do, considering he was the one who was supposed to marry Alina in the first place. That Nico ended up falling for another woman and graciously offered me up instead is just my rotten luck.

And however much the idea of being the sacrificial stud in this arranged marriage circus galls me, I can't put the marriage off for much longer without causing a rift in the Outfit.

Sal's teasing voice breaks through my thoughts. "You could at least pretend to be excited, Dante. Even Nico managed to act besotted while his engagement with Alina lasted. But you? You're openly sulking, and it's not a good look."

His words sting but sadly ring true. "I know it's hard, but you should try to mind your own fucking business once in a while, Salvatore," I snap.

Sal only laughs. *"Dio mio*, you're usually a better actor than Nico. A bigger asshole, yes, but you've always been great at hiding your true feelings. Or lack of thereof."

"I feel plenty," I counter, taking off the single earbud, no longer needing the frenzy of the heavy metal to ground me. I'm not even sure why I'm wasting my breath arguing with Sal. I know what he's doing.

Sal knows how tense I've been lately, and his way of helping is getting me to talk about the things that annoy me.

But I don't want to talk. I'd rather take it out on a punching bag or kill something. Feeling suddenly parched, I grab a bottle of water from the inbuilt cooler, unscrew the top, and take a deep drink.

"Dante, I meant feeling with your heart, not with your fists. Or your tiny junk."

Choking back a cough at his audacity, I retort, "You're a fine one to fucking talk about junk, *idiota*. When did you last talk to a woman for more than ten seconds? And no, that doesn't include your grandmother."

His grin widens, not the least bit fazed. "You're assuming there's a woman in the whole of Chicago that I want to talk to."

Sal is the youngest Capo, and for all his skill and brutality, he's still a virgin. I peeled him off the streets three years ago at twenty-one. A Harvard graduate, yet steeped in drugs and broken by trauma and loss. I helped him the only way I could. Therapy. And, of course, putting a gun in his hand.

Sal has since become the kid brother I never had. And let's just say, since knowing Sal, I've developed a new respect for Nico, who's lived with me for decades and somehow managed not to wring my neck for the things I must have put him through.

I take another swig of my water, then fix him a serious look. "Sal, it's not rocket science. Tell me what kind of woman you want, and I'll find her tonight."

"Alright." He shrugs. "I want someone different. Unconventional. Freakishly smart." Sal continues counting off the qualities of his ideal woman, but I don't hear any more as a flash of fiery hair and pouty lips flits through my mind like a neon sign.

Addy.

She's always there beneath the surface, teasing me with everything I can't have. Grating on my already thin resolve to leave her alone. But to go after her will be war.

It's been twenty-eight fucking months, my brain argues.

I clench my fist, willing away the reminders of her dark humor and quick wit. Of how ridiculously sexy she looked in my clothes. How she obliterated my self-control without even trying.

I shake my head, meeting his gaze. "Sorry, Sal. The woman you're looking for is too smart to get involved with men like you and me."

As if knowing the direction of my thoughts, Sal says, "You know, Dante, Alina will make you a good wife if you give her half a chance."

I snort. "*Sì?* And you know this because?"

"For one, she has a strong family name. Her father is the most powerful Capo, and her mother is a mafia princess from the famous Rinaldi family of New York." Sal's expression turns grave. "And most importantly, I'm sure she knows how to run a household of staff. I mean, what the fuck else could you possibly want?"

"For the life of me I can't imagine anything else," I reply, and we burst into simultaneous laughter.

As we settle, Sal tilts his head thoughtfully, a clear sign he's about to say something even more stupid.

"And let's not forget she's quite the looker too. Yes, probably not quite as breathtaking as Red Wine, but Alina holds her own."

My laughter instantly dies. "Don't fucking go there, Salvatore . . ." I warn, my hand curling into a fist I'd love to swing into his jaw. Red Wine is my men's alias for Addy.

"Fine, I'll drop it." He holds his hands up in mock surrender. "I'm just saying. You've got a lot to work with in your fiancée. And speaking of work, when is Kira due to appear on the Chicago scene again?"

My jaw tightens as I feel a familiar wave of protectiveness at the mention of the name of my father's ward. "How am I supposed to know?" I snap. "And why the fuck are you suddenly interested in Kira's movements?"

Sal grins. "We're extremely testy and prohibitive today, aren't we, Dante?"

"Don't use up all your Harvard words in one go, Sal. You'll need to save some for after I punch your lights out and you're reduced to babbles. Now what's your business with Kira?"

"Relax. I'm just looking to book her in for Resin Club launch night," Sal replies innocently, but a glint in his eyes tells me he knows exactly which of my buttons to push.

"So why don't you contact her agent?" I clip.

"Because I want to deal directly with Kira. I'm just checking to make sure that I won't catch a bullet for doing so."

I'm not stupid. I've seen the way Sal gets when he's around my father's ward. I just didn't think he'd have the guts to go there. I thought he'd want some easy lay as his first. The fucker is essentially taking permission to ask Kira out.

I should tell him to stay the fuck away from Kira. I want to say the words. I just can't get them past the tightness in my throat.

My resistance has taken its hardest hit in these past two weeks. Addy moving in with Kira has brought her another step closer into my orbit.

I have still managed to keep my distance, but something about the situation makes me feel like a kitten staring down a moving ball of yarn.

Imagine if Kira then decides that she likes Sal. My right-hand man and my father's ward spending time together will bring Addy another step closer to me.

How long before I take that inevitable leap at what's mine and let the shrapnel fall where they may?

I drawl, "I can't say for sure if you'll catch one or not, Salvatore. Why don't you try it first and see?"

Sal only laughs off my warning.

Before we can say more, an alarm blares from the building we've been watching, shattering the brief interlude.

"Here we go," I mutter, leaning back in my seat. My blood thrums with anticipation, every nerve ending coming alive. I live for this: the thrill of the job, the adrenaline rush.

We watch as people pour out of the place like ants from a disturbed nest. And then a curl of black smoke rises from behind the building, adding to the mayhem.

"You sick bastard," I say, shooting Sal a glance. "I told you to create an excuse to get the fire guys here, not to burn the place down."

He chuckles, completely unfazed. "Relax, it's just a desk. It won't cause too much damage before our men arrive."

I grunt in acknowledgment but keep my eyes trained on the unfolding scene. And then the sound of sirens pierces the air, growing louder by the second.

"And we're in business." Sal's smirk widens as fire trucks pull up to the curb, lights flashing like some twisted Christmas display.

A reluctant smile lifts the corner of my lips. The plan so far is going even better than I anticipated.

People mill around outside, talking hurriedly and casting nervous glances back at the building.

And then I spot him—Pietro, the man who went in for the sample in the thick of the distraction.

His black trench coat and hat, big stocky frame, and average looks blend him into the backdrop of aimless bystanders. But to the trained eye, his deliberate, unhurried gait, the tense set of his shoulders, and the watchful eyes scanning the area stand him out as a man with a purpose.

Which is why the street cameras have been disabled.

Pietro joins the crowd, acting every bit the concerned bystander. After a few moments, he saunters away from the assembly point, hands casually in his pockets as if he's just taking a leisurely stroll.

Then the car radio crackles to life with Pietro's voice, calm and composed. "It's done."

I let out a sigh of relief. "Good."

I focus on Pietro's retreating figure until he disappears around a corner, and the tension in my shoulders eases completely.

"Let's get out of here," I say.

Sal nods and starts the engine again, pulling us away from the scene as smoothly as we arrived.

As we drive off into Chicago's urban sprawl, my phone buzzes in my pocket, a jarring interruption to the satisfaction of a job well done. I fish it out, glancing at the screen. It's my brother, Nico.

"Fratello," I answer.

"What's your location?" Nico's voice crackles through the speaker, a hint of tension lacing his words.

I glance out the window at the passing cityscape. "Heading to Urban Elixir to see Martelli's lawyer. And then it's to the docks at midnight with the Senator's people."

There's a pause, then, "Great job with Ecolab. Now, forget Urban Elixir. You need to go home, you and Sal, there's something—"

I interrupt him. "How do you know the Ecolab job is done?"

Nico huffs out a laugh. "You're not as unpredictable as you like to think, Dante. You never fail to deliver where it counts. If only you'll stop juggling five things at once."

I suppose I should be flattered for being such a forgone conclusion. "You're catching on to how awesome I am," I smirk, "I dare say Sophie is finally rubbing off on you. How are she and the twins, by the way?"

"Very much mine, fuck you," Nico bristles, and I laugh. My brother's possessiveness of his pregnant wife is off the charts. Not that I blame him. She's the woman who holds the heart—and balls—of the ruthless Don of the Chicago Outfit in her dainty hands, after all.

"Listen," Nico continues after a slight hesitation, "We've got company. The Irish are here."

My eyes nearly pop out of my head. "You have got to be shitting me." I put him on speaker, so Sal can hear and know I'm not hallucinating.

"Afraid not. They're at the Urban Elixir as we speak. De Luca reported it himself. They're not causing a scene, but they ought to know who owns that club."

My grip tightens on the phone, knuckles whitening. "The fuck are they playing at?"

I can't believe what I'm hearing. The audacity of these Irish pricks, waltzing into our territory like they own the place. It's a goddamn slap in the face.

Nico's voice cuts through my seething. "Listen, Dante, I called you because I want you to steer clear. The last thing we need is another incident like last time."

The memory floods back, unbidden. Those two Irishmen hurling slurs at Addy. My vision had gone red, and bullets were flying out of my pistol before I even registered the thought. It had been a fucking mess, reigniting the simmering war between us and the Irish Mob.

I take a breath, trying to calm the rising tide of anger. "But they can't show up like this, Nico. Not after everything."

"I know, I know. Just let me handle it, alright? I don't want you running into them and starting another war."

That's where Nico and I are different. I shoot first and ask questions later. He likes to do things the other way around.

"But another war is exactly what they're asking for, *fratello*."

"You don't know that *fratellino*," he replies. "There has to be a reason for their presence. This time, Dante, I want answers, not bodies. Therefore, you and Sal are off tonight. Enzo and Orlando will handle it."

Like hell they will.

"Nico," I protest, "I'm literally minutes from the place right now. You'll be hard-pressed to drag Enzo from under a mountain of vomit and diapers."

Enzo is a high-ranking Capo and the proud and exhausted father of four-month-old sextuplets. He's a sharp and dependable soldier, but since his babies arrived, he's become one of those people who completely switch off when they're off duty.

"Still, better Enzo than you," Nico snaps. "I don't trust nor expect you to shoot straight with the Irish—not since that crap you pulled two years ago. Go home, Dante. I don't want you doing anything stupid tonight. *Capisci?*"

I grunt in acknowledgment and end the call, shoving the phone back in my breast pocket with more force than necessary as Sal executes a smooth U-turn.

What the fuck do those Irish want? I've stayed away from their precious little princess for the sake of peace, even though it killed me to do it.

I've not even stepped into Boston for two years. I've been a choir boy, playing by their rules. But do I get a medal from the smug pricks? No, instead, we get shit hurled at us.

I lean back in my seat, my jaw clenched tight. "Turn around, Sal. We're heading for the Urban Elixir Club, after all."

"The Urban Elixir? But didn't Don Vitelli just say—?"

"I know what Don Vitelli said," I snap, "But we've got some Irish gentlemen who seem to have lost their way. The least we can do is stop by and help them find it. Have Pietro meet us there."

Sal's eyes widen, but he doesn't argue. He nods and changes course again, and I catch him trying to suppress a grin. Sal lives for moments like this too. Unpredictable. Dangerous. Besides, there's nothing like a good old confrontation to reset eroding boundaries.

I may have promised Nico I wouldn't do anything stupid, but I never said anything about not doing something necessary.

It's time to remind those pricks just whose city they're in.

CHAPTER FIVE

Adele

"I'm so sorry, Ms. O'Shea," the woman at the front desk apologizes as she puts the phone receiver down. "The sixteenth floor has been evacuated. The elevators are out of service, and maintenance is still assessing the damage from the fire."

I've been sitting in the huge lobby of the tower that houses Ecolab for the past hour, waiting for an update from Jim Pearson's contact, or anyone from Ecolab. I'm too high-strung to have the steaming tea offered, I suspect, in a bid to pacify me, so I just cradle it in my hands, letting the heat soothe my jangled nerves.

This was not how I imagined my day in Chicago going. I arrived at the tower to find half a dozen fire trucks pulling out of the premises, and most of the Ecolab's staff gathered at the fire assembly point on the front lawn. Apparently, a fire had started from a wastebasket and caught a desk or something.

What was most surprising, though, was the number of fire trucks that attended to such a small fire. Must be a Chicago thing because back home, the entire tower would have to be engulfed in flames to get that kind of fire response.

When after almost an hour of hanging around and no one could explain what we were still doing out on the lawn despite the fire having been contained, I marched into the lobby and demanded to either be allowed up there or have someone from Ecolab come down and speak to me.

I wonder if I look as miffed as I am, or if the woman, whose name badge reads Jenny, is just a naturally anxious person.

"I'm sure someone from the company will be able to give you an update soon," Jenny says, then hurriedly picks up the phone blinking with an incoming call.

After about a minute of listening, Jenny finally puts the phone down. "Um, Miss O'Shea, I'm really sorry, but I've just been informed that Ecolab will remain shut for the rest of the week."

I raise a disbelieving eyebrow. "Because of a wastebasket fire?"

She fidgets with a pen, her eyes avoiding mine. "Well, it's not just that. I've been advised the entire floor is inaccessible as it is now flooded due to the, um, heroic efforts of the fire unit." Jenny has the grace to look mortified. Quickly she adds, "Besides, there is to be a police investigation."

I want to laugh and cry at the same time. Heroic efforts to put out a wastebasket fire? The whole floor flooded in a bid to put it out? It sounds like it's the Chicago Fire Unit who need to be arrested to have their heads re-screwed on.

"So what now?" I snap angrily.

"I'm afraid you'll have to reschedule," she says, then shrinks back as if expecting me to explode.

I take a deep breath, trying to quell my rising irritation. "Reschedule? I flew all the way from Boston for this sample. It's crucial that I get it today."

She bites her lip, clearly flustered. "I understand that, but there's nothing I can do right now. There's no one up there to attend to you."

The tea in my hand is no longer comforting; it's just hot and annoying. "When can I return for it?"

"I'll need to check with Ecolab logistics and maintenance," she stammers. "But it could be weeks before that floor is cleared for operation again."

"Weeks! I don't have weeks."

She looks about to cry, and I almost feel bad for yelling.

"Look," I say, softening my tone, "I need that evidence as soon as possible. Is there any way you can get someone from Ecolab to give me an update?"

She nods vigorously. "I'll email the logistics team first thing tomorrow and copy you in on it."

"Thanks," I mutter, though it doesn't feel like a victory. Doug Harrison will be livid. He'll somehow find a way to blame me for this. And I can't even imagine what Jim Pearson will do to Doug.

I step outside the deserted lobby and pull my coat tighter against the biting autumn wind. Anxiety gnaws at me, each step heavier than the last. The evidence retrieval was supposed to be a simple task, but nothing about this trip is turning out simple.

I flag down a cab. "O'Hare Airport, please," I tell the driver as I slide into the backseat and settle back against the worn leather.

He nods, merging into the flow of traffic. I close my eyes and sigh, pushing away the growing frustration.

We drive in silence for half an hour until traffic starts to build, gradually slowing us down to a crawl. And then it becomes a standstill.

The cab inches forward every few minutes, the driver fidgeting with the dashboard knobs, frantically changing radio stations as if searching for traffic updates.

Minutes slowly turn into an hour, dusk giving way to a moonless night, and we've barely moved. I lean forward, peering out through the windshield, seeing traffic stretch as far as the eye can see—a sea of red brake lights and honking cars.

"What's going on?" I ask.

The driver shrugs. "No idea. Never seen it build this bad so quickly before."

I check my watch for the hundredth time. At this rate, I'll be lucky if I even make it to O'Hare by midnight. Maybe tomorrow's flight. Maybe never.

I press my forehead against the cool glass of the window, watching as people start abandoning their vehicles, slamming doors with excessive force before marching off to investigate the holdup. I briefly consider joining them but decide against it.

Why ruin a perfectly good evening stuck in traffic by actually finding out what's causing it?

My phone buzzes, lighting up the dark interior of the cab. It's Dad. Again.

I stare at it, my finger hovering over the "End" button before letting it go to voicemail. The man has called me about a dozen times since he hung up on me this morning. Did he seriously think the fact that he hasn't forgiven me for that first time, or his tantrum today would stop me from doing my job?

What's his issue with me leaving Boston anyway? He needs to fucking chill out with the paranoia and take up a nice, relaxing hobby.

Like volcano climbing.

Instantly, a pang of guilt twists in my gut, as it always does when I chafe at his odd behavior or his overprotectiveness. I really can't blame him for being the way he is.

I finger my thin red scar through my shirt, a souvenir from an open-heart surgery at the age of five. One of a few aimless bullets had missed my heart by a hairline.

The bullets came from a deranged gunman who had opened fire in Airydale Children's Park. I was one of the many who survived.

My dad—who is, in truth, my uncle—however, lost everything that day. His wife, his two boys, his brother—my father, and his sister-in-law, my mother.

Stricken by grief, he'd nursed me back to health and adopted me. But as if the universe wasn't finished toying with him, I got thrown out of a car when a drunk cleared us off the road on the way to a hospital appointment, shattering my right hip in the process.

But here's the real kicker: all of that happened in Boston.

So why the fuss about never leaving Boston? My life has been more at risk in Boston than anywhere else on earth. But I suppose I'll never get it.

After I let yet another call go to voicemail, I decide to type him a reassuring text.

Daddy, can you stop worrying? I'm still in one piece, and no, I've not spoken to any boys. I'm now, in fact, on my way back. No alien abductions to report. Yet.

I switch off my phone before he takes that as an invitation to call—in other words, monitor my progress by demanding a minute-by-minute update on my location. Because nothing says, "I trust you not to get yourself killed," quite like real-time surveillance.

The cab driver leans out his window and shouts to a man walking back from the front of the traffic jam. "Yo, what's the holdup over there?"

The man shakes his head. "Some idiots in Porsches managed to wrap themselves around two huge Escalades. It's a real mess up there, but can you imagine there are no emergency services on the scene yet?"

"No shit," the driver responds. "How would they get through to the wreckage in this gridlock?"

"That's the other thing, though, man. Ain't no bodies over there. Given the pile-up you'd expect bodies, but . . . the cars are empty. It's a fucking mystery."

The forensic analyst in me is already putting the puzzle together. Four expensive cars in a pile-up. No emergency services. No bodies. It has 'unnatural' written all over it. Deliberate even. I shut off my overactive brain before it conjures up a whole conspiracy theory to torture me with.

The driver thanks the guy, then turns back to me grimly. "Miss, it doesn't look like you're getting to O'Hare in time for your flight tonight."

I already suspected that, but having the man confirm it lends a note of finality. With a sinking feeling, I switch on my phone and start tapping, searching for hotels nearby, desperate for a warm bed and a moment of peace after such a hellish day.

I stop my scroll on The Chicago Marston, just less than a mile away.

"Hey, you know this place?" I ask, showing the driver my screen.

He squints at it and nods. "Yeah, nice hotel. Just off Wellington Avenue, not too far from here. It's that high-rise building you can see all the way from here."

I glance out the window, weighing my options. The hotel beckons, promising a hot soak and soft pillows to ease the day's stress.

The driver eyes me warily. "You're not seriously thinking of walking there, are you?"

I shrug. "It'll be faster than waiting for this gridlock to clear."

He frowns, his gaze drifting to the darkened overpass in the distance. "I wouldn't recommend that. Just wait a bit, miss, and I'll take you there once we start moving again."

His warning sends a chill through me, but the hotel's allure is too strong to resist. My phone buzzes again with another incoming call from Dad. I ignore it.

"Thanks, but I think I'll walk," I say, handing the driver a few bills. "I could use the fresh air."

He shakes his head, his expression worried. "Be careful, miss," he calls as I leave the cab.

The sounds of idling engines and honking horns envelop me as I weave between the motionless cars. The air is thick with exhaust fumes, and the glare of headlights illuminates the frustrated faces of drivers trapped in the gridlock.

I reach the median, pausing to catch my breath. The Chicago Marston looms in the distance, the skyscraper a beacon of comfort amidst tonight's chaos. The din of the highway starts to fade away as I dart across Wellington Avenue, the sound of engines slowly giving way to the chirping of crickets.

I reach the quiet side road and approach the overpass entrance, which looks like a gaping maw of darkness. I quicken my pace, my footsteps echoing off the concrete as I walk right past the entrance and cross onto the sidewalk, clutching my bag tightly. The cuboid shape of the empty evidence box digs into my side, mocking me with a reminder of the day's failures.

I sigh in relief when I finally take the small steps off the sidewalk and into the Marston's huge parking lot. The lot stretches out before me, the high-rise building standing out like a promised land.

As I begin the final trek, an eerie stillness hangs in the air, the silence broken only by the distant hum of traffic and the crunch of tiny loose gravel beneath my kitten-heeled boots. The lot is pitch black, which strikes me as highly unusual, but the soft glow of the hotel's lights urges me on. I allow myself a small smile.

Maybe things are looking up after all.

Suddenly, a loud pop shatters the quiet, echoing through the night. I freeze, my heart slamming against my ribs. That sound . . . I know that sound. It's the unmistakable sound of a gunshot.

My eyes dart around the lot, searching the darkness, but the cars obscure my view. The shot came from the far end. That much I'm certain of. Every fiber of my being screams for me to turn and flee back the way I came, and the driver's cryptic warning rings in my ears, but the thought of returning to the gridlocked hell when salvation is just a few hundred yards away is too much to bear.

I take a deep breath, trying to calm my racing thoughts.

Maybe it wasn't a gunshot. Maybe my mind is playing tricks on me, conjuring up childhood fears of masked gunmen lurking in the shadows.

I force my feet to move, then I break into a jog, ignoring the dull ache in my right hip.

As I reach the middle of the parking lot, another pop rips through the air, stopping me in my tracks. This time it's followed by a scream.

Shit. That was definitely a gunshot. Without thinking, I dart behind the nearest parked vehicle, which, thankfully, is a large delivery van. I crouch low, my heart pounding so hard I can feel it in my throat, my breaths pumping out in a light smoke in the night's chill.

I think I hear another groan in the distance, but I can't be sure. More than anything, I need to get myself out of this rapidly evolving nightmare.

What the hell is it about Chicago, and why, of all things, do I find myself in the middle of a shootout every fucking time?

Once more, I look toward the Marston, its promise of soft pillows and a warm bath rapidly evaporating. I'll take staying alive over all of that. It's not worth the risk of walking into a criminal operation.

I stay crouched for another ten or twenty minutes, ignoring the biting cold and my joints aching from holding the same position for so long. When I don't hear any more sounds, I straighten and begin retracing my way back to the safety of the gridlock traffic. With any luck, I might even find my cab driver.

Suddenly, my phone vibrates against the metal evidence box in my bag, causing me to jump and accidentally drop my bag. The small metal briefcase clatters noisily onto the asphalt and spins a few feet away.

As I bend to pick up the case and my things—a pen, a tube of lip gloss, and a case of Tic Tacs—scattered onto the ground, my worst fears come to life: Footsteps.

Oh shit. Someone is coming this way.

I can't tell from which end of the van they're approaching, but I know they are not the footfalls of someone walking briskly to their car. No. These are much too slow. Heavy, deliberate. As if looking for someone in hiding. Terror slithers down my spine.

I can't stay here. Whoever fired those shots might have seen me from across the lot, and I don't imagine they'd be thrilled with the thought of having a witness.

I take the chance and with a sudden burst of energy, bolt from my hiding spot, running back toward the road.

Cursing my utterly moronic idea of wandering around in the dark in a strange place, I dare a quick glance over my shoulder to search for any sign of pursuit, relieved to find none. Still, I don't slow my pace.

Just when I think I might have escaped whoever was looking for me, I slam into a solid wall of muscle.

I scream as the impact sends me back sprawling on my ass, my skirt hiking up dangerously as I hit the asphalt. Pain shoots through my elbow and shoulder, but I barely register it over the terror gripping my soul.

As I scramble to readjust my skirt, my eyes travel up the imposing figure standing over me.

He's built like a linebacker, with a weathered face and a deep scowl that raises the hairs on my nape. A black trench coat hangs from his broad shoulders, the fabric flapping in the breeze. I try to scoot back, desperate to put some distance between us, but he bends over, grabs my arms, and hauls me up as if I weigh nothing at all.

Visions of how I might end the night flash through me. Pumped full of bullets and thrown into . . . *shit, what's the name of the river now? Yeah. Lake Michigan.*

No, that'd be stupid. They can't throw me in the lake. My body would be too easily discovered. They'd bury me in a thick forest where no one would ever find me. But then again, they could drown me if they tied my feet to a concrete—

Focus! I screech at my racing mind and face my captor.

"I swear on my mother's grave, I didn't see anything. I didn't hear anything, and I won't say a word," my voice comes out in a trembling rush.

The man stays silent, his dark eyes boring into mine for an unusually long time, almost as if he's trying to work out what species of animal I am.

I take the opportunity to catalog his features: a sharp jawline that probably hasn't felt a razor in weeks, the scar cutting through his left eyebrow, the deep-set eyes that don't miss a thing, and the faint scent of mint clinging to his black trench coat. Clearly, this is a man who takes his oral hygiene seriously, if not his grooming habits.

He notices the metal briefcase which has slipped out of my bag and onto the ground again and bends to pick it up. "What's that?" His voice is rough, like crushed stones.

"It's a case," I respond automatically.

He glares at me, looking slightly insulted. "I know what it is. What the fuck is in it?"

My mind spins with possible lies I could weave. Nothing clever comes to mind. "Jewelry," I finally respond. I deftly slide off my bracelet and let it roll onto the ground. It's not much, but it's the start of the trail I need to leave.

"Stolen?" he asks, narrowing his eyes.

Something about the assumption irks me despite the fear. Can't I own precious jewelry? "It was my grandmother's," I say with as much indignation as I can muster under his intimidating gaze.

He jiggles the case and gives me a look that suggests he thinks I'm full of shit. "You always tell ridiculous lies?"

Apparently, yes. "You wouldn't believe me if I told you the truth."

"Which is?"

"It's empty."

My heart pounds as he fumbles with the case. I'm hoping this goon does not find the work ID I tucked in one of the pockets of the case holder. Working in the DA's office won't do me any favors with a criminal.

He glares at me again. "You're right. I don't believe you."

"Well, there's a shocker."

"Open it."

"I can't," I say truthfully, but I know he won't believe me. Although all it's going to take is swiping my fingers one by one along the fingerprint pad.

The Hulk doesn't seem too interested in the box because he picks up my bag, tosses the box back in it, and then asks for my name.

"Addy," I reply.

"Uh-huh," he murmurs, clearly unconvinced by everything coming out of my mouth.

"And what are you doing here, Addy?"

"I needed a place to crash."

He looks over his shoulder and jabs a thumb at the Chicago Marston. "You wanted to crash there?"

I nod yes.

He grunts. "And, how did you get here?"

"I took a cab."

"Right." He studies me again intently before asking if I'm alone.

"Yes, I'm alone."

"And are you Irish, Addy?"

I shake my head so fast that I dislodge my bun, causing my thick curls to tumble down my back. "I'm American."

Apparently sick of our conversation, he rummages through my bag and removes my wallet. He pulls out my driving license.

"Adele O'Shea," he reads out loud, noting my Boston address. His eyes swing back to me with shock and a glimmer of something that looks suspiciously like recognition.

I open my mouth to tell him I'm pretty sure we've never met before, but his face smooths into a frighteningly cold mask that makes me shut my mouth.

"You're coming with me, Red Wine," he growls, and then his hands become iron bands around me as he hoists me over his shoulder like a sack of flour.

CHAPTER SIX

Dante

The roar of engines and blaring horns pulsates through me as I stand on the pitch-black overpass, watching a monstrous gridlock engulf the I-90.

Forty-five minutes. Forty-five fucking minutes, and the wreckage hasn't moved an inch. The Irish scumbags were just pulling out of Urban Elixir when we gave chase and finally managed to turn their expensive asses into scrap metal with a well-timed four-car pile-up.

I bark into my phone. "What the hell is happening? Those pieces of metal are not further apart from each other than they were half an hour ago!"

The idiot on the other end, who is probably a temp filling in for the Traffic Control Operator, mumbles about clearing the road in another thirty minutes.

I snap, "You'll be clearing your desk for life if that highway isn't up and running in ten. Do you understand?"

I hang up, shove the phone back into my breast pocket, and swipe away the rivulet of blood trickling down my left temple and onto my suit jacket. More quickly replaces it, so I reach into my jacket for a handkerchief to staunch the flow.

I don't remember getting the scratch, but it's an insignificant price to pay, considering the magnitude of the crash. One car managed to escape, but the other two weren't as lucky.

As I descend the pitch-black incline of the overpass and back to the Marston, the sound of a gunshot reaches me.

Sal had better not be getting carried away down there.

I usually prefer interrogating in a closed space, where I can control the environment, but tonight we don't have that luxury. Still, it's some small comfort knowing the Marston is ours, so getting the lights and cameras down was light work.

I return to find Sal standing before a kneeling Irishman, his other three friends sprawled on the ground, lifeless. Pietro must have left to check the perimeter again because I don't immediately see him.

"Salvatore. I leave you at a hotel with four guests, and in two minutes, three of them are dead. What does that say about our hospitality?"

Sal shrugs. "Two were already dying before you left. And one was chatting shit."

"And that one?" I cock my head at the only man left out of the four we captured.

"We only need one voice to sing, and his accent isn't so thick," Sal says, and I just huff and shake my head. As if the accent would be an issue for Sal or any of us.

An unspoken rule in our world is that you learn the languages of friends and foes alike, or you don't survive long. Be it the lilt of the Irish, the harsh consonants of the Russians, or the rapid-fire Spanish of the cartels.

But Sal is playing games, as usual.

"You'd better hope you're right about his singing voice," I mutter, then take a few steps toward the kneeling man. He's a big fellow with a ruddy complexion and a shock of dirty blond hair. His eyes, though filled with fear, maintain a defiant glare.

"What's your name?" I ask him, my voice deceptively calm.

He says nothing, just glares back at me with a stubborn set to his jaw.

"That's fair. I wasn't expecting you to answer. So, I'll rephrase. How many of you are still out there?"

He spits on the ground, hatred filling his eyes. "Don't need to answer that either, wop."

I chuckle. "Wop, huh?" I raise my gun and fire, targeting his right rotator cuff. I roll my eyes when he screams like a baby.

Disappointing.

"Keep it down, lad," I gently chide. "You don't want to scare the neighbors or lose your other arm, do you?"

He immediately quietens. That reaction alone tells me Sal is right. This one is worth taking back home. He should sing quite nicely, which is convenient for us, but I shudder to think that this might be someone's soldier. I cannot imagine any of my men being so easy to break.

I shoot Sal a look and dip my head in a nod. Job done, I holster my gun. "Third basement," I say, referring to one of the warehouses purpose-built for holding and questioning.

"Sure, Dante. And what about them?" Sal gestures to the other three on the ground.

"What about them, Sal?" I ask, already knowing he's about to suggest something deeply disturbing.

"Should we not box and mail them back to Boston?"

I grin when I'm proven right. "Nah, bury them. I'm sure the ones who escaped will fill in their friends back home on what happened. By the way, Sal, you might want to talk to Nico's wife about the shit show that goes on in your head."

He grins. "Yeah, I know. I already tried, but she kicked me out after three therapy sessions."

"Three? I'm sorry for being a self-righteous prick, then. You lasted two sessions longer than me."

We both guffaw, but our laughter is cut short by Pietro's sudden return; his usual sure strides are hesitant, and his face is lined with worry.

"Phenomenal work there, Pietro," I say, gesturing toward the I-90.

"Thanks, Boss." Pietro's brows are still furrowed.

I'd taken the wheel from Sal when we reached Urban Elixir. Sal's acute self-preservation instincts would never let him deliberately crash a car, so Pietro and I did it. And from the looks of things, the big man didn't even get a scratch.

"What is it, Pietro?" I ask.

"Two things. First is Don Vitelli. I can't reach him. As Underboss, in his absence, you call the shots . . ."

"I'm aware of that, Pietro. And since you didn't disobey a direct order from your Don, you've got nothing to worry about."

"I wasn't worried at all," Sal pipes up.

I glance back at Sal. "That's because you're an idiot. Pietro here isn't." I turn back to Pietro. "Nico will have to go through me before he gets to you, so you're good."

"'Preciate that, Boss."

I'd gladly take a bullet for any one of my men, but once again, a deep sense of affection and respect for my brother fills me. I'm almost certain that Nico didn't take Pietro's call because of me. Nico guessed exactly what I would do tonight, and giving a contradicting order would make the men pull back and leave me vulnerable.

"Pietro, you said there were two things?" I remind him.

He nods, glances at our hostage, and then approaches my ear. "I found . . . something else lurking on the far end of this parking lot."

I rear back and recount. We dragged out four Irishmen from the wreckage. Two died from their injuries, Sal offed one, and the last one is currently groaning at my feet. "Another one?"

He nods.

"How? Have those ones who escaped come back for their friends?"

Pietro shakes his head. "I don't think so. She was alone and on foot."

She! I gape at Pietro. I would have laughed at the absurdity except for the grave look on his face. "A woman?"

"You should see for yourself, Boss." He cocks his head toward one of the cars in the lot. "She's in there."

"Was she armed?"

Pietro's face darkens with annoyance. "No. But she's feisty. Was feisty," he amends. "She's out cold now."

At my puzzled glance, he explains. "She bit me. Got sharp teeth, too, and it hurts like a bitch," he grumbles. He then turns his back to me and shrugs off his coat and suit jacket, pulling aside the collar of his shirt to show me his shoulder blade.

Pietro was wearing leather overalls, so I don't know what the fuck he expects me to see there. The man has taken bullets without flinching, and yet at a woman's bite, he looks about to cry.

I suppose everyone has their tolerance. Holding back a chuckle, I say, "There are no puncture marks, Pietro, if that's what you're worried about, but you can still get tetanus shots later if you're really concerned."

"Unless you thought she was a vampire," Sal chortles, "in which case you're fucked."

"Sangue di Cristo!" Pietro crosses himself several times, which makes Sal laugh harder.

"Come on, show me," I say, following Pietro's hulking frame to a black car with the windows freshly broken, I suspect, by Pietro's elbow. I'm still wondering how the man managed to break into the car without triggering the alarm when I bend to peer through the shattered glass.

The first thing that hits me is the mass of red curls shot through with gold and chestnut. Thick, glossy, and thoroughly disheveled. I pull back as raw need slams into me, knocking me into an involuntary step backward. Then, almost immediately, my brain catches up, and I do a double take.

Because fuck me. There is only one person on earth who has hair like that.

I fling open the back door and grab her sleeping form, dragging her down the backseat toward me. And there she fucking is. Out cold, but there she is.

Adele.

What the fuck?

I stare. I can't help it. Porcelain skin, a dusting of freckles across high cheekbones, a pert nose, and full pink lips. My chest suddenly feels too tight, and I can't draw in air.

Without my permission, my index finger trails over her pale face and her chin, and finally brushes along her lip. She's wearing a prim shirt tucked into a skirt. *A fucking skirt!*

"Addy?" I murmur.

Her lids flutter open, but her green eyes are soft and unfocused, bringing back unbidden memories of the last time I watched her sleep.

Everything inside me wants to crush her against me and seal my lips to hers, but instead, I jerk back and away from the car.

Pietro looks at me curiously, but I ignore him.

Then when I trust myself to speak, I command, "Untie her, Pietro. Then get me a few joints and a car."

Pietro hesitates. He knows I haven't had a smoke in six months, and only recently, I'd been proudly bragging among the men about having finally kicked the habit.

He hesitates. "Boss—?"

"Now," I bark.

Pietro inclines his head. "Boss." He grabs a pocket knife and crouches into the car. Then he straightens and leaves without a backward glance. I never speak to my men that way. But I don't have the presence of mind to feel remorse. I have no capacity to feel anything apart from blind lust.

I hear her moan and start to shuffle around. Any moment now, she'll come out of the car.

And my carefully crafted control of the past twenty-eight months and six days will go up in flames.

If the Irish wanted to destroy me, they found the perfect weapon.

CHAPTER SEVEN

Adele

I wake up with my skull throbbing like it's hosting a rave party. For a second, I'm lost, my brain scrambling to make sense of my surroundings.

The musty smell of the car assaults my nostrils, and it all comes rushing back like a tidal wave of "oh shit."

I bit that hulking gorilla who had the audacity to throw me over his shoulder like a sack of potatoes. Guess he didn't appreciate my dental work, considering he tossed me to the ground like a possessed harpy.

My head must've bounced off the ground, knocking me out cold.

Passing out during a kidnapping? Real clever, Addy.

I gingerly touch the back of my head, half expecting my hand to come away sticky. Thankfully, there's no blood, just a goose egg the size of Texas. My wrists ache like they've been in shackles, but somehow, they're free now. Small mercies.

The wide-open car door screams "trap!" but my legs have a mind of their own. I'd rather crawl back to the road on my hands and knees than stick around for round two with Hulk.

I scramble out of the car, my head spinning like a top. And that's when I see him.

Not Hulk, but someone else. Someone who just might be the forbidden man who haunts my dreams and waking thoughts and makes me shake with need like a crack addict.

His back is turned, his head bowed, and his hands shoved in his pockets like he's posing for a GQ shoot. Six foot five, impossibly broad shoulders, and that glossy black hair pulled back in a messy man bun? Unmistakable.

This . . .

This simply cannot be happening. I promised myself there was no way the universe would let me run into this man. Not only did the universe let me down, the bitch decided I'd meet him while looking my absolute worst.

I'm barefoot—courtesy of my simian abductor, my hair is like a bird's nest, and I'm pretty sure my skirt is ripped in more than one place. Not exactly the reunion to relish.

I blink hard, hoping to clear the haze and the man from my vision, but there's no mistaking him. It is Dante Vitelli, in the flesh. My heart drops into my belly then flips over itself, which is ridiculous considering all the acrobatics it's been doing all evening.

I take a step forward, gravel poking into my bare feet. "Dante?"

He turns, his steel-gray eyes locking onto mine, and I lose my breath. Dante is the embodiment of danger—a walking, talking hazard sign. And no matter how much I hide, it seems danger always finds me. It's like a freaking curse.

I swallow against a suddenly parched throat. "How are you here?"

"I could ask you the same thing, Addy," Dante snaps angrily, hands still clenched in his pockets. "What the fuck are you doing skulking around in my city at night?"

His city? His tone gets my back up. Arching a single eyebrow, I shrug. "Oh, you know, I just thought I'd pop by Chicago for the world-famous 'Get Kidnapped by Goons' tour. It's all the rage now in Boston, you see."

His jaw clenches, a muscle ticking in his cheek. "Are you with the Irish?"

I stare at him in confusion, remembering how the Hulk asked if I was Irish. "Why the hell would I be with the Irish? What Irish?"

When he simply continues to watch me, I say, "Oh right, of course. Because every half-Irish redhead automatically comes with a built-in leprechaun squad, right?"

"Don't play dumb with me, Addy," he grits. "What the fuck are you doing in Chicago? I thought Daddy doesn't let you leave Boston."

I bristle at his mocking tone, my own temper flaring. "First of all, screw you. And second, I don't need anyone's permission to go where I please."

"Don't you?"

Just then, a large black SUV pulls up and my captor hops out. He tosses the key to Dante and says something in Italian, which Dante replies to with a curt nod. Then he disappears without another word.

Dante gestures to the car. "Get in. Let's get you out of here."

"Why don't you fuck off? I'm tired and in pain, and I need to crash right," I point to the Marston, "there."

He sighs, then starts to move toward me, but he seems to think better of it and stops. Even so, I feel the shrinking distance between us, like a force field that is getting stronger. "That place is mine."

Dear Lord. Is there anything he doesn't own?

"I suggest you come with me."

I cross my arms, standing my ground. "Are you insane? You expect me to come with you after you've been killing people tonight? I heard the gunshots."

A flicker of something dark crosses his face. "I haven't. Not directly."

It dawns on me that he means the accident. "The pile-up on the I-90 . . . that was you?"

Dante doesn't answer, but his silence speaks volumes. So I launch into a lecture, my voice rising with each word. "Do you have any idea what you've done over there? The thousands of lives and schedules you've disrupted? I had plans tonight as I'm sure all those other people had. Did you even stop to think about that?" I finish on a yell.

"Not really," he says icily. "But right now, I'm thinking about your Irish friends who escaped to find reinforcements. Now, unless you're planning on catching a bullet or two in that pretty head, you'll shut up and get in the fucking car. Now."

My knees instantly weaken at his tone, and I grit my teeth in annoyance. "Jerk," I huff, but the fact still stands. It's either I sit down in the next ten seconds or collapse in a heap. "Where are you taking me?"

"Away from here." Dante moves to the black SUV and opens the door for me; the perfect gentleman if you ignore everything else he's been up to tonight.

I catch a whiff of him as I go past him to get in the car. His scent is just as bold, musky, and exciting as I remember. Lord, I've missed the way he smells. Before I can help myself, I take in another lungful of him. And then another as he yanks the seatbelt and secures it without touching me.

God, he smells good.

I'm seconds away from burying my face in his neck when he jerks back and then slams the door.

Wow, Addy. Desperate much? Even he is trying to give you a wide berth but you? You're busy drowning your survival instincts in 'Eau de Bad Decision'.

"Is Hulky your man?" I ask as soon as he gets into the driver's seat. "The one who caught and bundled me into the car?"

Dante's lips twitch like he's fighting a smile, as he merges into traffic. The gridlock has magically disappeared and traffic is flowing as normal. "Yeah. You upset him, though. He doesn't appreciate being bitten."

There's something in his tone that makes heat pool in my belly. Memories of a different kind of biting threaten to surface, but I shove them down ruthlessly.

"You're right. Innocent women should politely ask their kidnappers for their preferences before they defend themselves."

"Innocent?" Dante scoffs, his eyes meeting mine. "Adele O'Shea, what the fuck are you doing here right now?"

I hesitate, weighing my options. I could lie, but Dante's always been able to see right through me. "I was trying to get to the airport," I admit. "But thanks to you, I've missed my flight."

"Why did you come to Chicago?"

"Work sent me."

His eyes flick to me then he scoffs, "You're the one Jim Pearson sent to Chicago?"

How does he know Jim Pearson or where I work?

I purse my lips, a stubborn refusal rising in my throat. I can't tell him about the case or the evidence I was supposed to retrieve. "No."

"Addy," Dante growls, his voice low and commanding. "Don't bother lying. You're terrible at it. Did you come for the sample?"

I stay silent, my heart hammering against my ribs. I can feel his frustration, but there's something else beneath that. Something that feels a lot like concern.

Still, I keep my mouth shut.

"Two and a half years, and you're still afraid of me," he shakes his head slowly, his voice softer now, almost vulnerable.

"I'm . . . not," I say, the words sticking in my throat. But it's obvious, even to me, that I'm not being truthful. Dante scares me, although not for all the reasons he should.

That last night, after I'd crawled out from under the table, I wouldn't let Dante come near me. He'd had to call me a cab straight to the airport. I was terrified, but more than that, I was confused as to why seeing Dante kill those guys for insulting me didn't turn me off.

For weeks, I tried to process what I was feeling, and I was horrified to realize that the deepest, darkest part of me liked it. A lot. I liked the way the air around him crackled. It was like watching a paranormal being shift. I found his dominance riveting, and his readiness to kill to defend my honor warmed me in a twisted way.

And that's the part that scares me.

Dante swears under his breath. "Addy, you know I'd never hurt you."

I do know he won't hurt me. But I still don't say anything. Instead, I study his profile, the strong line of his jaw, and the curve of his lips.

Even the blood trickling down from his temple to his jaw. I want nothing more than to catch it with my thumb and then . . .

What? My brain screams at me.

I tear my gaze away from him and ask, "How do you know where I work, Dante?"

Dante responds with a question. "Tell me who sent you to Chicago."

I hesitate, but something in his eyes, a glimmer of genuine concern, compels me to tell the truth. "My boss. Jim Pearson breathed down my boss's neck, and he sent me here."

His grip tightens on the steering wheel. "You came for the sample." It's not a question. I remain silent, but I don't need to say anything because he asks, "Why you, though? Why didn't they send someone from logistics? And where's your security detail?"

I shrug. "There wasn't time to do things by the book."

"Fuck," he swears again, dragging a hand down his face. "Why couldn't you just move to some small town and become the bounty hunter you always dreamed of?"

My lips twitch involuntarily. I know he's just trying to get a rise out of me. "I never said that, jackass."

The grooves in his cheeks flash briefly. "Might as well. You're obsessed with digging into crimes."

"And you live to create those crimes, don't you?" I retort dryly, and then it hits me: pieces of the puzzle falling into place and Kira's theory about the mafia funding Tommy Martelli's defense.

"Oh my God. The fire starting on the sixteenth floor, the fire unit's response . . . it wasn't a coincidence. You did that, didn't you?" I accuse. "You're sabotaging the Martelli case."

Dante doesn't deny it. He just keeps driving. When he finally decides to say something it's to ask, "Does your father know where you are, Addy?"

"I told you, Dante, I don't need his permission—"

He interjects, "I hear you. But does Benjamin O'Shea know where you are right now?"

I roll my eyes at his persistence. "We're not exactly on speaking terms, but yes, I mentioned it to him."

"Why aren't you speaking to him?"

I hesitate, considering whether to tell him, then I blurt, "Because he's a criminal."

Dante tenses beside me, wordlessly asking me to elaborate. And I find that I do. Like old times I used to be able to tell Dante anything.

"He . . . um. See, I found out that he deals with counterfeit money."

"And?" Dante seems to be waiting for more.

I snap, "What, like that's not enough? He's always been a man of high morals and brought me up to detest crime. How could he just turn around and do that?"

Dante huffs a disbelieving breath. "That's the reason you stopped talking to him?"

Irritation makes my fists clench. "I know for someone like you, that's like a kid taking candy from a shop, so I completely understand how you can be dismissive of what he's doing."

"Someone like me, huh . . ." Dante murmurs, then suddenly pulls the car over to the side of the road. He turns to face me, his gaze hard and searching.

"Addy. I and the Irish Mob are enemies. Did you know that every time you've come to Chicago, the Mob has deliberately trespassed on my turf? Now, if I were a man given to superstition, I'd conclude that you bring them with you."

"Well, it's a good thing you're not superstitious then," I snap, feeling a sudden urge to smack his too-handsome face. Insinuating that I might somehow be involved in a criminal gang just because of my Irish heritage makes me see red.

He watches me for a beat and then says, "You're right, I'm not superstitious." His voice softens. "In any case, you should leave tonight. Now, actually."

"What do you think I've been trying to do?" I say, nearly yelling. "I want to leave this damned city! I told you, I missed my flight."

"I'll get you on another flight," Dante clips.

I'm not prepared to examine why his determination to get rid of me stings. "You can't. That was the last one today. The next flight leaves tomorrow morning."

I watch in disbelief as Dante whips out his cell phone, his thumb moving at lightning speed across the screen. He brings the phone to his ear and speaks in a low, urgent tone. "Yeah, I need the jet. No, just a skeletal crew. Make it fifteen minutes."

He clicks off the call and tosses the phone onto the dashboard. "You're leaving tonight, Addy."

He's flying me out on his jet? Memories of the last time that happened assail me. When he dragged me onto his lap and fucked my brains out in the confines of his tinted SUV. "You can't just fly me to Boston, Dante. That's . . . insane."

His lips curve into a humorless smile. "You should take the chance before I change my mind."

Change your mind and do what? I don't dare ask.

He starts driving again, and this time, he doesn't spare me another glance.

I, on the other hand, can't seem to stop ogling. He radiates so much animal magnetism, and after over two years of no contact, my senses feel overwhelmed by his proximity.

I glance at his profile again and notice the muscle ticking at his jaw, the rigid set of his shoulders, and the white-knuckled grip on the steering wheel. His eyes blaze with intensity, but his demeanor is cold and detached.

Like the eye of a hurricane.

His restraint is palpable. Dante is holding himself back, and the effort is etched in every tense line of his body. I can almost taste the words he wants to say, the actions he wants to take, but he's reining them in.

Why? What does he want? What is he hiding? What does he know that I don't?

The questions burn in my throat, but I push them back, afraid of the answers. Afraid of the truth that might shatter my razor-thin resolve.

Silence stretches in the car, the air between us redolent with desire and unspoken words as Dante speeds through the night.

Before long, my skin begins to prickle with the need to touch him. But I know it'd be stupid to try it. Instead of doing what my body screams for—to reach across the console and place my hand on his bunched thigh, I lean back and slide my hand over my own thigh, rubbing small soothing circles, imagining it was Dante's callused hand.

Dante instantly floors the accelerator, shooting beyond the already breakneck speed. I should be terrified by how fast the man drives, but he handles cars so smoothly it hardly feels dangerous.

Subtly, I drag the hem of my skirt an inch higher. I know I'm playing with fire right now, but a part of me, a part I've denied for too long, wants to get burned.

A private airstrip—a strip of asphalt illuminated by the harsh glare of floodlights—materializes out of the darkness, ending my unnoticed strip tease.

The SUV screeches to a halt a few hundred feet away from a sleek black jet. The engines are on, and the sound is unnaturally loud in the otherwise empty airstrip. I see a lone man with a high-vis jacket waiting at the bottom of the idling aircraft.

"How do you even have a jet waiting so quickly?" I ask, my voice barely above a whisper.

Dante's jaw unclenches. "I just returned to Chicago not long ago myself. Go." His voice is steely, brooking no argument.

I hesitate, my hand on the door handle. Dante still hasn't looked at me. I hate how he can maintain control while I'm completely unraveling.

Forcing myself to open the door, I step into the cool night air and make my way toward the waiting jet. Every step away from Dante feels like I'm dragging my feet through thick molasses.

The man at the bottom greets me as I reach the aircraft steps. *"Benvenuta, signorina."*

I nod, my throat too tight to speak.

The low rumble of the jet engines vibrates through my chest as I take the first few steps. Suddenly, I can't go any further. My hand clenches around the cold metal handrail, unwilling—unable to let go.

It's as if there's an invisible string connecting my back to that SUV, and I've now reached the end of the tether.

Don't look back, Addy. Please.

After what feels like hours of battling with common sense, compulsion wins out, and I turn back, my eyes seeking out Dante.

He's stepped out of the SUV and is leaning against the side of it, all coiled tension and barely restrained power. A cigarette glows between his fingers, the tip a bright ember in the darkness.

The thought of leaving like this, of never seeing Dante again, is unbearable. Before I realize it, I'm walking back to him.

Dante goes statue-still as I approach, but his eyes, much like a predator's, track my every move.

"What do you want, Addy?" He bites out, his baritone rougher than usual.

"I hate it when you smoke," I blurt.

His lips twitch with a ghost of a smile. "Is that what you came back here to tell me?"

"Yes," I lie, my heart pounding against my ribs.

Dante holds my gaze for a long moment, then tosses the cigarette to the ground and slowly crushes it beneath his shoe.

"Done. You can leave now." He nods toward the plane, his message clear.

But I can't move. I can't tear my eyes away from him. I stand there, drinking in the sight of him, committing every detail to memory.

After what feels like an eternity, Dante moves. In one fluid motion, he uncoils and pushes off the car, grabs my bag, and tosses it to the ground.

Then he pulls me roughly against him, and his mouth crashes down on mine in a kiss that sears me to my bones.

CHAPTER EIGHT

Adele

Dante crushes me against the car, his mouth devouring mine with a desperation that matches mine. The kiss is savage and electric, sending lightning bolts straight to my core.

His hands tangle in my hair as he tilts my head back to deepen the kiss, and I moan, arching into him.

It's been so long, too long, and pent-up desire explodes between us.

His tongue traces the contour of my lower lip, demanding entry, and I open for him with a whispered curse. And then he invades my mouth, exploring every inch of me like he's been starved for a decade. And maybe he has. Maybe I have too. The years apart melt away as our bodies collide in a frenzy.

His scent—musk and sandalwood—teases me, and I lose my breath, trying to suck in more of it. My fingers clutch at his shoulders, digging into the fabric of his jacket. I can feel the hard planes of his body, the restrained strength beneath the surface, and it sends another thrill through me.

Dante's hands roam, skimming over my hips, my thighs, pulling me tight against him. I whimper as he grinds his arousal into my soft belly. Then he pulls back, his eyes dark with desire and growls low in his throat. "Fuck, I missed the way you taste."

My response is a breathless laugh. "Did you really?"

He only licks his lips, and then his mouth claims mine again. This time, the kiss is deeper, wilder. Our teeth click together, our tongues falling back to our old rhythm, only it's harder and more urgent.

His cock twitches against my lower belly, and I know I'd die if I don't feel that solid length inside me again. He groans into my mouth as his hands grip my hips, and then he starts to slowly grind me against his cock.

Goosebumps cover my skin. I love it when Dante does that with my hips—uses me for his pleasure. Still driving me insane with his mouth, his hand slips beneath the hem of my skirt, then goes straight for the jagged scar on my right hip and starts to stroke it in slow, perfect arcs.

"Jesus. Dante. Please." I sigh against his mouth.

He knows how sensitive I am over that knot of wrinkled skin and what would happen if he touched me like that. Dante is telling me he's not messing around.

He wants me now. Here.

Mindless with lust, I tug at his jacket. With a roll of his shoulders, he shrugs it off and then tosses it on the ground. Then his hand slides under my shirt, stroking my belly and waist, and I shiver at the feel of his calluses.

"How are you so fucking soft?" he murmurs, his lips nibbling a path along my jaw. I cling to him, my fingers digging into the rolling and bunching muscles of his wide shoulders and sinking into his thick silky hair.

Dante grabs the edge of my skirt and hikes it up, baring my thighs. A cool breeze teases my skin, sending more goosebumps across my flesh.

His fingers trail higher and higher until he's tracing the edge of my panties. The delicate lace does absolutely nothing to hide my arousal from him. I gasp as Dante traces the seam of my labia, catching the wetness that has gathered there.

"Do you want me to stop?" he murmurs, his breath hot against my ear.

"Yes, jackass," I moan, my nails digging into his back as I spread my legs wider.

He chuckles wickedly against my skin as his thumb starts to rub my clit. I bite back a moan, my hips bucking involuntarily, and bury my face into the fragrant skin peeking between his partially open shirt, his necklace cool against my heated cheeks.

"I am so fucked," Dante murmurs, and suddenly, he snaps the crotch of my panties and slips a long thick finger inside me.

"Dante!" My brain short-circuits as my inner muscles clench tight around him in a way they never do for anyone else. It's as if my body remembers what to do. What it was taught to do.

Deep and fast, he thrusts his finger in time with the insistent beat of my heart as pleasure swirls inside me. I can feel my orgasm nearing, coiling tightly in my belly like a spring. My head falls back against the car window, and I claw at his back, urging him on as he finger-fucks me with reckless abandon. My hips buck against his hand, seeking more friction, more of him.

He adds a second finger, stretching me wider, and I start to hear myself above the hum of the jet engine nearby. Which means I'm getting outrageously loud, but I'm too wound up to care. I'm teetering on the edge of climax, waiting for that final nudge.

As if reading my mind, his fingers curl with just the right amount of pressure, hitting my G-spot repeatedly. My vision sparks bright, and I shatter.

White-hot pleasure rips through me, and my body convulses. I cry out his name as wave after wave of pleasure washes over me. Dante groans with me as if he acutely feels my pleasure. He continues to pump his fingers inside me, drawing out my orgasm until I'm trembling.

Even when my vision clears, his fingers remain inside me, his face buried in the crook of my neck. My nails are still digging into his back, my arms still gripping him just as tightly.

He's not ready to stop. Neither am I.

When he finally drags his fingers out of me, I whimper at the sudden loss. He raises his head and pins me with his scorching hot gaze. For a long minute, neither of us moves, and it feels like Dante is staring into my soul, sifting through every decadent thought.

Thoughts of wanting to touch him . . . taste him.

And then he proves he sees through me when he gruffly commands. "Do it."

My lids flutter closed as my cheeks flush. He's read me like a fucking book. With shaking hands, I obey, undoing his fly and zipper, then I reach for his thick cock. He jerks in my hand as I stroke him, triggering a wave of lust so intense I bite my lip.

He's so big that I'm no longer sure what I want more. His cum on my tongue or his girth stretching my pussy. Still, my mouth waters for a taste of him. My foggy mind begs me to make true one of its deepest fantasies.

I've never had Dante in my mouth before; there was only so much of each other that we managed to explore over the few nights in a three-month period, one of which I was a blushing virgin.

I run my thumb back and forth over his glans, catching a drop of precum. Immediately, I raise my hand to my mouth, but Dante stops me. He catches my wrist and instead suckles my wet thumb into his own mouth.

I gasp, shocked and aroused beyond words and more desperate than ever for him. Dante kisses me then, and shamelessly, I run my tongue along his, trying to discover the taste of his essence, but it's too faint.

I draw back, lust warring with irritation. "You're such a tease," I whisper.

He shrugs. "There's plenty more of it, Addy. You know what to do."

I don't even hesitate. I start to sink to my knees, but Dante shakes his head and slips a hand under my ass, hoisting me back up against him. "Wrap your legs around me."

My breath hitches at the command, and I do as he says, my skirt riding up to my waist. I feel exposed, vulnerable, the cool night air teasing my bare pussy. Dante's hands skim my hip, and I shiver.

Then I feel the broad head of his cock nudging at my entrance. In one smooth thrust, he buries himself to the hilt, filling me, stretching me too full. I bite my lip to stifle a moan, the sound emerging as a whimper.

Dante's hands tighten on my hips then he growls, his voice rough with restraint, "Are you okay?"

For a moment, I can't speak. My hips move of their own volition, struggling to accommodate his size. I forgot just how *much* Dante feels like. And then I nod. "Fuck me."

He swears, a string of Italian curses, then his hips pull back, withdrawing almost all the way out before slamming back into me. I scream as pleasure explodes in my pelvis.

The car shakes with the force of his thrusts, the sound of flesh slapping against flesh filling the night air. I cry out with each thrust, my body a live wire of sensation. Dante's hands slide up my torso, palming my breasts through my bra, his thumbs teasing my nipples to tight peaks.

"Dante," I cry out. My head thumps against the car, but I hardly feel it. Dante sinks his fingers into the hair at my nape to steady me even as he pistons harder and faster into me.

"Oh God, Dante. Fuck!"

"You take me so good, Addy," he groans.

But even amid our frenzied passion, Dante remembers my hip. He supports my right hip with a big hand, massaging my scar with his thumb as he thrusts. The gentle pressure sends sparks radiating through my body, amplifying my pleasure in my core.

And then it becomes too much. My back arches clear off the car as my orgasm hits like an avalanche. "That's it, Addy," Dante growls. "Come on me."

I'm still shuddering with the force of my climax when his thrusts become jerky and less controlled. With a hoarse shout, he lifts my hips just so, changing the angle as he plants himself so deep that he drives me right onto that knife edge of pain-pleasure.

My breathing goes shallow. It's too much. "Fuck, Dante, please," I whimper, squirming, unable to stand the pleasurable ache blooming in my pelvis while my walls stretch to take the whole of him. He's never been this deep before; he never made me take his entire length before.

With a muffled shout against my neck, Dante starts to come, his release scalding hot. I moan, twitching and helplessly milking his cock as he spills himself inside me.

When our breathing slows. Dante raises his head, peppering my neck and shoulders with tender kisses. We remain in that position for long moments until, slowly, he pulls out of me and sets me on trembling legs. I whimper both at the pulsing emptiness between my thighs and the satisfying feel of his cum sliding out of me.

Once I'm steady on my feet, Dante drags me against his chest, his arms banding tight around my back and waist. His lips stroke back and forth over my temple, not quite kissing, just . . . letting me feel him. Smell him. Hear his heart pound hard against me.

How does this hug feel even more intimate than everything else we've just done?

"Christ, Addy," Dante curses, his voice rough. "You're lethal, you know that?"

Dante holds me until the fog of lust lifts. Then, one by one, the brain cells that sparked out the moment I laid eyes on Dante start to spring back to life and process what just happened.

I fucked Dante. A hardened criminal. The same criminal who's sabotaging our case.

I wait for the panic to set in, but it doesn't. Instead, I become increasingly aware of how much my skin tingles for. . . *him.*

"Addy," he whispers, leaning back. "Look at me."

My heart lurches when I finally muster the courage to meet his gaze. His eyes are ablaze with a raw, primal need that sends goosebumps on my skin. I know that look all too well; Dante wants more.

He's going to ask to take me home. And I'm not entirely sure I wouldn't turn into a giant stupid clit and say yes.

Mustering every ounce of willpower, I shake my head and say, "I should go."

Without a word, Dante steps back and starts adjusting my clothes. Then he takes a few more steps back, presumably to give me space.

The silence between us stretches, and neither says anything to break it. I turn to leave, feeling the weight of his gaze as I slowly walk back to the jet, cursing my kitten heels, which, right now, may as well be twelve-inch stilts for how steady I feel.

I grit my teeth, forcing my trembling legs into an even gait. It's silly that I'd happily let Dante pull up my skirt and fuck me right in the open, yet my face flames with embarrassment at the thought of him watching me limp.

As I reach the waiting plane, Dante calls out. "Adele," his voice carries across the distance between us.

I stop.

"Don't ever come back."

His words cut through me like a knife. He's right, of course. I should never return to this world, to him. But hearing him say it out loud hurts more than I expected.

"I'll still need to return for the sample." The words feel strange on my tongue, knowing he was the one who foiled this attempt to collect it.

"There's nothing to return for. Jim Pearson will find out soon enough that the sample is gone." His voice is steady, unwavering.

I whirl and stare at him in disbelief, my eyes widening. "What do you mean, it's gone?"

He shrugs, his expression unreadable, a mask of indifference. "It's been taken care of. Destroyed."

I don't know whether to marvel at his audacity or be disgusted by his blatant disregard for the law. I eye him again as if seeing him for the first time. His tall frame, broad shoulders, and arms thick with muscles honed from years of doing God knows what in the name of the Outfit.

His glossy hair is disheveled, long strands grazing his chiseled jaw and neck. I must have yanked off his hair tie in my frenzy, lost in passion. If I didn't have the sticky evidence running down my legs, I wouldn't believe that this cold, detached criminal was just inside me, taking me to heights of pleasure I forgot existed.

And now, he stands there, calmly telling me that the evidence, the very reason I came to Chicago, is gone. Destroyed. As if it meant nothing.

"I see," I respond. As I study him, I am hit by just how different our worlds are.

He operates by a code of his own, one that's written in blood and whispered in shadows. It's a world where the rules that bind the rest of us are just suggestions, and I can't help but feel a twinge of envy.

I wonder what it might be like to live like so, to be unburdened by the constraints that hold down the rest of society.

Without another word, I shake off the traitorous thoughts and take the steps up the obsidian jet. The footman who had been present earlier is now conspicuously absent.

As I ascend the steps and step into the cabin, the extravagance sparks a sense of deja vu—the buttery leather seats, gleaming wood panels, and sparkling chrome accents all exude an air of indulgent luxury that reminds me of that day Dante showed me his true self.

Only after I've settled into my seat do the crew emerge from behind the closed doors. Suddenly I understand the reason for their brief absence and a fresh wave of heat suffuses my cheeks.

Yet the crew maintain an air of utmost professionalism, greeting me warmly and offering refreshments and a steaming towel. I can't help but wonder if this is a common scene for them—Dante bringing various women aboard and ravishing them in plain sight.

As the jet takes off, I pull out my phone and see that I have missed eight more calls from Dad. I ignore them all, not wanting to deal with his incessant questions and demands, especially considering what I've been doing. I switch off my phone.

All I can feel is the ache and slickness between my thighs, the smell of Dante's skin, his taste, the blood from his temple smeared over the side of my face. I'd forgotten just how addictive he is.

From that first moment he approached me at the LBU gym, I'd been hooked on him. His confidence, his looks, and his raw sexual energy had drawn me in like a moth, and oh how sweet the burn was. Still is.

I shake off those thoughts and instead try to focus on how to break the bad news to Doug tomorrow. But it's no use. My mind keeps drifting back to Dante, to the way he'd touched me, the way he'd made me feel. I clench my thighs together, trying to quell the desire that still courses through me.

Kira might be onto something with these damn Italian men from Chicago.

As the jet soars through the clouds, I close my eyes and take a deep breath, telling my still painfully thumping heart it'll be okay.

That I just need to get back to Boston and forget about Dante.

That I'll never ever see him again.

But as I drift off to sleep, I can't drown out the voice that tells me I'll be back.

And soon.

CHAPTER NINE

Dante

THREE WEEKS LATER

The desperate words of Jim Pearson, a wiry man with a receding hairline and a pinched expression, crackle through the surround sound system in my study.

The only light comes from the flickering screen of the large, wall-mounted TV, bathing the dark wood paneling in an eerie glow. I lean back in my leather armchair, a glass of Macallan 18 cradled in my hand, savoring the aftermath of today's courtroom fiasco with a twisted sense of satisfaction.

Pearson now stands outside the courthouse, surrounded by a swarm of reporters, his once iron-clad case unraveling. Two of his key witnesses changed their minds at the last minute and another two have disappeared.

He knows that his witnesses didn't just change their minds on a whim—they were persuaded. Strongly.

Tommy Martelli's lawyers also played their cards right—the cards I dealt them.

"Do you think the judge will dismiss the case?" a reporter asks Pearson.

I turn off the TV and sip my whiskey, savoring the smoky burn and knowing that the dismissal of the case is practically in the bag.

Dismissing the trial is only the beginning. Tommy Martelli is a dead man, no doubt, but a twinge of regret grips me when I think of his family. No one should have to pay for the sins of their father. I wonder just what strings I'll have to pull to save Tommy's sons from the grave their father dug them when my phone buzzes beside me with an incoming text.

I don't need to look. I know it's from my wife-to-be.

Alina De Luca is nothing if not predictable. She sends me a dirty text every night at precisely eleven-thirty. Which then makes me glance into my phone screen to see Addy. And then I go a little crazier every night.

And so with a wry smile, I glance at my phone display. Addy's photo stares back at me as usual, a reminder of a world that should never have collided with mine.

My heart clenches, the familiar ache spreading through my chest. Three weeks ago, I'd taken that photo as she walked away from me, her fiery red hair flowing in the wind, my blood, sweat, and cum on her.

For twenty-eight months, I've tried to respect the Mob's wishes and stay away. To keep her oblivious to the realities of her life. But every night, the lines blur a bit more. And then, three weeks ago, the universe dropped her right in my lap. And still, I let her go.

I feel like a fucking saint at this point.

Needing to drown the driving urge to do something about this aching emptiness in my chest, I crank up the volume of my AirPods until Metallica's thunderous riffs blast through my ears. Then I open Alina's text.

> **I cant wait.▨▨▨**

Real classy, doll. What are we, twelve? I roll my eyes and run a hand down my face, suddenly feeling every one of my thirty-one years. Why do her texts feel so . . . juvenile? Each one is a reminder of the commitment I'm being shoehorned into.

The eight-year age gap between Alina and me feels like a chasm, even though it's the same as the one between Addy and me. But that's the thing with Addy, though. Her soul is . . . ageless.

If anyone had told me a woman's scars would drive me insane with need, I'd think they were high as a kite. But no, suddenly, a survivor of a bullet graze to the pericardium is the hottest fucking thing I've ever seen.

I fish the plain engagement ring out of my pocket and stare at it. I should've given it to Alina three weeks ago, the very day my red-headed witch waltzed back into Chicago and turned my life upside down again.

Screw it. I need to rip off the Band-Aid.

I dial Nico's number, giving zero fucks that it's almost midnight. Nico, until about a year ago would usually work out until midnight. But I know he's not in the gym right now. He's in bed with his wife.

Not that I blame the guy. He's happier, wealthier, more efficient, and with a lot more allies. The entire organization is in a better place because he's wrapped around that woman every night.

He picks up on the sixth ring. "This better be good," he grumbles, his voice rougher than sandpaper.

"I can't marry De Luca's daughter," I say, skipping the pleasantries.

Dead air. Then, "Are you shitting me? We're fresh out of Vitellis to trade with. You're the last horse in the stable."

I snort. "Why even bother with the horse when I can provide a gallon of premium Vitelli juice to knock themselves up with?"

It's a low blow, but I'm not feeling charitable right now. It's not Nico's fault that Alina changed her mind at the last minute, and no one knows the real reason why.

It's been the story of our lives since high school. The girls want one brother until they meet his lookalike, and then they want him, too. After a while Nico and I started sharing just to save time. At first, it was fun. And then it became inconvenient. Now it just fucking grates on my nerves to be reduced to a walking service stud.

"Christ, *fratellino*, you sound like a whiny brat," Nico yawns. "What, you've found a better bloodline to line up your genes with? Or are you just bitching about getting hitched?"

He sounds groggy, but I know he's not the least bit sleepy. He's just thrown me a challenge—daring me to admit something.

I say nothing.

"Dante, is there someone else?" Nico presses, proving me right, and for a moment, I wonder if one of my flight crew has talked.

No, it can't be any of them. They know better than to breathe a word about the things they see. Not unless they fancy breathing through a new orifice. Sal, though? That motormouth would sing like a canary on crack if Nico looked at him funny. But Sal wasn't there that night, thank fuck.

"No," I lie through my teeth.

"So, what's the problem? Alina's a knockout, and this marriage is crucial for the family."

"I need more time."

He curses colorfully, every pretense of sleepiness out of the window. "More time for what? To moon over Red Wine? Yeah, I know about the guy you have tailing her. Real subtle, Dante. Why don't you just skywrite 'I'm fucking obsessed' while you're at it?"

Fuuuck. Why can't Sal keep his trap shut to save his life? He's the only one who knows about the guy I hired to watch Addy from afar.

"She's under my protection," I say, trying to keep my voice level.

"Bullshit. Protection from what, her own family? You're fixating, and you know it."

"I'm not." I am.

Not many things hold my attention, but when they do, it's hard for me to let go. In Addy's case, what am I supposed to do when Benjamin O'Shea doesn't give a fuck that his daughter leaves one crime scene after another and cycles around Boston at all hours? She might as well wear a neon sign screaming 'Kidnap me! I'm fun!'

But that's all fine with Benjamin, just as long as the Italian bogeymen don't touch his precious daughter. Because clearly, we're the only danger that exists in the world.

"You are fixating, *fratellino*." Nico insists. "You can only control that impulse for so long and not if you keep obsessing. And it's only a matter of time before you snap."

"You make me sound like a fucking psychopath. I've kept it under control for over two years, haven't I?"

"Oh, you want a medal for keeping your word? Staying away from O'Shea's daughter is the price we paid for what you did in that restaurant."

Like I need to be reminded. "I know."

"Dante, you've not lost a mental battle since . . . forever. But you'll lose your mind if you don't take it off Red Wine."

"What, now you're a shrink because you married one?" I sneer.

"Dante, come on. You can't resist setting fires to rules that don't make sense. You're a pyromaniac in a world made of matchsticks."

I roll my eyes, but I have to admit that Nico is right. "Sounds like you've been peeping into the good doctor's notes. Or maybe you're lifting quotes directly from your own therapy sessions."

I hear Nico's heavy sigh, as if he's carrying the weight of our entire empire on his shoulders. Which, to be fair, he is.

"Dante, we have spent the last few years cementing the cracks of the broken city we inherited from Father. Orlando De Luca is a major fault line we can't afford to gape any wider. Any rebellion now, and we could lose our heads. Father, Mother, you, . . . Sophie."

Nico's voice catches on his wife's name and my heart squeezes like it's caught in a vice.

My brother loves his wife more than anything, which is why he's afraid of De Luca's rebellion. The rest of us he can risk, but he's terrified of Sophie getting a hangnail, let alone seriously hurt.

No Caporegime should be allowed to wield this much power over his Don.

"Nico," I say gently, as if talking down a spooked horse. "You do realize that a bullet in Orlando De Luca's brain would guarantee the peace you want, much more than a ring on his daughter's finger, don't you?

Nico grunts like he's entertaining the idea. "Really? And how would that work?"

I lean forward to press my point. "A handful of seasoned ghost assassins. Spaniards or Russians. We take out Orlando, Bianca, Bianca's father Don Rinaldi, and her three brothers. All six of them in one fell swoop."

Nico contemplates this for a full minute. I can practically hear the gears grinding in his head. "Tempting, Dante. Very tempting, but no. I'll take a marriage over a massacre. Less paperwork, you know?"

I shrug. "I knew you'd say that. You always were a hopeless romantic."

Nico's tone goes hard as nails, every trace of humor drained out. "Anyway, here are your orders, Capo. First, pack in the stalkfest. Get her out of your system, or keep her as a side piece. I don't care what you do as long as you don't bring her anywhere near Chicago."

"And second?"

"You have six weeks to marry Alina De Luca. *Capisci?*"

"*Sì, capito*, Don Vitelli," I drawl, the words like ashes in my mouth.

The line goes dead, leaving me alone with my thoughts like a mobster in solitary.

I take a minute to mull over my 'orders.'

Get her out of my system? Might as well try to win a marathon without a finish line. In hell. Wearing lead boots.

But I could marry Alina, then I wouldn't need to try to purge my brain of her because Addy wouldn't touch me with a ten-foot pole. Hell, she'll probably have my head on a platter if she finds out I was spoken for when I fucked her three weeks ago.

Flashes of memory light up my brain. The way her body spoke to me, a language more compelling than any omertà. The way her cries echoed over the idling jet engine. The way she looked when she'd finally taken all of me—like she'd found Nirvana in the ninth circle of hell. The way she moaned as I spurted deep inside her.

And far above all that, how fucking right she felt as her heart pounded against mine, asking me to keep her safe. To keep her. Period.

Before I picked up the phone to call Nico, I knew he'd never agree to kill De Luca. Just as I know Nico heard me loud and clear. I'm not going to marry De Luca's daughter. Not even if hell freezes over.

Which is why I know, without a doubt, that Nico is lying wide awake right now and planning contingencies. He probably has a whole playbook of 'What To Do When Your Brother Goes Rogue' scenarios.

What he doesn't know, though, is that Chicago will be getting a lot of Red Wine—and very soon.

Because I've already lost it. I have every intention of breaking my word and taking what's mine. Even if it means setting fire to this empire and watching the streets turn red.

Fuck me. I need another drink. Or ten. Something strong enough to make me forget I'm about to start a war over a girl.

Again.

CHAPTER TEN

Adele

"Ah, Adele! Ye've returned!" Ms. Ida, our full-figured, sixty-something-year-old housekeeper's round face splits into a beatific smile as soon as she spots me in the grand foyer of our stately home. She hurries toward me, her heavy footsteps echoing on the marble floor, to envelop me in her signature maternal hug.

The air smells, as ever, of wood polish and fresh flowers, mingling with the faint scent of Dad's cigars. As much as I hate to admit it, I've missed home.

In a thick Irish brogue, she gently chides, "Yer Pa's been worried sick over ye. I don't tink he's slept a wink in de past year."

"I left just a little over a month ago, Ida," I smile, feeling the warmth of her embrace seep into my bones.

"Aye, I know, but it feels like a whole year, child. Ye know he can't help bein' a worry wart, after everyting dat happened to his family . . . and yer poor ma and da."

Guilt lances through me, sharp and cold. My Dad may have lied about being morally upstanding, but nothing can take away the grief of him losing his family in a single day. And nothing should come between me and the only father I've ever known.

I nod, my throat suddenly tight. "I'm sorry, Ms. Ida. We had a fight, but I've come to smooth things over."

"Good on ye, child. Now what'll ye be havin' before lunch is done?" She proceeds to offer a range of snacks she has at the ready, her hands fluttering excitedly.

I have zero appetite, my recent debacle at work is all too fresh in my mind. Someone brought rum cake to work today and I must have overindulged because out of nowhere I'd gotten sick and thrown up in Doug's office. The bitter taste of bile still lingers in my mouth.

Terrified of catching something contagious, he'd immediately given me the rest of the week off to sort out whatever virus was plaguing me. Suddenly with so much free time and worsening guilt, I decided to take a cab home.

"I'm not hungry, Ida. I had a big breakfast this morning, and it's only after two." My stomach churns at the mere thought of food.

She shakes her head, her gray curls bouncing, clearly not having it. "I knew it. Dat's why ye've lost so much weight. Ye're not eatin' well. See?" She gently gathers my loose shirt in a hand so my small waist is obvious under my oversized shirt.

I smile, trying not to roll my eyes at her age-old mantra. It doesn't matter that my boobs and ass more than make up for my small midsection or that no matter what she feeds me, my waistline never changes.

"Okay, fine, I'll have scones," I concede, knowing it's easier than arguing. "Where's Daddy?"

"In his office waitin' for ye. He ran dere to wait de moment he spotted ye at de gates from de CCTV. Now ye know yer Pa. He'll act all aloof, but he was tearin' his hair out—what's left of it anyway, so be gentle wit' him," Ida cackles as she moves toward the kitchens, her laughter echoing off the high ceilings.

I stand for a moment, staring after her. Ida's knack for spinning reality has always been a constant in this house. Whether it was explaining away Dad's absences or interpreting scathing words as a sign of deep, unspoken affection, Ida seems unable to see or accept any other reality except that of a loving family. I've known for a while now that her perspective isn't always accurate, yet I can't resist wanting to see things through Ida's kind, rose-tinted perspective.

As I make my way to Dad's office, I find myself smiling despite the tension of the day. Her ideas about Dad's worry linger in my mind, painting a picture of a man anxiously pacing, sleepless with concern. It's a comforting image, one that Ida has always been skilled at creating.

As I walk through the familiar hallway, memories flood back: Running through these corridors as a child. The soothing sound of Dad's voice echoing off the walls as he carried on endless meetings with clients. The smell of his cigars always lingering in the background, even though he knew I hated it.

I remember how he would drop in unannounced during painful physiotherapy sessions, through my tough and dreaded Taekwondo lessons, and as I fumbled through violin class. He'd show up every time I felt like quitting, and suddenly, I'd want to try a little harder and be a little better for him.

I pass by the library, my only sanctuary, where I spent countless hours lost in books, escaping into worlds that both mirrored and were far removed from my own pain and isolation. The musty smell of old books wafts out as I pass, comforting and familiar.

When I reach his office, I pause, taking a deep breath before pushing the door open. Dad looks up from his desk. His receding hair, mostly faded with age to a cross between ginger and mousy brown, catches the light from the window. His hazel eyes light up as they take me in and the corner of his lips quirk up in a ghost of a smile as his gaze rakes over me.

Dad has never had an issue with my choice of baggy clothes. Quite the opposite, he seems to like it. Actually, there isn't any one of my choices he's kicked against—except for Chicago and the knowledge that I'd been secretly dating a bad boy. That seemed to torture him to no end.

Despite working from home, he dresses the same way on weekdays: an expensive tailored shirt rolled up at the sleeves and a waistcoat that masks a growing paunch. There's a half-smoked cigar between his fingers, the smoke curling lazily in the air.

"Adele," he says blandly. "Took you long enough."

I shrug, trying to appear nonchalant even as my heart races. "I didn't want to come at all, so don't push me, Daddy."

He smiles, the corners of his eyes crinkling. "Alright. Maybe what I should say is that I'm glad you've come home."

We remain silent for a beat, simply staring at each other. I get the urge to go and throw my arms around him, a move he never returns but still makes him flush with pleasure. We both need it, but I stamp it out, fully resolved not to forgive him too easily.

He gestures to the seat opposite him. "Why don't you sit down?"

I remain standing, crossing my arms tightly over my chest. "I'm good here. You said you wanted to explain. So explain."

He sighs and gestures to the seat again. "Please, Adele, sit. This could take a while, and I want you to be comfortable."

Reluctantly, I sink into the chair, the leather cool and firm against my skin. I watch him as he relights his cigar, his movements slow and deliberate. Instantly, the pungent scent wafts through the air, a contrast to the complex aroma of pine and fruit when Dante smoked three weeks ago. I'd tasted it on him too. Sniffed it on my hair that night and remembered it every night after as I laid awake in bed, craving the impossible.

Pulling my thoughts from that dangerous path, my eyes scan the bright, airy room.

Multiple monitors take up an entire wall, displaying stock tickers and financial news, while leather-bound books and awards line the shelves on the opposite side. I used to love this room. The very few times Dad allowed me to come in, sit on his desk, and tell him about something I'd read. Now, it feels like a cage.

"Adele, I know you're upset with me. And you have every right to be," he begins, his voice soft. "I want to explain everything to you, but first, I need you to listen with an open mind."

"Why do you do it, Daddy?" I ask quietly, my fingers tracing the intricate patterns on the armrest. "All those years, I thought you, this . . ." I throw my arms out, gesturing to the room, "was all legitimate."

He leans forward, resting his elbows on the desk. "Legitimate is a subjective term."

I feel a rush of irritation, my jaw clenching. "Oh, come now. You and I know where the law stands. What you're doing is a crime, punishable by law."

"It depends on who's making the law," he counters. As he leans back on his seat and takes several puffs of his cigar, his eyes begin losing their softness.

My voice rises slightly, betraying my frustration. "There's only one entity capable of making laws, Daddy. One government. One moral code."

"Yes, I know I've brought you up to think like that. But now I'm telling you, it's not true. There's more than one—"

"Let me stop you there, Daddy." I put my palm up to interrupt him. "It wasn't you who taught me to think that way. That is how the world works."

His smile is cold, indulgent, and designed to make me feel about two inches tall. But that was before. Now, it just irritates me.

"The world you knew of, Adele, is different from the one I'm going to spell out for you in the next few minutes. But before I do that, I want you to remember that everything I've done, and everything I will do from here on out, is to protect you."

"Protect me from what?" I ask, my heart starting to pound. I expected regret. An explanation of how he derailed from the straight and narrow. How he got enticed into a life of financial crime and money laundering. I didn't expect him to be cold, detached, and unremorseful. "Protect me from who, Daddy?"

"From the kind of people I work with," he admits, the hardness in his eyes now becoming steely. "I work with powerful people. Together we make a very formidable unit. But that also means that I don't always have the freedom to make independent choices."

I shake my head, trying to process his words. "I fail to see how you engaging in an elaborate money laundering scheme protects me."

He sighs deeply, rubbing his temples. "It's not just about the money. There's more to it than you know."

"Then explain it to me," I say, my voice trembling, already fearing what he might reveal. "I want to understand. What are you trying to tell me?"

He looks at me for a long moment, then his tone takes on a sudden urgency. "Adele, look, you're not safe out there on your own. You really shouldn't have moved out of here. And you should never have gone to Chicago. Or at least you should have informed me well ahead of going there."

A chill settles in my bones, goosebumps rising on my arms. "What do you mean?"

"There are people who would do anything to get to you," he states calmly, and a part of me wonders if my dad has gone off the rails, his paranoia finally tipping him into a mental breakdown.

"Who are these people out to get me, Daddy?"

He stands and goes to the window, taking a deep puff of his cigar and staring out into the back gardens. "Do you remember the incident at Airydale Park?"

I absently finger the scar on my chest. I was only five, so I can't actually recall the incident. But I remember crying myself to sleep the night before another surgery. I remember the physiotherapy sessions, and I remember being homeschooled until ninth grade. And I have the scar to show for it, so yes, it's safe to say that I was there.

"Of course," I say. "It was a random attack by a crazed gunman. We just happened to be in the wrong place at the wrong time."

He closes his eyes for a moment as if gathering his strength. "It wasn't a random attack, Adele."

"What do you mean it wasn't random?" My voice comes out as a whisper. "Daddy?"

He opens his eyes and turns to me, and I'm shocked to see his face pinched with cold hate. "It was an assassination attempt. And it didn't happen in Airydale, or in Boston for that matter. You were in bed with your mother in Chicago when it happened. You were shot six times, your mother eighteen times. She shielded you with her body, taking most of the hits."

The world around me blurs as I try to make sense of his words.

Shot multiple times? In Chicago?

My mind tries to piece together fragments of memory, but all I get is the smell of old books mixed with the acrid stench of smoke, the copper taste of blood, a woman's screams, and a masked gunman. My dad told me those were nightmares.

Apparently, they weren't dreams. They were memories, and for some reason my dad had me doubting my own reality.

An unpleasant buzzing begins in my ears, the sound making me want to plug them shut, to run and find a dark silent room, but I need to know.

"But . . . but what about the playground incident?" I ask in a trembling voice. "It's on record. The June 14th Airydale attack."

"Yes, the Airydale events are true, and they did happen that year," he admits, his voice heavy with regret. "But you weren't one of the victims. You were in bed with your mother when the gunman came. My sister was killed that night, but by some medical miracle, you survived against all odds. And you continued to survive through dozens of surgeries. I had to protect you and hide the fact that you didn't die that night."

My eyes widen in confusion, my breath coming in short gasps. "Hold on. Wait a second. How can my mother be your sister? I thought my father was your brother, Joshua O'Shea?"

His fists curl, his face contorting with rage as he snarls, "Your father is *not* my brother."

His sudden vehemence puzzles me, and his use of present tense isn't lost on me. There's a swarm of questions in my head, hovering like angry bees, but somehow, this is the first that tumbles out of my mouth.

"If only my mother and I were attacked that night, what about the rest of our family? My father? Your wife? Your sons, Brody and Baswell? Were they also assassinated?"

He looks down, his face pale. "No, because they never existed. I was never married, Adele. I don't have a brother—well, none you know of. And I never had children—well, except for you."

"But . . . but that's . . . impossible." I sputter out a disbelieving laugh as my gaze flies to the photo on the desk . . . One of him, his wife, and two ginger-headed boys with toothed smiles, taken around eighteen years ago.

There are dozens of similar photos dotting the walls around the house and in photo albums. His sons' old rooms are still immortalized to this day. We cry and put lilies on their gravestones every year . . . It's just not possible.

But I look into the cold unrepentant eyes of Benjamin O'Shea, the man I call Daddy, and I see the gut-wrenching truth lining his weathered face.

It was all a big, fat, elaborate lie.

The magnitude of the deception and the mockery that my life has been suddenly floors me.

My chest feels too tight, my breath coming in short puffs as I continue to stare at him, shock slowly giving way to horror, rage, then disgust.

And then fear. Fear that I have no clue who this man standing before me is.

He leaves the window and comes toward me, and I immediately shoot out of my chair, screaming. "Don't you dare come near me, you crazy lying son of a bitch!" I grab the back of the chair, the only barrier between me and him, as my eyes dart around for a weapon.

He puts up both hands in a reconciliatory gesture, his face a mask of calm. "I understand how betrayed—"

"Betrayed? Betrayed!" I scream, tears gathering and falling in swift rivulets.

"—you must feel." He continues in that chilling tone as if I hadn't spoken. "But I promise you, there is a very good reason why it had to happen that way. I'll explain just as soon as you calm down."

Calm down? Is he for real?

"The fact I'm not trying to get your skin under my nails right now should inform you how calm I am!" I yell, my hands shaking. "So don't fucking push me, you fucking bastard."

"Adele, I can't talk to you when you're like this."

I try to force my voice to a lower octave, but it doesn't work. "Fine. Answer me one thing then. What the hell was I doing in Chicago the night I was shot?"

My dad returns to the window, and I breathe a little easier with the length of the room between us again. Still leveling those cold eyes on me, he says, "You were born and raised in Chicago."

That knocks the breath right out of me. My legs feel weak, and I grip the chair tighter to stay upright. "But my birth certificate states that I was born in Boston."

His slow head shake confirms my worst fears.

"Does my original birth certificate bear another name?" My voice comes out as a hoarse whisper.

He remains silent for the longest time, his gaze fixed on some point in the distance. When he finally speaks, his voice is barely audible. "Adele, just know that you're not safe out there. And you shouldn't ever go back to Chicago. Move back in with me. Please."

Suddenly, it's too much to take in. The room seems to spin around me, and I feel like I might be sick again.

"Move in with you? Are you fucking insane? I don't even know who the fuck you are anymore, Benjamin." I spit his name at him and get a flash of satisfaction when he flinches. But I need more than that. I need to hurt him.

"What? You're shocked you don't get to be called 'daddy' anymore?" I wag my index finger, my whole arm trembling. "Ah-ah. Fuck that. You're not my father. You're the coward who's lied to me all my life.

For all I know, you could even be the deranged psycho who killed my mother and stole me."

I see a crack in his composure as a sheen of tears turns his hazel eyes glassy. But instead of sick satisfaction, I only feel . . . guilty. I've never ever seen him cry before. But he's lied to me all my life, first about who he was, and now, this. The liar even went as far as creating elaborate fake identities of his wife and children just to deceive me.

So, I steel myself against softening toward him and turn my back to him, my entire body trembling. The buzzing in my ear has become a full-blown screeching of nails on a chalkboard.

"I need to get out of here," I whisper.

"Adele, please. There's much more I need to tell you." His voice cracks, a desperate edge creeping in.

"I've heard enough!" I yell even as my heart pounds with the need to run. "I can't take any more of this twisted, fucked up life."

As I walk out of the study, I see Ida. Tears are running down her cheeks, carving paths through her makeup. She was obviously eavesdropping. She looks distraught. But rather than being shocked, she looks angry.

Angry at me.

I can tell straight away that Ida knows everything and that she's on Benjamin's side. She has always been on Benjamin's side. My favorite book in middle school flashes before me, a ratty, dogeared copy of George Orwell's *Animal Farm*.

Ms. Ida isn't just our housekeeper. She's Napoleon's Squealer, a tool of manipulation and mental shackling.

Suddenly desperate to escape the tangled web of lies, I turn and hurry down the hall, my footsteps echoing loudly in the silent house

"Ungrateful lass, ye are," she calls after me. The hard edge and assertiveness in her voice stops me in my tracks. Ms. Ida has never spoken to me like that.

Ida continues in her thick Irish brogue, each word hitting me like a physical blow. "For de last eighteen years, we have lived for not'ing except to protect ye, Adele. Ye owe yer life to dat man in dere, and ye should show him more respect, if not gratitude."

The door opens and my father's voice floats to me, calm and controlled once more. "Let her go, Ida. It was never going to be easy to break the news, so it's only fair that we give her some space to process it."

And that was the final straw proving I'm not who I thought I was. I was a doted-on, sheltered child, and now I'm a hunted orphan who should be grateful to her protectors.

I break into a run, not stopping until I'm outside the house, the cool air hitting my flushed face. Then I take several deep breaths, trying to steady myself. The scent of freshly mown grass fills my nostrils, a stark contrast to the turmoil inside me.

Everything I believed about my past, my family—it's all unraveling. The only place I can go is where I call home right now . . . my best friend's house.

But as I climb into the backseat of the cab that's still waiting in the driveway, I can't shake the feeling that I'm heading into an even darker unknown. The leather seats creak beneath me as I settle in, the driver's eyes meeting mine in the rearview mirror with a mixture of curiosity and concern.

As the car pulls away, I watch the house—the only home I've ever known—grow smaller in the rear window. It looks the same as it always has, grand and imposing, but now it feels like a beautiful lie, a facade hiding ugly truths. I turn away, unable to bear the sight any longer, and face forward, steeling myself for my next steps.

If only I had a clue what those would be.

CHAPTER ELEVEN

Adele

The second I step into Kira's penthouse hallway, the explosive beats of DJ Snake and Lil Jon's *"Turn Down for What"* fill the room, the powerful bass making the walls vibrate.

Shit. People. Today, of all days.

I shut my eyes, leaning heavily against the door. If only I could just disappear.

Kira mentioned this morning that she was having a few friends over to celebrate her latest gig—she's the official DJ for some new club launch. But I completely forgot in the chaos of the day.

The shouts filtering out from the living room make it sound like the whole of Boston is crammed in there. I promised Kira I'd be up for a few drinks after work, but right now, all I want is to lock myself in my room and have a full-on breakdown. My life has become a monumental joke in just one afternoon.

But a promise is a promise, so I huff out a deep breath, shove my racing thoughts into a cold, hard box, and force myself toward the living room. The bass thuds through my chest, growing stronger with every step.

Entering the living room, I take in the scene. There are about thirty people, a kaleidoscope of brightly colored hair, glittering jewelry, and designer clothes as they dance and mingle. Laughter and the clinking of glasses rise above the pulsing music.

My gaze lands on Kira, who's laughing with an arm draped around the shoulder of a guy with a shaved head and enough bling around his neck to sink a small yacht.

"Resin is going to be sick, Kira, you're a rockstar!" the bald guy yells over the music.

Kira beams. "So, does that mean y'all are coming or what? I know it's out of town . . ."

"Girl, are you trippin'?" a woman with pink braided hair and more piercings than I can count yells, giving Kira a high five. "VIP passes to the launch night? I'd crawl on my hands and knees to get there!"

I plaster a smile on my face, hoping it hides the turmoil brewing inside me. Only night owls like this lot would throw a party bang in the middle of the day.

"Hey, you must be Addy," a guy with rectangular glasses and a beanie perched on his head spots me leaning against the doorway.

There's a boisterous chorus of "Oi, Addy!" and I can't help the smile that tugs at my lips. As I approach Kira, someone hands me a glass of pink liquid with mint leaves floating in it.

"You made it, babe," Kira throws her arms around me. "And early as well. My friends just got here." She shouts over the booming music, "Hey, Zeddy! Where the hell are you? Addy's home." She leans in and whispers, "He's been dying to meet you."

"Zedd as in . . . the guy whose shirtless torso graced our wall all through college because you thought he was a God or something?"

She had a crush on Zedd, and it was one I got to experience with her since I was the one who had to describe the guy every day. By the time I'd gone over his looks a few thousand times, he'd started to grow on me. Until Dante happened, that is.

Kira has the grace to blush as she waves me off. "Yeah, well, we're friends now, and ever since he saw your picture, he's been obsessed with you."

Before I can say more, a tall, slim guy with spiked platinum hair saunters over, and I try not to choke on my saliva.

It's really Zedd in the flesh. The famous New York celebrity DJ. "You're serious! How is he even here?" I whisper.

"Same circles. By the way, close your mouth, babe," Kira teases, correctly guessing what my face is doing. "You'll give yourself away."

"Excuse me?" I snort. "Don't you mean give you away?"

She only gives me a playful nudge before Zedd reaches us.

"Hello, Addy," Zedd's voice is a rich tenor. His dark brown eyes warm over me. I already suspect he's interested. I should feel flattered. My heart should be racing, and my palms sweaty. But I feel . . . nothing.

Kira hovers while I smile politely and attempt to make small talk with Zedd. He's surprisingly easy to talk to, and within minutes I find myself starting to relax—until he asks, "So you're coming to Chicago too, aren't you?"

"Chicago?" I repeat, not quite following.

"Yeah, Chicago. The launch party this weekend."

Chicago. The city where my mother and I lived until she was shot twenty-four times.

Everything I learned today comes rushing back.

The gruesome attack.

The oppressive silence when I asked if my original birth certificate bore another name.

Bile rises up my throat, and I take a gulp of my drink to wash it down.

Bad move.

The cocktail, which should taste like lime and mint, lingers dangerously close to stale urine territory. Fighting nausea, I put my glass on the closest surface.

"Addy's coming to Chicago," Zedd tells someone behind him.

I'm already recoiling and shaking my head when Kira interjects.

"Zedd, Resin Club is actually in Evanston."

"Same thing," Zedd shrugs. "It's twenty minutes away from downtown Chicago. So, Addy, We'll be taking my new tour bus."

My mind scrambles for an excuse. "I . . . uh, have to work the day after."

"You work on a Sunday?"

Shit. "Yep," I say, feeling Kira tense beside me at my blatant lie.

"What do you do, if you don't mind me asking?"

"Um . . . forensics," I manage, taking deep breaths to calm my roiling stomach. My voice sounds strained even to my own ears. "I do forensics. I'm a forensic analyst," I repeat, just because I need to sound like a complete idiot.

Mortified at my blunder, I excuse myself and make my way to the terrace.

As I move through the crowd, desperate for air, I plaster on a strained smile, trying to appear enthusiastic. But my dad's and Ms. Ida's words twist like knives in my stomach, and the urge to vomit grows stronger.

Shit, I should have gone straight to the bathroom, not the terrace.

Once outside, I take deep gulps of air and lean against the frosted glass railing. Below, Boston stretches out in all its afternoon glory; cars crawl along the streets like metallic beetles, their horns muted from up here. I wrap my arms around myself—a self-soothing act that feels hollow when what I really need are answers.

A soft touch on my elbow makes me jump. It's Zedd.

"You okay?" he asks, genuine concern on his handsome face. "You seemed a bit off just now."

"No, I'm good. I just needed a bit of air, I guess."

He hands me a drink—another concoction that looks like liquid gold. I accept it out of politeness and pretend to sip. My stomach feels like a washing machine on high spin, and the earlier drink nearly had me losing my lunch all over the living room floor. The last thing I need is an encore of today's office disaster.

Zedd flashes a dazzling smile that I'm sure sends women weak in the knees. "I take it, loud music," he gestures toward the party raging in the living room, "isn't really your scene, is it?"

"No, I don't mind it, to be honest," I say.

My idea of unwinding used to be curling up with a book, but knowing Kira—who lives and breathes sound on such a profound level—has made me realize that a little noise isn't always such a bad thing.

And Dante finds music calming. He always had some rock band playing in the background when we spoke and classical music in the hotel room the few times he visited.

"So, do you not like to travel then?" Zedd's heavy-lidded gaze sweeps over me slowly, taking in my baggy trousers, red Metallica T-shirt, and sneakers. Hardly lust-inducing attire, but the way Zedd looks at me, I might as well be naked.

"No, I'm good with traveling." Except to Chicago.

"In that case," he continues, leaning closer, his voice a low murmur in my ear. "Would you be open to attending one of my shows in New York as my personal guest? You can bring Kira if you want," he adds when he sees my less-than-excited expression.

His hand brushes against my arm, and I instinctively pull back. My response isn't lost on him, and a flicker of something unreadable crosses his face.

"That would be . . . nice. Thank you, Zedd." My voice comes out flat and emotionless. I can't even muster up the energy to pretend like I'm interested. And even if I were interested, I couldn't flirt to save my life.

Unless it's with a certain gray-eyed criminal, and then my mouth has a mind of its own. The things I've let that man do to me—things I've begged him to do to me—make me blush just thinking about it.

"That was a no, wasn't it?" Zedd says ruefully.

I give him a genuine smile, glad that he caught the hint. "A little bit, yes."

He holds my gaze for a beat too long before shaking his head and retreating back into the throng of partygoers.

I release a pent-up breath as soon as he leaves. If I didn't know better, I'd blame my abysmal afternoon for not being a little bit nicer to Zedd.

But I just don't like being stared at by men.

As an only child, I used to look forward to Dad having his business partners and their children over for dinner.

When I turned thirteen, I started noticing the lingering looks from some of his business partners. And as I got older, it only got worse.

At first, I thought it was my limp drawing attention, so I trained myself to mask it.

When that didn't work, I started dressing like a boy—baggy clothes, baseball caps, anything to deflect unwanted attention. At one point, I even considered cutting my hair, but I just couldn't do it. My thick, wavy red hair is my one vanity.

"Addy?"

Kira's voice, soft yet firm, startles me out of my thoughts. I turn to see her leaning against the sliding glass doors, a worried crease between her brows. "Is everything okay?"

"Yeah. I'm just getting some air."

"You kinda spaced out there. Are you alright?" she adds, her tone laced with concern. Even with the music thumping behind her, Kira has an uncanny ability to sense when something's off. Especially with me.

I manage a weak smile. "Yeah."

"You don't sound like it, Addy."

"Just have a lot on my mind, that's all."

"Is it work? Your boss still blaming you for the lost sample?" Kira picks her steps carefully on the cobbled terrace and moves toward me.

Doug just wouldn't let it go, always insisting that if I'd taken that earlier flight to Chicago like he ordered, I would have reached Ecolab before the fire.

"Everyone still blames me for that, but today's debacle had more to do with the fact that I threw up on his shoes."

"You what?" Kira gasps.

"It's been a crazy day, believe me," I say. "One minute I was trying to act like I had it all together, and the next I was decorating his shoes. Needless to say, he threw me out and gave me the next couple of days off to sort my shit out. Unpaid, of course."

"Oh my God, Addy. You threw up! You never do. You can't even gag."

I snort. "Trust me, I gagged plenty today."

"Remember that norovirus outbreak at Loyola? We were puking and shitting our guts out, and all you did was rub your nose."

"I had a very itchy nose," I say with a smile. "It was awful."

"Sorry, babe, not the same thing as severe diarrhea. Not even close. Anyway, so is that what's bothering you? The unpaid leave?"

"No, actually. It's not that."

"It's your dad then."

I shake my head, already feeling the weight of her sightless gaze. "Seriously, don't worry about me. This is your day, Kira. Let's celebrate. Enjoy it." I gesture vaguely at the party raging inside.

Kira, however, isn't easily deterred. She crosses her arms, her expression turning serious. "You finally went to see him, didn't you? How did it go?"

I hesitate for about two seconds before I cave. "Pretty fucking terrible," I blurt out.

I immediately regret saying anything. The last thing I want to do is bring Kira down with my messy family drama, especially not today. But it's too late; the words hang in the air between us.

"What happened, Addy?"

How do I even begin to explain it? How do I tell her that my entire world feels like it's been tilted on its axis? That the only father I've ever known, the man who raised me to be loyal and honest, also nurtured me on lies?

My mind is still spinning from the revelation, from the sheer magnitude of his deception. And now, faced with Kira's innocent question, I realize the full impact of it all. I have no idea who I am anymore.

"I don't know him anymore, Kira. He's . . . changed. Things can never be the same again."

Kira reaches out until she finds my hands and links our fingers. "Hey, Addy, he's your father. The man raised you into the phenomenal woman you are today. That part will never change. The rest, you guys will just have to figure out."

I nod, grateful for her unwavering support. "Kira, I'm so sorry for how I was earlier. It just hit me out of the blue. I had no idea the club launch party was in Evanston. I thought it was here in Boston."

"I know. It's a swanky new club, and they're offering me an ungodly sum to DJ for the grand opening and to bring my friends. But it was pretty much last minute." Then her voice brightens. "Zedd wants to take us. It'll be so much fun, you know."

I hesitate. "About Chicago . . ."

Kira raises an eyebrow. "What, don't tell me you won't come?"

I swallow hard, my throat suddenly dry. "I, uh . . ."

What exactly do I say? That someone tried to kill me in Chicago eighteen years ago? That I've been banned from stepping into Chicago?

"I really shouldn't be going there."

"Addy, did something happen on that last trip? You've been acting odd since you got back three weeks ago."

I take a deep breath. "I ran into my ex." I brace myself for her reaction and the inevitable barrage of questions.

Kira's eyes widen. "Your ex, as in Dan?"

"Yes."

"The New Yorker?"

I shake my head, my brows furrowing. "No, Kira, he lives in Chicago."

"Wait, what? You said he lives in New York."

Oh shit. I did, didn't I?

Dante's right. I'm a terrible liar. I close my eyes and say, "It's a long story. Anyway, we had sex," I add, hoping to distract her from calling me out on my lie.

"Bullshit!" Kira gasps, pulling her hands away from mine. "How? Where? Spill, dammit!"

My face burns as scorching memories wash over me again. I still can't bring myself to regret how I let myself go with him. "I missed my flight, so he dropped me off in his jet."

"Hold up, hold up, hold up." Kira raises her hands. "Dan has a jet?"

I nod. "Did I not mention he's filthy rich?"

"No, babe, you left out that key detail." Kira cocks a sardonic eyebrow. "So, you ran into the Chicago-based billionaire and then joined the mile-high club. Or should I say, revisited the club?"

"Actually, no. We, um, kinda lost our heads in the moment and ended up doing it on the tarmac, right against his car."

Kira's jaw drops. "Fuck me sideways! Girl, you did not do that!"

"I did. I so did, Kira."

"Wow. That is off-the-charts hot!" She steps back, her sightless gaze raking me up and down as if seeing me with fresh eyes. Then her expression turns grave. "I cannot believe you'd do something like that."

"I know. I can't believe it myself—"

"That you would keep it from me, I mean," Kira interjects, her voice laced with hurt. "I tell you everything, Addy."

Actually, Kira, you don't.

Kira is quite well off now due to her celebrity status, but even back in college, she always had the most expensive things—designer bags, clothes, perfumes—and she was never short of cash.

She never once explained where they came from, and I was much too polite to probe into how her single mom, who worked as a housekeeper, could afford to give her that lavish lifestyle.

"I'm sorry I didn't say anything, Kira. He was so different from any other man I'd met, yet we had this insane connection . . . like we owned each other or something. It was frightening and . . . it felt forbidden."

A slow smirk spreads on her face. "So, was it still as good as it was when you were dating?"

Better. Oh God, it was so much better.

"Yes," I say blandly, firmly resisting the urge to elaborate.

There's absolutely no need to say that I can still feel the cords of his back muscles shifting under my fingers. Still hear his deep grunts and feel the sharp edge of his teeth sinking into the soft skin of my neck as he drove inside me. That my pussy still clenches at random times, as if in withdrawal from his thick cock.

So, a simple yes will have to do.

"Is he still married?" Kira asks.

"What do you mean? He's not married."

"But isn't that why you broke up with him? You found out he was married the whole time you were together."

Double shit.

CHAPTER TWELVE

Adele

See, that's the thing about lies. They're savage little beasts that come back to take a big bite out of your ass when you least expect it. Unless you're a psychopath with an IQ of 180, then maybe you can pull it off indefinitely. Like my dad.

And tonight is proving that I'm as dumb as bricks, because I can't even tell a single lie and make it stick.

I debate backtracking, covering up with another lie, but I'm sick of wallowing in so much deception that I decide to come clean.

"Actually, Kira," I begin, grateful that she can't see my flush of shame. "That wasn't why I broke up with him. He was never married. I lied."

Kira blinks, looking utterly lost. I might as well be speaking a different language.

I force the next words out, each syllable heavy with dread. "I broke up with him because he's a criminal."

"Really? That's why you broke up?"

"Isn't that reason enough?" I snap in irritation. Kira's tolerance for crime and criminals almost borders on the romantic. While I may find the dark world fascinating, it's not one I fancy myself living in.

Most of the time.

Kira scoffs, rolling her eyes. "Please, Addy. He's a billionaire. Loads of rich people are criminals; they're just too smart to get caught. Insurance fraud, tax evasion—"

"He's not that type of criminal, Kira." My voice comes out sharper than intended. "He's the type that kills people."

That brings her up short. "And how would you know that, Addy?"

I take a deep breath. "Because he shot two men. Right in front of me. All because they crashed our dinner and insulted me. *That's* why I broke it off."

Kira goes still, her playful demeanor vanishing like smoke.

"I see," she murmurs, but other than that, she seems unruffled. "So what happened after he shot those men?"

"Nothing," I say. "Not a fucking thing. That's what I couldn't wrap my mind around. He acted like he'd just swatted a couple of flies! He couldn't even understand why I was so freaked out about it. He's . . . he's not a normal person."

"No, babes, it would seem not," Kira muses.

Glad that Kira gets it, I continue. "So, do you see why telling you about him was hard for me? I kept looking over my shoulder, wondering when I'd get questioned for being a witness to a double homicide."

"Hardly likely," she scoffs, her voice deceptively soft now. "But I'm curious, though—Dan, is he even American?"

"Of course. Well, he's Italian-American—"

"Shocker," Kira interjects. "What's his full name? Daniele?"

I shake my head. "Dante."

Kira goes still again. "What?"

"Dante," I repeat.

"Shut the fuck up." Kira's voice is like a whipcrack. "Dante? Vitelli?"

I do a double-take. "How did you guess his surname?"

"Dante Vitelli!" Kira screeches, her hazel eyes as wide as saucers. "Dante Vitelli is your ex? And you hid that from me, you fucking secretive cow?"

"First of all, the operative word is ex. I'm never going back there again." I sputter, my head spinning. "Secondly, how do you even know of him?"

"What the fuck do you mean how do I know of him? I grew up in Chicago! Dante Vitelli is the shit. He's the absolute fucking shit of the Outfit. He's the Underboss."

I stare at her blankly. "You've lost me. What's an underboss?"

Kira throws her hands up in the air. "You were with the guy for three months, and you don't know? In Medieval Rome, you could be fed to lions for this."

I roll my eyes. "It was a long-distance relationship, Kira. We mainly talked on the phone. And it's not like he opened every conversation with his criminal resume."

And when he did visit, we were too caught up in each other to do much else.

"You talked," she scoffs. "About what, the weather?"

"Kira—"

"Okay, fine. Since you apparently learned nothing about him, let me educate you. An underboss is like . . . the heir apparent. Second in command. He calls the shots when the big boss isn't around. His brother, Nico Vitelli, is the Don."

My stomach flops, and I swallow the lump in my throat. I can't even say I'm surprised because I know firsthand the degree of danger the man exudes. Still, it's quite jarring to hear that he's just not a common member of the mafia.

Kira's voice drags me back to the present. "So, you ran into mobster ex and banged him like a drum, then broke up again or whatever. What has that got to do with you not wanting to go to Chicago?"

I heave out a sigh wondering whose version to tell. My father's or Dante's. I choose the latter. "He told me to never come back to Chicago."

Kira scoffs in disbelief. "Or what? He'll shoot you on sight?"

"Of course not." I snort.

"Good," Kira snaps. I can see she's working hard to rein in her temper. I don't think I've ever seen her this annoyed and I wonder why.

"I don't care if he drew a line in the sand and warned you not to cross it, you're coming with me," Kira states.

"Kira, really I wish—" I begin, but she cuts me off.

"You lied to me, Addy. For two fucking years. So, no, you don't get a say in this. If you don't agree to come, I'm going to cancel the entire gig."

She jabs her thumb behind her shoulder. "And I'm telling everyone in there that you pissed on their parade."

Her words hit me like a punch to the gut. I think of Kira's friends inside—the excited chatter, the anticipation for this gig. And I know she's right; I'd be public enemy number one if I messed with their night.

I sigh, defeated. "Fine," I say, throwing my drink back. It's not like Dante will know I'm there. I force down the cocktail, wincing at the trail of fire it leaves down my throat. It doesn't taste as bad as the pink one, but it's three times as strong.

But apparently, my promise to be at Evanston isn't enough for Kira because she continues to fume. "I'm so annoyed with you, Addy. It's just so unfair to me."

I wonder why Kira is so upset. Yes, I lied to her, but she's acting like she knows Dante personally or something.

Kira continues, "Can you believe I was coming out here to tell you how much Zedd likes you and then to be blindsided with all this?"

"Zedd?" I scrunch up my face. "But we've just met."

"And you've hit him like a thunderbolt. He's begged and is still bribing me to get you to come to Chicago. And I thought, why not, the girl has not had a date in over a year. Little did I know you've been busy screwing Dante Vitelli."

I ignore the last part, take another gulp of my drink, deciding it tastes like gasoline, and instead ask, "I thought you had a crush on Zedd?"

She waves a dismissive hand, "Like, eons ago. Anyway, he's into you. Do what you will with that information."

She turns and storms inside while a wave of nausea hits me so hard, I gag. For the second time, I put my glass away, turn my face to the wind, and take steadying breaths.

This time it doesn't work.

By the time I start to taste the cocktail I drank a minute ago, I know there's no stopping its messy reappearance. I glance at Kira's retreating back and the sea of bodies inside, cursing because there's no way I'll make it to the guest bathroom.

I rush to the corner of the terrace, which I hope is out of eyeshot to those behind the sliding glass doors, and promptly throw up right on the floor. It's loud, it's messy and so humiliating that tears sting my eyes. I'm not even drunk, and I'm puking my guts all over the place. Again.

What the hell is wrong with me today?

"Addy!"

Shit. Kira is too perceptive. She was practically back in the house, the music thumping loudly and the sounds of the city drowning my retching, but still, she heard me.

In moments, I feel cool fingers creeping up my back and my shoulder and gathering my hair up while I continue to empty my stomach contents onto the floor.

When I'm done, Kira pulls me into a hug.

"Kira . . . I'm sorry about the mess."

"Shh. Addy. It's okay." Her palm rubs soothing circles over my back.

"No, it's not okay." I pull out of her arms. "We have guests, and I need to clean up this crap before someone sees it or, God forbid, slips in it, tumbles over, and smashes their skull like an egg all over the concrete sidewalk two hundred feet below."

"Sheesh, you're so morbid," Kira grins but grabs my forearm as I start to leave to get a mop.

"Addy. Are you ill?" She puts the back of her hand on my forehead and then my neck.

"No, I'm just . . . exhausted, I guess."

"Exhausted and therefore puking like a dog? You threw up on your boss's shoes for chrissake."

"Kira, have you tasted these cocktails? They are absolutely vile." I snatch my arm away and go to fetch the mop and bucket.

It takes twice as long because not only do Kira's friends stop me with smiles and random chats, but Zedd also wants to know what the mop is for. I gladly inform him of my mishap, and like magic, he lets me go.

I'm surprised to see Kira still standing there, finishing my drink, brows furrowed in contemplation as I work.

"Addy," she calls as soon as I finish. "I may be going out on a limb here, but I strongly believe you've got a bigger mess to deal with than the one you just made here."

"What do you mean?"

"We sync, don't we? Every time we live together. Our cycles sync."

"Yeah, so?"

"So, I'm on my period right now. Are you?"

My eyes pop when I realize what she's suggesting. "Kira, stop, that's not even funny."

But my heart has already started to trip over itself.

She gets into my face. "You banged your ex right in the middle of your cycle. And three weeks later, you're here puking on everyone. I probably don't need to ask if you used a condom."

My lids fall closed. *No, you don't.*

Kira bends and gives me a sound peck, then leaves me reeling.

"What a wonderful world," she singsongs, mimicking Louis Armstrong's deep baritone as she expertly picks her way through the terrace into the lounge.

The mop clatters to the floor as my mind serves me a red-hot visual of the way Dante drove himself deep inside me. How stars burst behind my eyelids as his cock dragged tightly against my G-spot. The scorching heat of his semen as he filled me up. And I know without a doubt that he got me pregnant that night.

Hell. Do I even need a test at this point?

CHAPTER THIRTEEN

Dante

The clang of iron reverberates through the gym as I pump the weights, my muscles screaming in protest. I'm not even breaking a sweat, but pretending to listen to Sal as he drones about tonight's security protocol is exhausting.

"So, we're all set for your meeting with the Senator. Cameras have been angled to cover blind spots. No one's getting in without a key card access and a hand job."

Sal's voice crackles over the phone, a momentary pause before he continues, but it's enough for me to hear his deliberate slip-up, which is aimed at jolting me back into focus.

I interrupt him, smirking, "That's some spicy security measure you've got going there, Salvatore."

Sal chuckles on the other end. "I meant to say hand-print scans. I've got to keep your attention somehow, *fratello*. The point is, security will be tighter than a nun's knees tonight."

I grunt in irritation. "It's still a stupid location, Sal. The club's going to be packed tonight, and too many people will spot the Senator. Why not meet him in one of our warehouses?"

Sal's response is swift. "Bill Sheridan is a businessman, but he's also a politician, Dante. The man has the eyes of the public and media on him every time. In the club, we can at least control what they see compared to out there on the docks."

Sal's logic hits home, as much as I hate to admit it. "You're right," I concede.

I just hate club openings. Too many celebrity appearances, too many free drinks and VIP passes, and too many influencers hoping to create drama.

"As long as you keep the guest list sane, Sal."

"Sure thing. The upstairs VIP lounge will be on lockdown. The only people allowed there will be us and Sheridan . . . Oh, and also . . ." Sal's voice takes on that knowing, musical tone that usually means he's about to tell me something I don't want to hear.

"What," I snap, although I already know what he's going to say.

"Alina and her friends are with us too."

I slam the weights down, the metal groaning in protest. "Did I not make myself clear about her showing up there?" I don't need her suffocating me with her perfume and eyelash batting while I'm trying to conduct business.

"Come on, Dante," Sal coaxes. "It's our club opening. What's it gonna look like if your own fiancée isn't there?"

"Like I have a brain in my skull? Like I don't need a fucking ball and chain to validate my existence?" I growl, wiping the sweat off my forehead with a towel.

Sal, sensing we're not about to agree anytime soon, deftly steers the subject to safer ground. "Kira's coming, you know. She's the celebrity DJ."

"Yes, I know," I snap, wondering why Sal feels the need to bring this up every five seconds.

Unfazed by my irritation, Sal continues. "She's bringing a bunch of friends from Boston—the usual celebrity DJ circle. Red Wine is—"

"Sal, spare me the social calendar, will you?" I cut him off, not needing to hear more about his obvious obsession with Kira. And I especially don't need to know that Addy won't be there as she's not a celeb or a DJ.

"Sure," Sal drawls, and I get the sense the little shit is trying not to smile.

"Just make sure the Senator isn't photographed or recorded. Or wearing a wire."

"Done," Sal says.

"And get Alina and her minions seated far enough away and well entertained. Now, speaking of entertainment . . . It's been three weeks, has that Irish prick not said anything interesting yet?"

"Oh him? I'm afraid he's a little dead, *fratello*," Sal says casually.

"Awesome, Sal," I murmur testily. "Way to piss Nico off. Did he at least give up any good info before he kicked it?"

"I wouldn't call it good," Sal replies. "He said he and his boys were there to distract us from spotting their princess while she waltzed around Chicago."

"Hmm," I grunt. A ploy that only managed to land her squarely in my clutches. "Is that all you got out of him?"

"More or less."

"Then why did it take the prick three whole weeks to give you dead info?"

"Now you see why he vexed me. He could have saved me the trouble had he quietly whispered this on the first day. But no, he chose to die screaming it . . ."

. . . whisper . . . die . . . screaming . . .

The world shrinks, and the metallic scent of the gym fades as Sal continues talking, oblivious that I've stopped listening.

Life whispers, but death screams.

Loyola Boston University. Two and a half years ago.

It was enemy territory, but I was there on Nico's orders to negotiate a fresh peace treaty between us and the Irish Mob.

I'd promised Kira's mother that I'd check in on her daughter. Kira was meant to perform at some college event. A part of me was curious to see if she was any good so I dropped in on her during the event.

The music had thrummed through my bones as I stepped into the crowded college gym, the scent of sweat and cheap perfume assaulting my senses.

I'd scanned the crowd and immediately spotted Kira on the raised dais. She'd looked quite at home with the vibrant lights pulsating around her, her fingers dancing effortlessly across the mixer, creating the rhythm that filled the room.

And then my eyes had snagged on Addy.

She'd stood in the far corner of the gym pretending to be engrossed in the information on a bulletin board. Petite, with a hint of lush curves but she was dressed like a boy.

She should have been invisible, her allure swallowed up by her baggy clothes and baseball cap. Except for her hair, a long thick braid poking out of her cap and snaking down her back. A rope of fire that drew me in like a lasso.

I found myself crossing the room before realizing I'd moved. Something about her closed body language warned me she didn't like her personal space invaded. So, I took in her profile from a few feet away, my chest feeling too tight.

Porcelain skin, a smattering of freckles across her nose. And those lips, fuck me. Full and pouty, begging to be nipped, sucked on, and wrapped around my cock.

I must have made a sound because she turned to look at me. Her eyes, clear green pools hit me like wrecking balls. She instantly looked away. Then, after a few moments, she deliberately looked back, and this time, she didn't stop.

Her eyes boldly held mine and even when the blush crept up her neckline and stained her cheeks a deep crimson, she still didn't take her eyes off me.

I'd have given anything to know what she was thinking just then, but what surprised me more was her lack of shame in blushing for me.

My cock hardened painfully, and I had to rein in my lust before I did something stupid. Like push her against the wall and dry hump her.

I glanced away from her face, and my eyes instantly caught on the black folder she held across her chest like a shield, a battered thing covered in doodles and scribbles.

And there, in the corner of the folder, were the words that sealed my fate:

Life whispers, but death screams.

"Did you write that?" I asked, my voice rough to my own ears, laced with a need I couldn't quite place.

She startled, as if surprised I'd spoken to her. "What?"

I cocked an eyebrow at the folder. "The quote. Is that you?"

Her eyes followed my gaze until she saw what I was referring to, and then a wry smile tugged at her lips. "Oh, no, that was just the red-eyed, caffeine-overdosed, sleep-deprived version of me."

It was such a dark and unexpected quote from someone so shy and innocent-looking. I wanted to explore her eclectic mix of purity and provocation. To take her innocence and revel in the depravity lurking behind those clear green eyes.

"I couldn't agree more," I said, extending my hand. "Dante Vitelli."

She slipped her hand in mine and told me her name.

The moment my hand closed over her small hand, a needle shot through me like a drug, branding me. With a certainty that almost terrified me, I knew I would be unable to let her go.

I should've stayed away then. Instead, I marked her as mine through the things I taught her to crave. And in return, she broke me for other women.

Adele O'Shea was everything promised and so much more: A forbidden mafia princess with no clue who she was.

"Fratello? . . . Dante!"

Sal's voice snaps me out of my reverie, only to find myself hard as a fucking rock.

"I should go," I say, putting away the weights and straightening.

"Dante. Did you hear what I just said?" The chill in Sal's voice stops me from brushing him off.

I grab a bottle of water from the cooling rack, condensation dampening my fingers as I twist off the cap "What?"

"I asked you if you thought Benjamin O'Shea was lying when he claimed his daughter was betrothed?"

"Who cares what that lying prick said?" Even if he wasn't Irish, Benjamin O'Shea remains high on my shit list. What kind of father keeps his daughter in the dark and lies to her every single day? "Why do you ask?"

"Because in the last three weeks, there has been a flurry of activities in Boston."

I grunt, not bothering to ask Sal how he knows. Sal lives and breathes intelligence. From bugs to hacked communications to a robust network of spies.

"Do you know why the Mob is getting restless?" Sal pushes, and I tense. From his tone, I know I won't like his next words.

"Why are they restless?"

"Because there are rumors that you plan to break the treaty. To take Red Wine."

Fuck. Someone has been talking. Only seven people were there that night, including the pilot, Addy, and me.

I huff out a laugh, hoping it doesn't sound as hollow as it feels. "Why the fuck do the Irish think they know what I'll do?"

"Is it true, though?" Sal prods.

"I'm not a fucking caveman, Sal," I say, deflecting. "If there's going to be any taking, she'll be a willing participant."

"Sure. Well, in any case, Boston is beefing up their ranks as if gearing up for a world war. And you know there's no one on earth they hate more than us. We're talking negotiating alliances. Setting wedding dates."

And finally, I see where Sal is going. He's telling me Addy could be married soon. The question is, why he's telling me this?

"It's not possible. Sal, Addy doesn't even know who her father really is. She won't be marrying any mobster soon."

"You forget that the Mob and their affiliates don't require a courtship or even voluntarily said vows, to seal their deals. Only a consummation."

The thought hits me like a tornado, and my vision goes red. Cool water sloshes over my hand as the bottle crumples in my grip.

Over my fucking dead body.

If I didn't know better, I'd think Sal was warning me not to violate the treaty. Quite the contrary. He's telling me that I'm running out of time.

Unable to continue that line of thought without getting violent, I snap, "I'll see you tonight, Sal."

I disconnect the line, the only sound in the gym my ragged breathing, and Black Sabbath blaring through the speakers. My heart aches like a raw wound, the anger a living thing inside me, consuming me from the inside out as I contemplate the implications of Sal's words.

I need to move, to do something, anything to release this fury. I head into the bathroom, stripping off my clothes as I go. The icy spray shocks my system, but it's exactly what I need to clear my head.

Yet, even as the frigid water numbs my skin and cools my anger, my cock remains rock hard and throbbing with rage and need.

Addy is mine. All mine. I clench my jaw against the surge of arousal that courses through me.

I brace a hand against the marble wall of the shower, emitting a groan as I cup my heavy sac. I let my fist slowly slide up and down my rigid length. What happened three weeks ago was just a small taste; I need more. We both do. A proper reunion is long overdue.

I'll have to pay her a visit right after my meeting with the Senator. And tonight, there'll be no holding back. I imagine her soft, pliant body writhing under me, with those too-full breasts and tight, rosy nipples. But it's that pink scar running down between the twin swells that calls to the darkness in my soul. It's the most potent aphrodisiac I never knew existed.

Christ. It was so hard not to go overboard with her in those three months. She was untouched, yet depraved. Inexperienced but ravenous. It was hard to stay away, but she had such a hair trigger; it was dead easy to get her off just by talking to her.

And when I went to see her. Fuck. She was insatiable. She wanted to try everything. A flash of memory assails me. How she asked to suck on my balls. How she got on her knees and drove me insane until I lost it and came in her hair like an untried teen.

My hand fists my cock tight, and I moan as I imagine pushing my cock past her soft pillowy lips. I'll watch as her lush green eyes grow glassy with lust and tears as she learns to breathe around my cock.

My fingers find their way to my throbbing tip, and with a shudder, I begin to pump faster. My hips buck forward uncontrollably, seeking release.

I've taught her to take all of my cock, but she needs to learn to crave it, to deliriously beg for it when her neglected pussy drips as her ass clenches around me.

I no longer feel the cold water as it streams down my clenched abs. I grit my teeth against the oncoming climax, my other clenching into a fist on the wall as I lose myself in my rhythm.

I imagine Addy's luscious body convulsing with pleasure while my hand wraps around her neck, forcing her to decide what she needs more: air or the orgasm just out of reach . . .

I arch my back and let loose a growl as raw, unfiltered pleasure explodes within me, painting the walls of the shower in thick, white streaks. My groans echo off the marble walls, muffled by the cleansing water, my heart pounding in sync with each ragged breath I take as I come down from the intense high.

As I shudder with remnants of the heights of pleasure I owe to my red-headed witch, my mind empties of rational thought except for two certainties.

That I'll be buried inside that woman tonight.

And that the day Addy marries someone else is the day she will be widowed.

Hell. Maybe I am a caveman, after all.

***

Four hours later, Sal, Pietro, and I enter the club through the private entrance to find it packed. Kira is already doing her thing, the bass thrumming through the floor, and the air is thick with the scent of citrus and alcohol.

We make our way upstairs to the meeting spot at the VIP section, a private booth overlooking the dance floor.

Alina is on the other side of the room, holding court with her gaggle of friends. She catches my eye, and her gaze heats and fills with promise. I simply incline my head in greeting, feeling like a heel for not returning a sliver of her feelings.

I scan the club, looking for the Senator or his aides. He's late, of course. Fucking politicians.

Pietro must sense my irritation because he slips away to track down our wayward guest. Sal, ever the charmer, goes over to Alina and her friends to greet them, his smile wide and disarming. I watch, scowling as the women giggle, their heads thrown back, their throats exposed. It's all so fucking pointless.

I lean back in my seat, my jaw clenched tight. How the hell do I tell Orlando De Luca that I'm not going to be his son-in-law without sparking up a rebellion? Or make Addy mine without starting another war?

There's no way to avoid both.

The thought makes me want to put my fist through something. Or someone. But I can't. Not here. Not now. So, I sit, my posture deceptively relaxed as my fingers drum against the leather of the booth, my eyes scanning the club for any sign of trouble.

And all the while, her face dances in my mind, teasing me. It's as if now that I'm resolved to take her, I can't seem to wait anymore.

I stand, take my drink, and wander to the glass wall, a spot that offers an unobstructed view of the writhing sea of bodies downstairs and the massive C-shaped bar. I'm no stranger to nightclubs, but all the ones Salvatore designs never fail to stand out. Sal does know a thing or two about luxury, the little shit.

I throw back my drink, feeling the liquor burn a familiar path down my throat, but it does little to ease the tension coiling in my gut.

And then, to my utter disbelief, I see a flash of distinct red hair at the bar downstairs.

"Fuck me," I murmur, feeling the last shred of my control splinter to dust.

"Signor Vitelli."

I reluctantly turn away from the tantalizing sight to face Pietro, who has returned with a pale-faced and sweaty Bill Sheridan. I force myself to my feet.

"Senator," I greet, with a cold smile, taking his hand firmly. "I trust you found your way okay?"

I lead him to our booth, the need to get this negotiation over with beating down on me like a tidal wave. I have a more crucial business to attend to.

The last time that woman wandered into my lair, I let her go. Now she's tumbled right back. Even the Irish have to know that every man has his limits.

CHAPTER FOURTEEN

Adele

Resin nightclub is impressive. I'll give them that.

The place is a sensory feast. From my vantage point at the bar, I take in the scene. Strobe lights bounce off the polished marble floor and the air is scented with lavender and citrus, a refreshing change from the usual overpowering scent of sweat and cloying perfume.

Plush velvet booths line the walls and colorful reflective lights lend an interesting flickering glow to the place.

Across the room, bathed in the glow of the revolving disco ball, Kira effortlessly spins a set that has the crowd raving. I catch the girl with the pink braids and the rectangular-spectacled guy from the other day and wave back with a smile.

"Sure you don't want to dance?" Zedd asks beside me.

I take a steadying breath and pray that he respects my personal space today. I really don't want to have to give him a dressing down on a night he seems to be having so much fun.

"No, I'm good for now, Zedd. You go on."

The last thing I want to do is dance. I'm feeling too self-conscious in the white dress I talked myself into wearing. Although I didn't have a choice.

I couldn't exactly wear baggy jeans and a T-shirt, especially when Kira was dressed in a sparkly black number. The white dress was the only one I had.

"You've had an ungodly long drive here, Addy. You should stretch your legs on the dance floor," Zedd coaxes.

I didn't want to go on Zedd's tour bus because fourteen hours of being stuck in an enclosed place with his eyes burning holes into me wasn't my idea of a fun road trip. And as Kira isn't a great fan of flying, we rented a Corolla, and I drove us down here.

"No, seriously. Go have fun. I'll watch you from here."

"Well, in that case, we can stay here and people watch together."

Oh, Lord. I thought the guy could take a hint. If the last half hour is any indication, it seems he plans to stay glued to me all night.

I shrug and take a sip of my apple juice since I've clearly become allergic to alcohol. I mean, I wasn't going to knowingly drink while pregnant, but this baby has ensured that every drop of alcohol that entered my body after she did, came flying back out.

Kira and I haven't spoken about the pregnancy since I tested positive. She understood that I needed time to process my next steps.

"By the way, you look beautiful, Addy," Zedd breathes. "White is definitely your color."

"Thanks," I murmur tightly, discreetly tugging at the hem of my dress again, regretting why I didn't go with Kira to get a different dress.

While there's nothing wrong with this one, it's just that it belongs to another life. The last time I wore it was on my twenty-first birthday dinner date with Dante. I push down the memories threatening to surface and focus on why I'm here.

I'm here for Kira.

My gaze drifts back to her and instantly snags on the person standing next to her in the DJ booth.

An attractive man in his mid-twenties wearing an expensive suit. Tattoos snake up his neck, and a silver necklace peeking beneath his open shirt. Their heads are close together, almost touching as he speaks. She listens raptly even as her hands fly over the mixer. And then she throws her head back and laughs.

An unwelcome shiver races down my spine.

There's something about him—a familiarity that feels like a slap to the face. But it's Kira's reaction that's most unsettling. Kira is relaxed and at ease. Enjoying herself.

They know each other.

"Zedd?" My voice is barely audible, drowned out by the pulsing music. He leans close to me, his eyes brightening with hope and excitement.

"Do you know that guy Kira's talking to?" I keep my voice casual despite the unease prickling at the back of my neck.

Zedd follows my gaze and lets out a low chuckle. "Oh, him? He's one of Kira's people."

He says that like he expects me to get it. When I continue to stare at him blankly, he moves even closer to me, his face etched with disbelief.

"Wait, how long have you known Kira?"

I'm pretty sure I've known her longer than you, I want to snap, but somehow I sense he's not trying to mock me.

"Since college," I admit, feeling like the idiot who missed the joke. "We were roomies." His eyebrows almost rise to his hairline and something tells me I don't know Kira Sibel at all.

"I mean, she went back home to Chicago shortly after we finished college while I stayed back. We only just reconnected a few months ago when she returned to Boston."

And by the time Kira returned, she'd somehow become a nightclub sensation.

Zedd's nod is weighted as if debating what to say.

"In that case, you should ask Kira who her people are when you get back home."

"Zedd, come on. Please." I give him my best puppy-dog eyes.

"Okay," he mutters, his resolve instantly crumbling. "But you didn't hear this from me."

"I swear," I say quickly, my eyes still pleading for him to spill.

"So," Zedd begins, "does the name Vito Vitelli mean anything to you?"

I stop breathing. *Please. No. Hell fucking no.*

"No," I squeak. But it does. It really, really does.

He continues in a hushed tone. "Well, Vito is the patriarch of the Vitelli crime family—he's retired now. His son Nico is in charge now. I only got to know this myself when I was DJing in a Chicago club a few years back. Kira was new to the scene, and I think she was a little starstruck by me. We got talking, and she got tipsy. Nothing happened between us," Zedd puts his hands up when he sees my expression morph into disgust.

"Anyway," he continues, "Vitelli is Kira's godfather or something."

I snort out a laugh, my tension dissipating. "Oh, please. A drunk Kira told you that? And you believed her? Kira has a thing for Italian men and the mafia."

Absently I run my fingers through my curls, lifting the strands off my shoulders to let cool air reach my skin. The instant I see Zedd's heavy-lidded gaze heat up, I snap out of it. I'd hate for the guy to think I'm flirting. "Look, The Godfather is like her scripture, so I'm not surprised she'd fantasize that Vito Vitelli, a retired mafia don, is her godfather."

Zedd only gives me a wry look. "Alright. I see how that might be a stretch to believe. Can you at least believe that her mother is the Vitelli's housekeeper?"

The smug smile falls off my face.

Seeing he's got my attention, Zedd presses on. "Did you also know Kira's mother was trafficked from Turkey to America by a rebel syndicate, and Vito intercepted the cargo and saved them? Kira was so young and had no way of coping with her new disability."

I clasp my hands together in my lap to stop the trembling.

"Vito Vitelli took them in and raised Kira like a daughter, or well, like a god-daughter," Zedd finishes as if he just told me that Kira won a spelling bee.

My heart breaks for what Kira and her mom went through, and I am unable to imagine what would have happened to both of them had Dante's father not intervened. Yet hot betrayal burns in my chest at Kira's deception.

Kira's obsession with the Mafia isn't some audiobook fantasy. She lives with them.

Kira knows Dante Vitelli.

Kira knows I'm pregnant with Dante Vitelli's baby.

And suddenly, I feel like I'm the punchline of a joke I didn't even know I was part of.

I swallow my rising panic and the urge to run out of the club and out of Chicago like a crazy woman.

"So back to him," I nod at the tattooed guy still standing next to Kira. He appears to be whispering something to her. "You said he's one of Kira's people? Is he here to support Kira?"

"No, he's some sort of mafia genius and he designed this place." Zed throws an arm out. "His boss, Dante Vitelli, owns the club. Or maybe Nico does. Anyway, one of them does. It's hard to tell which way is up with the Vitelli brothers."

My blood turns to ice even as my rage simmers.

This is—could be Dante's club.

Kira knowingly brought me here.

Dante could show up at any point because Kira may have told him I'm pregnant with his baby.

My heart races, pounding against my ribcage like a trapped bird desperate to escape. The room spins, the flashing lights and pulsing music blurring into a dizzying mix. Here I am, already drowning in the bog of my family drama, yet the universe decides my life still isn't complicated enough.

Zedd must sense my discomfort because he places a reassuring hand on my arm. "Are you alright, Addy?"

Fighting to keep my expression neutral, I force a smile and say, "Zedd, I need to leave."

"What? Now?"

"Yep." I jump off my stool as panic claws at my throat. I need space to breathe, to think. I can practically feel Dante's presence, a phantom heat radiating through the crowd.

Zedd catches my arm, holding me in place. "Whoa, hold up, Addy." His words are playful, but his grip tightens. "Look, I didn't mean to scare you. I promise you're safe here. No one will hurt you. Actually, no one can. You're Kira's friend."

Kira is a lot of things right now, but my friend isn't one of them. I yank my arm free, stumbling back a step. "I just remembered something I have to do back in Boston." My excuse is beyond lame. I really need to be a better liar.

Like Kira, and Benjamin O'Shea, I think, anger surging through me, hot and bitter.

"What? Are you serious?" Zedd moves to block my path, his brow furrowed. "You can't just bail on Kira's big night. You drove her here!"

"I'm sure she'll have no shortage of mafia men to ferry her wherever she needs to go," I spit.

All those years, and all through the fourteen-hour trip here, she could have mentioned that she knew Dante. That Dante is her god-brother or whatever they are to each other.

I can only conclude that she wanted me here for her big night, not even caring that it would put me in an awkward position, especially being pregnant with the man's baby.

Zedd places a hand on my shoulder. "Look, I'm not stupid. I get that she didn't tell you any of this. She doesn't tell anyone. She still deeply regrets spilling the beans to me. As much as she is grateful for that family, she wants to live a normal life, and to be able to do that, no one can know that she's linked to them."

"I'm not no one. I am—was her best friend, Zedd."

His voice softens, his eyes searching mine. "Talk to her. Work it out. I'll get her for you right now if you want."

I hesitate, torn between the urge to flee and the realization that Zedd might be right. Leaving won't help, except to hurt Kira. And while I would derive perverse joy in hurting her back, I really don't want to.

I take a deep breath, trying to steady myself. "Zedd, I can't pull her in the middle of a gig so we can have a chat."

"Are you going to wait till the end of the night?"

I grab my purse. "Hell no."

He sighs, running a hand through his perfectly styled hair. "Then I'm not going to be the reason her best friend abandoned her in a club on her big night. Wait, I'll get her for you and take over from her. I'm sure the crowd won't mind."

I sigh in defeat. "Okay, hurry. I can't . . . I shouldn't be here right now."

Zedd nods, squeezing my shoulder before approaching the DJ booth. I watch as he reaches Kira, leaning in to whisper something in her ear. She glances in a random direction, unable to locate where exactly I am, and my heart squeezes tight.

I'm so angry with her but still in awe of her at the same time. I often forget she can't see.

Just then, a movement to my left catches my eye, and I turn to see a stunning woman in a slinky gold dress. She's tall and slender, with sleek dark hair and a figure that could make a nun swear. Her lips are curved in a cool, predatory smile, but her dark brown eyes are like ice chips, sending a bolt of unease through me. She perches on the barstool to my left.

I smile in greeting, and in response, she stares pointedly at my hair, scoffs, then rolls her eyes and turns away.

Fresh out of patience for catty nonsense, I snark. "Is there a problem?"

"Not unless you make one, hun," she replies, not sparing me another look. "Just a friendly heads-up, by the way, the man you're looking for is now permanently off the market."

I blink in disbelief. Who the fuck does this woman think she is? "I'm not sure which fortune teller told you I was looking for a man, hun, but you might want to ask for them for a refund." I retort.

Kira and her friend arrive, distracting me from the bitch next to me. Kira slips onto the plush seat, and the big tattooed friend stands next to her, watching me with an unsettling intensity. He inclines his head slightly as if in recognition.

"Addy, what's going on? Zedd says you're trying to leave," Kira's voice is tight and urgent, her unseeing eyes fixed on a point just over my shoulder.

"Oh, you know, just thought I'd cut the night short," I reply, my voice dripping with sarcasm. "Turns out I'm allergic to surprise mafia connections. Who knew?"

Kira's eyes widen. "Addy—"

"How could you, Kira? All this time, you knew Dante, and you never said a word."

Kira's jaw clenches, and her hands curl into a fist. The tattooed man looks over at the catty woman sitting on the opposite side of me, bends and whispers something to Kira, then leaves.

Kira immediately lowers her voice to a whisper. "You're one to talk about keeping secrets."

"That's different, and you know it," I snap, my voice rising. "I explained why I did it. You, though. You have no leg to stand on. I thought we were friends, Kira. I thought we trusted each other."

"Exactly," Kira retorts, her words clipped and icy. "I trusted you. Both of you. You obviously met during the Rho Theta party in our senior year, right under my nose. Do you think if I could see, both of you could have kept that secret from me?"

I shut my mouth, guilt twisting in my gut. She has a fair point there. Looks like we're both competing for the 'Friend of the Year' award.

"Look," I say, my voice low, trying to get a grip on my swirling emotions. "Can I just go? Please? I don't want to be here. I told you, Dante warned me to stay away from Chicago."

"Addy," Kira continues in a cool voice, "he's here. And he now knows you're here. So, you might as well stay and talk to him."

My heart leaps to my throat, my eyes widening in disbelief. "Kira, are you serious? I have to leave." I grab my purse, but then something awful occurs to me. "Did you tell him?"

Kira's brows furrow as she shakes her head, and then she reaches for my hand. "Of course not. I'd never do that. It's not my place."

I yank my hand away from her. "But you thought it'd be okay to make me look like a stalker, right?" The thought sends a fresh wave of humiliation through me. "I mean, he already has dozens of women throwing themselves at him; what's one more, right?"

"You only say that because you don't know how he—" Kira starts, but the silky voice to my left interrupts our heated exchange.

"You know, you being a pathetic stalker might be the one thing we can both agree on."

I whirl around, facing the catty brunette again. "Look, I've had it up to here with your nonsense. I don't know what your problem is or who you think you are—"

"I'm Alina De Luca, the woman he's marrying in a few weeks. So, I think I've earned the right to demand that you keep your filthy paws off Dante."

I roll my eyes, not even about to rise to her wild claims. "Right. And I'm the Queen of Boston. Lovely to meet you, too."

"Oh no," Kira murmurs beside me, and I whirl on her.

"Addy," Kira grabs for my hand again, and this time her grip is like a vise. "You're right, Addy. You should go. You can um, come back later."

Kira's reaction tells me everything I need to know.

Suddenly I don't want to leave. "Is it true? He's getting married?"

Kira nods imperceptibly and murmurs, "Arranged marriage," under her breath.

Rage. Jealousy. And a few other ugly, painful emotions I can't be bothered to name rush through me. I let out a sharp, humorless laugh. "Oh, wow. An arranged marriage. How charmingly medieval. What's in the clause? A dowry of goats and a public bedding ceremony?"

Here I was, secretly—stupidly, apparently—loving the idea of a part of Dante growing inside me. And now, I find out he's getting married to someone else.

I guess that gives me the clarity I need. Along with a heaping dose of humiliation.

I take a deep breath, forcing down the whirlwind of emotions swirling inside me. As I turn back to the woman, her pretty face marred by that smug, ugly sneer, the truth hits hard—she's somehow enjoying this.

"Well, Alina, it would seem congratulations are in order then," I say, my voice steady despite the turmoil churning beneath the surface.

She arches an eyebrow, her eyes gleaming with satisfaction. "I would wash that garish hair dye right off, hun. It's no use. Clearly, he doesn't do redheads anymore."

My jaw drops. The audacity of this woman! Before I can come up with a suitably scathing retort, I notice people are stopping, staring, and whispering behind their hands.

"Alina." A deep voice cuts through the tension like a knife, bringing the temperature in the room down a few degrees.

Dante.

He materializes beside Alina, his face tight with tension and a muscle ticking in his jaw. He looks gorgeous with his black tailored shirt clinging to his big frame like a second skin, tanned tattooed throat peeking out of his partially buttoned shirt.

He doesn't even spare me a glance, yet, like a besotted fool, I can't tear my gaze from him. My breath catches as I stare. I don't think a time will ever come when I'll get used to Dante's presence, his aura. His beauty.

And right now, his hand is resting possessively on Alina's lower back.

Well, isn't that just perfect?

"Come with me, *cara*," Dante says to her.

I watch as Dante helps Alina off her stool. She follows him, her gaze filled with undisguised hunger. It occurs to me as Dante and Alina disappear into the sea of bodies that I've never seen him touch another woman before. It's torture. It makes me sick to my stomach to think of Dante with her.

Touching her.

Making love to her.

Putting his baby inside her.

A wave of disgust hits me, and I know I should turn away, but I can't stop watching, staring at that hand hovering on the small of Alina's back.

CHAPTER FIFTEEN

Dante

"Come with me, *cara*." I guide Alina off her stool, my fingers barely grazing her back.

The saccharine smile I plaster on my face feels like it could crack at any moment. I'd much rather be facing down a rival family than having this conversation.

The bass thrums through the floor, vibrating up my shoes as we weave through the crowd. Alina's designer perfume, all roses and sophistication, mingles with the scent of sweat and spilled alcohol. Yet somehow, Addy's sweet vanilla smell is burned into my brain, cutting through everything else.

And that fucking dress. My eyes keep drifting back to the bar, where Addy stands out like a beacon in that white number. It had taken everything in me not to march downstairs and snap that DJ's neck as I watched him slobber over her. I barely heard Senator Sheridan as he pitched his plans for re-election, my mind filled with images of Addy in that dress that should be illegal for what it does to her curves.

Knowing she rarely goes out like that in public sparks up a deep possessiveness in me, a primal urge to yell over the crowd that she belongs to me. But I can't. Not yet. First, I need to deal with Alina.

As we ascend the curving stairs, Alina stumbles. Instinctively, I catch her elbow to steady her. When she takes that as a cue to press close and rub against my side, I immediately drop my hand and put some distance between us.

"Watch your step," I mutter, scanning the room. The VIP area is an oasis of relative quiet, the music muffled enough for conversation. I notice the absence of Alina's usual entourage.

"Where are your friends?" I ask as I settle into a booth, angling myself to keep the main floor and Addy in my line of sight through the glass wall.

Alina slides in opposite me and then shrugs. "They were boring me."

I nod as if it all makes sense to me, though I'm surprised. Alina usually thrives on attention. It occurs to me this is the closest I've been to her in . . . ever.

Now that I've finally got her away from Addy, I can't think of one thing to say to ease her into the impending breakup. Fuck, this is going to be harder than I thought.

I flag down a waiter. "Whiskey, neat. And water for *Signorina* De Luca."

She pouts, her lower lip jutting out. "I don't want water."

"Tough," I reply, noticing the slight glaze in her eyes. She's well on her way to getting tipsy, and a drunk Alina would be far from ideal right now.

"Dante, who is that redhead?" Alina starts to drum an impatient rhythm on the table, her perfectly manicured nails clicking against the polished wood.

"Not your concern." I accept my whiskey, taking a measured sip. The smoky liquid burns a path down my throat, steadying me.

Alina's lips curl, her eyes narrowing. "Not my concern! You're my fiancé and she's clearly one of those whor—"

"Choose your next words carefully, Alina," I cut her off, my voice low and dangerous. I can feel my control slipping, and the urge to defend Addy is overwhelming.

She leans in, undeterred. "Did you not see how she looked at you? Like you're a tall glass of water, and she's parched."

The waiter appears, bringing Alina's water. She huffs, then takes an exaggerated sip, arching both her brows as if to say "Happy now?" I tip my glass in response, biting back a sarcastic retort.

"You know, Dante," Alina continues, her voice taking on a wheedling tone, "this is the most attention you've given me in months. I could do naked cartwheels, and you wouldn't notice. But I talk to some redhead, and suddenly you're all over me." She gathers her silky dark hair, twirling it coquettishly. "Maybe I should dye my hair red too."

I can't help but snort. "It wouldn't suit you."

Her face colors. "You're impossible!" Alina snatches up her glass of water, her movements jerky with frustration. "We're supposed to be getting married, for God's sake."

Here we go. I lean forward, bracing my elbows on the table. "About that. It's not going to happen after all. As of now, the wedding is off."

"What?" The glass slips from Alina's frozen fingers and shatters on the floor. Without thinking, I stretch my foot over the broken pieces of glass, shielding her from any splinters while I summon a cleanup crew. They appear almost instantly, efficiently dealing with the mishap.

Alina leans back in her seat, barely taking notice of the woman cleaning her mess. I suppose she's reeling and needs a few minutes to digest what I just dropped on her.

"You . . . you can't be serious, Dante," she finally sputters, her eyes wide with disbelief.

I hold her gaze, letting her see the finality in mine.

Suddenly, she throws her hands up, nearly hitting a passing patron. "I knew it! I fucking knew it! I should have just stuck with Nico! But no, mama said—" She clamps her mouth shut, realizing too late what she's revealed.

"Go on," I say dryly. "Mama said what?"

She shakes her head, looking everywhere but at me. "Nothing. I only agreed to wed you because . . . because I like you a lot. And I thought you were so much nicer than Nico, but it turns out you're not," she finishes lamely, her cheeks flushing with embarrassment.

I'm pretty sure that's not Bianca's reasoning for wanting me instead of Nico, but I'm too relieved to be free of her schemes to care anymore. Still, I soften my tone, feeling a pang of sympathy for Alina.

"You deserve better, *cara*. You deserve a man who wouldn't ignore you. Who'd die before he hurts you or lets you go. And he's out there somewhere."

She snaps, "Don't patronize me, Dante," but there's a quiver in her voice that tells me she's desperate for the same thing. It's just too bad that she'll likely end up in another arranged marriage situation.

I continue, ignoring her false bravado. "So, if you ever find yourself hitched to a man you don't want, come and talk to me. Okay?"

"Oh, bore off." She rolls her eyes, but I know she heard me loud and clear. "I'm going home."

She stands, and I signal to her guards, who instantly materialize in a protective formation around her. She turns back on her way out, chin lifted in a show of defiance.

"I expect you'll be hearing from my father first thing tomorrow, and then we'll see if you really have the balls to back up your bluff. So go do your thing tonight, but I know you're not stupid enough to fuck this up over some random lay."

She flicks her hair gracefully and leaves.

I release a breath, feeling the weight of an unwanted future lift from my shoulders as I watch her go, her gold dress shimmering under the lights as she weaves through the crowd. Alina is beautiful. A spoiled mafia princess, yet untouched in so many ways. She deserves better than to be a pawn.

Through the glass floor, I spot Addy at the bar, toe-to-toe with Pietro, and my lips curve into a wolfish smile. Her wild curls bounce as she jabs a finger at his chest, and even from here, I can practically feel the heat of her anger.

Pietro steps back from her and rubs his chest, his usually expressionless face twitching like he's about to laugh or cry. He'll probably whine to me later about the bruise he got from being poked in the chest.

Thinking those two would get along really nicely in the coming months, I straighten my jacket and head for the stairs, anticipation thrumming in my belly.

She's mine, she's on my turf, and oh so fucking ripe for the picking.

CHAPTER SIXTEEN

Adele

Watching Dante leave with his fiancée feels like having a hole carved in my chest with a blunt knife. Unnatural and brutal.

As he guides her up the steps, I notice Dante's usually loose-limbed gait seems forced, his shoulders tense under his tailored jacket while Alina strains to get nearer to him. It seems obvious to me that he doesn't return her affections, but then again, that might be the stupidly hopeful part of me thinking that.

Whatever the case, though, Dante is committed to her. He's marrying her. He wouldn't even spare me a glance while she was there.

Suddenly, I understand why he was so conflicted the last time we were together. Why he needed to smoke so badly. Why he told me never to come back.

It had nothing to do with the Outfit's so-called war with the Irish or our roles in the Martelli trial. It's because he was engaged to Alina.

The man was just being nice, and I threw myself at him, pushed his buttons, and even flashed him my legs.

Really, what did I expect from Dante after I did all of that?

And now, there's nothing more to do than leave him alone. The pulsing beat of the club suddenly feels suffocating, the flashing lights disorienting.

"Well, Kira," I say, forcing a wry smile and slipping off my stool. "As far as dramatic ex reunions go, this was soap opera gold."

"Addy," Kira's hand stops me with a hand on my arm. "Dante won't marry her. He's just biding his time until he can break things off."

"Oh please, Kira. I don't need any platitudes here. I'm a big girl," I say, wrapping my arms around myself.

"Trust me, babe, that's not what I'm doing. Dante Vitelli only does one thing: What he wants to do. And he clearly doesn't want Alina."

No argument there. Still, I'm not about to stick around for crumbs. Coming here was a big mistake in the first place. "Well, good for him. I'm leaving."

"You're going back on a fifteen-hour drive to Boston now?"

"No, of course not. I'll find a motel, and come back at dawn when you finish up. And I promise I'll be fine, don't worry," I say to reassure her when I see her brows knit with concern.

Kira throws her arms around me. "Okay, babe. Thanks. For everything. And I'm sorry. I just thought that if you saw him again, you'd get some clarity on the . . . situation."

"It's okay, Kira. I understand. You're an amazing DJ, by the way," I whisper, my chin resting on her shoulder. "Way, way better than your idol, Zedd."

She chuckles, kisses my cheek, then steps back and lets the tattooed man guide her away. The man inclines his head to me in a gesture I can only interpret as respect before he leads Kira away.

As soon as the duo disappears into the throng of gyrating dancers, I get the urge to escape and breathe. Maybe cry a little too. I need to process everything that just happened tonight.

I grab my purse and turn to leave.

But I don't even make it two steps before a large hand clamps down on my arm, stopping me in my tracks.

"Not so fast."

I jump and almost scream in alarm, and then I see it's none other than Hulky. His massive frame towers over me, his grip firm but not painful.

"For fuck's sake, get a real job, Hulky. Manhandling women is about as classy as a fart in church," I spit, my free hand balling into a fist at my side.

His grip on my arm remains like a vise. "Says the woman who bites like a rabid chihuahua," he retorts, his face impassive save for a slight twitch at the corner of his mouth. "Anyway, Boss wants a word with you."

"Oh really? Well, tell Boss that he can go fuck himself."

Hulky doesn't budge, his stance as solid as a mountain. "His instructions were to wait."

"To wait for him while he gets his rocks off with his fiancée?" My nostrils flare with rage, and I jab my finger into his chest. "Even you must know that's a little excessive. If you're allowed to form an opinion, that is."

Hulky's eye twitches, but his face is otherwise impassive.

Instantly, I regret what I just said. "I'm sorry, that was rude."

"Save it," Hulky snaps, rubbing at his chest in a way that makes me wonder if I have ice picks for nails. I double-check just to be sure, but nope, they're smooth and buffed into blunt ovals.

"Can you at least let go of me?" I ask. The warmth of his hand on my arm is becoming uncomfortable.

Hulky instantly drops my arm as if I'm on fire, then steps back. "If you try to leave—"

"What, you'll take my shoes and knock me out cold?" I cross my arms over my chest, shifting my weight to one hip.

"—you won't get very far, I meant to say. But now that you mention it, that could work too."

I sigh, my shoulders sagging in defeat. It's no use. Hulky won't let me leave. I'm trapped here until that jerk returns. Seeing no other choice, I return to my bar stool.

"What's your name, anyway?" I ask, my fingers fidgeting with the hem of my dress.

"Hulky Hulk," he replies with a straight face, and I can't help the chuckle that bubbles out of me.

"That's a good, strong name," I remark.

"Thank you," he replies. As if those words were a secret code, Hulky visibly relaxes. He takes a step back, widens his stance, and folds one hand over the other. I'm pretty sure I only said 'thank you' and not 'at ease,' but something tells me there's no point trying to figure out Hulky.

As he shifts, I catch a glint of gold on his ring finger. A wedding band. *Huh.* Why does the fact that Hulky is married surprise me?

"He cares for you." As soon as the words tumble out of Hulky's mouth, he stiffens, his jaw clenching as if he wants to snatch them back. I'm about to dig into what he just said when I see Dante approaching, and my stupid breath catches again.

Dante's eyes—like embers of smoky quartz—hold mine captive until he comes to a stop right in front of me, his thighs brushing the front of my knees.

He's close enough that I can feel the heat radiating off his body, his spicy cologne mingling with the scent of expensive whiskey on his breath.

His gaze slowly sweeps over me, taking in my dress, my hair, and my face until I can almost taste the tension crackling in the air between us. Despite my irritation, a throb begins between my legs.

"I'll take it from here, Pietro," Dante says, still not taking his eyes off me. He looms over me, making me feel small and vulnerable.

"Boss." Hulky—Pietro, apparently—nods and moves a few steps away, but I notice he doesn't leave. His footsteps fade into the background noise of the club.

"Let's go talk," Dante murmurs, and the low rumble of his voice vibrates through me.

"I think we're way past talking," I snap, crossing my arms over my chest and trying to school my face into a mask of fury. I fail miserably, but at least my voice doesn't waver. "Why don't you go back to your . . ." I wave a hand dismissively toward the VIP lounge, ". . . fiancée?"

Dante ignores my question and instead continues to sear me with his gaze. His jaw clenches, a muscle ticking visibly. "Now, Addy," he commands.

"Fuck off." The words come out as a hiss between clenched teeth.

Something flashes across his face, and then he leans over me, bracing both hands on the bartop, caging me in and closing the gap between us. The nightclub disappears as my world contracts, and all I see is him. My gaze travels up his muscled chest and neck before finally meeting his molten silver gaze.

He's too close. His heat surrounds me, his breath fanning against my lips. I raise my hands to his chest to push him away but somehow get distracted by his nearness, so they hang uselessly on his lapels, the fabric smooth under my fingers.

"What are you doing?" My hands finally cooperate and push against his muscled chest, but whether I haven't applied enough force or he's too stubborn, I can't tell because he doesn't budge. His body is like a wall of solid heat.

He bends his head, letting his lips trail along my temple before he whispers into my ear. "I want to talk to you. Alone." His stubble scratches lightly against me, raising goosebumps on my skin.

The last dredges of my anger evaporate as my body completely betrays me. My nipples harden into painful points as my fingers find their way into his partially open shirt, running against the warm inked skin beneath. But even while his big body forms a warm cocoon, I'm not completely lost on the fact that there are other people sitting at this bar.

"You're making a scene, Dante," I say in a hushed tone.

"What, you're worried your boyfriend will get jealous?" His breath tickles my ear, sending a shiver down my spine.

"He's not my boyfriend. And you should be more concerned about your own fiancée. You know, the woman you're going to be married to in a few weeks, jerkhole." I push against his chest, trying to create some distance between us.

He rears back and looks at me with an unreadable expression. Then his arm snakes around my waist, and he drags me off the stool and right against his body. I'm still trying to tug down my hem when he grabs my purse and steers me away from the bar without letting me go.

Bodies part as he walks us toward the door, my body plastered against his side.

"Stop fidgeting and smile for the cameras," he bends to whisper in my ear. "We'll be all over the internet by morning."

And that's when I notice the raised phones.

How is this even happening to me right now?

The moment we get outside and the cool night air hits my flushed skin, I snatch my purse from him and wrench myself out of his arms. "Get off me, Dante. I have a life and job, you know?"

I notice Pietro has followed us outside, his hulking form stands guard a few feet away.

"It's not a crime to be photographed with a man, Addy," Dante says.

If only he were just a man. "I know that. I'm just not prepared to deal with unnecessary online speculation."

And if what my dad said is true, whoever is out to get me shouldn't know that I'm in Chicago right now.

Dante takes a step closer. "So why did you come here tonight, Addy? What do you want from me?"

"You think I came back for you?" I scoff, tossing my hair over my shoulder. "Please. Don't even flatter yourself."

"What am I supposed to think when you keep showing up uninvited in my house?"

I shake my head, not even willing to dignify that with a response. I simply spin on my flats and start to walk toward my rental car, trying my damnedest not to limp.

His voice stops me. "Adele."

My lids fall closed. It's unfair that Dante Vitelli calls me like that, drawing my name to three syllables. Raspy, musical, provocative. I hate what it does to me.

"What?" I ask, not turning around.

"Tell me you came here for me tonight. That you couldn't get me out of your mind, so you tagged along with Kira, wearing that dress and letting some asshole put his hands all over you to get my attention."

"I didn't come to get your attention."

"Well, you have it now. All of it."

I feel myself melting, so I grit my teeth and stiffen my spine. "I don't want it, Dante. You can shove it up your ass. I'm leaving."

"The hell you are." The next thing I know I'm up in his arms and he's stalking toward a huge black SUV.

"Dante, where are you taking me?" I push against his chest, my hands meeting solid muscle.

"Home."

"Oh my God. You wouldn't fucking dare." My heart races with a mix of fear and excitement.

"I told you not to come back, Addy. What I didn't warn you about was what would happen if you did."

"So, what, you'll keep me prisoner?" I squirm in his arms, but his grip is unyielding.

"No. I'll let you decide if you still want to leave when we're done."

"Done doing what?"

He only smiles, then pulls open the passenger door and unceremoniously dumps me into the front passenger seat. The leather feels refreshingly cool against my heated skin.

"You're engaged, for fuck's sake."

"Did you see a ring on her?" His eyebrow arches as he leans over me.

I violently shove down the hope swelling inside me. "I don't care. You're planning to marry her. You're promised to wed. You already gave your word. You're betrothed. Avowed . . ."

"Are you done with the synonyms or would you like a thesaurus?" He grabs the seatbelt and buckles me in, his hands brushing against my thigh.

"Fuck you," I spit, my hands clenching into fists.

"You will, baby. Soon."

My core clenches at his words. What on earth has Kira gotten me into? I scramble for an excuse. "Seriously, I–I can't go home with you."

"Why not?"

"What do you mean, why not?" I sputter in disgust. "You're getting married. Doesn't that mean anything to you?"

"For the last time, Addy, I'm not marrying Alina. And you should know I've never touched her."

"You did. Tonight," I can't help grumbling, crossing my arms over my chest.

He rears back to stare at me for a full minute. "Well, then since we're being jealous. Why the fuck did you let him put his hands on you?"

"Who, Zedd?"

He cocks his brow. "Whatever the fuck he calls himself. I was that close to snapping his neck."

"Good. Now you know how I felt."

Dante suddenly throws back his head and laughs, and that's when I realize I said that out loud.

Shit. "Look, I need to leave."

His thumb traces my bottom lip slowly, and I have to tamp down an insane desire to suck on it.

"No, Addy, you don't want to leave. You want to spend the night with me buried deep inside you."

My lids flutter closed. That's it, game over. My body had thrown in the towel. But my mind stubbornly refuses to cave, coming up with another excuse.

"I can't. I have to return my car to the agency first thing Monday morning or lose my deposit . . . and Kira—your godsister or whatever—she has some of her things in the trunk. She'll need them. I'll talk to you here, but I can't go home with you."

"Where's the rental car?" He leans close to me, his body tempting me with his nearness.

"It's in section 2B. A black Corolla." I fidget with the hem of my dress, avoiding his gaze.

"Give me your keys."

"Dante, wait."

He simply reaches for my purse and fishes out the car keys. He straightens and tosses the key to Hulky. "Corolla in 2B. Get it returned to Boston."

"Boss." Pietro leaves, his footsteps fading into the night.

"Pietro will take care of it, alright?" Dante dips his head and murmurs against my lips, his breath hot on my skin.

"Dante—"

His lips capture mine in a kiss that I instantly feel all the way to my toes. Teases my lips until my mouth goes slack with need, then slants his lips over mine and shoves his tongue deep inside my mouth in a clear stake of ownership.

He's rough and demanding, shamelessly sucking, nibbling at my lips, and pulling tortured moans out of me as I feel a rush of wetness coat my panties. Without words, Dante has just told me that he's going to fuck me tonight and I'm going to let him.

I swear there's no man alive who can communicate more eloquently with his body the way Dante can.

And then, as suddenly as the decadent kiss began, Dante tears his mouth off me only to plant a chaste peck on my forehead, a complete one-eighty from the way he's been plundering my mouth just now, apparently because I still need a final mindfuck.

Wordlessly, he steps back, slams my door shut, rounds the car, then gets into the driver's seat while I meticulously pick my scattered brains off the floor.

I'm still catching my breath when the engine roars to life, and Dante backs out of the parking spot. I see Pietro in my rental car already idling at the entrance of the lot.

Just as Dante approaches the waiting Corolla, a deafening explosion rips through the night, its force rattling the SUV.

Dante immediately throws his body against my chest, knocking the wind out of me as the car rocks violently. My ears ring, and the world becomes a mix of reverberating echoes and alarming cars. Heat, smoke, and debris fill the air, and the smell of smoke stings my nostrils.

"Addy!" Dante calls, his voice tight and urgent.

It's only when I feel his hands running over my face that I realize my eyes are tightly shut and I'm screaming. I open my eyes a fraction and nod. "What was tha—"

Before I can finish, Dante swears loudly and throws open the door. "Under no circumstances should you leave this car, do you understand me?" he barks, and then he's out of the car and running, his hand already reaching for the gun in his back holster.

It takes me a moment to peer beyond the smoke and commotion to realize what just happened.

A bomb. But it's not until I undo my seat belt and crawl into the driver's seat, deftly avoiding the deployed airbags, that the full weight of the situation crashes down on me, stealing my breath and leaving me paralyzed with shock and terror.

Smoke billows from the charred metal that remains where the Corolla had been a minute ago. A shoe with the foot still in it lies a few feet from the smoking ruins.

I swallow a wave of nausea as the horrifying facts hit home. Hulky – Pietro. Dante's man. He was inside my rental car.

The car that just exploded.

That should have been me in pieces all over the parking lot.

And then Dante is in my line of vision, striding toward the burning ruins, disbelief etched on his features. He stands close—too close to the smoking ruins, frozen in shock.

Suddenly, he tears off his jacket and launches it at the rubble, then drags his hand through his hair and throws his head back. I can hear his almost-inhuman roar of grief and feel every bit of his devastation and an inexplicable urge grips me.

I need to go to him.

Before I can think better of it, I grab the door handle.

Just then, Kira's tattooed friend appears from nowhere and grabs Dante, dragging him away from the inferno.

"*Fratello*," he yells, pleading with Dante, his voice breaking, "Go. I'll finish here."

Dante spins around, his face a mask of anguish and fury, his voice a raw snarl. "Who would dare?" He struggles against the man's grip, and I see his control, always so absolute, shattering before my eyes. It's the most rattled I've ever seen him, the most vulnerable. His gray eyes are glassy with tears and blazing with a desperate fear I've never witnessed before.

Something inside me snaps. I can't just sit here and watch. Dante needs me. He needs someone. Anyone.

I open the SUV door and stumble out, my legs shaky beneath me.

"Dante!" My voice is a choked whisper, lost in the roar of the fire and the panicked shouts of the crowd starting to gather at a safe distance.

He hears me, his eyes widening as he sees me standing there. "Get back in the car, Addy," he shouts. "Right now!"

His words are laced with panic and a terror that chills me to the bone. But beneath it all, I see something else in his eyes. It's not anger. It's terror. For me. He wouldn't be this afraid if it weren't for me.

My heart aches for him, at the raw pain on his face. He looks like a wounded animal, trapped and desperate.

"Red Wine," Dante says to the man holding him, his words clipped and strained. "She goes off-grid effective immediately, do you understand me?"

Just as he's about to leave, Dante pulls him back and looks into his eyes. "She's in your hands, *fratellino.*"

"I understand, Dante."

And without another word, without a backward glance, Dante turns his back on the chaos and strides toward the club, leaving me standing there with a hollow ache in my chest.

The smell of smoke stings my nostrils, but it's the sight of Dante's retreating form that truly burns.

CHAPTER SEVENTEEN

Adele

I'm still frozen in shock when Dante's man ushers me into the back of another SUV, frozen until the door slams shut with a finality that makes me flinch, the sound echoing loudly in the confined space.

For a moment, all I can hear is my own ragged breathing and the pounding of my heart against my ribcage. Each beat is a painful reminder that I'm alive while Hulky . . . isn't.

I squeeze my eyes shut, but it doesn't help. Dante's face haunts me—the anguish etched into his chiseled features, the tears glistening in his stormy gray eyes and the raw grief and rage radiating from his body. And Pietro, reduced to scattered pieces on the pavement.

All because of me.

The SUV's interior suddenly feels suffocating. I press my palm against the window, feeling the cool glass against my skin. Outside, the city lights blur as we drive.

We're moving at a speed that should terrify me, the force pressing me back into the seat. But I'm too numb to care. Dante's man is a wall of barely contained emotion. In the moonlight filtering through the tinted windows, I see the rigid set of his shoulders, the white-knuckled grip he has on the steering wheel, and his jaw so tight a muscle ticks reflexively.

The silence is charged with unspoken accusations. This man and Hulky worked together. Maybe they were even friends. The memory of the glint of gold on Pietro's finger flashes in my mind. Hulky had a wife. Did he have children too?

Guilt claws at me, threatening to choke me. I need to say something, anything, to break this suffocating silence.

"Red Wine," I murmur, the phrase foreign and heavy on my tongue. I've heard Dante and his men use that phrase more than once, so it must mean something to them. Or maybe it's just a foolish, desperate attempt to get a reaction from this man who must surely hate me.

His dark, haunted eyes meet mine in the rearview mirror, widening slightly in surprise. For a moment, neither of us speaks.

"I'm so sorry," I finally choke out past the lump in my throat. "I'm so terribly sorry."

The man's expression softens almost imperceptibly. "It's Sal," he says, his voice gentler than I expected.

"What?"

"My name is Salvatore. You can call me Sal."

I nod, grateful he's talking to me.

His eyes flicker back to the road before meeting mine again in the mirror. "And Red Wine is the code name Don and Dante call you."

His words sink in slowly, each one a pebble dropping into the still pond of my shock. Dante and the Don have a code name for me. They talk about me. That sends a mix of fear and something else down my spine.

But the guilt is quick to follow, a bitter reminder of the price of my presence in Dante's life. What would the Don think of me now, the woman who caused the death of one of his loyal soldiers?

My lids slide shut, spilling out hot, salty tears. If only I had listened to Daddy—Benjamin. If only I'd never left Boston like he warned, none of this would have happened.

He was telling the truth. Someone is really out to get me.

The fact makes me double over in pain, my forehead almost touching my knees, arms wrapped tightly around my midsection as if I could hold myself together through sheer force of will.

"Oh God. It should have been me," I mutter. "It should have been me."

"Addy!" Sal's voice is like a whip, snapping me out of my guilt-ridden chant. I straighten and his eyes meet mine again in the rearview mirror. "I don't think you realize how lucky we all are that it wasn't you."

His words are drowned out by the ugly voice in my head screaming that this is all my fault. The stench of smoke and rubber from the explosion clings to me and Sal, a constant reminder. It's in my hair, on my dress, on Sal. My lungs burn with the need for fresh air, for escape.

And suddenly, I can't breathe anymore.

"Stop the car," I gasp, my voice tight with panic.

"I can't do that, Addy," Sal says, but his words barely register. The need to get out, to escape the guilt and fear, beats down on me. My fingers scrabble clumsily at the door handle but it's locked.

"Please, Sal," I plead, bile rising in my throat. I clamp a hand over my mouth, my stomach roiling. "I'm . . . I'm going to be sick."

For a moment, nothing happens. Then, with a curse, Sal wrenches the steering wheel to the right. The SUV lurches, tires screeching against the pavement as we veer off the road. The sudden movement sends me sliding across the leather seat, my shoulder slamming into the door.

Before the vehicle has fully stopped, I fumble with the door handle. This time, it gives way, and I tumble onto the rough asphalt. The impact jars through my body, but I barely notice. I'm too focused on the burning in my throat, the acid taste in my mouth.

On my hands and knees, I retch violently. The contents of my stomach splatter onto the ground, the acidic smell mixing with the exhaust fumes. I heave until there's nothing left, until I'm bringing up nothing but bitter bile.

My body shakes with the force of my sobs, tears streaming down my face to mingle with the mess on the ground.

I'm vaguely aware of Sal a few yards away, a silent shadow in the darkness. The cool night air raises goosebumps on my skin, a stark contrast to the heat of shame burning through me.

When the heaving finally subsides, I remain on all fours, gasping for breath. My arms tremble with the effort of holding myself up, my hair hanging limply around my face. I've never felt so utterly wretched, so completely undone.

After what feels like an eternity, I hear Sal's footsteps approaching. He crouches down beside me, and when I finally gather the courage to look up, he's holding out a bottle of cold water, his face filled with quiet concern.

With shaking hands, I take the water and rinse my mouth then drink, the cool liquid soothing my raw throat.

"Thank you," I whisper hoarsely.

Sal nods. "Think you can stand?"

"Yes," I say, though I'm not entirely sure I can. When I wobble on my feet, Sal puts an arm around my waist and guides me back to the SUV.

The car feels less confining now, more of a sanctuary from the harsh reality outside. As Sal shuts the door and rounds the vehicle to the driver's side, I lean my forehead against the cool window.

We continue on in silence, the only sounds are my ragged breathing and the muffled rumble of the engine. I close my eyes, and my thoughts center on Dante. Need, hot and fierce burns inside me. It's the same inexplicable heat I felt when I saw him roar in anguish at the parking lot. I want to be with him right now.

Soon, the glittering city lights fade, replaced by sprawling estates and perfectly manicured lawns. We pass through wrought iron gates emblazoned with a large crest and start up a winding driveway, but I barely notice them.

Not until a mansion rises high out of the ground and above us do I sit up and look at a fortress of stone and glass. The silhouette of turrets and high walls stands out against the night sky. The moon casts a silver glow over the landscape, highlighting the gnarled branches of ancient trees and rolling hills.

"Where are we?" My words come out as a hoarse whisper, my throat raw from crying.

"Dante's family home," Sal answers as he takes a detour off the winding driveway to the side of the main building. He stops in front of what seems like a solid stone wall, but as Sal gets out and gestures for me to follow, I realize it's a hidden door.

My legs feel like lead as I exit the car, the cool night air a refreshing balm on my heated face and stuffy nose. Immediately, the door opens to reveal an extremely tall man with snow-white hair and a stooped posture. He ushers us inside quickly, his movements sharp and efficient despite his age. He and Sal only exchange nods as he stands to the side, and Sal leads me deeper into the dimly lit hallway.

The old man, the house butler, perhaps, shrinks into the shadows as we pass, but when I glance back, his eyes are wide with shock as he stares at me. Unnerved, I turn away and follow Sal into the maze of corridors, my heart pounding a frantic rhythm in my chest.

The carpets muffle our steps as we move deeper into the mansion, taking flights of stairs down. This house seems like a scene straight out of a gothic novel, with cold stone walls and sconces of flickering yellow light casting eerie shadows. The air hangs heavy with an oppressive silence, as if the mansion itself is holding its breath.

Sal guides me through the maze of corridors, his hand a steady pressure on the small of my back. Finally, he stops before an ornate door, its dark wood gleaming in the low light. He pushes it open, and I step inside, my breath catching in my throat.

It's a large but windowless room, having air conditioning vents in the walls instead. A king-sized bed dominates the space, its dark silk sheets an invitation to indulge in luxury. But it's the mirrors that catch my eye—floor-to-ceiling, they reflect the room back at me.

"You'll be safe here," Salvatore says. He gestures to an intercom panel just beside the bed. "Food, clothes, anything at all, just call. Falzone, the old butler, will get you anything you need."

I nod my thanks. Although right now, the only thing I need is Dante. His absence is starting to feel like a hollow space in my chest.

As Salvatore turns to leave, I reach out, my trembling hand grasping at the sleeve of his suit.

"Sal," I say, my voice breaking, "What about Dante? Will I see him tonight?" I hate the neediness in my voice, but I can't mask it.

Sal shakes his head, and my heart sinks. "He's grieving, Addy," he says gently. "He loved Pietro like a brother."

But that is exactly what I want. I want his grief, his pain. I want him raw and uncontrolled.

"Please, I need to see him. Need to . . ." I trail off, unsure how to put into words the dark hunger that gnaws at me.

I want to take away his pain, even if it means taking it into myself. To be the one to comfort him, to soothe him. To let him use me . . . hurt me . . . break me.

The thought terrifies me, even as it sends a dark thrill through my veins. I don't understand it. I don't want to understand it. All I know is that I crave Dante with an intensity that borders on madness. My fingers tighten on Sal's sleeve, knuckles white with the force of my grip.

Sal's dark eyes meet mine, and something like understanding flickers in their depths. He gently pries my fingers loose. "Give him time, Addy," he says, not unkindly. "He'll come and see you. The Don is away, so Dante is sorting out the mess and making sure everyone else is safe."

I feel another pang of guilt. I'm so wrapped up in my head that I forgot about the others. And Kira . . . God, Kira. Vulnerable in the chaos because of her lack of sight. The rest of her DJ friends. In danger because of me.

"Kira?" I lick my dry lips, tasting salt from dried tears. "Is she okay . . .?"

Sal's gaze softens further as he assures me, "Kira is safe. She was inside the club when . . ." He trails off, his jaw clenching, and I know he's thinking about Hulky.

My stomach twists, and I swallow a wave of nausea and I try to focus on the present, to be grateful for the people who are still alive.

"Get some rest, okay?" Sal says, his hand briefly squeezing my shoulder. Then he turns and starts to leave.

"Sal?" I croak.

He pauses at the door, waiting.

"What was his full name?"

He stays silent for a long time, and I start to think he won't respond when he says on a soft exhale. "His name was Pietro. Pietro Potenza."

And then all I hear is the sound of the door softly closing behind Sal.

And I'm left alone with my thoughts and the accusing stares of my reflections.

In the end, I can't bear the softness of the bed or the luxury surrounding me. So I curl up on the carpet instead, my knees hugged to my chest. I rock back and forth, my mind spinning with dark thoughts and darker desires.

I need Dante. Yearn for his hands on me, his body against mine. I want him to hurt me, to punish me, to absolve me.

My fingers dig into my arms, leaving crescent-shaped marks on my skin. I welcome the pain, a poor substitute for what I truly crave.

And so I wait, lost in the labyrinth of my shockingly twisted longing. The ornate clock on the mantel ticks away the seconds, each one an eternity. The mirrors reflect my huddled form, multiplying my misery, but sleep eludes me.

The only way I can cope with the crushing guilt is to imagine Dante striding through those doors. To imagine his hands on me, gentle at first, then bruising hard. His lips on my skin, teeth marking me, making me forget, just for a moment, the horror of what's happened.

CHAPTER EIGHTEEN

Dante

Smoke stings my eyes as I approach Ron Higgins. The head of the bomb squad is bent over the mangled remains of the Corolla, his movements precise and methodical, while my muscles tense, fists clenching and unclenching as I fight to maintain control.

"The other feds are gone, Ron. So, for fuck's sake, did you find something or not?" I growl. It's probably the tenth time I've asked him tonight, each repetition grating on my already frayed nerves.

My fingers twitch at my sides, itching to do something, anything. The urge to lash out, to destroy, pulses through me with each heartbeat. Instead, I force myself to stand still, to appear calm even as chaos rages within me.

The first nine times I asked, all Ron did was grunt. I know he found something; I'm sure of it, but he wouldn't say anything in front of the rest of his fellow agents. Now, with the area cleared and only us remaining, I wait for him to talk to me.

Ron is loyal to the Outfit, which means he won't report or file anything without passing it through me first.

It was almost impossible to keep the authorities out of this due to the overwhelming number of witnesses, but we at least managed to keep the media away. The PR team is doing damage control on the internet and seems to be steering the narrative so far, but my mind barely registers these small victories.

All I can think about is Pietro, my friend, and Addy . . . Christ, Addy. The image of her, pale and shaken, flashes before my eyes, and I have to suppress a shudder.

What if it had been her?

The question pokes at my brain every five seconds, driving me insane with the absolute horror of it.

"Dante." Grim-faced, Ron finally straightens from his crouch, holding up a small, charred piece of metal.

"What's that?" I ask, even though I already suspect the answer.

"It's the detonator," Ron says.

I nod for him to continue, my entire body tense as a coiled spring.

"It's military grade."

I grit my teeth, rage surging through me again, threatening to break free of my carefully constructed control. It's not an amateur attack. But I already knew that in my gut. Only two groups have access to those kinds of weapons: the US military, and people like me.

I clap him on the shoulders, my grip perhaps a little too tight. "Good work, Ron. You know what to do."

"Sure," he replies, understanding the unspoken order.

As Ron moves away, I'm left alone with my thoughts, each one more volatile than the last. Someone wants Addy dead, and they're ruthless enough to use a bomb. But last time I checked, I was the one who's in the habit of pissing off the Irish . . . so why her?

Although every single time I've pissed them off, Addy has been with me, so there's that.

And there's the issue of her father's enemies who may be seeking retaliation.

A million possibilities, each more terrifying than the last, race through my mind. It's like trying to grasp smoke. The need to hit something, to release this pent-up energy, weighs heavy on me. But I can't. Not yet. I need to stay focused, stay in control.

For Addy. For Nico. For everyone counting on me to fix this fucking mess.

I stalk into Resin, my blood still boiling. The club is empty now, save for a few trusted men. Sal is leaning against the bar, nursing a scotch. He looks up as I approach, then pours me a glass without a word.

The amber liquid sloshes in the crystal tumbler, catching the dim light. I down it in one gulp, relishing the burn as it slides down my throat. It's not enough to dull the edge of my anger, but it's something.

"When are we going to see his wife and kids?" Sal's voice is rough with emotion.

I shake my head, pouring myself another drink. "Not we. I'll go see Sylvia and the boys as soon as I leave here. You are going to identify that bomber. And I want something before dawn."

Sal nods. "I'll see what I can do. But shit, it still feels like a dream." He pauses, a sad smile tugging at his lips. "Pietro was the best sniper we had, you know. Could shoot the dick off a mosquito from a mile away."

I chuckle despite the heaviness in my chest. "Yeah, and he was a cocky bastard about it too. Always bragging about his aim."

We lapse into silence, the weight of Pietro's absence hanging between us. He was more than just a soldier, more than a friend. He was family.

Sal drains his scotch, his eyes glinting dangerously in the low light. "Whoever is behind this blast had better give themselves a clean death now before I find them."

I see the look in his eyes and almost feel a flicker of pity for whoever is responsible. Almost. Sal can be creative when he's angry, and right now, he's livid.

"Kira and her Boston friends?" I ask, forcing myself to focus on the practical matters at hand.

"In good hands. My men have settled them in Hydrea Hotel."

I nod, relief mingling with the cocktail of emotions swirling in my gut. Then I ask the one question I've been dying to know, the one that's been burning in the back of my mind since I sent her away. "How's she?"

Sal clears his throat, his eyes meeting mine. "Red Wine? Not good. She's asking for you."

I tense, my grip tightening on the glass. The crystal edges dig into my palm, grounding me. She doesn't know what she's asking for. I'm dying to see her, to touch her and feel with my own hands that she's okay, but I'm feeling too raw right now.

I need to be in control with her, but right now, I'm barely holding it together.

"Not tonight, Sal," I say, but even I can hear the lack of conviction in my voice.

"Sure." He scoffs as if he knows that my resistance is currently in a watery puddle at my feet. "With or without the blast, the moment you saw her tonight, there was only one way it was going to end."

I force a smirk, trying to deflect. "You know, for a virgin, you seem to have a lot of insight into these matters. Did you finally get the birds and bees talk?"

"Maybe," he says with a secret smile that tells me I'm better off not knowing more. The corner of his mouth twitches, and then he changes the subject, his tone turning serious. "When do you need me tomorrow?"

I take a deep breath, the scent of whiskey and smoke filling my lungs again. "Be at the Fortress with the rest of the Caporegimes for an emergency meeting at noon tomorrow."

Sal's eyebrows shoot up. "But Don Vitelli is away."

Nico was in Paris with Sophie but has had to cut their vacation short and is on his way back now.

"Don Vitelli will be there," I finish grimly, the words leaving a bitter taste in my mouth.

Sal's eyes widen slightly. "Shit. Did you tell him everything?"

Everything except the part about Addy. I figured we could always light that powder keg when he returns. "I told him just enough to get him packing up."

I drain my glass, setting it down with more force than necessary. "Sal, I'll handle Nico. You just make sure the Capos are there tomorrow. And stay hot on the bomber's trail."

"*Certo.*"

My voice hardens as I continue, "And Sal? I want every fucking thing there is to know about Benjamin O'Shea's dealings. Someone desperately wants his daughter dead."

"Consider it done," Sal says, his voice laced with deadly intent.

I pour another drink, the amber liquid sloshing against the crystal.

Someone and their entire family are going to bleed for this. And I won't stop until I find out who.

CHAPTER NINETEEN

Adele

I wake up with a scream, remnants of my vivid dream of being torn apart in a bomb blast all too real.

My ass feels numb. I must have dozed off, but now, the events of the night come rushing back like a tidal wave.

I squeeze my eyes shut, but the images flash relentlessly behind my eyelids: the fireball erupting into the sky, the twisted metal of what was once my car, and that single foot that should have been mine.

My chest constricts, and a choked sob escapes my throat, quickly followed by another. I clamp a hand over my mouth, trying to stifle the sound, but it's like the dam has broken again. The tears come in a torrent, hot and salty, wetting my chest and soaking into the neckline of my suddenly too-tight dress.

I drag myself to my feet, legs trembling, and stumble toward the en-suite bathroom. I grip the edge of the sink and force myself to look in the mirror.

My hair is a tangled mess. Mascara streaks down my cheeks in inky rivulets. My skin is pale, almost translucent, making the dark circles under my eyes stand out in stark relief. I look haunted, broken.

With shaking hands, I turn on the tap, letting the water run until steam fogs the mirror. I splash my face until the water scalds, but I welcome the pain.

When that stops working on the tearing ache in my chest, I lurch back into the bedroom, desperate for anything to numb the pain. My gaze lands on the crystal decanter on the mantelpiece, the amber liquid within glinting invitingly in the low light.

I'm reaching for it before I can stop myself. The stopper yields with a soft pop, the scent of aged whiskey sorely tempting. I might throw up, but maybe if I drink enough quickly, I could knock myself out before puking. My mouth waters, my body screaming for the oblivion the alcohol promises.

But I can't. I can't do that to my baby. To Dante's baby. With a frustrated cry, I hurl the decanter at the marble fireplace. It shatters with a satisfying crash of glass and liquid.

And yet, beneath the frustration, the dark hunger grows. It coils in my belly, a desperate need for distraction. Sick of resisting, I grab the hem of my dress, and I yank it over my head, then I crumble to the floor.

Almost of their own accord, my hands begin to roam my body, seeking relief. I cup my breasts, thumbs brushing over pebbled nipples, then I pinch them. I gasp at the sensation, a jolt of pleasure amidst the pain.

My fingers trail lower, dipping between my thighs to find myself already slick with need. I circle my clit, hips bucking into my own touch, chasing the release that hovers just out of reach.

Dante's name falls from my lips, a broken plea. I need him. Need his hands, his mouth, his cock. I need him to take me out of my head, to make me feel something, anything, other than this crushing guilt.

I'm so lost in my desperate pursuit of oblivion that I don't hear the door. It's only when I feel a presence looming over me that my eyes snap open, and I realize that I'm no longer alone.

CHAPTER TWENTY

Dante

It's 3:30 AM. The relentless beating of my fists against the punching bag echoes through the empty gym. Earlier, all I could think about was coming here, hitting something until my hands bled or my shoulders gave out, whichever came first.

Now, even as sweat drips down my face and my knuckles throb, it's not enough to drown out Sal's words echoing in my skull.

She's asking for you.

It's like a siren's call, a hook in my gut that I can't shake loose.

I throw another punch, harder this time, feeling the impact reverberate up my arm. But the physical pain does nothing to quiet the storm in my head. Neither does the music blasting through my AirPods.

Not when every fiber of my being is screaming at me to go to her. To give her what she wants.

Me.

I step back from the bag, chest heaving, and run a hand through my sweat-soaked hair.

What happened tonight changes everything because she's dead to the world she used to know and now alive in mine.

Addy has taken every part of me except for the part that truly matters. That I live by a certain moral code that I need her to be okay with. Heck, she has to be ready to live by it too. Addy can't even stand to be near a gun, and she still hasn't been told who she is.

My hand twitches with the need to wring Benjamin O'Shea's neck for keeping his daughter in the dark about her true identity all this while. The rage bubbles up, hot and familiar. Although, as of tonight, Addy has stopped being an O'Shea.

From now on, she's mine. And I don't plan to hide anything from her.

Mind made up, I leave the gym, shower, and then change into a suit. I grab a couple of spare T-shirts for her.

I'm out the door, car keys in hand, and in a matter of minutes, the cool night air hits me like a welcome punch.

Sal was right after all. This night is only ending one way: with Addy wrapped around me.

The drive to the Fortress is a blur. The streets are empty, the city asleep, but my mind is wide awake. Every stoplight feels like an eternity, every mile stretching out before me like a goddamn marathon.

By the time I pull up to the side entrance of the Fortress, my heart is pounding. The gravel crunches beneath my tires as I park the car, the sound harsh in the stillness of the night.

And then I'm there. Standing right outside her door. My hand pauses on the knob when I hear it. A soft cry, muffled by the heavy door. And just like that, my heart breaks open for her. I twist the handle and the door swings open on silent hinges.

I lean on the door frame, rooted to the spot as the cadence of the pulse pounding in my ears completely drowns out the strains of heavy metal rock emanating from my AirPods. Because nothing could have prepared me for the sight of Addy's grief.

Her desire.

Her guilt.

And her dark, desperate need for me

CHAPTER TWENTY-ONE

Adele

He stands there, looking like something straight out of my fantasy, his damp hair falling like a curtain around his face. His eyes flash with unmistakable heat as he takes in the sight of me—naked and touching myself and moaning his name while surrounded by the remnants of the shattered decanter. Only there's no shock in his eyes, no judgment. Just a calm understanding that shakes me to my core.

He gets me.

"Dante..." I feel a flush creep up my neck, spreading across my cheeks. He says nothing but simply holds my gaze, the intensity in his eyes pinning me in place as surely as any physical touch.

"Please," I breathe, the word catching on a sob. "I need..." But I don't even know how to finish that sentence. I don't know how to put into words the desperate, clawing hunger inside me.

Dante takes out his earbuds and lets them fall to the floor. Then he tosses what looks like balled-up T-shirts onto one of the couches in the room. He slowly sheds his suit jacket as he takes a step toward me, then another.

Finally, he crouches low right before me and wraps a big hand around my throat. Then he rises, gently bringing me to my feet with nothing but the hand around my throat.

"Tell me, *tesoro*," he murmurs, his voice low and soothing. "Tell me what you need."

My hands clench into fists. The scald on my palms stings with the movement, a sharp reminder of reality amidst the surreal tension of the moment. Dante's other hand reaches out, fingers ghosting along my jaw. The touch is feather-light, barely there, but I feel it in my core. His thumb brushes over my bottom lip, and I can't help the small sigh that escapes me.

In one fluid motion, he grips the back of my neck, fingers tangling in my hair. It's not painful, but it's firm and assertive. He tilts my head back, forcing me to look up at him. Our faces are inches apart, and his breath is hot against my skin.

"Talk to me, Addy," he murmurs.

I want to speak, to explain, to apologize about tonight—but the words stick in my throat. Instead, I lean into his touch, seeking more contact. My hands finally uncurl, and I reach up to touch his face.

Dante catches my wrist before I can cup his jaw, then turns my palm up, examining the red raw skin. His jaw clenches, a muscle ticking in his cheek.

"What have you done to yourself?" he asks, his tone unreadable.

I open my mouth to respond, but all that comes out is a choked sob. The tears I thought had run dry well up again, spilling over onto my cheeks. Dante releases my wrist, his hand coming up to cup my face. His thumb brushes away my tears, the gesture achingly tender.

The contrast between his gentle touches and the power emanating from him is intoxicating. I sway on my feet, lightheaded from a combination of grief and sheer want. Dante steadies me against him, his hand leaving my throat to wrap around my waist. The feel of his clothed body against my bare skin is electrifying, and I press closer, seeking more contact.

He allows it for a moment before pushing me back gently. "Words, Addy."

The loss of contact is almost a physical pain, and I can't suppress the whimper that escapes me as my body sways toward him again, drawn like a magnet. This time, Dante doesn't stop me.

I start to rub against him, moaning at the heady feeling of the hard planes of his muscles, loving the way his shirt buttons catch my nipples and his steely erection pushes against my stomach.

Dante's pupils swell at the sight and sound of my desire. The intensity of his gaze is almost too much to bear. I feel exposed and vulnerable—not just because I'm naked. It's as if he can see right through me, past all my defenses, to the darkest, most hidden parts of myself.

His free hand comes up to tangle in my hair again, tugging hard. The pain sends a jolt of pleasure through me.

"Tell me what you need, Addy. Now."

I shudder at his words, at the feel of his breath against my skin. What do I need? The answer is simple and terrifying all at once.

"You," I whisper. "A lot of you."

He pulls back slightly, his eyes searching mine. Whatever he sees there must satisfy him because the last vestiges of his control seem to snap.

In one swift movement, Dante carries me across the room until he's pressing me against the wall of mirrors. The cool surface is a shock against my overheated skin, making me gasp and arch into him.

He takes my mouth, swallowing my gasp. And then I feel his desperation for me too. It's in the way his mouth hovers over mine, the way he hungrily seeks out my tongue, the way he waits for me to exhale and then takes in my breath.

The guilt, grief, and confusion all fade into the background, overshadowed by the sheer force of our desire. His callused fingers leave a trail of fire as they stroke down my torso, following the dip of my waist to the flare of my hip.

And then he's cupping my ass cheeks in his big rough palms, kneading gently, then more firmly.

Nerve endings I never realized were there start to crackle. I moan into his mouth, arching into him. And when he squeezes harder, hard enough to hurt, to leave the prints of his fingers over my ass cheeks,

I feel an answering throb in my clit and, surprisingly, a tension in the pucker of my ass. He's never touched me like this, and I never realized how much I want him to.

When I start to mewl, my leg lifting of its own volition to curl around his thigh, he runs a hand through my folds. I nearly shout with relief.

"Dio mio," he groans against my neck as he sucks on the sensitive skin there, then bites down hard as he slides two fingers inside my aching pussy.

I jerk. "Dante, please . . ." I'm not even sure what I'm asking for. All I know is that I need him, need this, need something to make the pain and the guilt go away.

He rears back to look at me. "Is this what you want?"

I can feel my heart pounding in my chest as Dante's fingers slide in and out, then curl inside me, hitting that spot that makes me jolt in pleasure.

"Dante," I gasp.

His response is to spank me hard, the sting of it sending a shockwave through my already sensitive nerve endings. I cry out, both in pain and pleasure, as he kisses me deeply, his tongue exploring every inch of my mouth while he spanks me again and again.

Tears sting my eyes even as pleasure ripples out from my pussy. And then he slips his fingers out of me while my own fingers dig into the back of his neck, silently begging him not to stop.

I can feel my wetness all over my thighs, the evidence of my arousal taunting me as I struggle to regain control. But I'm powerless against the insane craving that consumes me.

"Do you want my fingers back in your greedy pussy?" he whispers against my lips, his breath hot and heavy.

I nod frantically, my hips bucking against his hand, but he pulls away, denying me what I crave.

"No," he says. "I think you want to feel something else."

Dante's fingers glide over my folds, gathering moisture from my pussy. And then he's stroking the pucker of my ass.

"Ah. Ah." I sigh. The sensation is foreign and intoxicating, teasing me with the promise of more. I spread my legs wider, my ass moving to time with his strokes.

Dante emits a throaty growl, sucks on the skin of my neck, then breaches that forbidden hole, pushing his finger inside. My nails sink into his back as my breath hitches.

I'm trying to work out exactly how it feels when he starts to slowly thrust in and out. My thoughts scatter, and my body arches into his touch as he rears back his head to watch me intently, his eyes dark with desire.

"You want that?" he murmurs, and I nod. He bends and sinks his teeth into my collarbone, making me jerk in pleasure and pain, then follows the bite with a soothing slide of his tongue, only to do it again.

And again.

My eyes cross with the need to feel more. The need to chase that unfamiliar sensation blooming in my pelvis every time he slides his finger knuckle-deep.

Without thinking, I reach behind me and circle his wrist, then push it against me in a silent plea to go deeper.

"You're fucking perfect, aren't you? You gorgeous, dirty girl."

That's it. It's dirty. It's more than just a word. It's a feeling that kicks up my heart rate and makes my skin prickle with lust. It's the same way I felt when he fucked me up against his car in full view of his crew. I can't deny it anymore. This is who I am, who I've always been beneath the surface. With Dante, I can finally be myself, raw and unfiltered.

"Yes," I moan, my voice barely audible.

Dante smiles wickedly and adds a second finger, then plunges deeper, stretching me in a way I never thought possible.

"Ah, fuck!" I cry out, the sensation almost too much to bear. I can't believe I'm here, in this position, with Dante's fingers buried deep in my ass and me loving it and craving more.

I don't know if I can come like this, but I know I don't want him to stop. I want him to push me out of my comfort zone and take me out of my head. I bury my face in his fragrant shirt to muffle the moans pouring out of me.

His other hand trails into the hair at my nape, using it to pull my head back. "Look at me," he growls, his voice low and commanding as he starts to finger fuck my ass harder.

I feel completely exposed to him. The more he pumps his fingers in and out of me, the more I feel myself slipping into a state of pure pleasure. It's not just about what he's doing to me. It's about who he is and what I'll let him do. My eyes go hazy, but I continue to look into his gray eyes, pupils blown with lust.

And then my vision blurs as I feel my pussy tighten around nothing. A gush of wetness leaves me, and my moans grow louder as he continues to work his fingers in and out of my ass.

"Look at you," he murmurs, his voice husky with desire. "Dripping all over my hand. You were fucking made for this, baby."

I feel a surge of lust at his words, and with every slippery glide, every stretch of my tight, forbidden hole, the pleasure swells higher inside me, a wave that's threatening to crash. My cries are no longer muffled against his chest but right against his ears, in tune with his softly whispered curses.

His head is tilted close to me as if he wants to catch every whimper, every plea, every ragged moan as I completely unravel for him. I'm mindless with the need to come.

And then, I'm right there on the brink, my whole body taut.

"Oh God, Dante," I cry as I tether, desperate for my orgasm. Dante bites down on my neck again. Then his thumb presses hard over my swollen clit.

That single touch pushes me off the brink and sends me tumbling into ecstasy. My mouth opens on a soundless scream, and my vision goes black. My ass tightens around his fingers as he starts to rub my clit in tight perfect circles, drawing out my climax.

"Fuck!" The pleasure-laden cry tears out of me as my nails dig into his shoulder muscles, seeking purchase against the overwhelming pleasure blooming in my pelvis. I gasp in surprise when I feel wetness running down my thighs.

I've never come like this before, never this much, and I'm shocked by its intensity. I drift as I slowly recover from my climax, yet still suspended in a haze I can't quite name.

"You want more, Addy?"

I look up to meet Dante's gaze and take him in. His strength, his words, his warmth. It's as if he's unlocked something, a deep connection, an anchor even as grief threatens to pull me under.

CHAPTER TWENTY-TWO

Adele

I can't look away from Dante's eyes. Large, black pupils rimmed with molten silver irises that make me feel like I'm tumbling into a bottomless pool. It's both unnerving and exhilarating.

"Addy. Do you want more?" Dante's voice is hoarse with need. His raw tone jerks me out of my trance. I also hear the undertone of grief beneath his tightly restrained desire, and I know he needs to lose himself in me, too.

I swallow and whisper, "Yes."

"Louder," he demands, wiping his hand on my thighs and spreading my wetness everywhere. If it wasn't clear how much I squirted just now, I just got a clear idea.

My hips buck against the hand that's still between my thighs as I grow more desperate for his touch. "Yes! Fuck me like you mean it, Dante."

"Alright." Dante steps back and starts to unbutton his shirt, and cocks his head at the bed. "On your knees," he commands. "I want your arms stretched out and your cheek right against the pillow."

My heart races as I scramble to obey, my face turned to watch him undress. The play of his muscles makes my mouth water with the need to trace each precisely cut one with my tongue, marveling at how each one stands in stark relief against the ink on his torso.

My arousal swells as Dante bares more of his skin. The moment his long, thick, veiny cock springs into view, I start to squirm.

Thankfully, he doesn't make me wait. He gets on the bed behind me and folds himself right over my back. I arch into him, seeking fuller contact, but he winds his fist around my hair to hold me down. A mixture of pain and pleasure courses through me, and I raise my hips, silently begging for more.

Dante rears back and enters me in a single long, unending thrust. My body stiffens, and I let out a loud whimper as he fills me completely. Immediately he starts to thrust into me, fast and deep, his hips slapping against my ass, his balls hitting my swollen clit.

My fingers clench into the sheets, my cries muffling into the pillow. Each stroke is masterful, stretching and filling me and slamming hard enough to set me right on the knife edge of pain and pleasure. My mind goes blank, emptying of everything except the feel of him as the tension starts to coil and stretch inside me.

Dante tightens his grip on my hair and pulls my head back so hard that it brings tears to my eyes. But the pain only heightens the pleasure, and I whimper, my body seizing beneath his.

"Let me hear you scream my name, *tesoro.*"

And that's when I realize what I've been crying out almost non stop into the pillow.

His name.

My mouth snaps shut, heat spreading over my face and neck. But when he pulls my hips back against his cock and changes the angle of his thrusts, pleasure washes over me, so intense it makes me tremble. I do as I'm told, too far gone to care about anything else except surviving my impending climax.

Dante gets louder, too, each harsh breath punctuated by a curse every time he bottoms out inside me. His other hand leaves my hair and slides beneath me to cup my breast, his fingers pinching my hard nipple.

"Ah, fuck! Dante," I scream as I orgasm, my trembling turning into full-body shudders.

My knees buckle, and I'm about to collapse on the bed, lost in pleasure, but Dante holds me up and sinks his cock balls-deep.

"Don't go anywhere. Stay right there and milk my cock, Addy," he commands, holding me tight against him while I helplessly convulse around him.

His hand slips into my hair again, gripping tight. "I want to feel every squeeze. Every last twitch of your tight sweet cunt."

It feels too much. Too intense. The way he goes completely still, watching me, taking in my orgasm while I shatter around him. This is the part of Dante that both excites and scares me. There's something utterly irresistible about the way he hyperfocuses. It draws me like a moth every single time he does it.

When I'm completely spent, Dante releases his grip on my hair and then lets me go. I crumple onto the bed in a boneless heap. Dante leans over me, and I feel his warm breath on my neck as he whispers deliciously filthy things that make me tighten around his still-hard cock.

Within a few minutes, he has me aching and squirming for more just from his words alone. Then he pulls out of me, turns me onto my back, then smoothly enters me again. My back arches off the bed, and I gasp.

I'm sore from all the pounding I just took, but the sensation of his weight on me, the sight of him, the desire in his heavy-lidded eyes, his gorgeous face tight with pleasure, his big, ripped torso brushing over my tight nipples are enough to have me spreading my legs wide for him to take what he wants again.

However he wants it.

I'm so wet that he glides in easily. But instead of hard thrusts, he holds himself still inside me and then starts to kiss me softly. His tenderness is a sharp contrast with his earlier roughness, and it breaks me open.

I whimper softly as his lips trail over my cheekbones, my jaw, and my collarbone. And then he links our fingers together and puts his forehead to mine, his hair falling like a dark curtain around us. His gray eyes bore deep into mine, then slowly, ever so slowly, he starts to move, angling his cock so he's hitting my G-spot with almost clinical precision.

I shiver in pleasure and something else. I'm completely bared to him, and it's as if he's taking everything I have to give. And then offering himself to me in return.

"Ah, Dante," I moan, "I can't." *I can't lose myself in you.*

He chuckles wickedly. "Yes, you can do it, *tesoro*. You already are."

When my lids start to flutter closed, he tightens his hands around my fingers painfully, and my eyes fly open again.

"Addy," he rasps.

"Hmm?"

"No more running. No more hiding under tables. Do you understand?"

My chest tightens. He's stripping me. I'm scared of stepping into Dante's world, but I can't exactly run back to mine, which is even more terrifying. It's like being trapped on a crumbling cliff.

Dante pauses mid-thrust and waits until I meet his scorching hot gaze. "Do you understand?"

I shake my head as my chest goes tight. "I—I'm afraid."

"Then let's make it easier for you. How about this: you're mine. Body and soul."

Oh shit. That's supposed to be easier? "Only if you're mine, too," I reply.

Dante smiles. "*Tesoro*, I've always been yours."

If my chest goes any tighter, I might start to choke. "Dante. I—" I whisper, completely lost for words.

"It's settled then." He goes to resume thrusting, but I stop him.

"Wait, what's settled?"

He simply cocks an eyebrow. "If you ever run from me again, I'll fucking find you and drag you all the way back here by your pretty hair."

I must be sick because the image his words conjure makes my pussy tighten around his cock as a low whimper escapes me. Heat spreads across my cheeks, and my gaze flies to his, somehow hoping he didn't notice my reaction to his fierce declaration.

Of course, I'm not that lucky. Smirking, he tuts as he rears up, then wraps my legs around his waist. "And here I was trying to make love to you, but you have to go and get all slutty on me."

I bite my lip as my pussy goes rogue again. "Oh fuck." And then I can't help lifting my hips in a plea for more. "Dante, please."

"Fine." He heaves an exaggerated, put-upon sigh and stretches my arms high over my head, holding both my wrists in his big hand. I grow tense with anticipation as he drags his callused palm down the side of my face, neck, and lower still, until he cups a full breast. His fingers close around my nipple, and he starts to pinch again, hard. His mouth covers mine, swallowing my cries as he begins slamming his hips into me, deep, fast, and punishing.

Pain and pleasure merge, and another orgasm suddenly crashes over me, so powerful it steals my breath. Dante fucks me through it, hard and relentless.

"Fuck!" he swears, when I start to shudder beneath him again. He bends to trail kisses down my jaw to my earlobe, sucking and biting. When his cock gets even harder and his thrusts are almost violent in their intensity, I know he's about to come too.

He rears up then, his hair falling in subtle waves around his face as he stares at me. His gaze rakes over me from where his glistening cock sinks in and out of me, to the curve of my belly, to my bouncing breasts and reddened nipples, and finally, his eyes lock with mine, moments before he emits a tortured growl and starts to come.

I gasp at the force of Dante's release. The pleasure on his gorgeous face is so intense, so overwhelming, it triggers a response deep inside me. I can't believe how sensitive I am, how easily he's setting me off again, and I find myself rolling my eyes at my own body's responsiveness even as another small wave of ecstasy hits me.

"Christ, Addy," Dante groans through gritted teeth, his voice rough and raw. He buries his face in the crook of my neck, his teeth sinking into my skin again and his breath coming in harsh pants as he rides out his climax.

"Tesoro," he whispers in my ear, his voice still ragged from his release. "You take me so fucking well."

Sated and exhausted, I bask in the warmth of his praise. But as I lay there, Dante's substantial weight on me, his words come back. I belong to Dante, and I own him in return.

What the hell does that mean besides the fact that he won't let me run away from my feelings? Are we back to where we left off two years ago when he was trying to bring me to his world? And if we are, how on earth do I exist in Dante Vitelli's world without losing my own identity?

As I drift off to a dreamless sleep, a mocking voice asks me what exactly that identity is.

I wake up to the sensation of heat, an insistent itch, then pins and needles rippling out from my right hip as callused fingers trail over my scar. Then the aroma of sex and Dante's unique scent and the warmth of his skin envelop me.

My lids slowly flutter open to meet his flinty gray irises. He's leaning on his elbow, watching me sleep. His eyes are glassy with tears, red-rimmed, and there are dark circles under them. Something tightens in my chest at the sight of his grief, stark and unhidden.

"I'm sorry, Dante," I whisper miserably, the guilt starting to creep back. "About Pietro."

He shakes his head slowly, his eyes never leaving mine as he starts to trace the thin red scar between my breasts, raising goosebumps on my skin. "I'm not sorry."

My breath catches in my throat, and I have to shut my eyes against the surge of emotion in my chest.

How is it that this man knows me so well? Well enough to utter the words I didn't realize I needed to hear. Three words that right everything in my world.

"Thank you," I whisper. "I know you two were close."

He smiles sadly. "I think you would have been good friends, too, if he'd stuck around."

"Somehow, I doubt that our paths would have crossed again after last night."

"I was coming to take you away from Boston last night."

"No way!"

"True. You surprised me by showing up. Although looks like someone wasn't surprised you were at Resin. They knew which car was yours and rigged it with a bomb."

Hearing Dante say those words out loud brings a chilling reality to it. I can't imagine who'd want me dead.

"Your father must have some enemies," Dante states.

"You mean someone he ripped off?"

Dante's eyes harden, and a muscle ticks in his jaw. I get the feeling he wants to tell me something, then thinks better of it. An inexplicable urge to snatch the words out of his mouth hits me, and I'm about to demand he tells me what he's thinking when he flops back onto the pillow and stares intently at the intricately carved murals on the ceiling. "It's entirely possible."

"Dante, I don't think it's someone from Boston, though."

He tenses. "Why do you say that?"

"My dad. You know he's always been paranoid about me leaving Boston. But earlier this week, he specifically told me someone was out to get me. Someone in Chicago."

To my surprise, Dante only scoffs. "Of course, he'd tell you that. It's not true, though. No one in Chicago would be stupid enough to let history repeat itself. And trying to kill another Irish woman on our turf would be doing just that."

My brow furrows in confusion as my heart starts to pound. I have about fifty follow-up questions, but one stands out like a beacon.

"What do you mean, history repeating itself?"

Dante runs a hand through his hair, disheveling it further, then turns to me. "It's not pretty, *tesoro*." His gray eyes search mine, seeking permission to tell me something I might find disturbing.

"Tell me," I plead, needing him to cement the puzzle already falling into place in my head.

"Some time ago," he begins, his voice tight, "Naomi Ritter, an Irish woman, and her child were brutally murdered on Brackendown Street in downtown Chicago. The son of a bitch emptied a whole magazine of bullets into them while they were asleep in bed."

Dante glances at me, no doubt checking that I'm not going green. "Naomi seemed like a simple bookstore owner, but it came to light after she died that she had hidden connections to the Boston Mob—the Irish version of the mafia," Dante clarifies for me.

My mother had connections to the Irish mafia? Through who?

Something tells me I already know, but I shove that thought to the same dark place I've kept all the questions my afternoon with Benjamin O'Shea roused in my mind.

Dante continues. "It sparked off the worst mafia war in the Outfit's history. The Irish were screaming for blood and revenge. They haven't forgotten to this day. I doubt they ever will. No one keeps a grudge like them, and that was a massive blow to their heart."

Goosebumps rise on my arms despite the warmth of the room. "Dante, Naomi Ritter's murder, was it eighteen years ago?"

Dante's eyes whip to mine. "Yes. Did your father tell you about it?"

"He's not my father."

"What?"

I nod, a sob catching in my throat. "I never told you this, but he's my uncle. He adopted me when I was five. He made me believe he was my father's brother, but he's really my mother's brother. He lied to me, Dante. My whole life has been a lie."

"Okay." Dante has gone as still as a stone now. "What else did Benjamin O'Shea tell you?"

The words pour out of me in a torrent. "He said that I wasn't born in Boston. That this," I trace the line between my breasts, "wasn't the only injury I sustained as a result of a gunshot."

I point to my right hip. "I didn't shatter my hip in an accident, and I didn't tear up my back falling on broken glass." I take a deep breath and continue. "Dante. I was deliberately shot six times when I was five years old."

"Holy mother of fuck!" Dante's face, already drained of color, twitches with shock.

"It was you."

CHAPTER TWENTY-THREE

Dante

The Irish Mob lied.

They have been lying for two decades.

My throat constricts, a vise grip of understanding tightening with each passing second. Addy was the child from eighteen years ago.

The little girl survived the assassination that sparked a decade-long war.

Benjamin O'Shea might have saved her life, but the son-of-a-bitch didn't raise Addy—the daughter of his enemy—out of the goodness of his heart. He took her, kept her, and rewrote her entire history.

THE MAFIA'S BROKEN VOWS

Addy is not his daughter. She's his hostage. A deadly bargaining chip for future use.

I hold Addy tight to me, murmuring soothing words into her ear as I rein in the shock, awe, and rage roiling in me.

My fingers trace the three parallel scars on her back, scars I now recognize for what they truly are: gunshot wounds, cleverly disguised as glass lacerations. Each line tells a story, one that has fascinated me from the start, but now consumes my every thought.

But it's not just Addy's real identity that's hit me. With it comes a far more staggering reality. One that could change everything.

Addy is half-Italian.

It's common knowledge that Naomi Ritter was involved with a high-ranking member of the Outfit. But there's a whispered rumor, shared only in the shadows and passed along in secrecy—a rumor I've always dismissed. One suggests that this high-ranking member was none other but Vito Vitelli himself.

My father's face flashes in my mind, the way his expression hardens whenever the events of that night are mentioned, as if guarding a secret too heavy to bear.

The pieces start to fall into place, the implications chilling me to the fucking bone.

Addy could be my half-sister.

Addy's voice, small and uncertain, breaks through my spiraling thoughts. "Dante? Are you okay?"

I face her, forcing my features into a mask of calm, then run my thumbs over her cheekbones, catching the drop of moisture hanging onto her lashes. I can't resist raising my thumb to my mouth and licking off her tears.

She sucks her bottom lip between her teeth, her green eyes open and trusting despite everything she's just learned. "You were silent for a while."

"I'm good," I say, reaching for her hand and linking our fingers. "Tell me what you're thinking, Addy."

Her hand moves to my chest, fingers tracing over my pecs and abs, sending currents of pleasure all over my skin.

"Growing up, I always felt . . . different," she says softly. "Like I didn't quite fit in with the other kids. I never felt comfortable in my own skin, and I thought it was because of the homeschooling."

"Something inside you knew you didn't belong there, *tesoro*."

"Yes." Addy's fingers dip lower, down my abs, and then lower until she lightly circles my cock. Then her fingers trace beyond the shaft to boldly cup my balls.

"Addy . . ." I warn. "You need to rest."

"I know. I'm just . . . admiring. Nothing more." Her eyes flicker down, and she licks her lips. "I really like these, you know."

Society would tell me to care. But Lord knows I don't give a flying fuck we could be half-siblings. "I know, you sexy little minx." I push her to her back and let my hands roam over her, too.

When I touched her earlier, my vision was clouded by lust. Now I take in her sexy form again. Her breasts are fuller than I remember, her areolas darker and more pronounced, and the deep red shade starkly contrasts with her pale skin.

"Addy? You look . . . different."

"Good different or bad different?"

My palm cups her breast, then moves lower to her hip, slipping a thigh between hers.

"Good. So fucking good."

"I feel different. I am different."

I watch as she takes a deep breath, her chest rising. When she speaks again, her voice drops even lower, almost inaudible. "Speaking of, I should tell you something."

"I'm listening."

"It's about the time we were together at the airstrip. Things didn't end there."

The casual way she says it, as if commenting on the weather, makes the impact all the more powerful. My body goes still, every muscle tensing as the meaning of her words sinks in.

Without a word, my hand slides from her breast, fingers skimming over the soft skin of her stomach before coming to rest on her flat lower abdomen.

I meet Addy's gaze, searching her eyes. She simply nods.

For a full minute, I just stare at my left hand as it spans her belly. My pinky finger brushes the short red curls on her mons, the same finger I wear my signet ring on. The crest of diamonds on the bezel of the ring sparkles in the low light, branding her as mine. A fierce sense of possession grips me, setting every nerve ending on fire.

Addy is pregnant. This changes every fucking thing. Half-sister or not.

"Dante? Please say something."

My gaze meets hers again, and I roll us over, pinning her beneath me. My lips crash down on hers in a bruising kiss, swallowing her gasp of surprise.

I pour everything I'm feeling into the kiss—the possessiveness, the need, the overwhelming urge to protect and claim. My tongue sweeps into her mouth, tasting, exploring, demanding. Addy responds with equal fervor, her hands sliding up my back, nails digging into my skin.

When we break apart, both panting, I growl against her neck, *"Tesoro,* there's nothing left to say. You're carrying my child." I punctuate the words with a nip to her pulse point, feeling her shiver.

"So?"

I pull back slightly, bracing myself on my forearms to look down at her.

"So what?"

Addy bites her lip, a gesture that never fails to drive me wild. "Does it mean you're excited?"

"Baby, I'll burn the whole fucking world to the ground to keep you happy and safe. Both of you."

Later, even after she's finally drifted off to an exhausted sleep, my hand continues to splay on her belly.

The clock on the mantelpiece ticks eerily loud in the room, which, except for Addy's rhythmic breathing and an occasional soft snore, is silent as a graveyard. It's too quiet for me to sleep. I eye my discarded earbuds scattered on the carpet near the door, but I don't bother to grab them. I know I couldn't sleep if I tried. There's too much swirling through my head.

I check the time again. It's nine in the morning, although you can't tell from the windowless state of this fucking dungeon. Nico should be back from Paris. I imagine he'd be grief-stricken. But he doesn't even know the half of it. Yet.

It's going to be carnage today.

Addy will be livid when she finds out why she won't be allowed to return to Boston. I can see Benjamin O'Shea and the rest of the Mob foaming at the mouth, declaring another war. And Orlando De Luca? Well, the man might as well start plotting my accidental demise.

Addy makes a soft mewling sound and burrows closer, drawing me out of my dark thoughts.

I take a moment to drink her in again. She's on her belly, her face turned toward me. The chandelier's light catches gold highlights in the wavy mass of red hair splayed across the pillow. I run a blunt fingertip along the smattering of freckles across her cheekbones, her full lips, slightly parted, still swollen from my kisses, and then I turn her over gently because I need to see all of her.

I lightly trace the thin pink line between her full breasts, and then my finger drifts lower to my favorite spot, the sensitive, jagged scar on her hip. The reason she has that sexy hitch in her step, one she tries her damnedest to mask.

She'll probably think I'm a fucking creep if she knew how hard I get just watching her walk.

I trace the curve of her thighs with my finger, seeing the drying evidence of her juices and my cum smeared all over her skin. We were at it until she fell asleep half an hour ago.

And I want her again.

But instead of spreading her thighs and sinking into her slippery warmth, I plant a soft kiss on her forehead and make myself slide off the bed and get dressed.

I need to see Nico, and Addy needs to rest. She could possibly do with some space too. I've never been anything but gentle with her, and last night was a small departure from what she's known with me.

She needs to see the bruises and handprints on her porcelain skin and decide that she's okay with it happening from time to time.

She needs to get used to the fact she's just been shoved into the plunge she couldn't take two years ago. And ultimately, her life in Boston, her job at the DA's office, her blog, everything she used to be, is over.

So, with one last look, I head out of the room, heading toward the conference room where a pissed-off Nico will be nursing a scotch. It's almost uncanny how well I can predict my brother's thoughts and actions. I know Nico will be in the room, jet-lagged and exhausted yet unable to sleep. He'll be bent over the laptop, studying the CCTV feeds and police reports from last night and trying to piece together what the fuck happened.

CHAPTER TWENTY-FOUR

Dante

The scent of leather-bound books and old paper greets me like an old friend as soon as I push open the heavy double doors of the Vitelli conference room. Bookshelves of rich mahogany line the walls, and a large fireplace crackles in the background.

A long, polished woodgrain conference table, designed to seat twelve, forms the centerpiece of the room. Built into its surface are secure laptops—our sole connection to the outside world. A dozen high-back, black leather chairs surround the table, each assigned to a specific capo.

Only one seat has swapped owners since the capos gathered here three years ago. Nico's seat is now positioned where Father once sat as Don.

I find that my earlier intuition was spot-on. My brother is sitting at the head of the table, a glass of amber liquid in front of him. Except that his laptop is closed. And he's not alone.

Sophie is in Nico's lap, dressed in one of his shirts, and her face is buried in his neck. I can't see their lower halves, but from the way my brother's head is thrown back and the dazed, ecstatic look on his face, I know his wife is doing something incredibly erotic to him.

"Sorry to interrupt," I snort, leaning against the doorframe, not in the least bit sorry.

They jerk apart. Sophie looks more than a little guilty, but Nico only smirks and pulls her back in for another kiss.

"Guys, look, just say the word. I can come back in two minutes," I tease.

"Shit timing, *fratellino,*" Nico growls, his eyes narrowing at me.

"It's okay, Dante," Sophie pipes. "Nico just needed another cuddle, that's all. It's been a rough night."

Normally, I'd have a sarcastic comeback to that, had I not just now rolled out of Addy's bed myself. I guess I, too, needed a bit of a cuddle, if that's what we're calling it now. "For us all, sis," I reply.

Sophie slips off Nico's lap and comes to me, her steps graceful despite being six months pregnant.

"*Ciao bella,*" I greet her, and just to annoy Nico, I envelop her in a tight bear hug that never fails to make Nico scowl. I'm sure if he had his way, he'd be the only man on earth who could look at or touch his wife.

She whispers in my ear before leaving, "I have to meet this woman driving you to public madness, Dante."

I snort out a laugh. The photos have gone viral then. "You'll see Addy soon enough," I whisper back.

Nico would have been briefed by the PR team the moment the photos broke. And Nico tells his wife everything, either because she's a therapist or because Nico just can't help himself. And with the way his gaze follows Sophie as she leaves the room, I'll bet it's the latter.

As soon as Sophie is gone, Nico's expression becomes grave, the dark circles under his eyes a testament to the grief and sleepless night we've all endured. He leans back in his leather chair, the rich material creaking slightly under his weight.

I clear the lump in my throat, my gaze dropping to the amber liquid swirling in the glass he holds. "How are you holding up?"

"Peachy," Nico murmurs with a sardonic smile, his free hand rubbing at his temple. "Just got in an hour ago." He motions to the decanter on the desk between us. "Want one?"

I shake my head, waving off the offer. There's too much brewing today, and I need to keep a clear head and sharp reflexes. I might need them to survive the next few hours. "I'm good."

Nico's fingers tap against the glass as he glances at the huge Roman numeral clock hanging between the tall, book-lined shelves. "How long before the Capos get here?"

I know he wants to know how much time we have to speak privately. I drop into my chair, the one just next to his. "About two hours. Where do you want to start?"

"De Luca." Nico throws back his drink then slams the glass down. He pins me with a look, his blue eyes fierce. "What in the actual fuck are you doing, Dante? Getting handsy with Adele. In public. You are supposed to be proposing to Alina."

"What's the point of proposing?" I retort. "It's not like the girl was going to say no. It was an arranged marriage, for fuck's sake. Although, as of right now, it's all gone down the drain."

"Yes, a proposal is redundant. Still, it would have been a nice thing to do, considering the woman loves you," Nico argues, his fingers drumming against the polished wood of his desk.

I shake my head, scoffing at his tone. I swear Nico has gone soft. "Alina does not love me."

"She picked you over me," Nico says, his tone exasperated, his eyes narrowing. "What the fuck do you call that?"

I chuckle, the sound harsh in the stillness of the room. "Good taste?"

"Dumbass." Nico smiles wryly, the expression not quite reaching his eyes. "But seriously, Alina wants to be your wife, Dante. I could think of worse things than that."

"No, Nico. Bianca wants to be my mother-in-law. There's a difference." I lean forward, my elbows resting on the table, my gaze intense.

Nico's eyebrows shoot up in surprise, his fingers stilling on the desk. "Switching grooms was Bianca's idea?"

I nod, my jaw clenching. "Are you surprised, though?"

Orlando may be the Outfit's highest-ranking Capo today, but he started out as an orphan boy who clawed his way up from the dirt by serving three generations of Vitellis.

Orlando's wife, on the other hand, is a spoilt mafia princess, the last child of the wealthy Rinaldi family in New York. She was raised to know the difference between power and pedigree and wants nothing more than for her daughter to become a Vitelli.

Nico's brows furrow. "No, I can't say I'm surprised. Although, if Bianca is that ambitious, why would she turn down the Don of the Outfit . . . for the Underboss?"

"She must think I'm hotter or something," I shrug, and we both laugh, the sound momentarily easing the tension in the room.

I continue, every trace of humor now gone. "Anyway, like I said, Nico, it's all down the drain. I called time on it last night."

"You what?"

"I've broken it off with Alina. I'll make it official with De Luca when he comes in today."

Nico sighs wearily, then leans forward with a dark glower, his elbows resting on the desk. The vein on his temple is starting to pop out—a clear indication of how much he's fighting for patience—and a part of me almost feels bad for him. It would be healthier if Nico yelled from time to time. But no, he keeps his emotions tightly in check.

"Dante," he grits. "Orlando De Luca is my most powerful Caporegime, the one whose loyalty to the Outfit happens to be hanging by a thread. His wife has the strength of the New York mafia behind her. Do you have any fucking idea what would happen now that you've broken your promise to him?"

I shrug, my posture relaxed despite the gravity of the situation. "Best case scenario, mutiny. Worst case, an outright rebellion."

"Exactly." Nico's eyes become flinty, his voice cold, his jaw clenching. Every ounce of my big brother is gone. In his place is Don Vitelli, and his empire comes before anything else. "And you think I would let you tear my house down, Dante?"

I meet his gaze without flinching. "Not only would you let me, you'd throw the first punch—bullet, so to speak, for me."

"Why the fuck would I do that?" Nico's voice finally rises in the stillness of the room.

"Red Wine. I've put her off-grid. She now lives here for the foreseeable future," My words hang in the air like thunderclaps. "Somehow, I doubt that Alina could deal with a groom with that much baggage."

Nico leaps to his feet, his chair scraping against the floor, his hands slamming down on the desk. "You've got to be fucking kidding me. I ordered you to get her out of your system, and you take her and bring her under my roof—"

"She's mine, Nico. Boston will have to suck it up." I interrupt, my gaze steady.

"Suck it up? You take the Mob's princess, fake her death, and expect them to take it lying down?" Nico's voice is incredulous, his eyes wide with disbelief.

I explain with a calm belying the storm building in my gut. "Nico, sit down. I told you that a bomb killed Pietro. What I didn't say was that bomb was meant for Addy. Her car was rigged last night, and Pietro got into it instead of her. Someone wants to kill her and pin it on us."

Nico freezes, and then as if he's suddenly run out of energy, he falls back into his chair. "And yet you in your wisdom, choose to put her off-grid. What the fuck, Dante? You realize you just made it possible for the Mob to do exactly that? Pin her death on us."

He continues when I remain silent. "Eighteen years ago, some sick bastard killed Naomi Ritter and her daughter on our turf and shoved the smoking gun in our hand. We were dragged into a war for something we didn't do, all because Father couldn't keep it in his pants."

Looks like Nico believes the rumors, too.

I ignore his grave warning and smirk instead. "A point of correction: Eighteen years ago, Naomi Ritter and Addy were shot while in bed. Addy survived and was adopted by Naomi's brother, Benjamin O'Shea."

Nico sits up so fast the air whooshes, his eyes wide with shock. "Red Wine? It was Red Wine?" he yells, his voice echoing in the room.

I almost feel sorry for Nico. I don't remember him ever raising his voice. But I can understand his shock. The weight of this revelation must have hit him like a sucker punch.

I nod, my gaze steady. "Yes, it was her, Nico. A carefully hidden secret, even from Addy herself. She only fully pieced it together this morning. She's their hostage. That's why they lose their shit when she comes near Chicago. And now someone wants her dead."

A low whistle escapes Nico's lips, his hand running through his hair. "Fucking hell." I can see the wheels turning in his head, his brows deeply furrowed. "Someone is desperate to start a war again."

Nico leans back in his chair, his expression grave. "So, do you now see how you can't possibly hold her here? I'll negotiate a deal with the Mob to get her for you. We might need to give up a few thousand kidneys, but it's doable. In the meantime, you will return her to Boston. ASAP."

"I will do nothing of the sort."

"That wasn't a suggestion, Dante."

"I can't let her go."

"Dante, at the risk of sounding like a fucking scratched record, you know the stakes. If that woman isn't returned to Boston tonight, we're looking at a war. And without De Luca, our strength is halved. We are in no position to face the Irish and the fuckers they're probably joining forces with, in a full-out war. So for the last fucking time, return Red Wine to the Irish and fucking kiss and make up with De Luca," Nico commands, his voice rising with each word.

"I can't. I'm in love with her, Nico." It feels incredible to be able to say it out loud.

I see Nico's eyes go soft for a second, then his face hardens again.

"She's your half-sister, *fratellino*."

I point to myself. "Do I look like I give a shit?"

"She might give a shit." Nico counters.

"Or not."

Nico only shakes his head. "You're fucked up way beyond redemption, you know that?"

"No argument there."

"Anyway, you still need to let her go, *fratellino*. Only for a few weeks. I swear I'll bring her back here myself once we smooth De Luca's ruffled feathers and once the dust of your betrayal has settled."

I'm not sure which one of us is more stubborn. I'd say Nico because I'm sure deep down, he's always known this would happen, but he chose to ignore it. "Nico, I couldn't let her go even if I wanted to."

Nico drags his fingers through his hair, clearly frustrated now. "Why the hell not, Dante?"

"Because she's carrying my child."

Nico goes still for a long moment, his face frozen in shock. I'm beginning to think he didn't hear me when he suddenly roars, "Fuuuuck! You always have to be a fucking inconvenient pain in the fucking ass, don't you, Dante? This is a fucking unsurvivable war. You know that?"

I chuckle. "Calm down and look at the bright side. At least we get to die with honor. Nothing beats going down as human shields for the women we love."

"Seriously?" Nico thunders, his eyes flashing. "You still have the guts to talk out the side of your neck after pulling this shitstorm?"

I shrug, my nonchalance a deliberate provocation. I watch him, silently begging him to erupt. I want to hit something. I need it. We both do after last night.

I almost sigh in relief when, in a flash, Nico leaps off his seat and rounds the desk. He grabs me by the collar and slams me into the nearest wall, his face mere inches from mine, his breath hot against my skin. "I swear to God, I'll kill you with my bare hands before this is over."

"You can fucking try," I growl.

Just then, the door flies open. Father strides into the conference room, his footsteps echoing on the polished floor. He takes in the situation, his sharp gaze lingering on Nico's hands bunched in my shirt, and my defiant smirk.

"Why am I not shocked?" Father shakes his head, a wry smile tugging at the corners of his lips.

Nico immediately releases me, but not without a parting fist to my face. Already anticipating the move, I duck, the rush of air from my quick movements ruffling my hair. I return swinging, sending my own fist into his hard jaw. It lands with a satisfying impact on my knuckle. Nico staggers back, his eyes wide with surprise, anger, and a grudging respect. He used to have much faster reflexes than me.

"You've gone a bit soft, *fratello*," I taunt, rubbing the salt in. "I suggest less cuddling, more training."

Father deftly steps between us and pushes Nico away before he tackles me to the ground. While Nico and I tower over him, the strength in Father's muscly frame is unmistakable.

"Enough, both of you," he barks, pushing against our chests to send us further apart. "We have more pressing matters to attend to. Such as a family breakfast."

The mention of breakfast captures our attention because we have never ever had breakfast together as a family and I don't eat before noon.

Father faces me, "Dante. Your Irish woman has been extracted from where you thought you were hiding her. She's in the kitchen with your mother and Sophie as we speak."

My heart skips a beat as protectiveness rises in my chest. "She's where right now?"

"They're making her breakfast." Father tosses his head in the direction of the kitchen, the light catching the silver in his hair. The implication is clear: Sophie and Mother are pumping Addy for information.

I clench my fists. For fuck's sake, the woman is still reeling from last night's close shave. I was hoping we could talk more and lose ourselves in each other for one more day before unleashing my family on her.

"How the hell did they even find her?" I ask. Addy was still sleeping when I left her half an hour ago.

Father only shrugs. "You know nothing happens under this roof without your mother's—or Aydin's knowledge. Come on, enough scuffling for one morning. Let's go join them."

I grab his arm before he can leave, the wool of his suit rough beneath my fingertips. "Wait, Father. Don't you want to know what Nico and I were fighting about?"

He looks from me to Nico, his gaze calculating. "I imagine it had to do with Pietro's death. Or the guest you shouldn't have brought home last night."

"But Father," I press. "Adele isn't just any Irish woman." I ignore Nico's subtle nudge for me to shut the fuck up, and continue. "She's actually Naomi Ritter's daughter. She's the little girl from eighteen years ago. Can you believe she's been alive all this time?"

Father's expression becomes unreadable in the flickering light of the room as he murmurs thoughtfully, "Is that so?"

Nico and I share a look, a silent understanding passing between us. Father knows. He's always known exactly who Addy is.

"So, Father," I continue pushing, the sound of my raging pulse loud in my ears, "did we ever find out whose mistress Naomi was?"

Father's eyes become shadowed, a flicker of something very much like guilt passing over his features and the lines of his face deepening. "Your actions will trigger a war unless you do as your brother tells you, Dante. It's the only way."

He turns to leave, his shoulders slumped, no doubt weighed down with secrets long kept, secrets that now threaten to unravel the very fabric of our family.

As I watch him walk away, my mind reels with the implications of his words, or lack of thereof.

Nico's hand lands heavily on my shoulder. "So, did you get the reaction you were digging for?"

My jaw clenches as the question hangs in the air. "All I know is he looked guilty as hell just now."

Nico squeezes my shoulder. "You gave him a chance to come clean, and he didn't. So, I've got your back, you fucking twisted prick. Do what you need to do. Just know you're diving headfirst into this bog of shit you're dragging us into."

"You bet, *fratello*." A smile splits my lips, a rush of affection washing over me. Despite our differences, Nico and I are one constant in this world of shifting shadows and uncertain loyalties.

But right now, my heart is with Addy, and I'll be damned if I let pesky little things like another decade-long mafia war or being blood relatives stop me.

CHAPTER TWENTY-FIVE

Adele

I pad into the bathroom, my bare feet silent on the cold marble tiles. When I came in here last night, I was drowning in so much grief and guilt, I took no notice of my surroundings. Now I gasp as I take in the space, all gleaming surfaces and golden fixtures. A massive jacuzzi tub dominates one corner, while a glass-enclosed shower big enough for a small party takes up another.

My eyes are drawn to the enormous gilded mirror spanning the entire bathroom wall, but I avert my gaze, not quite ready to look into my own eyes. It was easy enough to avoid the mirrors in the bedroom with the room being so large, but here, it might be a little tricky.

I focus on my purpose: wash the smoke and grit out of my hair. The scent clings to me, a constant reminder of the sure death I escaped. Drowning myself in Dante got me through last night, but waking up this morning without his big body wrapped around me left an odd ache in my chest and my mind free to replay last night's disaster.

Yet, as I pass the mirrors, something catches my eye. Before I can stop myself, I glance at my reflection then do a double-take. My breath hitches as I take in the sight before me.

My skin is a canvas of Dante's desire. Love bites pepper my collarbone, descending in a trail down to my breasts. Finger-shaped bruises mark my hips, a stark reminder of his grip as he pulled me against his thrusting hips. I turn, craning my neck to see my back. More marks adorn my ass and thighs.

Heat floods my cheeks as memories come rushing back. Dante's hungry gaze as he explored every inch of me. The way his hands and mouth roamed my body, pleasing me, claiming me.

I bite my lip, surprised by the thrill that runs through me at the sight of his marks. Am I sick for loving this? I've never been one for rough treatment or macho bullshit. Even the thought of men gawking at me makes my skin crawl. But Dante's lust . . . it sets me on fire.

Surprisingly, my face, neck, arms, and legs are unmarked, but from my collarbone down to my thighs, it's savage town. It screams deliberate. Controlled. That he likes to be rough, yet he knows where and how to draw the line. Fuck if that doesn't make me want him more. I finger each faint mark, responding to the sensory memory of Dante's touch.

I step into the shower, unable to shake the image of my marked body. Dante's hands, his mouth, his eyes—they're all I can think about.

As the hot water cascades over me, I find a bottle of shampoo, and lather it into my hair, scrubbing away the smoke and grit. I rinse thoroughly, letting the hot water wash away the suds and the memories of the previous night.

With my hair clean and the stress starting to melt away, other thoughts rise in my mind. What do the events of last night mean for my life and my future? What will Dad—Benjamin—do when he hears that I almost died?

I think about work. Doug Harrison will be expecting me to show up. And I'm already a week overdue on my blog.

And I need to talk to Kira.

After my shower, I head to the vanity table and rummage through my purse for my cellphone. When I come up empty, I recall Sal tossing it into the smoking ruins of the Corolla before we left the club last night.

Shit. No phone, only an intercom to a hundred-year-old butler.

I glance around the room, taking in the tall ceilings with no windows, the intricate patterns on the vintage furnishings, and the ventilation that easily distracts the mind from what this place really is: a fortress designed to keep people like me safe . . . or trapped.

Did Dante lock me in here?

I wrap the towel more tightly around my body and venture toward the door. I turn the brass lock, beyond surprised to find it unlocked.

But as I step forward, the towel slips, and I freeze. I can't go wandering around this place half-naked. I need clothes. My dress and panties lay in a heap on the floor, but there's no way I'm getting into my ruined panties and soot-stained clothes.

My gaze snags on the T-shirts draped over the chair. And now I know that Dante brought them for me.

It's either I put on Dante's T-shirt or call the old butler. It's an easy decision. I've always preferred loose-fitting clothes, but I particularly love wearing his clothes.

I reach for one of the shirts, the fabric soft and worn, and pull it over my head. It falls to my mid-thigh, the sleeves extending past my elbows. His smell instantly surrounds me, a heady mix of his musk and sandalwood. I grit my teeth, steeling myself against the wave of arousal.

This is so not the time, Addy, I chide myself. I must stay focused and figure out what the hell is going on. I head to the door, throwing it open with more force than necessary.

And then, it's absolute chaos.

A blur of brown and green feathers darts between my legs, the unexpected contact causing me to screech and leap back into the room, jumping on the bed and burying my head in the pillows.

A woman's distant laugh makes me raise my head. But I don't see a woman. All I see is a huge mallard duck, wearing what appears to be a diaper, standing in the middle of the room with its head cocked to one side, observing me with a kind of detached curiosity that only a bird can muster.

I didn't know ducks could be this fat, or wear diapers for that matter, but here we are. An obese, diaper-wearing duck.

What in the world?

Before I can fully wrap my head around the absurdity of the situation, a woman who looks like an older version of Kira rushes into the room. She's dressed in a smart black shirt dress with a white collar and cuffs and a white apron tied around her waist. Her dark hair is pulled back into a severe bun, but her eyes hold a familiar warmth. I already know who she is.

"Oh, dear, I'm so sorry about that," she gestures to the bird, who has lost interest in the clueless human and waddled to the wall of mirrors, moving this way and that in what I can only call a preen. "That's just George. He's a little . . . eccentric."

I stand there, gaping, as she scoops up the duck and cradles it in her arms like a baby. George quacks contentedly, as if this is the most normal thing in the world, to be held to a human's chest.

The woman gives me a reassuring smile. "I'm Aydin, Kira's mother. You must be Addy. Kira's told me so much about you."

Even though I already guessed who she was, it's still a little jarring to see. I stretch my lips into a toothed plastic smile, a testament to my nerves.

Kira's mother is really the Vitellis' housekeeper. I'm really in the Godfather's mansion.

She sets the duck down, dips her hand into her pocket, and tosses a few treats on the floor for him. And suddenly, I get why George would be obese.

Aydin turns her attention back to me, her eyes softening with concern. "Are you alright, dear?"

I snap my mouth shut when I realize the smile is still frozen on my face. "I'm good, thanks."

"You look a bit shaky. Understandably, after last night's trauma," she says, holding out her hand to help me off the bed. I can stand on my own, but I don't want to appear rude, so I let her guide me. "Maybe some breakfast?" She asks.

I nod, still trying to process everything. "Um . . . that would be nice, thank you," I manage in a steady voice, still watching the duck busily peck the treats off the floor.

Aydin chuckles when she sees me staring at George. "This place can be a bit . . . much at first. But you'll get used to it. So, about breakfast. Would you like to join the rest?"

"The rest?"

"Oh, just the two *Signora* Vitellis. Don Vito and Don Nico's wives. They can't wait to meet you."

"Where's Dante?"

"He's in a meeting."

"I—ah. I don't know." I shake my head. Something in her expression makes me ask, "Am I allowed to say no, though?"

Aydin laughs. "Of course you are. Although I wouldn't say no."

As I put my face in my hand and softly groan. George emits a loud quack, and I startle again at the unexpected sound. The duck looks at me as if waiting for an answer.

"I thought . . ." I trail off. I don't know what I expected today. I didn't think beyond reveling in Dante's arms.

"Did you expect that he'll keep you locked in here?"

Actually, I did. I certainly did not think he'd be siccing his family on me. "I'm hardly dressed for a family meeting, Aydin." I gesture at my bare feet and oversized T-shirt.

"You're perfect. It's just breakfast. Come on." She spins on her heels, her hand gently nudging my elbow, and I have no choice but to follow her out.

The twists and turns of the stairs and corridors seem to go on forever, each one identical to the last. A sense of unease begins to settle in the pit of my stomach as it dawns on me that I could wander these halls for hours and never find my way back to where we started. This place is really a prison.

I glance at Aydin. "Is there any cell service here?"

She shakes her head, a sympathetic smile playing at the corners of her lips. "No, dear. No mobile signal can penetrate these walls. It's part of what makes this place so secure."

Secure. The word echoes in my mind, taking on a sinister edge. I'm trapped here, cut off from the outside world, and at the mercy of a man whose very existence threatens to consume me. What the hell have I gotten myself into?

As we continue, the narrow stone corridors and antique sconces give way to a modern space. Marble and glass replace the dark, heavy decor. Huge windows offer stunning views of rolling vegetation and distant hills, making it feel as if we're outside.

I'm surprised at the transformation. The mansion now feels open and alive, shedding its oppressive atmosphere. Sunlight streams through the glass walls, casting patterns on the floors.

Aydin leads me through the main living areas. We pass a spacious living room with modern furniture arranged around a grand piano. The walls feature contemporary art pieces that contrast sharply with the vintage paintings in the basement.

Finally, we enter the kitchen, a space so large it feels like a dining hall. One entire wall is made of glass and light pours in through the wall, making the room feel alive. There is a large round dining table off to the side.

Two women stand by the huge double oven, chatting like old friends catching up on gossip. The first, presumably Dante's mother, has a plate of something delicious-smelling in her hand. Her shoulder-length dark hair is threaded with silver, but her eyes sparkle with a youthful energy.

The other woman munches on a pastry and like me, is wearing a man's shirt. Hers is a white button-down folded up at the sleeves.

The material looks like cross between cotton and silk and screams God-awful expensive. Her hair is in a thick braid flowing over her shoulder and past her very pregnant belly.

They spot Aydin and me and straighten up. The pregnant one, whom I assume is Nico's wife, moves with a grace that seems impossible for someone about to give birth to a small planet, and strides toward me.

"Addy!" she exclaims, smiling radiantly. She pulls me into a hug before I can even register what's happening. When she draws back, her amber eyes twinkling, she says, "Oh, my God, you are fucking gorgeous. I'm Sophie, Dante's sister-in-law."

I smile back in greeting.

Sophie glances back at Dante's mom, a mischievous glint in her eye. "Mama V, I told you Dante is screwed!"

Dante's mom just chuckles, shaking her head as she approaches. "*Cara,* thank you for joining us. I'm Antonella—"

"She loves to be called Mama V," Sophie chirps.

"I hope you don't mind us getting you out here? Left to my son, he was going to keep you hidden in that basement for days. We didn't want you staying there all by yourself after what happened last night."

"Uh, no. It's fine," I say, fighting the urge to run back to the safety of that luxurious windowless room.

Antonella heaves a relieved sigh while Sophie just chuckles. "Of course she minds, Mama V. She hardly knows us and probably still needs to process everything." Sophie gently nudges Antonella toward the oven, then she turns back to me and pulls me to the windows. "Come on."

The view from the glass wall takes my breath away. Rolling lawns extend outward, meticulously manicured and dotted with clusters of vibrant flowers in perfectly designed gardens.

Beyond the manicured gardens, a serene lake shimmers under the soft light of the early sun. The water is so clear that I can see the reflection of the surrounding trees and the sky, a perfect mirror of the world above.

"Oh my God," I breathe.

Sophie smiles at my reaction. "I know, Addy. Hard to believe a place like this exists, right here in Chicago. It was a crime to make you stare at mirrors and wall murals when you could look at this!"

I nod, still absorbing the view. The contrast between the dark, hidden basement of the mansion and this bright, open expanse is striking. It's like stepping into a different world altogether.

Sophie drops her voice to a whisper, "In case you were wondering how we found you, it was Falzone, the butler who told Aydin that Sal brought you here. You see, nothing in this house ever gets past the staff. Anyway, I figured if you're going to be stuck here for a while, it might be better if you didn't feel like you were in a prison."

"Oh, I'm not staying," I say. "Sal just brought me here to crash after . . . last night."

Sophie doesn't respond, but her expressive eyes say it all. I might as well be dreaming.

"What?" I ask.

"I don't know if you've noticed the labyrinth in the belly of this place and the glaring lack of cellphone signal. This isn't really a place to crash, Addy. It's a place to disappear."

CHAPTER TWENTY-SIX

Adele

It's a place to disappear.

Sophie's words echo in my head. The logical part of me knows she's telling the truth as I piece together everything that has happened since last night, but the stubborn part of me refuses to accept it.

Who would choose to live like this, and why? Does it mean the people within this mansion are cut off from the world?

I glance back to see Antonella retrieving something from the oven. She hums a tune that sounds suspiciously like a funeral dirge, yet her floral loungewear clashes cheerfully with the somber melody. She shoots me a kind smile before returning to her task.

My gaze shifts to Sophie. Faint smudges under her eyes hint at a sleepless night, but her skin still radiates health, her cheeks rosy with the glow of pregnancy. Like me, she's barefoot and she's paired Nico's shirt with soft leggings.

They look like a normal family, not a crime syndicate living in a luxurious black hole.

"Does everyone live here?" It's certainly big enough to house a small village.

"Here?" Sophie's face takes on a look of mock horror. "Oh, hell no. Only Nico's parents live here. Although, after what happened yesterday, Nico has been hinting about me staying here until the twins are born."

My eyes make a beeline for her stomach again, and I try not to wince. I can't imagine what she's going through with a twin pregnancy. And then it occurs to me that I don't even know what or how many I'm carrying.

Shit! I need a scan, pronto.

Sophie, oblivious to my mini-meltdown, continues. "I was fully prepared to kick up a huge fuss, but maybe it won't be so bad being cooped up here. I'm sure we can both find enough trouble to get into."

Her open friendliness pulls at me, and for some reason, I find myself trusting her. "Sophie, I really can't stay here. I've got work and a dad back in Boston. They're expecting me at work tomorrow."

Sophie nods thoughtfully. "How long did Dante say you'd be here for?"

Good question. "I haven't had time to . . . talk to him." We've been too busy doing other things.

I look away to hide the flush in my cheeks, but not before catching the knowing glint in her eyes.

"You know, Nico and I just got in a few hours ago, so I've not had a chance to speak to Dante properly either. He and Nico are talking now, which is code for someone's probably getting a black eye, but he'll soon be free to talk to you."

"Sophie, what does it mean to be 'off-grid'?" I ask.

"What?"

"I heard Dante tell Sal to put me 'off-grid' or something."

Sophie's eyes widen, her full lips pouting into an O.

"What does that mean?" I insist.

She looks as if she's debating telling me. Then she suddenly pulls me into another hug. "Dante can be impulsive, alright, but his instincts are never wrong. If he tells you to stay here, I'd do it, Addy."

Her answer does nothing to reassure my peaking nerves, but before I can press further, Antonella speaks up.

"Okay, enough with all the hushed voices." She gestures to the large round dining table with half a dozen chairs around it. "Let's sit down, have food, coffee, and some proper gossip, shall we?"

I'd prefer tea. But asking for it might invite questions about why. Or it might not. Still, it's better to keep things simple and accept a coffee instead. As soon as we settle around the massive kitchen table, Sophie starts to give me a crash course of who is who among the family and the house staff but she doesn't get far before the older woman gently cuts in.

"So, Adele, tell us a bit about yourself. What do you do?"

And this is where it all goes south. "I work at the DA's office in Boston."

A long silence follows, during which I wait for the other shoe to drop.

Antonella, who paused in the process of sipping her coffee, carefully puts her mug back down. "The Boston DA's office?" she asks with an overly bright smile. "That's amazing."

"What Mama V is wondering is," Sophie pipes up, her eyes twinkling, "what your job role is and specifically, where you stand in a certain man's trial."

"Sofia Lauren!" Antonella scolds.

"What, Mama V?" Sophie laughs. "I'm a therapist. And you're the definition of wearing your thoughts on your sleeve. Anyway, Addy, where do you stand with Tommy Martelli?" Sophie prompts me.

I shake my head. "I'm just one of the forensic guys. I'm supposed to be neutral and not have an opinion either way."

The tension in Antonella's shoulders reduces a fraction, but I can still see the furrow of concern on her brow.

Sophie leans forward, her elbows resting on the table. "Forensics. It could be worse, Mama V. At least Addy isn't on the prosecuting team. Not that Dante would care. He'd eat that shit up."

"Where did you and Dante meet?" Antonella continues, her plate of pastries forgotten.

Before I can respond, the deep baritone that never fails to send thrills through me, cuts through the room. "Boston."

I turn to see Dante standing in the doorway. His shirt looks wrinkled around the collar, and his hair is unbound and tousled, but that doesn't detract from his allure. My breath catches in my throat as our eyes meet. Electricity crackles between us. His eyes look almost as stormy as they did the last time I saw them.

When he was deep inside me.

I quickly look away, subtly clearing my throat and desperately wishing I had Sophie's olive complexion as I feel my cheeks heat and my heart rate kick up. It would be so embarrassing to react to him this way in front of his family.

Out of the side of my eye, I see that instead of coming to the table, Dante heads straight for the glass wall and sits on the counter beside it.

Behind him, two men who I assume are Dante's brother, Nico, and his father file into the kitchen. I'm struck by how stunning they are. Tall and muscular with jawlines that could cut glass, they look almost identical, and as if they've walked off a runway. The Vitelli genes are clearly something special.

Dante is the bigger of the two brothers, but Nico exudes an aura of danger and authority that instantly sends a shiver of fear down my spine.

Vito is an older version of his sons and carries himself with a quiet dignity, his presence commanding respect.

"So good for you boys to join us for breakfast," Antonella chirps, then puts an arm around me. *"Carissimo,"* she says to her husband, "look who I found. It's Adele."

Vito comes to me and I stand. His blue eyes are somber when he kisses both my cheeks.

"Welcome to our home, Adele. I'm Vito." His eyes look like they are saying more, but since I'm not skilled in reading the subtle expressions of made men I've never met, I simply smile and murmur a soft thank you. He gives his wife a quick kiss, then sits at the table while she fetches more food.

"Nico." Nico simply acknowledges me with the barest hint of a smile and a curt nod, then makes a beeline for his wife. I thought his greeting was a tad frosty, although I can't blame him. He's the Don of the Chicago Outfit and, therefore, entitled to be as grumpy as he wants, I suppose. Not to mention that I more or less killed one of his men yesterday.

But then I see another side to Nico when he wraps an arm around Sophie and takes her mouth in a kiss that is so not fit for public, although no one else seems to care that they have their tongues down each other's throats.

Vito watches me silently. His gaze is warm and kind, but I don't miss his slightly furrowed brows. I can't decide if it's puzzlement or irritation.

Everyone else has taken a place at the table except Dante, who seems more content to perch on the counter across the room, staring at me. Or rather, staring at his shirt on me.

Antonella puts a fresh plate of pastries on the table and then moves to the coffee machine, then begins handing out coffees to the men. Nico's is black, while Vito accepts a flat white from her.

"So, Boston, did you say? When was this?" Antonella presses.

I get a feeling that everyone at this table already knows enough about me, but I reply. "It was back in our final year at LBU. Dante, you came over to see Kira perform, didn't you?" I say, trying to shift the spotlight away from me.

Dante unfolds from his perch, then reaches up into a cupboard and takes out a teabag from a small tin. My eyes follow Dante's movements as he pours in steaming water then adds some honey.

"I saw Addy standing by the wall, trying to be invisible," Dante says as if to himself. "But it was quite the opposite. She stood out to me like a fucking beacon. So fucking stunning."

He comes to the table and places a perfectly brewed green tea in front of me before returning to his spot. My face heats up at that simple yet intimate gesture.

I notice a soft look enter Antonella's face while Sophie simply smiles like a Cheshire cat. Nico's face remains unreadable, while Vito's has deepened into a scowl as if the milk in his coffee has just curdled.

"Dante, come on. I was dressed like a boy," I point out, trying to diffuse the thickening tension.

His gaze, which hasn't once left mine, heats up even more. "Exactly. Spellbinding. Sexy as fuck."

Everyone else recedes into the background, and I find myself unable to look away from Dante, not even when Vito clears his throat loudly. And not when Antonella finally hands Dante his drink.

I notice Dante's coffee is in a much larger mug.

Why did she make his larger? What's in it? Why is he not having any food? Suddenly it seems like the most important thing right now.

How could I date the man for three months and have no idea how he takes his coffee or that he doesn't eat breakfast? So what on earth did we talk about?

Mostly, me.

Dante's sole focus was on me. And I was too busy enjoying the thrill of his attention to want to know more about him. Or perhaps I was too afraid of the danger I sensed was lurking beneath the surface and didn't want to find out?

Partly out of curiosity and partly wanting to take the spotlight off me again, I suddenly blurt out to Dante, "How do you take it?"

"This?" He raises his mug, and I nod.

Dante takes a large sip of his coffee, then cocks his head and mouths, "Come and see."

"Now?" I whisper.

His gaze sharpens into a command that has everything within me snapping to obey. My pulse starts to race as I'm caught in Dante's sensual web. The room completely disappears and as if in a trance, I stand and cross the kitchen to Dante.

CHAPTER TWENTY-SEVEN

Adele

As I reach him, Dante puts his coffee mug away, pushes off the counter, grabs my waist, and lifts me onto the counter. Then he spreads my thighs and steps between them.

All I see are his eyes, stormy pools of desire ringed by a darker rim of gray. "Dante." I suck my bottom lip between my teeth as undeniable excitement streaks through me. "Everyone can see us."

He smiles wickedly. "Yes, and we don't give a fuck." He wraps one hand around my jaw and another on my thigh, and every last shred of my resistance dissolves.

"So, you wanted to know how I take my coffee?" He starts to nibble softly on my lips.

I nod, unable to resist kissing him back.

"You tell me." His mouth covers mine and he kisses me fully. His tongue slides between my lips, and the bittersweet taste of mocha explodes in my mouth. It might be the best thing I've ever tasted. It's so intoxicating that I start to suck on his tongue as a throaty moan escapes me. My hands trail up his chest and into his silky hair, pulling tight. I feel his answering groan all the way into my toes.

The kiss goes on and on until my legs wrap around his waist, and I'm silently begging for more, but Dante only nibbles a path along my jaw, then finishes with an open-mouthed kiss on the sensitive skin below my ear.

"Do you know how I take my coffee now?"

The fog of arousal clears instantly, replaced by a dawning horror. My eyes snap open and I push against his chest. I look over at the empty table sporting half-eaten, abandoned food, then drop my head onto his shoulder.

"Oh God, Dante, that was so bad. Just take me back to the basement already."

Dante chuckles. "Trust me, we're good. Nico and Sophie are worse."

"You're joking!" My cheeks flush with a mix of embarrassment and excitement.

"Afraid not."

"What kind of people are you?"

Dante's lips curl into a devilish smirk. "Sometimes we don't always use words to get our points across."

"And what was the point here?" I ask, tilting my head to the side, my slightly-damp curls cascading over my shoulder.

"That they needed to quit with the sham breakfast, get lost, and let me talk to my woman alone," he replies, his fingers tracing lazy circles on my thighs while his other hand trails up my neck until his fingers spear into my hair, massaging my scalp gently. I suppress the purr working its way up my throat.

"Well, I'm here now, so use your words," I say, throwing his words from last night back at him.

His grin is a flash of white teeth and dimpled cheeks. "It's so fucking hot when you do that, you know? "Anyway," Dante's gaze drops to the bruises closest to my core, his fingers ghosting over the tender skin. "Do I need to apologize?"

"No," I admit, my breath catching. "I–ah. I liked it. Is that the worst . . ." I trail off, struggling to find the words. "Is there more where that came from?"

Dante's eyebrows arch in surprise. "You want more?"

I shrug. "I dunno. Maybe?"

Now his eyes are popping, his jaw slackening in disbelief. I notice how his nostrils are flaring, too, and the very slight flush staining his neck.

"Do you enjoy being hurt?"

"It didn't hurt, Dante—" I start, but he cuts me off, his grip on my thighs tightening.

"It fucking will if you want more."

"I mean, yes, it hurt a little in the moment, but there was so much—" I try to explain, but words fail me.

"Reward?" he finishes. His pupils dilate, the rim of irises around them becoming lighter than their usual stormy gray. I feel the tremor in the hand he has on my thigh and the way his chest rises and falls with each ragged breath.

My core tightens, need shooting through me again. I nod, my eyes locked on his. "Yes, it's . . . very rewarding."

"Addy." His hand comes up to cup my face, his touch gentle, a stark contrast to the fingers tightening on my thigh. "You like pain."

"No, Dante. I like this." I take his shaking hand in mine and raise it between us, my eyes never leaving his. "I like you. Trembling. Uncontrolled. I like the way you get overcome with what you're feeling. Your raw emotions . . . they're intoxicating. And I feel like I don't see them enough."

"Addy, you saw me two years ago in that restaurant and ran away," he reminds me, his voice rough with emotion, his eyes searching mine.

"I didn't understand what I felt back then. You were always so controlled, and you suddenly transformed, and I was shocked and horrified. But mostly, I was sickened by the fact that I wanted you more in that moment than ever." The words tumble from my lips in a rush, my heart laid bare before him.

A low, humorless chuckle rumbles in Dante's chest and the sound vibrates through me. He takes a couple of steps away from me and turns around, his fingers running through his head and grabbing hold. The muscles of his back tense under his shirt. "Christ, I am so fucked."

He takes a deep breath, holds it for a few seconds, then his shoulders sag with the release of air. He does this a few more times while I watch in fascination. By the time he returns to me, his hands have stopped shaking, his eyes are clear and focused, the storm within him temporarily quelled.

"Alright, Addy. Duly noted," he says in a steady, almost brusque tone. "Now, about this morning with Mother and Sophie . . ."

It dawns on me as he changes the subject that, for some reason, Dante needs to be in control of his emotions, to erect a fortress against the turmoil within. "What about them?" I reply.

"Were you uncomfortable?"

I love the way he's checking that I'm okay. I raise my hand and pinch my thumb and index finger together. "A little. It was . . . unexpected. First Aydin found me, and then there was George, who scared the living shit out of me—"

"Oh, you've met Sophie and Nico's spoilt brat, then—" he interjects.

"Oh my God, he's theirs!" The thought of Nico having such a ridiculous pet is unbelievable.

"Unfortunately, yes," Dante huffs, "which makes George immune to any kind of neck wringing, and the bird knows it. Anyway, what happened after Aydin found you?"

"She practically dragged me out, dressed in nothing but your T-shirt, through the maze of gothic underground corridors with cold stone walls, to this modern marble and glass paradise, to face hugs and kisses and finally being devoured alive by you in a roomful of people while your brother scowls at me like a bug he'd very much like to squash and—"

Dante laughs, the sound rich and warm, filling the kitchen with its melody. "Nico likes you, Addy. He just has the weight of the world on his shoulders. A weight I put there by claiming you."

I rear back in surprise, my eyes widening. "Claiming me?"

His smile disappears. "What the hell did you think this was all about?"

"I'm not a thing that can be claimed, Dante," I snap.

"Wrong word choice, maybe. But the facts of the matter remain." He places a hand low on my belly, his touch possessive, the heat of his skin seeping through the thin fabric of my shirt. "You're mine, remember?"

I raise an eyebrow, a flicker of defiance in my eyes, but my heart is pounding with excitement. "So what am I now, your prisoner?"

Dante's gaze flares with an intensity that steals my breath away. His finger traces the bruises on my thighs, raising goosebumps on my skin and making my nipples tighten beneath the thin fabric of my shirt. "If I wanted to hold you captive, you'd be in my house and tied to my bed right now. So no, you're not my prisoner."

Tied to his bed. Slave to his pleasure. I know firsthand how Dante. Doesn't. Stop. The memories alone are enough to make me chase the delicious ache between my legs as moisture seeps out of my core.

His wandering hand, a delicious distraction, makes my body quiver and threatens to derail my thoughts. I catch his hand and intertwine my fingers with his, trying to halt his slow seduction so I can concentrate.

Sophie's words echo in my mind, a reminder of the real reason I'm here. I take a deep breath and then ask, "Dante, what did you mean last night when you told Sal I'm to be off-grid?"

He hesitates for a beat, then speaks, his voice matter-of-fact, the words falling like a hammer blow. "It means you're dead."

My heart stutters, a cold dread seeping into my veins. "What do you mean, dead?"

Dante's grip on my hand tightens, but the stroke of his thumb over my knuckles is gentle. "Adele O'Shea ceases to exist. Date of death, obituary, gravestone, the whole works."

The room starts to spin, the marble countertop beneath me seeming to tilt and sway. It feels like I'm falling into a bottomless pit and the walls are closing in around me. "No. Hell no."

Dante's free hand comes up to cup my cheek, and his eyes bore into mine. "Addy, whoever tried to kill you needs to believe they succeeded; otherwise, you will be dead for real."

Panic rises in my throat, and my breath comes in short, sharp gasps. "But . . . I can't be dead. I have to work. And my dad. I'm all he's got. All he's ever had. I couldn't do that to him."

Something flashes in Dante's eyes, and he raises a single eyebrow. "Benjamin O'Shea lied to you."

"I know. But he's still all the family I've got."

Death is so . . . final. It means I'll never be able to return. Was that what he meant by 'owning' me? Did I make a mistake telling him about the baby? "And what about Kira—"

"It's done, Addy," Dante says with a note of finality. He steps away from me and reaches for his coffee mug. I watch as he takes an unhurried sip, the casual action a stark contrast to the storm swirling inside me. His jaw clenches as he swallows, and then he takes a deep breath and says, "Don't worry about Kira; she knows the truth. And for Benjamin O'Shea, the cops will be notifying him of your death today."

CHAPTER TWENTY-EIGHT

Adele

Rage explodes inside me, hot tears blinding my vision. "Abso-fucking-lutely not, you bastard!" I slip off the island, my bare feet hitting the cold tiles with a slap, the chill sending a twinge up my hip. "I will not let you destroy my life like that," I yell as I head for the door, my heart shattering with every step.

"Where are you going?" Dante calls after me, his voice echoing in the vast hallway.

"Away from you!" I shout, my voice cracking as I throw open the door and step into the large, unfamiliar space. Unsure of which way Aydin and I came from, I take the next right, fully expecting Dante to follow me. But he doesn't.

A winding staircase down and two right turns later, I find myself lost, the labyrinth of corridors seemingly endless. What kind of house is this anyway? I mutter, as I start to retrace my steps, my fingers trailing along the cool, smooth walls. Most doors have no handles, only sleek black handprint panels that mock me with their inaccessibility, a reminder of the world I'm not privy to.

The silence is oppressive, broken only by the soft padding of my bare feet on the carpet and the pounding of my heart. Where is everyone? I strain my ears, thinking I hear faint sounds—a deep chuckle, maybe—but I can't tell where exactly they're coming from.

Finally, sick of it all, I crumple to the carpeted stairs, my body shaking with sobs. It seems like ages ago that Kira talked me into going to Resin nightclub, a distant memory from another life, a life that was falling apart but a life nonetheless.

"Addy." Dante's voice is gentle as he suddenly appears beside me. His hand reaches out to comfort me, then he thinks better of it and lets it drop to his side. *"Tesoro,* I'm not destroying your life. I'm saving it."

"It doesn't feel that way, Dante."

Dante moves to the door opposite the staircase and places his palm against the sleek black panel on it. It swings open. He holds out his hand to me. "Come on, let's talk about this."

Seeing no other choice, I follow him into the room. It's a large space with a seating area off to the side where a rich gold velvet chaise longue sits. A pool table dominates the center of the room, with cue sticks lined up along the wall.

Dante leans against the table, his arms crossed over his chest, his eyes never leaving me as I drop into the velvet chaise lounge. "Until I know who was behind the blast, Addy, it has to be this way."

I shake my head, trying, and failing, to clear the fog of irritation. "But you said Kira knows the truth. Why can't my dad be told too? He may be a liar, but he doesn't deserve this." I remember the sheen of tears in his eyes the last time I was home. No matter what, he was still my father for eighteen years. "He'll be devastated, Dante."

"No doubt he will be," Dante agrees, but there's a hard edge to his voice. "In fact, the entire Boston Irish Mob will be devastated. Although vengeful and bloodthirsty is a more apt description of how they will react."

My spine stiffens as I welcome the familiar buzzing in my ears, that white noise that signals to me that it's time for me to bail, to leave a conversation I don't want to face. But this time, Dante seems to pin me in place with his piercing gaze, his eyes intense and unwavering, and I'm unable to move a muscle, my body frozen under the weight of his stare. It appears I am being forced to confront the truth that I refused to face the last time I spoke to Dad.

Still, I balk, my mind grasping at straws, desperate for any way out of this reality. "Dante, I'm talking about my dad, and you're going on about some Irish Mob. I don't see what one has to do with the other." My voice wavers, the words feeling hollow even to my own ears.

Dante's stare remains unwavering, his eyes boring into mine. "Baby, you do. Your father masquerades as an accountant, a paragon of morals, but deep down, you've always known. Tell me that even before finding out about the counterfeiting, you didn't know there was a darkness in him."

"I-I . . ." My voice trails off, my throat constricting with emotion.

"Benjamin O'Shea is not only a high-ranking member of the Boston Irish Mob. He's the second in command." Dante's words hang in the air, the truth of them settling over me like a heavy blanket.

I stare straight ahead, frozen to the spot as my world turns over again for what seems to be the tenth time in the past twenty-four hours. My heart races, my palms go slick with sweat as I try to process this new reality. After a few moments, I feel the seat dip as Dante sits next to me and pulls me into his arms, his warmth enveloping me like a protective cocoon, the scent of him both comforting and overwhelming.

"I can't believe . . . How is this my life?" My words are muffled against his chest. But deep down, I know Dante is right.

"Baby, this has always been your life. You just weren't living it." As if to emphasize his point, Dante's fingers graze the scar over my hip, the touch sending a shiver down my spine.

My mind reels with the implications of his words. "How long have you known all this?"

Dante's fingers tilt my chin up, forcing me to meet his gaze. "Addy, haven't you wondered why every time you've stepped into Chicago, the Irish Mob goes crazy? That day you came to Ecolab, the Irish showed up because of you."

I shake my head, clutching at straws, but the memories come, hitting me hard and fast. Dad's lies. His instructions to stay away from Chicago and the warning that there was much more he needed to tell me.

"Why? Why would they follow me around?"

"Your father's orders, I imagine. Remember when I told you that we and the Mob don't get along?"

I nod woodenly, recalling how he'd pulled the car over to tell me this. His eyes had bored into mine, his expression so earnest, as if he'd expected me to understand.

Dante continues, "After that night we broke up, a war broke out between us and lasted for months, until Benjamin came to draw a truce."

"My dad came to see you?" I sputter, my eyes wide with shock.

He nods. "He wanted to negotiate new terms of peace. He also told me to back off because you were his daughter and that you were promised to someone else."

For the longest time, I can't say anything, my mind struggling to process this new information. Finally, I find my voice. "He lied. I'm not engaged to anyone."

Dante doesn't look convinced. "Yes, an *engagement* would require that you know about it. But your father and his goons are not the most transparent sort. If you were promised to some mobster, there's a good chance he won't tell you."

"Come on! What's he going to do, blindfold me and take me to the altar?"

Dante says nothing and his silence feeds my frustration. "So, what happens now?"

"Now that you're dead at the hands of Italians, you mean?" Dante's words are blunt, the reality of the situation hitting me like another gut punch, but I nod wearily.

"Now, we go to war."

I drop my head into my hands, my fingers tangling in my hair. "Oh God, no. You can prevent this war by simply letting my father know that I'm alive."

"No. No one can know that just yet."

"Dante, I don't want a war. Guns, bombs, innocent people getting killed, their lives destroyed . . . so many people dying just to save one person. It's not worth the chaos—"

Dante cuts in roughly, his eyes flashing. "Don't you ever say that again, do you hear me? You don't dictate how much value I place on you. If I want to go through a thousand lives to keep you safe, it's my prerogative."

"Well, it's my life," I snap, my chin lifting.

"Sure, and that's my child you're carrying."

Dante's heated words hover in the air between us before descending straight into my core.

We stare at each other, at an impasse, my eyes brimming with angry, frustrated tears even as I start to throb with arousal. I want to smack his gorgeous face, almost as much as I want him to fuck me again. Desperately.

Which is my cue to run.

"Oh, fuck it. I'm tired. I'm going back to bed. Alone." I stand abruptly, my legs shaking as I storm off toward the door. "And I don't want to see you for the rest of the day," I throw behind me, more to my raging hormones than to him.

"Okay, Addy." Dante doesn't even spare me a look. He only leans back on the chaise, his head thrown back, eyes closing as if getting ready to take a nap. *Jerk.*

I push the door open with more force than necessary and step out, my heart pounding in my chest. And then I freeze. I don't know where I'm going, and I can't go back inside because the door has no handle, only a handprint scanner. Somehow, I don't think it'll recognize mine.

With a maneuver a stunt artist would be proud of, I slam myself back into the door before the final inch closes and fly back inside the room. I move back to Dante, my eyes narrowing as I take in his relaxed posture.

"Need something, baby?" Dante is still reclining on the chaise, hands knitted behind his head. His big torso is on display, his shirt stretched taut under rippling muscles. His gaze is literally ripping my shirt into shreds right now, and I feel my body respond, my nipples tightening and my core clenching with need.

God, it's too unfair for him to be this attractive.

"I can't find my way back," I admit, hating the way my voice trembles.

"Do you want to go back to the basement, or do you want to stay in my suite?" He tilts his head, studying me intently. "Don't worry, I don't live here."

For some reason, that revelation crushes me, and I have no idea why. "You don't?"

"No."

"I'll stay in your suite then." The words are out of my mouth before I can stop them, and I feel a flush creep up my neck.

Dante uncoils from the chaise with feline grace, closing the gap between us in a few long strides. "Do you want me to take you there?" His voice is low and rough, and I know exactly what he's asking me.

Unfortunately, there's only one answer to both questions, which annoys me even more. "What do you think?" I spin on my heels, not waiting to catch the smirk on his face.

But my pace is no match for his, and within seconds, he's caught up to me in the corridor, his hand slipping through my hair and around the back of my neck in a possessive grip. "The mansion is actually pretty simple to navigate. It's all in a circle, so you can't get lost," he says as we go up a curving staircase, his breath hot against my ear.

He starts pointing out different landmarks, explaining how they connect to the rest of the mansion. "See that painting of my grandfather over there?" He gestures toward a large oil portrait of a stern-looking man with piercing eyes that seem to follow us as we move. "If you take the hallway to the left, it'll take you to the kitchen. And if you go to the right, you'll find the library."

I nod, trying to take it all in and memorize everything, but it's hard to focus with Dante's body so close to mine, his scent wrapping around me like a seductive cocoon.

"And my suite is just down that way." He continues, pointing toward a set of large double doors on the other side of the room. "It's got everything you need, including my number."

"You're assuming I'll want to call you," I retort, trying to ignore the way my heart skips a beat at the thought of having him on speed dial.

He only huffs out a laugh, and the sound sends a delicious thrill through me.

When we reach the double doors, he takes my hand and places it on the handprint panel. I'm shocked to hear a soft click and see the doors swing open. I whirl back to face him, my eyes wide. "How?"

"I disabled it before. You've just reset it now." His eyes are dark and intense as he ushers me inside, his hand pressed firmly against the small of my back.

We step into the room, and immediately, I'm assailed by the brightness and acoustics. Heavy metal rock blares from hidden speakers, the harsh chords reverberating through my body. Dante touches a few buttons on the wall panel, drawing down the blinds and shutting off the music, plunging the room into a soft, muted light.

Like the kitchen, one entire wall is made of glass, offering a breathtaking view of the lush vegetation beyond. Dante's huge sleigh bed is positioned right next to it, making it feel like one is hanging right off into the greenery. I can only imagine how incredible dawn must be here, waking up to the first rays of sunlight filtering through the leaves.

"You said you don't live here. Why is there music?" I ask.

"No, I don't. Aydin sets it whenever I'm in the house." He shrugs, a small smile tugging at the corners of his mouth.

"Okay. Well, thanks." I glance pointedly at the door while ignoring the screeching protest in my ovaries.

His eyes roam over my body like a physical caress. "I'll let you get settled in then. Clothes are in the closet."

"Your clothes or mine?" The words are out of my mouth before I can rationalize them. Four words, seemingly innocent, but with the way Dante reacts, they may be the filthiest words ever spoken.

Dante goes still. His eyes widen as a look of feral hunger settles on his face. "Fuck, Addy," he growls, an animalistic rumble that makes my core pulse with heat.

"What?" I ask innocently. I may be melting into a puddle of lust, but that doesn't stop me from enjoying the effect my words are having on him too. "It was a simple and valid question, considering . . ." I gesture at my garb.

In a few long strides, he closes the distance between us. His hands grip my hips, and he pulls me flush against his body. I gasp at the contact, feeling the hard planes of his chest pressing against my soft curves, the heat of his skin seeping through our clothes.

"And here's your simple and valid answer: Feel free to wear my clothes and smell of me." His lips score the shell of my ear. "Since you're already wearing me on the inside."

My lids fall closed and I arch into him, my body responding to his words with a desperate, aching need. "Dante," I breathe, his name a plea and a prayer all at once.

"That's it, baby," he murmurs, his hands kneading my ass through his shirt. "Tell me where else you want me."

My head falls back as I surrender to the sensations coursing through my body. "Everywhere. Now."

CHAPTER TWENTY-NINE

Adele

Dante's answering growl is a sound of pure, masculine satisfaction, and then his lips are on mine, claiming me with a kiss that is both fierce and tender. He rips the shirt clean off my back, and I melt into him, my hands fisting in his hair, holding him close as he devours my mouth, his tongue sweeping inside to tangle with mine in a delicious, heady dance.

His hands return to my ass with a desperate urgency that matches my own. I tense in anticipation, expecting him to spank me, but he doesn't.

"Dante," I gasp, my head falling back as his lips trail down my neck, his teeth grazing the sensitive skin of my collarbone. "I want . . ."

"What, *tesoro?*" he murmurs, his voice rough with desire. "What do you want?"

I push against his chest, urging him to step back. He complies, his eyes dark and questioning as I sink to my knees before him, my hands reaching for the buckle of his belt. "I want you undone."

My fingers tremble slightly as I work to free him from the confines of his pants. The moment he springs out, hot, hard, and so fucking big, I suppress a gasp, then stick out my tongue and lick his shaft slowly from the root up to the large mushroom head. My eyes flutter closed, and I moan, enjoying the feel of the satiny skin and the salty taste of precum gathering at his slit.

"Christ, Adele." His groan is tortured. I open my eyes to watch his tongue peek between his lips, his fingers tangle in his hair as his head falls back in pleasure.

This . . . this is the Dante I want. Mindless, unhinged. I release his cock with a pop, then switch off my last rational brain cell, the one telling me to reconsider my next words.

"Fuck my mouth, Dante. I want you to fill my throat."

Dante's head snaps forward in disbelief, his eyes wide and unfocused. "Fuck, Adele O'Shea," he groans, "You are going to be the death of me."

He takes a few steps back, and for a moment, I think he's trying to leave, but he only goes to the panel at the door. He switches on all the lights and raises the blinds so the room is bathed with light. Then he turns on the heavy metal band to a volume so high that I flinch.

"You okay?" he asks.

I nod, glancing around as if searching for the hidden speakers. "It's really loud—"

"Do you trust me?"

"I do."

"Now, come here and put your mouth on me."

Everything inside me tightens at his tone, and I scramble to my feet.

"On your fucking knees, Addy."

My heart pounds like a solo drum while the sultry voice in my head goads me on. *You wanted him this way, Addy. So fucking take him.*

I fall back on my knees and crawl to him. Once I'm near enough, he slides his hand along my jaw and feeds his cock to me. The moment I wrap my lips around him and suck, I feel him tense. His hand slips into my hair and grips it tight.

I swirl my tongue around his frenulum, relishing the answering moan and jerking of his hips, which involuntarily pushes him deeper into my mouth.

His feel and taste are addictive—smooth, hot, and tangy, serving my mouth with a sensory feast that sends my senses reeling. I suck gently, stroking him with my tongue. I watch him through my eyelashes, loving the intense pleasure etched on his face.

I might be on my knees taking his cock, but fuck, this is heady. Dante is so responsive, it feels like every single lick and suck produces a different response altogether.

I take him deeper until he hits the back of my throat. The moment he does, Dante lets out a feral groan. It's a sound of torture and surrender that goes straight to my clit. But instead of driving deeper, Dante pulls back.

"Fuck, baby, take it slow, okay?" His voice is tight and rough, and I know he's struggling to do the same.

I don't want him to take it slow. I can't afford to, not if I want to drive him insane. He's so big that my jaw is bound to fall off before I can finish him off.

So instead of doing as he says, I wrap one arm around his thighs and cup his balls with the other. I relax my throat and let him all the way in until my chin brushes against the balls I'm gently fondling.

"Fuuuuck, Adele!" Dante bucks against me as if unable to control himself

I gag violently, but I don't pull off right away, instead letting my throat fight to expel him. His tortured groan drowns out the heavy metal band, and his fists tighten involuntarily in my hair. The resulting pain in my scalp makes me moan around him. When I start to feel lightheaded, I pull away from him and take a few ragged breaths.

"Jesus fucking Christ, Addy!" Dante looks like a man way past his limits. His mouth is slack with lust, his hands tangling in my hair to guide me closer to where he needs me most. "I get it. You want me off the rails. Give me a fucking safe word. Now."

"Red Wine," I whisper, not even having to think about it.

His answer is a deep, guttural groan that sends a pulse of heat between my legs.

"Come here, then." Suddenly, he takes control, or rather, he loses it. His hands grip my head, holding me in place as he thrusts deep into my mouth. I can feel the head of his cock reaching past the barrier of my throat, and the sound of my own gags filling the room makes me wetter.

He starts to move faster, his hips pumping as he drives in and out of my mouth. Tears leak from the corners of my eyes, and drool fills my mouth and spills down the corners of my lips only makes it all the better for him to fuck my throat.

The size and girth of him, the way he fills me completely, the way he uses my throat for his pleasure drives my lust to unbearable heights. When I start to taste more of the salty tang of his precum, I hear his groans get louder, and his muscles coil tighter, I know he's going to come soon.

I'm not so far off too. My pussy throbs, clit so swollen I know I'll shatter with a few strokes of my fingers. I slip a hand between my folds and start to rub, my moan of pleasure vibrating onto his cock.

"Hands on my fucking wrists," Dante barks. Heart pounding at his sharp command, I immediately wrap my hands around the thick wrists on either side of my head.

"Squeeze me if you need a break," he instructs curtly, and then he's dragging my mouth on and off his stiff cock. The fire between my legs rages on, my nipples hard as diamonds. With nowhere else for my pent-up lust to go, all I can do is squirm and take his rough treatment, wound as tight as a bow, eager for his pleasure, his orgasm, as if tasting his release would somehow bring me mine.

And then he's there. With a final savage thrust, he holds himself still, his cock buried deep in my mouth. I feel every single pulse, the way his cock jerks in time to his guttural sounds as he comes straight down my throat. I moan as I take all of him in, every last drop.

When he finally pulls away, I'm left gasping for breath and trembling, but so is Dante. I look up at him, and I can see the raw need all over him still.

"What the fuck, Adele?" he growls, his eyes black pools of lust. He looks like a stalking predator might do just before that final leap at their prey. "Just how greedy can you get?"

I let my gaze drop to his still-hard cock. "I should be asking you that, Dante. You're still hard as a rock after *that*."

I lean forward to lick off the cum dribbling off his tip. And I finally taste him. Thick and creamy. Salty sweet. I could certainly get used to it.

Dante holds me close as he slowly pulls me to my feet. My breasts drag across the hard planes of his torso, sparking fireworks as I go. He looks at me like he wants to devour me whole. And I know that's exactly what he's going to do.

Once back on my feet, I lean and wrap my arms around his neck, pulling him closer. His rigid cock pulses against my stomach. "Take me. Hard," I whisper hoarsely.

"Sure, you don't need a break?" Dante teases me softly.

"No," I moan.

Dante lifts me up, his hands gripping my ass as he carries me to the bed. He lays me down, then settles his big body between my spread thighs. He takes my mouth again, his tongue tangling with mine until I'm wantonly sliding my wet folds along his thighs and moaning as sensation ripples out from my clit.

And then he's slowly sliding inside me, inch by glorious inch, until he fills me up completely. I gasp, my nails digging into his back as I stretch to take all of him.

Still, I crave more.

"Harder," I beg, my voice strained with need.

Dante growls, and then his hips are snapping into mine with a force that leaves me breathless.

Then he wraps my right leg around his waist while bending my left leg so my calf is pressed right against his ripped torso. I'm completely open and vulnerable to his hard thrusts in a way I've never been.

His eyes never leave mine as he thrusts so deep that all I can do is gasp and squirm. "This hard enough, baby?"

I nod, moaning brokenly.

His fingers stroke my hip, thumb right over my hypersensitive scar, and I tremble. Then he starts pressing in deep, past the point of pleasure, past soothing tender muscles. Hard enough to hurt. To bruise.

"And now?"

"Fuck. Dante!" My leg spasms around his waist even as my pussy clenches around his cock. Identical responses, one produced by intense pleasure, the other, searing pain, transforming the experience into something ethereal as I race toward my release.

He doesn't let up, slamming hard and hitting spots inside me that make me tremble and jerk while his wicked thumb presses in harder and harder.

I lose my mind, caught in a flood of endorphins. I don't realize how much I'm screaming, begging him to end my torture. To never stop torturing me. To fuck me until I can't feel anything beyond how hard he's making me come.

And then I'm right there at the point of no return as the orgasm explodes in me. It's been swelling inside me and threatening to consume me since the moment we started arguing, and now I can only sob as he fucks me through it until I'm breathless and spent.

Dante shudders and follows me over the edge, his own release coming hot and fast.

We lay there for a moment, our bodies entwined, breathing in short, ragged gasps. His heart pounds hard against my breasts in a rhythm that feels identical to mine.

He rearranges us so I'm fully tucked under him, then supports some of his weight on an elbow. Other than that, he makes no move to get off me. Instead, his fingers start to stroke my bruised, still-spasming thigh.

And I'm terrified by how much I loved the way it hurt.

CHAPTER THIRTY

Dante

The harsh chords of heavy metal music blare from the speakers, a much-needed distraction and an anchor to my slowly unraveling mind. Because Addy is driving me insane.

The last twenty-four hours have been like a sledgehammer was taken to the shackles in my mind and now I'm left reeling with the dark satisfaction that I've broken every rule. Crossed every line.

I've always sensed this tantalizing part of Addy and have been inexorably drawn to it without fully understanding why. Now her cravings are another matter entirely. Fucked doesn't even begin to cover what I am at this point.

"Was that too much, *tesoro?*" I murmur against her skin as I massage the jagged scar on her hip.

"No, it was . . . good." She finishes in a throaty whisper that tells me just how good it must have been for her.

"And my weight?" I ask just to distract my wayward mind from conjuring hundreds of other ways to deliver on the pleasure-pain edge she loves, but it's the wrong thing to focus on because the thought of her delicate frame under my two hundred pounds of muscle triggers a fierce sense of protection . . . and another wave of lust inside me

"You are heavy." Her fingers stroke down my back. "But your bed is glorious. It feels like being pressed into fluffy clouds. Although I think my ears are bleeding. Do you need to have it on so loud?"

"Yep. I was going a little bit mad. I'll turn it off as soon as you stop gripping my cock so tightly, and it's safe to pull out without risking a penile degloving."

She giggles. "Ew, Dante, your pillow talk needs serious work if you think that was even remotely romantic."

I trace the thin scar between her breasts. "You don't do romantic, *tesoro*. You're a fucking cesspit of a thousand ways to die."

Addy's chuckles dissolve into full-on belly laughs, the sound vibrating from her small frame and through me.

"You ever think that something in your subconscious sensed that your life with Benjamin O'Shea was a lie? That maybe you need for answers may have led you down this forensics path?"

She nods, although her eyes appear shuttered. "For as long as I remember, I've had nightmares. They seemed so real, so graphic. I just didn't understand why I kept having the same dream. In time I accepted it. Embraced it even."

Addy lifts her gaze to meet mine. "Then I started to wish they'd go on for longer, so that I'd see more details, like the face of the masked man. Or glimpse the title of any books covering an entire wall. The woman had red hair like me, you know. I used to think it was the blood that made it red, but now I know."

I turn onto my back, taking her with me so she's sprawled on my chest, her ear against my pounding heart. "That was too much to deal with at that tender age."

"I know. I was about six or seven when I told my dad about the woman and the masked man in my dreams, but he brushed it off. He showed me pictures of my mom—a blonde woman—and my dad—a ginger like him. And in time, I started to see more photos around the house, and then we visited gravestones every year . . ." she trails off.

I shut my eyes against the rage churning inside me. What kind of sick bastard treats a child like that? I want to kill him almost as much as I'm grateful that he saved Addy's life.

She shrugs as if it's not a big deal and changes the subject. "Seriously though, Dante, do you have the music on so loud so people wouldn't overhear us? You didn't even scream all that much. I mean, yes, you yelped now and again, but on the whole—"

"Yelped?" I ask, suppressing a chuckle.

"Fine." She sighs. "I'll tell the truth then. It sounded more like screeching."

Suddenly, I shift her to the bed, rolling her to her stomach. Then grabbing her wrists in one of mine, I smack her ass. Hard. She yelps, glaring at me in mock indignation, but I already caught the lust swirling in her eyes the moment my palm hit her ass.

God help me with this woman.

I spank her until her ass cheeks are red with the imprints of my palms and she's moaning into the pillow, then I let go of her wrists and start to stroke the sting away.

"I sometimes need the music to anchor me, keep me from spiraling out of control when things are a little . . . tense."

She goes still, then turns on her side to look at me. "Is it like Kira, you know how she has a hypersensitive sense of hearing, smell, and touch? Do you feel too much sometimes?"

"It's not so much how I feel as how I sometimes process information."

"I have no clue what that means, Dante."

"I know, *tesoro*. I'll explain later." I glance at my wristwatch. "Right now, I need to go. Work calls."

I press a tender kiss to her neck, then reluctantly stand. As I shut off the speakers and dim the lights, I feel Addy's eyes following my movements. "You should get some sleep, Addy," I call over my shoulder, heading to the bathroom.

When I return, shrugging on a fresh shirt and carrying my suit jacket, Addy's still awake. She turns to watch me, her brows furrowed in concentration, fingers fidgeting with the edge of the blanket. Something's bothering her.

"So, I trust I won't see you for the rest of the day," she says, aiming for nonchalance but missing by a mile.

I can't help but smirk, "No, you won't. I wouldn't dream of boring you to death, so I'll go home after work."

"Where's home?" She sits up straighter.

"I told you it's a little place up on Shorecliff beach. Sunsets are awesome. You'll like it."

She hesitates, then asks, "Will you be alone?"

I go still, shocked that she feels the need to ask that. "What do you think, Adele?"

She shakes her head, looking away. "I'm sorry."

"Don't be. Talk to me." I move closer, perching on the edge of the bed.

She takes a deep breath. "It's stupid. It's just . . . Alina said something, and I wondered if you had a thing for redheads . . . women, in general."

Fuck.

Heat crawls up my face, a sensation so foreign I almost don't recognize it. I haven't blushed like this since third grade, when Mrs. Radcliffe caught me passing a note to some girl and read it aloud to the class.

Still, I don't hide my reaction from her. "I have a thing for you. Just you. And no woman has ever seen the inside of my house."

Addy's shoulders relax, a smile tugging at the corner of her mouth. "Really?"

I nod, holding her gaze. "Well, one did come close once, but she ran off screaming."

"Why did she run?"

"Something about the Halloween decor spooked her, I think. Although she's still intrigued, and she's now begging for a second chance to see it."

Addy's eyebrow arches. "Really? And you'll let her?"

I shrug, a playful glint in my eye. "Only if I know she won't run again."

"Maybe if you stop scaring her, she'll stop running away." She leans forward, a challenge in her voice.

"Not a chance." I stand, straightening my jacket. "Anyway, I'll be here tomorrow morning. Then you can tell me all about how you managed to do what you did back there without throwing up all over me despite being four weeks pregnant."

"Six," she corrects, her hand unconsciously moving to her belly.

"No, *tesoro*, we had sex four weeks ago. Do the math."

Addy starts to chuckle, the sound warming me more than I care to admit. "Oh my God, Einstein, that's so not how the math is done."

My brows furrow as I shrug on my jacket. "Do you know how many we're having yet?"

"What the hell is that supposed to mean?" She sits up straighter, eyes widening.

"Just saying. Enzo had six. Nico's having two. Might be something in the weed we smoke."

"Dante!" Her voice rises in alarm. "You still smoke?"

"Not unless I'm losing my mind." I walk over to the hidden compartment and take out two loaded guns, securing one in my waist and another in my ankle holster. When I turn back to Addy, I notice how the tension seeps into her shoulders, her fingers gripping the sheets tightly.

"This work you have . . . what's it about?" Her voice wavers slightly as she cradles her still-flat belly.

I finish adjusting my suit jacket, weighing my words carefully. "Just a meeting to discuss last night. Someone's probably going to catch a bullet. Usually happens when a war is brewing."

She groans and puts a hand to her forehead, closing her eyes briefly. "Do you think the same 'meeting' is happening in the Irish mob at the moment?"

"Without a doubt. Even if the cops haven't notified them, your tracker would have gone offline at Resin, and they would have heard about the bomb blast. Put two and two together."

Her eyes snap open, disbelief etched across her face. "My tracker? Are you saying my dad—Benjamin, would have a tracker on me?"

"You are a mafia princess, Addy. His hostage. I'd expect no less." I keep my voice gentle, knowing the weight of my words.

She swallows hard, her next words coming out in a rush. "Dante, do you have any idea who my real father is?"

A slow smile splits my face. "*Tesoro.* Believe me when I say it's not a discussion you want to have today. Certainly not right now."

Her eyes flash with determination as she throws off the covers. "Then you should let me leave. I want to confront that liar."

"Not this again, Addy—" I start, but she cuts me off.

"You can't keep me here forever. I can't stay in this world," she says, her voice trembling, each word a struggle. She wraps her arms around herself, as if physically holding her fractured pieces together.

I move closer, caging her between my arms, my palms pressed on either side of her head. Her breath hitches as I lean in, our faces mere inches apart. "I'm the scariest thing in this world, and you handle me."

A ghost of a smile touches her lips, but the fear lingers in her eyes. Her gaze searches mine. "Do I, though?"

"Like a fucking pro."

She closes her eyes, her brows knotting as she wrestles with the overwhelming reality pressing down on her. "Dante. You're so . . ." she trails off.

"What?"

"Bossy. Pushy," she says in a soft exhale. "I feel like you're nudging me down this path."

I nod. "Do you want me to stop?"

"No," she breathes so softly I almost don't hear it. When she opens her eyes again, they're ablaze with a fierce mixture of desire and desperation. Her fingers weave into my hair, tugging me down, her lips crashing into mine. The kiss is frantic, like she's trying to lose herself, to forget the fear in the familiarity of our connection.

With a final lingering touch, I break the kiss and pull back, my thumb tracing gentle circles on the delicate skin of her wrist.

"I know it's a lot to take in," I murmur, locking eyes with her, grounding her in the truth I see there. "But I meant what I said, Addy. You'll be fine."

"Alright." Her voice is breathy, her half-lidded eyes raking over me. She stops at my crotch, looks away, and promptly looks back as if she can't help herself. Then she sucks her lower lip between her teeth.

My gaze drifts over her full breasts and rosy nipples down to the trimmed red bush at the apex of her thighs. But it is the sight of her scars that triggers a fierce streak of possessiveness in me—as if the universe itself has marked her as mine.

Slowly, almost tentatively, Addy trails a hand from her belly upward until she cups a breast, rolling her nipple between her thumb and forefinger. The action is both sensual and desperate, a silent demand for connection, and I feel my cock jerk in my pants.

"Fuck, Addy, what are you doing right now?" I ask, my voice rough with desire.

"Nothing. You should go. You have a war to plan, don't you?" Her eyes and body are begging me to do the opposite.

She doesn't want me to leave her. And she doesn't want this war.

I huff out a breath, then lean over to remove her hand from her breast and bring it to my lips, dropping a tender kiss on her palm.

Addy is using sex as a coping mechanism, a way to ground herself in the disaster that has upended her life. So much has changed for her in the past twenty-four hours. Her past and future are irrevocably altered. Our connection might be the one constant she can cling to. I see her struggle, and my heart breaks for her.

"I see you, Adele." I brush back silky wisps of hair from her forehead. "I promise I'm here, and I won't stop fighting until you feel safe—in every way a person can be safe. Okay?"

She nods, her eyes glazing with a mixture of desire and exhaustion. "Okay."

"I'll see you tomorrow," I say, giving her a quick peck on the lips. "Get some rest. I've pushed you hard enough for today."

Addy nods, turning onto her side as her lids flutter closed. Within moments, she's snoring softly, the rise and fall of her chest hypnotic in the otherwise silent room.

My attention is drawn to the three linear scars that mar the otherwise flawless expanse of her back. They're a testament to the violence that has haunted her past, a reminder of the incredible strength and resilience she possesses.

She's survived the most impossible odds as a child. And while others were having playdates, she was enduring hospital appointments, multiple surgeries, and relearning how to walk.

And now, she's being targeted once again. But I'll be damned if I let them harm a single red strand of her hair this time.

Now she's mine. To protect, to love.

With a final glance at Addy's sleeping form, I quietly exit the room and head to the conference room, anticipation heavy on my shoulders as I imagine the fallout with Orlando De Luca and, inevitably, the Irish Mob.

How the hell do we fight on two fronts and win this war?

CHAPTER THIRTY-ONE

Dante

Eight pairs of somber eyes turn to me as I step into the dim conference room. The dim light casts shadows, matching the uneasy atmosphere.

Everyone knows I'm usually one of the last to walk into meetings, a conscious choice because those first few minutes of chin-wagging and dancing around the main point drive me up the wall. But today, Nico glances pointedly at the clock. I'm only three minutes late but he's in a mood. Everyone is, and understandably so.

Pietro's usual seat sits hauntingly empty, a cruel reminder of his death. Orlando's seat is also conspicuously empty. Which means I haven't missed much. The party will only start when the man gets here.

"Apologies, brothers," I mutter, making my way around the long pine conference table.

I clap Enzo on the shoulder as I pass. His face is drawn, perpetual exhaustion etched into his features—the price of fathering sextuplets.

As I take my seat opposite Father, I catch Sal's eye. A silent understanding passes between us. Apart from Nico and Father, he's the only other person here who knows that Addy is alive.

I hold Father's gaze longer than necessary, searching for any crack in his stony façade. My earlier display in the kitchen was meant to rattle him, to see if his reaction would reveal what he stubbornly refuses to admit—that Addy is my half-sister.

But he gives nothing away, only looking back at me steadily. The silence stretches, heavy with unspoken tensions and unanswered questions.

Finally, Nico's voice cuts through the quiet. "Salvatore, you have something?"

Sal leans forward, his eyes briefly meeting mine before addressing the room. "*Sì*, Don Nico. We found the bomber. He's a DC-based ghost who goes by the name Owen Novak. He has no fingerprints or dental records and never leaves a trace."

I exchange a meaningful glance with Nico. Ghosts are the apex predators of our world—assassins so skilled they're practically myth. Whoever ordered the hit is clever enough to use one.

"Yet you smoked him out in less than twelve hours. Impressive, Salvatore," Nico marvels in approval.

When Sal only grins in response, I mutter, "Well, don't be shy now, tell us how you did it, you evil genius. Finding a ghost's identity should be next to impossible."

Sal shrugs off our admiration. "I have a contact. Goes by the name Bonnie. She charges an arm and a leg, but she's an absolute magician. Told me who and where he was within minutes."

"She?" Nico leans forward, intrigued. "That's . . . extraordinary. She one of your Harvard buddies?"

Sal shifts uncomfortably in his seat, a slight flush creeping up his neck. "Nah, I don't think she even finished high school, *Signore*." He's a little miffed that this mystery girl has stolen his thunder.

I can't resist rubbing the salt in. "Well, fuck. You think maybe she could come work for us full-time?"

Sal shoots me a withering glare, but duty compels him to respond to his underboss. "I believe she works exclusively for the head of the Five Families of New York," he bites out. "She only did this as a personal favor."

Wow. Nico's New York best friend is a lucky S.O.B.

"Shame," I say, patting Sal's back. "Anyway, we've still got you. It's better than nothing."

"Fuck you," he fake-sneezes, and I struggle to keep a straight face.

The room's somber mood tempers my usual inclination for jokes, though. I clear my throat and get back to business. "So when can we pick this motherfucker up? I'd like to see just how many traces he doesn't leave while he's being flayed alive."

Sal begins to respond, "I can arrange—" but he's cut short as the double doors burst open.

Orlando De Luca storms in, his imposing frame filling the doorway. His ever-present toothpick twitches as his jaw clenches, pale green eyes blazing with fury.

The room falls silent, the sudden tension so thick you could cut it with a knife. I notice the flicker of unease that crosses Nico's face.

This will be bad.

Excitement thrums in my veins as I feel the reassuring weight of the guns in my side and ankle holsters. I can already hear the splinters and cracks forming in our enterprise—sides being taken between those loyal to Orlando and the old ways, and those aligned with Nico and me, who are trying to bring the Outfit into newer climes.

"What the hell is this?" Orlando demands, throwing a handful of photos onto the table and scattering them across the polished wood.

I catch glimpses of myself with Addy. One shows us leaving the club, her body plastered to my side. Another captures me carrying her. Her arms are wound tightly around me, and her face is buried in my neck.

An inexplicable warmth pumps through my veins. Seeing Addy draped around me stirs something in me. I like it. A lot. But I keep my expression neutral as I meet Orlando's gaze.

"I don't see how that's any of your business," I say coolly.

Orlando's eyes narrow, his voice dripping with venom. "It becomes my business when you're publicly cavorting with some mystery woman while you've left your vows to me unfulfilled. Who the hell is she, Dante? One of your little whores?"

I clench my jaw, suppressing the urge to bash his face in. Around the table, I notice the other men shifting uncomfortably, their eyes darting between Orlando and me.

"I suggest you watch your tongue, Orlando," I warn, my voice low and dangerous.

But he only grows bolder, leaning across the table until his face is inches from mine. "She's the same Irish woman from two years ago, isn't she? What, you're bored of starting wars, so you've moved on to setting fire to your own house? Grow the fuck up!"

The room goes deadly quiet. My entire body goes still, save for my right hand, which twitches involuntarily. I stare into Orlando's pale blue eyes, imagining the tidy red hole that will soon appear between them.

As a rule, we don't shed blood inside this room. Orlando knows that, which is probably why his mouth is running a mile a minute. But fuck it, there's a first time for everything.

Just as I move to blow out the man's brains, I catch my father's meaningful one-eyed glare. It's a look he created especially for me and one I've learned the hard way to heed over the years.

With great effort, I lean back in my seat and issue Orlando a low warning instead. "You're treading on thin ice, De Luca."

Orlando's eyes dart belligerently around the room, his rage unabated. "Where is the woman, Dante? I demand to know where you're hiding her."

His intensity is puzzling. Why is he so disturbed by me being with another woman? True, I should be putting a ring on his daughter, but faithfulness isn't generally something an old-school mafioso like Orlando would expect out of an arranged marriage.

Before I can respond, Nico interjects, his voice calm and authoritative. "The woman in the photos is dead. She was in the car that exploded last night."

The change in Orlando is instantaneous and unsettling. His face goes sheet-pale, and a violent tremor runs through his body. "I was told it was Potenzo . . . that died in the blast."

Watching the play of emotion on De Luca's face is confusing. So I do what I do best: poke the bear.

"She and Pietro were in the car," I say flippantly, ignoring the warning looks from both Nico and my father. "Not that it's any of your business, but I needed to make room for a few more whores in my car, so I made her ride with Pietro instead. Anyway, yes, she's dead, too."

You could hear a pin drop in the silence that follows. Tension radiates from every man present as their eyes dart between Orlando and me, waiting for the inevitable explosion.

"I see." Orlando's voice is tight with an unnamed emotion. He turns, takes a couple of steps back, then suddenly whirls to face me again. "And what's this I hear about you breaking off your betrothal to my daughter? Is that true?"

I meet his gaze with insolence, my voice even. "I'm afraid so, Orlando. I admit I may have put the cart before the horse and should have told you first. But the bottom line is that the horse is now hitched to the cart, and both are being kicked out. The wedding is off."

Orlando watches me with an unreadable expression, then suddenly hacks his throat and spits on the floor, his face twisted with disgust. The room collectively inhales, shocked at this blatant show of disrespect.

"You are a dishonorable little bitch, Dante Vitelli," he snarls. "If it wasn't for your father sitting in this room, I'd gut you where you sit."

He turns to face Nico, his contempt palpable. "And you are not worth the seat you're on for not reining him in, boy."

With that, Orlando yanks off his signet ring and throws it at Nico before storming off.

"De Luca!" Nico barks, his rage barely controlled. But Orlando doesn't stop. His shoulders are hunched, and his fists are clenched as he disappears through the doorway. The heavy door slams behind him, echoing in the stunned silence.

The room is frozen in disbelief. As Nico's Underboss, I should have already put a bullet in Orlando's head the moment he threw his ring at his Capo. But I'm rooted to the spot, partly due to the shock of what just transpired and partly because of the way Father has been glaring at me throughout this entire exchange.

My mind races. Orlando De Luca is a seasoned Capo, known for his cold, calculated demeanor. He rarely shows emotion, let alone loses control like this. There's something odd about his reaction, something that doesn't quite add up.

As the implications sink in, I realize Orlando has just signed his own death warrant. In a twisted way, I'm almost relieved. His singular action of openly dishonoring his Don means there will be even fewer sympathetic to his cause. We might be able to avoid a civil war after all.

Without being told, the top enforcers, Giorgio and Enzo, rise from their seats. Their hands simultaneously reach for their Glocks as they start to follow Orlando.

Suddenly, my father's voice cracks like a whip, stopping them mid-stride. "Sit down, Enzo. You too, Giorgio."

We all turn to my father, stunned. His stern expression and the authority radiating from him transport us back to when he was the Don. It's wildly inappropriate, given that his Don is sitting beside him.

I can almost hear the gears turning in everyone's heads, trying to make sense of this unprecedented situation.

Nico nods curtly, his jaw clenched, giving Giorgio and Enzo leave to follow Father's command, despite the clear undermining of his own authority. Then he stands to his full height and faces off with Father, his voice tight with rage.

"You forget your place, Vito."

"No, I don't," Father replies calmly, his eyes meeting Nico's gaze unflinchingly. "As Consigliere, it's my duty to advise you. And in this case, I would let Orlando go."

"Let him go?" Nico nudges the signet ring on the table. "So, I broke my word about giving him a Vitelli heir, yes, but De Luca has just earned himself an execution with that display."

I glance around, noting the anticipation on the faces of my fellow mafiosi. Giorgio's brow is furrowed, his eyes darting between Nico and my father. Enzo's hand still hovers near his holster, awaiting final orders.

Father looks at every man in the room, then announces, "Do you all think that was the rage of a disappointed Capo?"

He pauses, letting his words settle. "That was the anguish of a grieving father. A man who has lost something far more precious than a marriage deal. He's lost a daughter he was never allowed to love."

My pulse pounds in my ears as I watch comprehension dawn on each face around the table. Nico's jaw goes slack, and Sal's eyes widen, his gaze snapping to mine.

Orlando De Luca is Addy's real father. And he must have known for some time now that she survived.

Nico sinks back into his chair, the weight of this revelation clear in the slump of his shoulders. Another heavy silence descends upon the room as we all process this bombshell.

"Well, fuck me," a humorless chuckle escapes my lips as the irony hits me.

Looks like Orlando De Luca is still going to be my father-in-law one way or another.

Enzo clears his throat, his brow furrowed in concern. "So, what do we do now? Both Benjamin O'Shea and Orlando De Luca believe their daughter has been killed on our turf. And both are now our enemies."

After a long moment, Nico leans forward, his deep blue eyes scanning the room. "Do the Irish know it's De Luca?"

Father shakes his head. "Why do you think the war went on for that long? They wanted us to give up the man Naomi was sleeping with, but Orlando has always been smart. He kept his affair very well hidden till this day."

Nico digests this information, his jaw clenching and unclenching as he thinks. Finally, he speaks. "We let De Luca grieve for now."

Nico turns to me. "And when the time is right, Dante, you will pay him a visit. Let him know we're in on his secret. He'll crawl back into the fold if he values the rest of his family. Then we can decide his consequences."

"*Sì*, Don," I murmur in acknowledgment.

But Nico's not done. "Also, I want Owen Novak tied up, trussed, and ready to talk in three days." He shoots me a weighted look. "Again, you're doing the honors, Dante."

"Certo," I nod, a grim smile on my lips. I made the mess. I'm more than happy to clean it up.

Turning to Sal, I feel a spark of excitement despite the gravity of the situation. "Fancy a New York bounty hunt, Sal?"

Sal's eyes light up. "Always."

"Great," Nico says, standing. He squares his shoulders, once again the Don. "That will be all, gentlemen."

With that, he leaves the room, effectively dismissing us. As the other Capos file out, I remain seated, my thoughts churning.

The game has changed again—but the players haven't, and Addy is still right in the middle of it all.

CHAPTER THIRTY-TWO

Dante

In all the thirteen years I've been sworn by blood, I still haven't quite gotten used to its cloying metallic stink. I suppress a shudder as I wipe my hands with a white towel, the crimson stains seeping into the fabric.

Sal hands me a vial of epinephrine, his face a mask of concentration. Across from us, Owen Novak sits tied to a metal chair, the skin of his chest flayed and kneecaps missing. He silently begs for the release of death, but he doesn't deserve it. Not yet.

Smoking Owen out of the war bunker he'd holed up in, then dragging him back to Chicago, took a hell of a lot longer than planned. Meanwhile, the Irish have started throwing tantrums.

Urban Elixir Club and Colosseum Casino now lie in smoldering ruins. I've asked Nico not to retaliate as long as no one is hurt. As much as it pains him to do nothing while they torch our businesses, Nico has honored my wishes. He understands how difficult it would be to explain over dinner—or in bed—how you killed your woman's daddy.

And now time is running out. It's been a week since the meeting and six days since Sal and I left for DC. And all I have to show for it is Owen Novak, dying in front of me.

A grunt of frustration escapes me as I draw the pale fluid from the vial into a syringe. "Tell me what I want, and I'll let you die, Owen."

The room falls silent, punctuated only by his rattling breath. Blood pours from his nose and mouth, and his breaths are shallower. A punctured lung, maybe. How the hell did he even get that? But it doesn't matter anymore. This man will be dead in minutes.

It would have been more efficient to break him down slowly, torturing him mentally and physically over days or weeks. But we don't have that time. Already, it took too long to track the slippery motherfucker down, even with Bonnie's help.

So, it has to be this way: a cocktail of extreme brutality starting with excruciating pain to increase brain glutamate levels and give a heightened sense of despair, followed by Pentothal, to help loosen the tongue. Epinephrine shots keep them alive a little longer until they break. Or die.

This is a huge gamble, and especially for a hardened assassin like Novak, the natural way is way less messy and more predictable. But I've always been a wagering man.

"Why her?" I ask again because asking a ghost assassin, "Who sent you?" is as useful as trying to squeeze blood from a stone.

I hear a faint wheeze, and as I go to jab his bruised, swollen neck with epinephrine to keep him alive a little longer, I hear him speak.

"Unfinished business . . ." Owen gasps, his chest rising and falling unnaturally.

I tamp down on the hope bubbling inside me that he's finally breaking, but something about the way his head lolls to one side tells me Owen no longer has the strength to lie or resist. He's too far gone.

"What? Speak up, Owen," I cajole.

"T-the first hit . . . it failed . . ." His breath hitches, and I feel an unpleasant prickle at the base of my skull at having to wait with bated breath for his words.

I take a deep breath telling myself if the man could talk faster, he would.

"Come on, Owen, give me something fast so I can help you."

His head lols to the side. "Client c-came back. S-said the child. Didn't. Die."

My gaze flies to Sal, the shock on his face mirrors mine. Owen Novak tried to kill her eighteen years ago? I eye Owen skeptically. There's not much human left of him, but he can't be a day over twenty-five years old. He's simply not old enough to be the gunman from two decades ago. "You were the Brackendown road hitman?"

"It was Daddy, Emil N-Novak," he sputters deliriously. "He's . . . retired now."

Sal and I exchange another look, this time more horror than surprise. This is so much worse. The person after Addy is deranged enough to carry a grudge over two decades and truly means business. They won't stop until she's finally dead.

"I see." I fold my arms and lean against the metal table, where my instruments are laid out in neat lines, half of them caked with blood. "What happened to decorating torsos with dozens of small-caliber bullets at point-blank range, your usual fucked-up MO? Why did you use a bomb this time?"

He makes long choking sounds, and I'm surprised he can still talk. His wounds have stopped pouring out blood. Meaning his heart has stopped pumping effectively. "She . . . kinda h-hard to k-kill."

"True." A surge of dark pride overwhelms me. Addy survived half a dozen bullets at the age of five. While I've been shot a few times in my adult years, I've never taken six hits at once.

I decide to ask the next question since he's started talking. "So, who wants her dead so bad?"

Owen's breath hitches dangerously, and he sputters incoherently. "It . . . It . . ."

I lean closer to him, noting Sal instantly on high alert. I put up a finger to stop him. Owen can't do much right now.

"Who, Owen? Give me one name."

"P-p-pa . . ." He trails off again

"Who motherfucker!" I roar.

Owen gasps, then goes still.

"No, no, no. Not yet!" I jab him with the epinephrine.

His head falls back, his face a grotesque mask of blood and flesh, irises dilated in death.

It's over.

"Fuck!"

"Any point in CPR?" Sal suggests, already cutting his binds.

I look him over and sigh, shaking my head. "Nah. He's a mess. His ribs are broken, lung punctured . . . It's no use."

For a moment it looks like Sal still wants to go for it but then realizes it's pointless. Even if we restart his heart, he'd be brain-dead. Owen Novak will not be talking anymore.

"I should have gone slower," I mutter.

"And he wouldn't have broken," Sal says. "He's a ghost, Dante. Only you could make him even begin to spill his guts."

I toss the syringe and vial onto the metal table and head to the sink mounted on the far wall to wash off the blood and grime. A weary fatigue descends on me. This is one aspect of our lives that I loathe. But without it, we'd all be dead.

For the last thirteen years, every time I've taken a life, it's been to protect what I've sworn to protect: Blood. Duty. Honor.

And recently, a fiery redhead who embodies all of that.

Fuck, I needed that name. I have to find out who they are and stop them before it's too late.

We might have found a way to stop Orlando's rebellion, but I am still fighting on two fronts:

One enemy seen and the other unseen.

***

The smell of blood and fear still clings to my skin as I stride into the mansion. My muscles ache from the tension of the past week, but there's only one thought in my mind: Addy.

The marble foyer echoes with my footsteps, the surroundings a stark contrast to the grimy warehouse I've just left behind. Aydin appears from a side corridor, her expression brightening.

"*Signor* Dante," she greets, then adds without me having to ask. "Addy is by the pool with *Signora* Sophie."

My heart rate quickens at the mention of her name. It's been a week—a long, grueling week—and the need to see her, to touch her, is almost overwhelming. But I force myself to nod calmly.

"Thanks, Aydin. Any other news?"

She shakes her head. As much as I want to rush to the poolside, I know I need to shower first. The stench of violence clings to me, and I won't bring that to Addy.

I climb the grand staircase, my hand sliding along the polished banister. The house is quiet, but I can feel the undercurrent of tension. Everyone is forced to stand by while the Irish make moves, but we're on very high alert.

My suite door opens silently, and I'm immediately enveloped in Addy's sweet vanilla scent. My body responds instantly, a primal reaction I can't control.

I strip quickly and step into the shower. As hot water cascades over my skin, the tension from this gruesome afternoon ebbs away, replaced by a different kind of urgency.

Stepping out of the shower, I dry off quickly and pull on a pair of swim trunks. I catch a glimpse of myself in the mirror. My body is a map of tattoos, each one a reminder of the life I live. But for the first time, I wonder what Addy really sees when she looks at me. Do I still terrify her?

Would she be more comfortable if things were more nuanced, more hidden? If I *pretended* to be a good man like the devil she likes to call daddy? Did Benjamin choose a clean-skinned man like himself for her?

But there's no fucking point in what-ifs. Addy's getting me, and she'll have to get used to me.

No hiding, no shadows. Just all of me.

With a towel slung around my neck, I head toward the pool area. The faint scent of chlorine grows stronger with each step, bringing me closer to her. I can feel my heart rate picking up again, anticipation building with every moment.

A week has never felt so long.

CHAPTER THIRTY-THREE

Adele

I trace my finger along the cool, damp surface of my iced tea—which is more ice than tea—watching the condensation bead and roll down the crystal tumbler. Chlorine-scented air fills my lungs as I take a deep breath, my eyes wandering over the shimmering surface of the Olympic-sized pool. Sophie's rhythmic strokes break the water's stillness, her lithe form cutting through in a rapid yet graceful front crawl.

"Gosh, Addy, I feel like such a fraud," Kira mutters, stretching beside me on one of the white leather chaise lounges lined by the pool.

I take my eyes off Sophie and turn to face Kira fully. My friend's profile is set against the backdrop of gleaming tiles and tropical plants. The recessed lighting accentuates the furrow in her brow.

"Why do you say that, Kira?"

She pushes her slipping sunglasses back up her nose. "Because all my friends are refusing to book new gigs and going around like someone kicked their puppy to death while I'm there trying to remember to mourn, unable to tell them it's not that big of a deal."

"Really? Your friends are grieving for me?" Apart from Zedd, I don't really know Kira's DJ friends that well. I certainly didn't imagine they'd react that way to news of my demise.

It's been seven days since the world declared me dead in that car explosion and six days since Dante and Sal left for DC. I still can't believe how soon it took the Outfit to find out who he was and where to find the bomber.

Apart from scattered mentions of the incident on TV, I've had no way of knowing how the news has been received. I'm desperate to see what social media and my blog followers are saying about my death. But for now, my days are spent with Sophie and Aydin, while my nights are filled with longing.

When Kira, my last connection to the world I used to know, showed up this morning, smuggled in by Falzone and Aydin just before dawn, I'd nearly wept with joy.

Kira snorts. "Babe. You were blown to pieces right in front of them. Of course, they're traumatized and grieving."

I nod. "It's true what they say about friends and family, right? They are the ones that suffer."

Kira's lips turn down as she swirls her glass of cranberry punch, the ice cubes clinking softly. "I dunno. My best friend has never fake-died before, so I have no frame of reference here. I miss you, though."

"I know. Are things crazy back home?" I ask.

Kira shrugs and takes another sip of her drink. "Like you wouldn't believe. There are so many flowers, and the place smells like a rose garden. Condolences from neighbors I didn't even realize lived in our building. And don't get me started on Twitter. Zedd took it the hardest. I think he's doing a whole soundtrack dedicated to your memory."

I groan, my head falling back against the lounge chair. "Great. I'll be memorialized in EDM. And I spent a total of what, two hours with the guy?"

"I know," Kira grins. "I think when Zedd falls, he falls hard. But I could think of worse things. At least he's not a songwriter, so there won't be lyrics about how Adele O'Shea was torn to pieces."

"I suppose." And then, I think of Pietro again, the man who died in my place. "Kira, did you know Pietro Potenza personally?"

Kira shakes her head. "Contrary to what you may think, I hardly know these Capos. I only hear stories from my mom."

"What about Sal?"

"I'd never met him until a few weeks ago. He was the one who offered me the Resin job."

"Really? You two seemed like you'd known each other forever. Like childhood friends or something."

A blush stains Kira's cheeks. "Sal is the furthest thing from my friend."

"Kira? Are you—"

"No." She sighs as if she already knows what I'm about to ask her. "Am I wishing he'd stop trying to be friends and bang me, though? Fuck yeah."

I screech. "Kira!"

"What? Have you seen the man? He's insanely hot."

I stare at my friend like she's suddenly sprouted horns. "Yes, I know Sal is attractive, but Kira, I'm shocked you can tell. You have not seen him."

"Maybe not, but his voice is off the charts. Such a rich and layered texture to it. And he's so fucking smart. Like you have no idea how much of a turn-on that is."

She takes another quick sip of her drink. "Also, he also let me touch his face, so I got a good inkling what he looked like early on." Kira's voice drops to a whisper. "And, I, uh, I touched his hands too."

I stare at Kira as heat creeps up her cheeks. "Kira. You're blushing because you touched Sal's hands? Not his body. His hands."

She shifts in her chair and shrugs. "Well, Addy, if you don't get it . . . "

"Fucking forget it," I complete Kira's age-old mantra, laughing. It's her classic response when she's sick of explaining how she perceives something that she's never seen before, and I'm failing to picture it.

"But gosh, it must be . . . interesting." A part of me envies her heightened senses and her ability to feel so much more from physical touch and sounds.

"You have no idea, babes." She giggles as if in on a private joke.

As our laughter mingles with the gentle splashing of the pool, I watch Sophie again, marveling at her strength and endurance. I've lost count of the number of her laps—she must be on the fiftieth or sixtieth by now.

"She's so strong, isn't she?" I murmur, more to myself than to Kira.

"Sophie, you mean?" Kira nods in agreement. "Yeah. Makes you wonder what you might be like in the next few months?"

I down the rest of my drink. "Well, I already walk like a duck. So it's not hard to imagine what I'll be like when I'm as big as a whale."

Kira sputters into her drink then quickly wipes her mouth with the back of her hand. "Trust me, Addy, you don't walk like a duck. I've heard your footfalls, and . . . it's sexy."

I roll my eyes. "Yeah, right. I call bullshit on that, Kira."

Kira's shoulders shake with laughter. "Okay, fine. I'm blowing smoke. But I happen to know that Dante likes it."

The sound of his name triggers a familiar rush of longing and heat blooming in my chest. "Dante told you he likes how I walk?"

Kira leans back in her chair, crossing her legs. "No. Dante doesn't tell anyone anything. Sal does, though. He thinks Dante is obsessed with you. Like dark and twisted, I'll burn the whole world to keep you safe, obsessed." She pauses, her head tilting to the side. "Speaking of, how do you like it? Being here, I mean?"

I take in a deep breath, the scent of chlorine mingling with the fragrance of nearby orchids. I tilt my head back to watch the rays of the afternoon sun streaming through the skylights, casting a warm glow on the polished marble floors. My gaze then drifts to the glass walls that look out to the manicured gardens and to the gallery above the entrance that provides a breathtaking view of the poolside from the mansion's second floor.

"It's unbelievable," I marvel. "The Vitellis sure know how to treat a girl to luxury."

Kira nods, her dark hair catching the light. "Good. Because I don't think your baby daddy will ever let you go, Addy. Just saying." She adds with a note of finality.

I swallow the lump in my throat. Dante has made that fact crystal clear. I'm never going back. The thought of that triggers a panic inside me every time I think about it. "Speaking of daddies, has . . . has my dad been in touch?" I ask, keeping my voice carefully neutral.

Kira's brow furrows, her fingers drumming against her glass. "Surprisingly, not yet."

"You don't think he knows we came to Chicago together, do you?"

Kira frowns in thought. "I don't think so. Otherwise, he would have contacted me to find out what happened . . . for closure, you know?"

Or that he already knows I didn't die. My heart lurches with hope that my father has realized that I'm alive, so the Mob won't wage war against us . . . I catch myself immediately.

Us? Really? Since when did you become a member of the Outfit?

"There's something else, Addy." Kira traces the edge of the nearby stool and then puts her cocktail down. "Tommy Martelli is dead."

"What?" I sit up straight. The lounge chair creaks under my sudden movement.

Kira's hazel eyes are fixed somewhere over my left shoulder. "Why're you surprised? I told you he was a dead man."

A chill runs through me despite the warm sun on my skin. "Did . . . Dante kill him?"

He didn't say anything to me. Not that I expect him to come home bearing a list of everyone he's un-alived.

Thing is, I wouldn't mind if he did.

"No, Dante didn't have to lift a finger because Tommy died of natural causes. A heart attack. During sex, no less." Kira's voice is steady and matter-of-fact, but her face has an assessing look.

"Oh, come on Kira," I scoff. "You expect me to believe he just keeled over and died?"

"No, I expect you to believe that he had an autopsy." Kira's face remains impassive, but there's a slight quirk on her lips.

As the pieces click into place, I feel a strange mix of horror and dark fascination.

I tilt my head slightly, arching an eyebrow. "Autopsy huh? I'm sure they found he had clogged arteries and leaky valves. And he also smoked like a chimney. He also had traces of cocaine in his blood. I bet he'd just gotten high on coke and then fucked a twenty-year-old hooker. A classic case of a heart attack waiting to happen."

"Yep. We can't argue with a coroner's report." Kira's face breaks into a beaming smile.

"Just like you can't argue with my obituary," I murmur.

The same way you can't argue with gravestones and family photos.

"Exactly." Kira nods solemnly. "My tribute to you was particularly moving, if I do say so myself."

There's a beat of silence before we start to laugh.

Maybe Dante is right. Maybe this is my world, and I just haven't been living in it.

We're still chuckling when the rhythmic splashing ceases as Sophie pulls herself out of the pool, water streaming off her athletic form.

Her black one-piece clings to her curves, emphasizing the swell of her baby bump. She pads across the cool tiles, leaving wet footprints in her wake, then reaches for a plush towel from a nearby rack and settles onto the edge of the lounge chair next to mine.

I shift on my lounge chair, the leather creaking softly as I prop myself up on my elbows. "Sixty laps, and you're not even breathing hard," I say, watching as she dries off.

She leans back, supporting her weight on her arms, and turns her face toward me with a smile. "Says the woman who goes on a five-mile walk every morning."

I laugh, dropping back onto my chair and draping an arm over my eyes. "That's just to keep my muscles from stiffening up. Doctor's orders."

After a few minutes, the barman approaches. "*Signora* Vitelli," he says warmly, "your usual?"

Sophie sits up slightly, smiling at the bartender. "You know me too well, Diego. Yes, please."

Diego nods and retreats to the bar. Sophie, Kira, and I chat idly, the conversation flowing easily between us until Diego returns, carrying a silver tray balanced expertly in one hand. He places it on the small table between our lounges with a flourish. It's laden with an array of exotic fruits and a gleaming curved knife.

"*Grazie,* Diego," Sophie says, reaching for the knife. It's our daily routine now; her laps, followed by the platter of fruits while I pepper her with questions and get a little more spellbound by this life.

Sophie and Kira continue to chat, but I don't hear them anymore. I'm too engrossed with what Sophie is doing with the knife. She spins the knife this way and that, then peels and slices a dragonfruit with an expertise that doesn't strike me as natural. Normal people shouldn't be able to handle knives like that. You should need to study under a guru for that kind of skill.

"Coming, Mama!" My friend rises from her chair, her smart cane unfolding with a soft click. She navigates around the chaise lounges, the cane tapping rhythmically against the floor. Kira always uses her cane as an extra precaution when she's outside the house. She pauses by my side to squeeze my hand briefly, then does the same to Sophie's shoulder before continuing toward the house.

As Kira's footsteps fade, Sophie turns to face me fully, weighing a large mango in her palm. "Do you miss your old life, Addy?"

I answer without thinking, "Yes," but then I have to ask myself what exactly my old life was. A job I tolerated, a family built on lies, and a constant feeling of not quite fitting in. I realize with a start that none of it was real.

"I miss my blog," I admit more truthfully. "And I wish I could confront my dad. But the rest? Not really. It feels surreal, like waking up from a dream I didn't know I was having."

"You'll be alright, Addy." Her voice rings with the same conviction Dante exudes.

"Sophie, Dante told me about Orlando De Luca," I blurt out. "He's supposed to be my real father."

Sophie's hands pause, the knife hovering mid-slice, then she resumes her work. "And how does that make you feel?"

When the only father I've ever known turns out to be something completely different, I'm bound to think fathers are overrated. Still, there's a desire in me to know who I really am and where I come from. Unsure of how to answer, I just shake my head and watch the wicked-looking blade dance across the fruit, mesmerized by Sophie's dexterity.

"Are you good with . . . other weapons too?" I deflect, because asking if she knows how to use a knife just sounds silly.

A small smile plays on Sophie's lips. "I am," she simply says, a wealth of unspoken words in that admission.

"Like guns?"

Sophie sets the fruit down and faces me. "Those too."

My heart races as I voice the question that's been burning inside me. "How do you do it, Sophie? How do you cope with loving . . . being married to someone like Nico?"

Sophie's smile is almost relieved, as if she's been waiting for this question. "At first, it felt like I was being dragged back into the hell I was running from. But once I stopped running, I realized something crucial." She leans forward, her voice firm. "Nico is my home, Addy."

Wow. I've never quite heard it put that way before. "And what about your family? Do they approve of your husband?"

Sophie's eyes twinkle. "Oh, they love Nico." She pauses for a beat, her smile getting wider. "Or should I say, they would love to hate him."

"But they don't?"

She shakes her head. "No, they don't. Well, except for maybe my brother, Cade. I think he truly hates Nico's guts." She takes a slice of her mango and chews thoughtfully while I gape, intrigued by her family dynamics.

"Your brother hates Nico?"

"He hates Dante too. But the feeling is quite mutual, so they're all on the same page, which, when you think about it, isn't such a bad thing."

"Is it because of who—what Nico and Dante are?"

Sophie inclines her head as if to gauge my reaction to her next words. "That's only half of it. It's mainly because of who Cade is. He's an FBI agent. Specializes in dismantling organized criminal syndicates."

My eyebrows fly to my hairline, and my mouth opens in an 'O.'

"And how the hell does that work for family gatherings?"

"It doesn't work," Sophie chuckles. "Put them in a room together, and within seconds, it lights up like the Fourth of July. They think they want to kill each other when what they really want to do is hug each other so bad."

I huff out a nervous laugh. "That's interesting. But are Nico and Dante . . . safe? From government scrutiny, I mean."

Sophie just winks and says cryptically. "As someone who has loved and lived with each of those men, respectively, I can promise you that behind the guns and badges, they're exactly the same people." She pauses, reconsidering her words. "Actually, Cade might be worse than them."

My brows arch in surprise. "What do you mean worse?"

Sophie sighs. "Why spoil the surprise when you'll get to meet him yourself soon enough?"

Sophie has just opened up a whole can of questions about who her brother is, but before I can launch into it, the pool's ambient music shifts, transitioning from soft jazz to a familiar heavy metal rock.

Sophie's eyes light up, her head bobbing slightly to the beat. "Ah," she murmurs, smiling. "Sounds like Dante's back."

"How do you know that?"

As if summoned by her words, I feel a shift in the air, a prickle along my skin. I turn toward the door, my breath catching in my throat.

Dante appears in the doorway, tall, broad, and imposing. His damp hair falls loosely, framing his gorgeous face, while his torso remains bare save for a towel slung around his neck. His body—God, his body—a mesmerizing tapestry of corded muscles and ink, looks like a sin I'd gladly commit.

"Adele," he growls softly, his voice carrying across the poolside. My name rolling off his tongue feels like a long, slow lick between my thighs.

The world narrows, and everything fades except for him.

CHAPTER THIRTY-FOUR

Dante

The scent of chlorine reaches me before I see the water, mingling with the fragrance of tropical flowers from the conservatory. I pause at the entrance, taking a deep breath. Then, squaring my shoulders, I step out into the sunlight, my eyes immediately searching for her.

She's lounging on a chaise, engrossed in conversation with Sophie. For a moment, I just watch her, drinking in the sight of her voluptuous curves in a tiny blue bikini. Then, as if sensing my presence, she looks up.

The smile that spreads across her face is like a sunrise, brilliant and warm. And then she's on her feet in an instant, all pretense of cool abandoned as she runs toward me, her steps perfectly uneven.

I open my arms just as she reaches me, and suddenly she's there—warm, soft, real. Her arms wind around my neck, her legs around my waist, our bodies molding together like two parts of a whole. The scent of her—sunscreen, chlorine, and vanilla—fills my nostrils, making my head spin.

"Dante," she breathes, her voice muffled against my neck. I tighten my arms around her, one hand sliding into her hair, cradling her head.

"I fucking missed you, baby," I murmur, my lips brushing against her temple, then my tongue sweeps inside her mouth, and I groan as her taste seeps onto my tongue. One hand leaves the curve of her ass to find the knot of skin on her hip, and her breath stutters as she writhes against me.

A throaty laugh makes us break apart. Sophie is standing now, one hand resting on her swollen belly, an amused smirk on her face.

"And that's my cue to leave," she says, her eyes twinkling. "I still haven't recovered from the last time I had to go soak my eyes in bleach after one of your cuddles."

Addy laughs, the sound vibrating against my chest, but she doesn't let go of me. I feel a grin tugging at my own lips.

"Sorry, sis," I say, not feeling sorry at all.

She waves a hand dismissively, already turning to leave. "Just try to keep it PG-13 until I and the babies are out of earshot, yeah?"

As Sophie's footsteps fade away, I turn my attention back to Addy.

"How was . . . work?" Her green eyes are locked on mine, filled with avid curiosity and a blatant hunger. My attempt at a teasing reply instantly dies on my lips.

Instead, I say, "Work was good. Win some . . . lose some."

"Wanna talk about it?"

I huff out a surprised chuckle. "Do I want to talk about it? Sure. Which part do you want? Bright and shiny or dark and twisted?"

I cup her face in my hands, thumbs brushing over her cheekbones. She leans into my touch, her eyes fluttering closed for a moment. When they open again, they're on fire.

"What if I said twisted?"

Well, then. Without a word, I step backward, walking us into the shallow edge of the pool. The warm water envelops us, and Addy's legs tighten around my waist as I wade deeper into the pool.

Her skin is slick against mine, her breasts pressing against my chest with each breath. I can feel her heartbeat, or maybe it's mine—they seem to have synchronized, creating a rhythm that drowns out everything else.

"Ask me anything you want to know," I say then capture her lips with mine.

The kiss is hungry and desperate, a week's worth of longing poured into it. Addy responds eagerly, her fingers tangling in my hair, nails scraping lightly against my scalp. A low groan of pleasure escapes me, the sound getting lost in her mouth.

When we come up for air, we're both breathing heavily. Addy's cheeks are flushed, her lips swollen, and I've never seen anything more beautiful. I press my forehead against hers, content for a moment to just hold her, to breathe her in.

But I can see the questions in her eyes, the curiosity that's always there. She bites her lower lip, a gesture I've come to recognize as a prelude to a difficult question.

"So," she begins, her voice soft but steady. "You and Sal found the bomber, right?"

I feel my body tense involuntarily as I realize that she really does want to know. Something wild and uncontained takes flight in my chest.

Here I am, forcing myself to be patient with her and not scare her, and yet to my delight, she seems eager to lose herself in me.

"We found him," I say, keeping my voice neutral.

Her fingers trace patterns on my shoulders, a soothing gesture that contrasts with the intensity of her gaze. "And you managed to . . . talk to him?"

I almost laugh at her choice of words. "In a manner of speaking, yes," I reply, watching her face carefully.

She nods as if confirming something to herself. "How long did the 'talk' last?"

I sigh, closing my eyes for a moment. When I open them, Addy is still watching me, waiting. "About three hours," I admit.

Her eyes widen slightly, but she doesn't look away. "So then he died of a broken heart?" she asks, her tone making it clear it's not really a question.

"Excuse me?"

"I mean, you tortured him for information until his heart gave out," she says. It's not an accusation, just a statement of fact.

I incline my head, studying her. There's no disgust in her eyes, no fear. Just a calm acceptance that both relieves and worries me. "I'm concerned with your thought process here, Addy," I say, my brow furrowing.

She shrugs, the movement causing small waves to lap against us. "I can't work, I can't blog. All that morbidity has to go somewhere."

Her words hang between us for a moment. Then, to my surprise, she continues, "So, is that . . . is that what you do? For work, I mean."

I can't help the laugh that escapes me. "Did you not hear when I said bright and shiny? I have a life beyond killing people, baby."

She raises an eyebrow, clearly not satisfied with that answer. "So what exactly do you do for the Outfit then?"

"I'm surprised you've not pumped it out of Sophie yet, what with your daily gossip."

She giggles and slaps me playfully. "We don't gossip about you."

"Really?" I shift her in my arms, moving us to the edge of the pool where I can sit on the underwater ledge and keep her in my lap. "What do you talk about then?"

"Everything else."

"I see." I slowly loosen the tie of her bikini until her breasts spill into my palm, gratified when she doesn't bat an eyelash at being half-naked outside.

"I run a company called Voltex. It's a company based in Detroit that manufactures lithium-ion batteries for electric cars."

What I don't tell her is that half of Voltex is now a smoking pile of ruins as of half an hour ago, thanks to the Irish Mob.

Addy's eyes go wide, her mouth forming a perfect 'O' of surprise, and then her lower lip disappears between her teeth when I softly stroke a rosy nipple.

"What, did you think I spent my days lurking in dark alleys and mugging people?"

She chuckles, the sound ending in a moan when I pinch her nipple. Still, I can see the curiosity burning in her green eyes warring with her growing desire.

Then apparently making up her mind about what she wants more, she drags my hand down into the water and between her legs. I don't need to be invited twice. Nudging the crotch of her bikini to the side, I slide two fingers inside her hot depth. Addy buries her face in my neck and moans as I slowly finger her.

To my surprise, she continues to quiz me. "And . . . ah, the other gritty aspects . . . drugs? Prostitution? Gambling?"

I smirk, "Oh yeah, we've got those too, but that's your daddy's forte."

When I feel her small teeth playfully sink into my neck, my cock throbs in response. I stand and walk us to the smoother edge of the pool, then crowd her against the wall.

"Be serious," she chides.

"I am. Your daddy is the drugs and narcotics expert," I say deliberately, drawing out the word 'daddy'.

Addy still hasn't asked me anything about Orlando since I dropped that bomb. Instead, she's drawn closer to me. Which tells me she's still reeling. The more overwhelmed Addy is, the more she seeks physical outlets for her confusion.

Not that I'm complaining about how Addy is dealing with her trauma. I'm loving it. I'm also determined to give her the emotional space she needs to process this.

She'll ask me about Orlando when she's good and ready.

"The Outfit is a diverse group of companies and businesses," I tell her. "Some are illegal, but we're working on phasing them out."

Addy nods slowly, her fingers tracing over the muscles of my back. "But the violence . . . that's not going away, is it?"

I sigh, wishing I could lie to her and shield her from this reality. But I can't do it. So I meet her searching gaze head-on. "No, it's not. Until the end of time, we will always be a target. Defending the people we love is the hallmark of the Mafia, *tesoro*."

"The people you love," she repeats, her voice a low murmur.

"Person I love. You."

"You love me?"

"What do you think?"

She drops her face to my neck and resumes her slow torture, biting and licking until, unable to take more, I reach between us and line my cock against her entrance. I cover her mouth with my hand and slam home, swallowing her soft cry. I don't let up until she's convulsing around me.

As she comes down from her orgasm, I sense a residual tension in her, and I know there's more on her mind. But I can't talk to her while she's driving me insane, so I reach behind me to take her legs from around my waist, and I pull out of her, but she holds fast.

"Dante. I'm . . . not done yet," she protests.

I smile. She likes it hard. "I'll give you what you want after you tell me what's on your mind."

She looks up at me, worrying her lower lip. "Oh, I just want to ask you something. I dunno what you'll think of it."

I tense. "If it's about Benjamin O'Shea—"

She shakes her head, her damp curls bouncing. "No, it's nothing like that."

"What is it then?"

"Dante," she says, her voice steady, "could you teach me to defend myself?"

My cock jumps with excitement, easily giving away how I feel on the subject. But I tell myself what I'm thinking can't be what Addy means.

"You were taught martial arts, weren't you?" I ask, careful to keep my tone neutral.

She shrugs. "I tried to learn. Jiu-Jitsu and Krav Maga. But there was only so much I could do. I'm not that strong, not as fast, my hip—"

"Baby." I put my finger against her lips. With my other hand, I start to trace arcs across the sensitive scar on her hip. "You're as strong as you need to be."

She shivers in response but presses on. "Anyway, those skills are useless where it really counts."

"Where does it really count?" I prompt, waiting for her to explain what she means, although the dark part of me already knows where she's heading and is leaping for joy.

"Dante, most threats don't look like me. They look like . . ." She trails off.

"Me. Big, armed, dangerous," I finish for her.

"Exactly. I can't take down someone like you."

"Not naturally, no," I affirm. "But you don't need to know how to kick my ass, Addy. You only need to know how to kill me."

Her eyes go wide. And for the first time it's not fear I see in them. It's intrigue. And then dismay. "I can't use a gun. Or a knife, like Sophie."

My smile turns wicked, and my arousal is starting to ache like a wound. I need to fuck her again. Hard. "It's easier than you think. All you need is your mind."

"Teach me then."

I cup her face in my hands, searching her eyes. "You're sure?"

Addy nods, her gaze unwavering. "I am. I don't want to be helpless anymore. I want to be able to protect myself . . . and the people I love."

"The people you love?" I tease back.

She nods. "You."

A bone-deep joy spreads through me, warming me more than the sun ever could. Still with her legs wrapped around me, I stand up in the pool, water cascading off us. "Let's go."

"Now?" Addy asks, brows arched in surprise.

"Right fucking now, baby," I growl, already walking us out of the pool.

CHAPTER THIRTY-FIVE

Adele

"Dante . . . please," I beg incoherently, my spread thighs tense and shaky with need, my moans drowned out by the strains of Vivaldi pouring from the speakers.

I'm sprawled on the floor of the gym, back arching off the soft carpet, my hands cupping my breasts and pinching hard on my nipples in a bid to relieve the ache building in my core.

The featherlight strokes of Dante's tongue on my sensitive folds only stoke my lust. My hips rise eagerly against his mouth, a plea for more of him.

It's been this way for the last three weeks. My early morning walks have been replaced with intense workout sessions with Dante. He spends half an hour pushing my body to its endurance limit, then the next hour teaching me to tackle him. By the time I'm at my wits' end, he'll show me a new skill. Something innocuous yet deadly.

A crushing swipe at the Adam's apple. A jab into the eye or the angle of the jaw. Breaking the nasal bone just right. Targeting the intercostal spaces when stabbing at the heart with an ice pick. Anything could be a weapon, including my body. I've started to look at mundane things and see the deadliness in them.

By the time we're done training, my mind is full of dark possibilities, and my body is overwhelmed with pent-up desire. Sometimes he fucks me in the shower, but most of the time, we don't make it that far.

Like today.

My hand grows a mind of its own and starts to wander down my belly toward my neglected clit, only to freeze at Dante's curt command.

"I told you to keep your hands on your breasts." He raises his head to look at me, his eyes almost black with lust, lips glistening with my juices. Deliberately, his tongue darts out to slide across his full bottom lip. The sight of him this way is beyond provocation.

"Baby. Dante . . . please. I need—"

Before I can finish, Dante flips me over onto my belly, pulls me to my knees, and starts to spank me.

That . . . I needed that.

"Ah!" I cry out with each stinging blow. I can feel my wetness dripping down my thighs. He can, too, because he pauses, spanking me, and catches the wayward trickle with his tongue, then licks up from the middle of my thigh all the way back to my pussy.

Only he doesn't stop there. His warm, wicked tongue continues until it reaches the pucker of my ass, and he starts to eat me there too.

My moans get louder as my pussy starts to clench in need. Shamelessly, I spread my shaky legs wider to give him more room. "Fuck," I sigh. "Please more."

"My dirty girl wants me in here, don't you?"

"Yes, God, yes."

Dante sinks his teeth into the soft round curve of my ass, making me jump and shiver. Then he gathers my wetness on his fingers and starts to stroke the tight bundle of nerves between my ass cheeks. My ass flowers open for him and he presses both fingers deep inside me.

I feel full, stretched tight around his fingers, pleasure curling deep inside me. He thrusts his fingers hard and fast, faster than he usually does, and I tuck my mouth against my arm to keep from alerting the entire left wing to what Dante is doing to me, although I'm pretty sure by now everyone is fully aware of what goes on daily in this gym.

Just when I think he'll finally fuck my pussy and let me come, he spits on my ass and adds a third finger. "Oh fuck. Dante!" The stretching is unbelievable and the emptiness in my pussy worsens, an ache demanding relief now.

"Be good, relax and take it, and maybe I'll fuck your tight ass," Dante rasps against my skin.

My heart slams hard against my ribcage. He's going for it. After all this time of teasing and ass play, he's finally going to do it.

I nod frantically, canting my hips higher and whimpering with anticipation of how good he'll feel in my ass. How much he'll stretch me.

And then his fingers are gone, and he turns me over onto my back while he remains on his haunches between my spread thighs. Confusion furrows my brows, but he rasps, "I want to look deep into your eyes when I take your ass, Addy. I want you to see me as you ache for me."

I nod, lost in his gaze, as he takes hold of his length and slides it back and forth along my drenched pussy. When his cock is fully covered in my slippery juices, he lifts my hips from the floor onto his thighs, presses the fat head to the bud of my ass, and slowly starts to push in. My fingers dig reflexively into the soft carpet as everything inside me tightens. He's bigger than anything I've ever felt back there.

"Ah, Dante," I groan.

He stills. "Tell me how that feels, baby."

"Dante." I babble again, shutting my eyes tight against the pain and pleasure of the invasion, unable to form more words. But my body speaks eloquently as I involuntarily sink down on him, taking another inch of his cock.

"Ah, God!" He's too hard, too thick. Too fucking big, but I want him too much to stop.

Finally, I feel his balls on my ass, and I know he's slid his entire length inside me. The heat and incredible fullness make my breath catch. As there doesn't seem to be enough oxygen, my mouth opens to drag in gulps of air.

Drool gathers in my mouth, but I can't for the life of me figure out what to do with it beyond concentrating on breathing in and out and trying not to lose my mind in pain and pleasure.

I do lose my mind anyway because Dante starts to move.

He withdraws a little, then pushes back in, as much as my tightness would allow, but as the speed and depth of his thrusts increase, my ass, now a ring of pure fire around his large cock, sends bolts of panic to my brain.

My hapless pussy, on the other hand, contracts around nothing, begging for the same treatment my ass is getting. My brain seems lost between those signals of intense pleasure and the biting edge of pain, and all I can do is hold on for dear life and . . . feel.

Dante also looks tortured, his mouth open, moans mingling with mine, and his face drawn into a tight mask of pleasure even as he continues to drive in and out of me with a singular focus.

"Adele, every single part of you is mine. Say it," he commands.

"I'm yours," I babble. "Oh, Dante, I've always been yours."

And then he's fucking me even harder, deep strokes, driving me completely insane. My juices flow freely, dripping back between my ass cheeks and coating his cock with more than enough lubrication to let him fuck me hard and deep.

I feel my climax dancing just beyond reach. Teasing me with the promise of explosive pleasure. I want it more than I want my next breath.

He transfers both my wrists to one of his then finally, finally, slips his thumb between us and starts to stroke circles around my clit.

"Oh my God," I moan, my lids fluttering shut and eyes rolling back. I can no longer keep my eyes on his. And then my orgasm is crashing against me like an avalanche. I scream and buck as my pleasure takes hold and doesn't let go, suspending me in an endless vortex. "Fuck! Dante."

"Addy!" Dante growls as his thrusts lose rhythm and gain more force. He slams into me a few more times, his cock swelling. Still, he doesn't stop flicking my clit, and I don't stop coming.

And then, with a shout and a violent shudder, his thumb freezes on my clit, and he starts emptying into me. Hot, thick jets of cum spurt into my ass and spill out.

I come down slowly, languidly, basking in the wild intensity of my anal orgasm.

"Are you okay, *tesoro?*"

My body feels like lead, every muscle screaming in a delicious sort of agony.

"My ass might as well be on fire. And I don't think I could sit or walk in the next century. But other than that, I loved it. I'd like to go again, actually."

"Really! Right now?" A few more inches and his eyebrows might collide with his widow's peak.

I bite my lip and shrug. "What, like you can't go? You're insatiable, Dante."

He rears back to look at me in disbelief, yet, as we stare at each other, I feel his cock twitch in response, then start to get harder. I knew it.

He laughs, the delicious sound rumbling through me. "You have no fucking idea, Addy. But," he pauses then whispers against my ear. "Red Wine."

He withdraws from me, then drops gentle kisses on my collarbone, up my neck, and finally, my temple. When he doesn't make another move to touch me elsewhere, I realize what he's done.

"Did you just . . . safeword on me?"

He strokes his fingers across my face and down my neck, over my breasts before coming to rest on my still flat lower belly. "Someone clearly needs to learn their limits."

I roll my eyes. "Are you even supposed to do that?"

He stands, scoops me up from the floor then heads toward the shower. "Not sure. Why don't we check with the local police to see if that's allowed?"

I smile into his neck, and then something occurs to me. "Speaking of, have you ever been arrested?"

He laughs. "That's like asking ice if it's ever been cold. I'm the black sheep of the family. What do you think?"

"I didn't think a crime family could have a black sheep."

"Oh, trust me. I'm the only one of my living relatives who's seen the inside of a prison cell."

Dante's strong arms encircle me as he steps into the shower. With a gentle twist of his wrist, warm water cascades over us, the steady patter of droplets against tile filling the air. Steam rises and envelopes us in a comforting cocoon.

He settles onto the teak shower bench, cradling me in his lap. The water sluices over my aching body, and I let out a soft moan as the heat begins to work its magic on my sore muscles.

"What were you arrested for?" I ask, my words starting to slur with exhaustion.

His soap-slick fingers work on my lower back, kneading the tender flesh with just the right amount of pressure. "Uh, let's see. Dangerous driving. Assault. Drug possession."

I almost purr as his skilled hands move up to my shoulders, working out knots I didn't even know I had. The scent of sandalwood from the shower gel mingles with the steam, creating an intoxicating aroma. "Sounds like you were out of control."

"Pretty much. I was a bit different. Neurodiverse. Which was not an excuse to be an asshole kid."

"When did you stop?" I murmur, my eyes fluttering closed. The combination of the warm spray, his gentle massage, and the lingering endorphins from our session has me floating in a haze of contentment.

"Stop what?"

I yawn. "Being an asshole."

Dante pauses his ministrations, "Who says I stopped?" He teases, his words almost lost in the rhythmic sound of falling water.

"Dante, I'm serious—"

"Everything changed after I took the vows at eighteen. I suddenly had more responsibility. I've been on the straight and narrow since then."

"Straight and narrow my ass," I snort.

"Well, you'd know, wouldn't you." He kneads my ass for emphasis, and I giggle, drowsy with contented sleep.

***

The soft whir of the Fortress' library's climate control system cycles off, breaking my concentration. I take a deep breath and stretch languidly on the beanbag, feeling the satisfying pop of my spine, as I fill my lungs with Dante's rich scent. I can't resist grabbing the neckline of his T-shirt and inhaling again.

I'm surprised by how refreshed I feel, considering the intense workout and play we had today. Contrary to what I thought, I'm sitting and walking fine. I fell asleep in Dante's arms during the shower massage and woke up just as he was leaving for work.

I didn't bat an eyelash when he announced he was going to have a 'heart to heart' with Tommy Martelli's sons. My shock capacity has diminished considerably in the past few weeks.

Besides, I figured since he didn't use the word 'chat', it bodes well for the Martelli boys. So, I kissed him goodbye and found my way to this crazy, cozy nook he created for me.

The soft glow of the reading lamp beside me illuminates stacks of books, yellowed newspaper clippings, and manila folders filled with case files. My heart clenches again as I recall the way Dante casually showed me this reading nook.

"I had the cobwebs and mothballs cleaned out in this section just in case you want to start living here," he'd said simply while I squealed like a schoolgirl and leaped on him.

I inhale again, savoring the comforting scent of old paper and ink. The Vitelli library's crime section is far more exciting than any library I've visited, boasting rare first editions and even confidential files that I'm pretty sure aren't meant for civilian eyes. It's a treasure trove that would make any crime enthusiast drool.

Refocusing on the journal in my lap, I try to lose myself once again in the chilling profile of the late sixties' Zodiac Killer, but my mind drifts yet again.

Thoughts of restarting my blog have been nagging at me for days, and every time I come here, they sink their talons a little deeper. I'm thinking I could revive the Scarlett Holmes blog, not as herself but as an anonymous fan who is so invested in her work that they want to keep it going since Scarlett went AWOL.

It's risky, especially since folks at work, and I'm pretty sure Benjamin O'Shea, know I'm the author, but the familiar rush of adrenaline at the prospect of impersonating myself is hard to ignore.

I'm so engrossed in my internal debate that I barely register the soft knock at first. Looking up, I see Aydin's head poking around the heavy oak shelving, her expression a mix of apology and amusement at finding me sprawled on the plush oversized beanbag, surrounded by a fortress of books and papers.

"Sorry to interrupt," she says quietly, "but I have a note for you. From Dante."

"Dante?"

"Yes. One of his men just dropped it off now."

I check the time again and see it's almost midnight. And then I'm tearing through the black envelope.

Tesoro. I have to go to Detroit. There's been another fire at Voltex but it's nothing to worry about.

I will tell you this, though. Yer da is startin' to do me fuckin' head right in. Still, I'll try my best not to kill him. Yet.

I laugh out loud at his deliberate Irish brogue. Sometimes, I forget Dante speaks the language as well as a few others. I reread the paragraph, but this time register the subtle but chilling warning.

Of course, Benjamin couldn't have set the fire to Voltex himself. Dante just slipped his name in there because he wants me to know what could happen.

The war is starting to escalate. It's almost inevitable that those two would clash at some point.

The question is, how would I feel if Dante killed Benjamin O'Shea?

The fact that I'd take that scenario a million times over the reverse somewhat settles things in my mind about how I'd feel about it.

Taking a breath, I continue reading.

I should be done here by Saturday. Looking forward to getting you slick and ready for . . .

I turn over the note, my heart rate kicking up.

. . . our baby's first scan.

Ti amo. DV

"Jerk," I murmur, a goofy smile on my lips, hand cradling my flat belly. Beyond taking my vitamins every day, I conveniently forgot about everything else. Like scans and antenatal classes and baby names. I've blocked out everything else apart from Dante and our overwhelming connection.

Because if I haven't come to terms with who I am, how can I tell my baby who she is?

And now it's getting all too real. Come Saturday I'll see my baby for the first time and face the fact that she's a living, breathing human that belongs to Dante.

And me. Although that's the part I'm still working on.

CHAPTER THIRTY-SIX

Adele

The rhythmic thud of my fists against the punching bag echoes through the empty gym, a steady beat that matches the pounding of my heart. Sweat trickles down my back, soaking into the fabric of my sports bra.

I throw another jab, feeling the satisfying impact reverberate up my arm. My muscles ache, protesting the repetitive motion, but I don't stop. I can't stop.

It's been five days since Dante left for Detroit, and the physical exertion is the only thing keeping me sane. Well, that and the constant reminder that I'm going to see the spawn of Chicago's most dangerous today. Talk about life goals.

The gym is eerily quiet without Dante's presence. No low, encouraging murmurs as he corrects my form. No playful banter as we spar. Just the sound of my labored breathing and the creaking of the chain that suspends the punching bag. I knew it would be hard, but I didn't expect to miss him this much.

Or resent being off-grid this deeply. When he gets back, we're so going to have a chat about this arrangement.

"It was fun while it lasted, *Signore,* but playing dead is no longer working for me," I imagine saying to him.

I execute a particularly vicious right hook and a sudden wave of dizziness washes over me. The room tilts alarmingly, the polished wood floor seeming to rise up to meet me. I stumble, catching myself on the edge of the bag. The rough leather scrapes against my palm as I lean into it, trying to steady myself.

And then the now-familiar craving for ice hits me out of nowhere. It's an all-consuming need, as if every cell in my body is crying out for it. I can almost taste it—the cold, crisp sensation as it melts on my tongue. My mouth waters at the thought, even as frustration bubbles up inside me.

Despite the pregnancy vitamins lined up neatly on my bathroom counter, this craving won't leave me alone. It's always there, lurking at the edges of my consciousness, ready to pounce at the slightest moment of weakness.

I rest my forehead against the punching bag, trying to catch my breath. My heart is racing, whether from exertion or the sudden onset of the craving, I'm not sure. Probably both.

I was hoping Dante would be back in time for our workout this morning. Thanks to being dead, he hasn't contacted me again since he left, and I have only Nico's constant reassurance that he's fine.

I hate not having access to him.

The craving intensifies, pushing all other thoughts aside. It's a physical ache now, impossible to ignore. I give in, unwrapping my hands with trembling fingers. The tape clings to my skin, sticky with sweat, and I have to peel it off slowly.

Breaking my routine feels wrong, like I'm admitting defeat. But the need for ice overrides everything else. I head for the kitchen, my bare feet silent on the cool marble floors.

The halls of the mansion are quiet, the early morning sun casting long shadows through the tall windows. Since that first morning when we had breakfast, I've found that everyone pretty much does their own thing in the morning and lunchtime and that morning's attempt at breakfast was exactly as Dante called it: A sham.

As I enter the kitchen, I find Aydin standing at the corner of the island. She's bent over and sniffing but straightens as soon as she realizes she's no longer alone.

"Aydin?"

"Addy... um, *Signorina* O'She—" she stutters, her usually steady and unreadable voice trembling.

"Aydin, please, just Addy," I reply, suddenly self-conscious of my sweat-soaked workout clothes and messy hair.

Without a word, she grabs a glass and teabag, pours some hot water, then darts to the fridge for some ice, and the soft whoosh of the door opens, filling the silence. She returns with a glass mug, condensation already beading on its surface.

"Cold tea on the rocks," she says, offering it to me with a smile. Her eyes are clear and dry, almost as if I imagined her crying earlier.

I accept it gratefully. The ice clinks against my teeth as I take a long sip, the cool liquid soothing my parched throat. It's not quite the same as crunching on pure ice, but it helps take the edge off the craving.

"Thank you," I murmur, leaning against the counter. "Are you okay, Aydin?"

Aydin nods, turning back to resume polishing the marble counter, and I can't shake the feeling that something is wrong.

I watch her work, struck by the easy familiarity with which she moves through the space. It occurs to me that I know very little about Kira's mother, who seems to be everywhere at once in the mansion.

"How long have you been with the family, Aydin?" I ask.

She pauses to look up at me. "Fifteen years."

Wow. Fifteen years. That means Aydin must have known Dante since he was sixteen. When he was 'the black sheep,' as he said. Aydin must have watched Dante grow from a rowdy teenager into the man he is now. She probably knows Dante better than anyone.

"You must know Dante very well," I say, trying to keep my voice casual.

Aydin's lips twitch in a ghost of a smile. "I've known *Signor* Dante for a long time, yes."

I take another sip of my tea, the ice cubes clinking against the glass. "I miss him," I blurt out, surprising myself with the admission, but I immediately regret my words.

Should I be talking to Aydin about my feelings for Dante? Although why not? Aydin would have to be deaf, blind, and practically dead not to know how physical Dante and I are.

Sophie too, is just as affectionate with Nico and is very friendly with Aydin. But I notice she never talks about her relationship with Nico unless I ask. But surely that's just her right?

Aydin's expression softens slightly, a flicker of something—sympathy? understanding?—passing through her eyes. "The war has escalated," she says gently. "I'm afraid Dante may not make it today."

My eyes widen in surprise at her words, but somehow I can't believe that. "I'm sure he'll let me know himself if anything changes."

"He is letting you know now," Aydin says, her voice kind but firm. "I wasn't going to tell you until later. I begged him to write a note like before but . . . he couldn't do it."

Apprehension slithers down my back like drops of icy water along with an emotion I don't care to name but I know I detest. "What do you mean he couldn't do it?"

Aydin takes a deep breath. "Dante finds the dark aspects of this work revolting, although there's no one as brilliant as him at executing it. So whenever he has to deal with blood and gore, he wants to spare those he loves from the monster, if you will, he becomes."

Mild irritation starts to churn in my gut and I get the urge to turn and walk out of the kitchen yet I find myself asking, "Is he violent when he's like that?"

"Oh no, nothing like that. He's just distant . . . emotionally flat."

"He's not emotionally flat." I snap.

"You haven't seen him when he's doing those things. He retreats to this place . . . you just want to reach out to him, but hardly lets in anyone."

Tears sting my eyes. *So he should leave.* But even as the thought occurs to me, I know he can't. Dante Vitelli might as well have the Outfit growing out of his heart. To separate him from it would be a physical death.

He can't leave.

"I love him. Every part of him." I say, already done with the conversation. Something about it makes me feel like I'm sneaking behind Dante's back to dig for information about him. Besides, I'm still not convinced we're talking about the same person.

The Dante I know is different from the moody, conflicted man Aydin is painting. The dominant lover who demands my trust and craves my obedience, who laughs at my terrible jokes, who looks at me like I'm the most precious thing in the world, is unapologetically bad. And he's comfortable in his skin.

Part of me wants to stay and argue, to tell Aydin that she's wrong and doesn't know him at all. That he's not the same boy she used to know, but I respect her years of experience too much to dismiss her words outright.

Plus, arguing with the staff about Dante's personality seems like a great way to win the 'Worst Mafia Girlfriend' award.

As I turn to leave, Aydin's words stop me.

"You don't believe me, do you?"

I shrug without turning. "No, I don't. But it's alright. That's your opinion. It's just . . . it doesn't at all sound like Dante."

"There's something else you may not know," Aydin's voice drops slightly as if sharing confidence. "Dante has ADHD—Attention Deficit Hyperactivity Disorder."

That makes me stop. I turn back to Aydin. Dante has told me in so many words that he's neurodiverse. But I had no idea he ever had an actual diagnosis.

Seeing she has my full attention, Aydin continues. "He was almost unmanageable. He wouldn't sleep. He wouldn't tire. And he just wouldn't stop."

"Stop what?"

Aydin throws her arms out. "Everything. Anything he wanted to do. He was medicated for years, although the medicines never seemed to make any difference. Over the years, he's changed, but sometimes he can come across as having many facets to his personality."

Aydin pauses to take a breath. "You might notice some quirks when he's excited or stressed, which disappear when those impulses are controlled. With loud music, for example."

Tears spring to my eyes as I grab the counter for support.

I don't know much about ADHD, but a surge of protectiveness wells within me. I don't see what that has to do with Dante coming to see me today, and I fail to see why she would even need to bring that up with me. Sophie must know, yet never told me anything.

Still, I can't help all the emotions this news rouses inside me.

Guilt that I found this out behind his back, anger at Aydin for an unwanted, possibly irrelevant exposition of a painful, chaotic childhood.

Gratitude for some insight into the man I love.

A searing hurt deep in my chest that Dante hadn't told me this himself. Or maybe he would have with time but thanks to Aydin, I'll never know.

But above all, I feel a fierce, uncontrollable desire to just be with Dante. To be whatever he needs right now.

"Thank you for telling me," I say, putting away my glass of tea. The ice has mostly melted now, leaving the drink watery and unsatisfying. The craving for pure, crunchy ice is starting to resurface.

I'm about to make an excuse to leave, to retreat back to the sanctuary of my room when Aydin drops another bombshell.

"He's in Chicago, you know. He arrived this morning. He won't come here, though. Nico has declared full retaliation against the Irish, and

Dante is leaving for Boston tomorrow. He'll be gone until the war is over. Two, maybe three weeks."

Panic grips me hard. *Three weeks? I can't wait that long to see him.*

"How do you know Nico has declared a war?" I manage to speak past the lump in my throat.

Aydin only shrugs and turns away.

I feel a frisson of unease. I think it's wildly inappropriate that Aydin knows so much about the Outfit's plans. Does Dante know that his father's house staff are aware of his itinerary?

Suddenly, I can't wait to see him. Even if he can't be emotionally available, surely he'll be interested to know that the Fortress isn't as safe as he thinks it is.

"I'd like to see him."

Aydin shakes her head. "I can try to get him to scribble a note, but he won't come here."

"But I can go to him. Can you get me to him?" I hate the desperation in my voice and the fact that I'm having to reach a man I love through a go-between who, frankly, is pissing me off by how much she seems to know about everything. But I have no choice or pride left at this point. I want to see Dante too much to care.

Aydin pauses, then smiles. "I think you might be the one person in the world he needs to see right now. He loves you, Addy. He never stopped loving you. He's desperate for you. Maybe if he knew how much you accept him for everything he is . . ."

Aydin trails off, and I stand frozen, caught between the safety of the mansion and the pull of my heart.

"I can arrange a car to take you," Aydin's voice sounds firm, almost authoritative. "And Dante can bring you back in the morning."

On one hand, leaving the safety of the mansion now terrifies me. I've been hidden away here for weeks, presumed dead by the outside world. The thought of stepping beyond these walls terrifies me.

But on the other hand . . . Dante. The image of him alone in his penthouse, wrestling with the darkness of what he's had to do, makes my heart ache. And then there's the war. My father—no, Benjamin, I remind myself—is out there, potentially in Dante's crosshairs. The thought makes me sick to my stomach. If I could just talk to Dante, and make Benjamin understand that I'm alive, maybe we could stop this bloodshed before it goes too far.

I open my eyes, meeting Aydin's steady gaze. "Okay," I say, my voice stronger than I feel. "I'll go."

Relief flashes across Aydin's face, so quickly I almost miss it. She nods, already turning to make the arrangements. "I'll have a car ready in thirty minutes. Pack light—just essentials for overnight and come straight down and through these doors—they'll be open in exactly thirty minutes from now."

As she speaks, she moves to a locked drawer, extracting a small black device. I'm shocked to see anything remotely resembling a cell phone after weeks of being cut off. "It's a burner phone," she explains, handing it to me. "It won't work until you leave the grounds. *Signor* Dante's number is on speed dial 1. Use it only in an emergency."

Another frisson of unease runs through me. *Why would I need an emergency between here and Dante's beach house?* But I nod, clutching the phone like a lifeline. Its weight in my hand makes this all feel suddenly, terrifyingly real.

"Thank you, Aydin," I say tightly. "For everything."

She smiles tightly, watching me with an expression I can't quite decipher.

I nod again, unable to find the words to respond. As I turn to leave the kitchen, to go pack for this impromptu trip, a wave of dizziness washes over me. I stumble, catching myself on the edge of the counter.

"Addy!" Aydin's voice is sharp with concern.

"I'm fine," I assure her, straightening up. "Just a bit lightheaded. Pregnancy stuff, you know?"

She doesn't look entirely convinced, but she nods. "I'll have some snacks prepared for your journey. It wouldn't do to have you fainting on the way."

I manage a weak smile, touched by her thoughtfulness. "Thank you."

As I make my way back to my room, my mind is a whirlwind of thoughts and emotions. Fear and excitement war within me, leaving me feeling jittery and off-balance. I shower quickly, the hot water doing little to calm my nerves.

When I return to the kitchen, Aydin leads me through the quiet house, down to a garage I didn't even know existed. A sleek black car waits,

its engine already purring softly. The driver, an Italian man I don't recognize, nods respectfully as Aydin opens the back door for me.

As I slide into the plush leather seat, a wave of nerves washes over me. I'm really doing this. I'm leaving the safety of the mansion, venturing out into a world that thinks I'm dead.

Aydin leans in, her expression serious. "Remember, Addy. Keep a low profile," she pauses, something softening in her eyes. "Take care of each other."

I nod, unable to speak around the lump in my throat. As the car door shuts with a soft thud, a sudden chill runs down my spine. The plush leather seat, which was a symbol of luxury moments ago, now feels like a trap closing around me.

I can't shake the feeling that something is very wrong. The realization hits me with the force of a physical blow—I shouldn't have left the mansion. I should have spoken to Sophie.

I lean forward, trying to catch the driver's eye in the rearview mirror. "Excuse me," I say, fighting to keep my voice steady, "how long until we reach Dante's house?"

"About twenty minutes, *Signorina*," he replies, his voice professional and detached.

I nod, settling back into my seat. His response was normal, expected even. So why does this feeling of dread continue to grow, coiling in my stomach like a venomous snake?

As we turn onto a main road, the driver adjusts his grip on the steering wheel. And that's when I see it—a tattoo on the back of his hand, partially hidden by his sleeve. My breath catches in my throat. It's like spotting a 'Beware of Shark' sign after you've already jumped into the ocean.

Having spent hours tracing the tattoos on Dante's body and learning what different symbols may mean in the underworld, when I see the six-pointed star on his hand, cold fear grips me.

It's one favored by the Irish Mob. "Turn the car around, please. I forgot something."

"What did you forget, *Signorina*?" Perhaps because I'm now hyper-aware, I catch something in his Italian accent, the barest hint of an Irish lilt, so faint it's almost imperceptible.

My gaze flies to his. "Just turn around, please." I try to keep my voice casual, like I'm asking him to pass the salt instead of potentially saving my life.

He watches me for a few seconds and casually looks away. And then there's a soft click. The doors lock—or double lock.

Fuck. He knows that I know. "Stop the fucking car, you asshole!"

The driver's eyes meet mine in the rearview mirror, and any doubt I had vanishes. There's no warmth there, no humanity. Just a cold, calculated purpose.

Panic streaks through me as the clear glass partition between the front and back seats begins to rise. Just before the partition closes completely, the driver's hand darts back, tossing something into the rear compartment. A cloth, I realize, as it lands with a damp thud on the floor.

The air immediately becomes pungent, a sickly sweet smell that makes my head spin. Through the partition, I watch in horror as the man removes what looks like nasal plugs from his nostrils.

Chloroform. The word flashes through my mind, accompanied by a surge of terror.

I lunge for the door handle, yanking it frantically even though I know it's locked. With shaking hands, I unbuckle my seatbelt, using the heavy metal clasp to strike at the window. But it's useless—the glass must be reinforced. It doesn't even scratch.

The smell is getting stronger. I push the cloth as far away as I can with my foot, but I know it's futile. Already, my movements are becoming sluggish, my thoughts growing fuzzy around the edges.

As my vision begins to blur, a face swims into focus in my mind—Aydin. I see the expressions on her face as she spun her tale about Dante. The ones I couldn't decipher earlier. Now, with horrifying clarity, I understand.

It wasn't concern. It wasn't sympathy.

It was deception.

That's the last coherent thought I have before darkness claims me, dragging me down into oblivion.

CHAPTER THIRTY-SEVEN

Dante

I adjust my AirPods as I navigate the familiar streets to Sal's luxury condo, wishing I could replace the music with Addy's voice instead. I need to be done with this fucking war, get her safe so we can be a normal couple. I want to be able to call her anytime. Take her out. Live with her.

I'd just returned from the ruins that Voltex was left in. This second fire did so much more damage than the first and called for a forceful and excessive retaliation. But we need to put our house in order before engaging the Mob, which is why it's time to reel in Orlando De Luca.

I pull up to Sal's condo, my tires crunching on the gravel driveway. Sal's door opens before I can knock. "You look like shit, *fratello*," he greets me, a smirk playing on his lips.

I brush past him, my eyes scanning the apartment, and instantly note that something is off. The usual clutter is gone, replaced by an almost clinical neatness.

"Going somewhere?" I ask, unable to keep the edge from my voice.

Then I see the book on the coffee table, its cover embossed with raised dots. Braille. My gaze snaps back to Sal, who's watching me warily.

"What the fuck, Salvatore?" I growl, taking a step toward him.

Sal holds up his hands, palms out. "It's not what you think, Dante. I'm just learning to read Braille."

I freeze, my eyes darting around the room. Now that I'm looking, I see other changes—tactile markers on light switches and labels on kitchen cabinets. My chest tightens as understanding dawns.

"Kira," I breathe, the name both a question and an accusation.

Sal nods, his expression a mix of defiance and apprehension. I close my eyes, exhaling slowly. When I open them, I fix Sal with a hard stare.

"If you hurt her, Salvatore, I will tear your heart out. I'm dead serious."

"It's nothing serious. We're friends, that's all."

I run a hand through my hair, suddenly feeling the weight of the past few days. "I just hope Kira knows what she's getting into."

"I should be the one being asked that," Sal mutters under his breath

"You're on your own there, prick. Anyway, get dressed," I snap. "We're going to Orlando's."

Sal's eyebrows shoot up. "De Luca? Why?"

"We need him back in the fold yesterday. All our ranks need to be tight as shit."

I pace the room, tension making it impossible to stand still. "I've just returned from Detroit. A source tells me Boston is getting ready to strike a deal with a big syndicate."

Sal slumps against the counter and sighs. "You heard right, *fratello*. It's the Shadow Gang in Philadelphia. They're about five hundred strong."

I pause, surprised by this.

The Philadelphia Shadow Gang. Hired fighters, barbarians who've gotten rich by contracting themselves out to fight mob wars. They're a force to be reckoned with, but not an insurmountable threat to the Outfit.

"Sure, they have the numbers, but they're disorganized. They're mercenaries, not strategists. They fight for the highest bidder, not for loyalty."

Sal puts up his index finger. "That may be true, but they more than make up for it in brutality. Dante, these fuckers would carve up their pregnant grandmother if she crossed them."

"Which only shows how weak and desperate the Mob is to descend to that level."

"They mean to win this time by any means necessary. On the other hand, we should rethink this non-engagement rule and take decisive action against the Mob ASAP. Dante, watching them contract a five hundred-man army to fight us is like watching gangrene spread."

The weight of Sal's words sinks in. It's true, but Addy needs to know what this means for Benjamin O'Shea. It's a conversation I'm not looking forward to, but it needs to happen today.

"Agreed," I muse aloud. "We should act before they do more damage. I'll speak to Nico today."

"Fuck yes!" Sal does a subtle fist pump and then heads to his bedroom to change. His voice drifts back to the living room. "Though I do feel bad for the Mob. To have the Italians murder Naomi eighteen years ago and now lure and do the same to her daughter? That's cause for war in any book."

I snort. "Someone needs to tell them we might be fucked up, but we generally never carry a grudge for that long."

Sal emerges, buttoning up a fresh shirt. "I know. They're actually the ones that behave like pussies. No offense to Addy."

"None taken. She's not Irish. She's mine." The possessiveness in my voice surprises even me.

Sal looks ready to vomit. "Fucking kill me right now," he mutters.

I glance at my watch and snarl, "You might get your wish if you don't move your ass now. You have two minutes. We're on a clock here."

I need to get back to Addy. I promised her I'd be with her today. It's been five days. Too long.

As Sal disappears back into his room, my gaze lands on the Braille book on the coffee table. The raised dots seem to mock me, a tangible reminder of how this all began.

If Kira had seen me talking to Addy that day in Loyola gym, she would have warned her away long before either of us had the chance to sink hooks into each other irrevocably. And now, I can't help but wonder if Sal isn't already heading down a similar path with Kira.

God help Kira because Salvatore is messed up.

***

The tense silence in the car is broken only by the purr of the engine. It's unusually silent because Sal keeps fidgeting with his phone, dialing and redialing a number obsessively, and fiddling with his cufflinks, a nervous tick I've never seen before. It sets my teeth on edge.

"What?" I bark when I'm inches from planting my fist in his temple.

He shrugs. "You don't want to know."

"Sal, if you don't spit it out right now—"

"Kira's unreachable—her phone is switched off."

"You're right. I don't want to know. Maybe she's come to her senses and doesn't want your 'friendship' anymore."

"No, we're good. Very good, actually."

"You can't be all that good if she doesn't know that switching off her phone doesn't deter you from finding her."

"She knows I track all my friends and doesn't mind me doing the same to her."

"Really?" Part of Sal's job is keeping tabs on the Capos, which is a welcome layer of security should anyone get ambushed or kidnapped. To anyone else, it would be a gross invasion of their privacy. I'm surprised Sal is open about it, even more so that Kira lets him do it.

"So, what's the problem then?" I ask. "She probably forgot to charge her phone."

"Dante, the problem isn't the cell phone being off. The problem is where the phone is right now."

"Where is it?"

"Her phone has remained in a single spot at Logan Airport for the past four hours."

A dark chill settles in my bones. "Kira hates flying."

"Precisely. This is what is driving me up the wall, Dante. What the fuck is she doing at an airport with a switched-off phone for four hours."

Before we can say more, the huge composite gates of the De Luca estate loom. They slide open silently as we approach.

"He knows you're coming," Sal states the obvious.

"Of course. And I bet he also knows why."

The driveway, lined with perfectly manicured topiaries, winds its way up to a mansion that wouldn't look out of place in the Italian countryside.

"Jesus," Sal mutters, eyeing the stone fountains and marble statues dotting the expansive lawn. "Forget Intelligence, I should've been on the Narc's side of the business."

I shoot him a wry glance as we pull up to the front of the house. "You can't stand drugs anymore, Sal."

He chuckles wryly. "Yes, but fuck. It's easy money."

The front doors open before we reach them, and I'm hit with a wave of cool air, heavy with the scent of lemon polish and something floral. Bianca De Luca stands in the foyer, regal in tan pants and a flowery blouse, and not a hair out of place. She's slim and graceful, but her posture remains rigid, her eyes calculating and her chin jutting in hostility.

"Dante. What an . . . unexpected pleasure." She turns to address someone behind her. "I told you he'll be back, *cara*."

My eyes slide past her to Alina, hovering uncertainly in the background, and I groan inwardly. The hurt in her eyes is palpable, but there's something else there too, a resignation that makes my gut twist. No woman should ever be turned down the way I did Alina. But I wasn't thinking straight that night.

"Bianca," I nod, keeping my voice neutral. "Alina. I'm here to see Orlando."

Bianca's lips curve into a smile that doesn't reach her eyes. "Of course you are." Her words drip with venom as she turns to her daughter. "Vitelli men can never change. They'll trample on your heart every chance they get."

The bitterness in her voice makes me imagine—a younger, more desperate Bianca engaged to my father. Until he fell for another woman. Something tells me that if Bianca had not compelled Alina to choose me, Nico would have done the exact same thing I did to Alina. The same thing Father did to Bianca.

I push the thoughts aside, focusing on the present. "Let Orlando know I'm here."

A gleam of hope flashes in Bianca's eyes, but I can see that Alina knows better. Bianca must think I'm here to renegotiate the marriage deal, now that my 'mystery woman' is dead and the Irish are closing in on us.

"Certainly," Bianca's smile widens, becoming almost predatory. "Although Orlando's been sulking like a wounded dog since he threw his tantrum in front of the entire Outfit. But it looks like it worked. I'll go get him for you."

I exchange a glance with Sal as Bianca saunters off, leaving Alina standing uncertainly. That Bianca resents her husband is no secret, but that she'd be willing to openly disrespect him in front of his fellow Capos is shocking, to say the least.

"Alina," I say softly, taking a step toward the woman. "How have you been?"

She meets my gaze, her eyes a storm of conflicting emotions. "I've been better," she admits in a faint voice. "But I'm managing."

"I'm sorry, again."

"You're an asshole, Dante."

"That too."

Her lips twitch in response, and she rolls her eyes and leaves. Moments later, heavy footsteps announce Orlando's arrival. The man who enters the room is a far cry from the proud, powerful man who stormed out of the conference room weeks ago. His shoulders are slumped, defeat written in every line of his face.

"Dante," he says, his voice rough. "If you've come to ask for my daughter's hand now that you need to bolster your ranks against the Irish, I can tell you right now to fuck off."

Bianca hovers in the doorway, her eyes sharp and hungry. I say nothing but Orlando must see something in my eyes that makes him shift uncomfortably and turn to Bianca.

"Leave us," he commands, but his tone lacks conviction.

"Not on your life, Orlando. The Vitellis have fucked us over for too long," Bianca snaps, moving further into the room. "And now they've broken my daughter's heart. I'm staying to see that things are made right again."

I raise a surprised eyebrow. It's not that I disapprove of a woman having a say in her home—quite the opposite. But I'm taken aback that Orlando, whom I've always thought of as old-fashioned, allows it so openly.

Meeting Orlando's eyes, I choose my words carefully. "Orlando, is the snow fresh?"

It's a code, one that means, 'I need to tell you something in private.' Orlando's gaze flicks to Bianca, then back to me. He shrugs, a gesture of defeat that speaks volumes. He's not going to get her to leave.

"Sit," he says, waving toward the leather armchairs. "Say what you came to say, Dante. I doubt there's anything left that could surprise me now."

I lower myself into the chair. Sal remains standing, taking his guard behind me. The tension in the room heightens as I stare into Orlando's pale blue eyes. I take a deep breath and begin.

"Orlando, your Don wants you to reaffirm your loyalty to the Outfit. Just as soon as you pay the price for your disrespect."

Orlando's eyes narrow. "What price?"

"You and I know you should pay with blood. But Don Vitelli is willing to take your grievances on board. So instead, you're done with narcotics."

The words hang in the air for a moment before all hell breaks loose.

Orlando's temper explodes like a powder keg. He leaps to his feet, his face flushed with rage. "You come into my house after everything, and you dare—"

My voice cuts through his tirade like a whip. "We know Naomi Ritter and her child were yours. Eighteen years ago, the Irish asked for a name, and rather than give it, my father chose a decade-long war. You may want to consider your next words, De Luca."

Orlando becomes still as a stone. "You're blackmailing me? Either I join forces with you or you'll throw me to the Irish dogs?"

"In a nutshell, yes. Give up the narcotics, fall back in line, and never ever break faith again. Or face the Irish on your own." I pause, letting my words sink in before unleashing the killing blow. "And forget about meeting Naomi's daughter. Your daughter."

Orland freezes. "What? What are you saying?"

"She's alive, Orlando. Adele is alive. Like a phoenix, she survived Emil Novak's gunshots. And five weeks ago, she survived Owen's bomb. I put her off-grid."

I can see the physical impact of my words on Orlando. He staggers back, collapsing into his chair. The emotions that play across his face are raw, unguarded—shock, joy, and, most of all, an overwhelming regret that makes my chest tighten.

"Emil and Owen Novak?"

I nod. "Father and son. Both ghosts. Both are now dead."

"Do we know who sent them?"

I wince in regret. "No."

"But she's alive." He breathes.

"Yes," I confirm.

His eyes become glassy with unshed tears. It's a startling transformation, seeing this hardened mafioso stripped bare by a single word.

Out of the corner of my eye, I see Bianca pale as a sheet, her knuckles white as she grips the back of a nearby chair.

"Is it still fresh?" I ask, using our code to inquire if it's safe to continue.

Bianca hisses, her composure cracking. "How much more can there be, you fucking cheating bastard?"

Orlando waves a weary hand, gesturing for me to continue. He looks utterly drained, as if the weight of his past has suddenly become too much to bear.

I lean forward, my voice low and steady. "Let me spell out the terms again, Orlando. You lose the narcotics business and fall back in line, or we tell the Irish it was you. We'll end the war by letting them tear you apart, and of course, you never ever get to see her again."

Orlando drops his head into his hands, his next words muffled but clear. "My daughter is alive."

I feel a strange mix of pity and respect for this man who's been carrying such a burden. "And who knows? You may be getting a Vitelli son-in-law after all."

Orlando's head snaps up, his eyes boring into mine. "Really?"

I nod, allowing a small smile. "If Adele will have me, yes."

The expression that crosses Bianca's face is pure, unadulterated rage. It's gone in an instant, replaced by a mask of indifference, but I've seen it. A chill runs down my spine as I realize the storm that's likely to break in this household once we leave.

"Your Don wants an answer in twenty-four hours—" I begin, but Orlando interrupts.

"He can have it now," he says, his voice stronger than it's been since we arrived. "I'm in. My only condition is that I get to meet my daughter." He hesitates. "If she wants to, that is."

Bianca rolls her eyes dramatically and storms out of the room, the sound of her heels echoing on the marble floor.

I nod, acknowledging his terms. "That can be arranged."

Neither Sal nor I move to shake his hand. Not until Orlando gets back his ring—he hasn't earned that right yet.

"We'll see ourselves out," I say, standing.

As we make our way to the front door, I hear soft footsteps behind us. Turning, I see Alina, her eyes red-rimmed but determined.

"Dante," she calls softly. "Can we talk? Just for a moment?"

I glance at Sal, who nods and hangs back, giving us space. Turning back to Alina, I see the need for closure written plainly on her face.

"Of course," I say gently.

She takes a deep breath, squaring her shoulders. "So, the redhead didn't die?"

"No. And her name is Adele."

She nods. "Was she—is she the reason why you couldn't love me? Like, if . . . if she wasn't in the picture, do you think . . . maybe it could have worked between us?"

The question hits me like a punch to the gut. I owe her honesty, at the very least.

"Tell me something first. Who did you really want, Nico or me?"

She shrugs. "I'm not sure. I think I loved you since that Thanksgiving you put Paulo—my cousin in the hospital for beating me."

I furrow my brows, not having the foggiest recollection, although beating up a girl sounds like something Paulo Rinaldi would do.

"The party was right in this house. I was six, you were fourteen, and he was about twenty." Alina explains when she sees the look on my face

I snort. "Sounds like the fucker deserved it."

"Anyway, that was the last family gathering your parents let you attend because apparently, Paulo spent three months in the hospital after that. I didn't see much of you again. I saw Nico instead. And I think I fell for him too."

"So you would have married Nico if your mother hadn't interfered?"

"I guess so. You and Nico look so much alike, you know. You're literally the same people."

I want to burst out laughing, but I rein it in as a wave of protectiveness surges in me. Nico and I might look identical but we couldn't be any more different.

"No, Alina." I finally give her the answer she needs. "We wouldn't have worked out regardless. I'm pretty sure I would have made you miserable. And so would Nico."

She nods, a single tear escaping down her cheek. "Thank you," she whispers. "For being honest. I think . . . I think I needed to hear that."

I reach out, squeezing her shoulder gently. "And I'd like to amend what I said before. If you're ever asked to marry someone, whether you want to or not, come and talk to me, alright?"

With a final reassuring nod, I turn and walk out of the De Luca mansion.

As I slide into the driver's seat beside Sal, he breathes, "Hell, poor girl dodged two bullets there."

"Shut the fuck up," I say, fighting a smile.

As I merge into traffic, I think about Orlando. I've known the man all my life. He's a tough nut, famous for his near-pathological lack of emotion, and not at all one I'd pick as a father for Addy if it came down to choosing. But the man I saw today seems lightyears away from that person.

Still, I wonder if that's enough. Does he really want to get to know Addy, or does he just want her because she carries his DNA?

CHAPTER THIRTY-EIGHT

Dante

The drive back from De Luca's is tense despite having succeeded in bringing back Orlando into the fold. Kira's cell phone is still switched off and hasn't moved from that spot in Logan Airport. Sal's voice breaks the silence to beat himself up again.

"Something is wrong. She's not home, either. She had a gig in Boston. It was supposed to be her first in five weeks, so she really wanted to do it. Fuck. I should have protected her better."

I glance at Sal. "Did you take her to Boston yourself?"

Sal knows better than to associate with Kira, especially while she's in Boston.

Sal throws his head back against the headrest. "Yes."

Alarm bells ring in my head, and I turn to face him as I stop at a red light. "Did you spend the night with her, Sal?"

His face tells me everything I need to know.

I don't have to say anything. Sal knows he shouldn't have done it. It's bad enough that Kira stubbornly refuses to live anywhere except for Boston, but we've been careful about associating with her.

"She was scared, okay?" Sal says, throwing his hands up. "She's so self-sufficient that everyone just forgets how vulnerable she can be. She's all alone and terrified."

"Addy lived with Kira, Sal. You know as well as I do that the Mob would have eyes on Kira the moment Addy was proclaimed dead."

"I know. I fucked up, alright? The crazy thing is I knew I was fucking up with every single second I stayed with her. But I just couldn't leave her, you know?"

I know.

I urge him to calm down, but I can't even stop the dread that coils in my stomach. Kira is intelligent and extremely capable despite her disability. But she's still vulnerable because of that.

She wouldn't know if she was being followed.

She wouldn't see or recognize, let alone stop anyone who tried to hurt her.

She can't run.

My mind conjures a million other ways she is at more risk, and I desperately push the disturbing thoughts away.

"We'll go to Boston tonight, if need be," I say, my voice steady despite the turmoil inside. "Might as well get a head start since we're invading in a few days."

"Sound plan, Dante." Sal nods, his face flooding with relief, betraying just how much he cares for his 'friend.'

"See if you can find her current location first, so we're not just wandering around enemy territory," I say.

"That's the problem. I'll need to hack into hundreds of street cameras at once. It's doable within a day. But with an airport involved . . ."

"She could be outside Boston."

"Exactly, which means we'd need fifty people hacking into cameras in each state to determine which one she's in. There's only one person who can cast a net that wide . . ." Sal's voice trails off when I shoot him a murderous look.

My knuckles whiten on the steering wheel. Cade Quinn. Sophie's brother. I want to kill the smug bastard so bad I can taste it. It's too fucking bad we share the same sister.

"Alright then," Sal murmurs. "Kira had better still be in Boston then."

The Fortress' silhouette offers no comfort tonight. As we enter, Falzone greets us, his usually impassive ruddy face tight and pale with concern.

"Don Vitelli wants to see you both now, *Signore*."

My plan was to go straight to Addy and then debrief with Nico later, but I make my way to the conference room, Sal following closely. Each step increases the weight of foreboding pressing down on my chest. I push open the heavy oak door, and the scene before me stops me.

Nico perches on the table's edge, his posture rigid with fury. But his eyes . . . they're not only angry, they're devastated. He looks betrayed, an expression I don't see very often.

Sophie stands beside him, a soothing hand on his arm. Her eyes are red-rimmed, her usual poise cracked.

And then there's the real kicker: Aydin, crumpled at Nico's feet, her sobs muffled against his shoes. The sight is so incongruous, so wrong, that for a moment, I can't process it.

When Nico finally raises his gaze to meet mine, time seems to stop. I know, with a certainty that chills me to my core, that my worst fears have been realized.

"Kira?" I ask. As awful as it sounds, I hope this is about Kira going missing because my brain can't process the other scenario.

"Gone." Nico inclines his head tightly. "Taken by the Irish."

Nico pauses, and I can see him steeling himself for what comes next. "Addy too, I'm afraid."

The words hit me like a punch to the face, and I stagger backward, my hand finding the doorframe for support. Beside me, Sal's sharp intake of breath is the only sound in the suddenly airless room.

"What the hell?" The word comes out as a strangled whisper; I hardly recognize it as my own voice.

Aydin's sobs grow louder, and suddenly, everything clicks into place.

"What the actual hell?" This time it's a roar, the sound tearing from my throat. Rage and anguish propel me toward the woman on the floor.

Nico moves swiftly, pulling Aydin roughly to her feet and pushing her toward Sophie. "Get her out of here, now," he growls.

Nico grabs my shoulder, his hold on me restraining and comforting as Sophie quickly leads Aydin away. Sophie's golden eyes are huge and pleading as she trains them on Nico, mouthing something that sounds like 'call him, please,' but I can't hear over the roaring in my ears.

I struggle to breathe, to think. The world has just tilted on its axis, and nothing makes sense anymore.

"How?" I manage to push past the tightness in my throat, a single word laden with a thousand questions.

Nico's voice is clipped, emotionless. "They picked up Kira from her concert in Boston. She confessed that Addy is alive. They threatened Aydin to give up Addy in exchange for her daughter and so she convinced Addy to leave. As soon as your woman left, Aydin confessed to Sophie."

Each word is a nail in the coffin as the future I dared to dream of crumbles before my very eyes.

"I'm getting her back," I say, my tone brooking no argument. "Tonight."

"Dante—" Nico starts, but I cut him off.

"Tonight!" I roar.

Nico sighs, running a hand through his hair. "We don't know exactly where she is. Although Aydin gave Addy one of our trackable phones."

Sal moves to one of the laptops on the conference table and starts typing on the keys. He finally straightens. "It's no longer live but it was last in O'Hare airport."

Nico leans over to peer at the screen, too. "She must have been taken back to Boston."

"Then Boston we shall go—" I begin, but Sal holds his hand up, cutting me off.

"Hold on," Sal continues typing on the keyboard. I peek over his shoulder to see that he appears to be chatting with someone. "She might not be in Boston, Dante."

When Nico and I simply look at Sal, he explains. "It looks like the deal with the Shadow gang is being struck today. Sounds like the top guns of the Mob, including Benjamin O'Shea, are in Philly tonight."

I nod, but it still doesn't make sense. I rake my hands through my hair and grab hold of the strands. "If they're wrapped up in a crucial deal tonight, how the fuck do they have time to pull something like this today of all days?"

"Because they're desperate to take their only leverage against us?" Sal replies. "With Kira and Red Wine in their grasp, they could ask us to fall on our own swords, and we'd do it."

"Or," Nico levels his gaze at me as he voices the worst possible scenario, "it could be that they need Addy for the deal."

An unnatural chill settles inside my bones. What I feel is beyond rage. Beyond despair. It's a cold, monstrous vengeance demanding blood. A reminder of why I would choose this life over and over again. The freedom it gives me to create my own justice.

I will personally flay every inch of skin off the bones of anyone who so much as touches the mother of my child.

I pull up a chair and make myself sit because giving into a fit of anger will achieve nothing. Instead, I let all the rage coalesce into a hot, tight ball in the pit of my belly.

Sal taps a few more buttons, pauses, and then starts up again. Finally, he straightens from the laptop and confirms. "Confirmed. Half of Mob are in Boston, the other half is at a wedding in Philadelphia."

I huff out a bitter laugh. *A wedding, huh? She's about to become a widow.*

Between Sal and me, it'll be a piece of cake to locate Addy, considering the Shadow gang isn't the most innovative.

But it'll take several hours, if not days, to extract her. I need better. I need a fucking demon who can do it in minutes.

I tell Sal while leveling Nico with a stare, daring him to contradict my next words. "Sal, get me Cade Quinn."

"Absolutely not," Nico says, deadly soft. "Since we already know where Addy is, all we need is—"

"Cade fucking Quinn!" I roar. "Now, Salvatore!"

Nico stares me down for a full minute, then snaps. "Fine." He stalks out of the room, obviously not wanting to be here when I speak to Cade.

He pauses at the door and throws behind him, "We've had enough. Call everyone in. We move within the hour. The moon rises red in Philly and Boston tonight."

I love you too, fratello.

CHAPTER THIRTY-NINE

Adele

Cold.

That's the first sensation that penetrates the fog in my mind. A bone-deep, teeth-chattering cold that has me curling into myself before I'm even fully awake.

The next is the pounding in my head, a relentless drumbeat that makes even opening my eyes an uphill task.

When I finally manage it, the world is a blur of unfamiliar shapes and shadows. I blink, trying to bring things into focus. A four-poster bed looms around me, its dark wood starkly contrasting with the bare mattress beneath me. No sheets, no blankets. Just me, shivering in my lacy pink underwear.

Where the hell are my clothes?

I push myself up, ignoring the wave of nausea that accompanies the movement. The room spins for a moment before settling. It's large, opulent even, with high ceilings and what looks like antique furniture. But it's not my room. Not Dante's suite.

Dante.

His name brings a flood of memories. The gym, Aydin's deception, the car ride. And then . . . the pungent smell. The cloth. The driver's cold eyes in the rearview mirror.

My stomach lurches, and this time it's not from the lingering effects of chloroform and whatever else drug they used on me. Aydin. Aydin did this. Has she been working with the bombers all along?

And Dante. God, he'll be livid. I can almost see the rage in his eyes and the tension in his jaw when he realizes I've been kidnapped.

A new smell cuts through my spiraling thoughts—food.

My gaze lands on a table across the room, laden with an array of dishes. My stomach growls traitorously, reminding me that I have no idea how long I've been unconscious. But the memory of that drug-soaked cloth is too fresh, the taste of fear still bitter in my mouth. I'd rather starve than let them poison me.

The soft click of the door opening has me tensing, every muscle coiled tight despite my weakened state. But it's not a threat that enters—at least, not an obvious one.

A small woman with a round face and bone-straight black hair steps into the room and bows slightly. Her smile seems genuine, but the sadness in her eyes makes my chest tighten.

"You wake," she says in broken English, her voice gentle but laced with an undercurrent of something I can't quite place. Pity? Fear?

"Eat?" She gestures toward the table.

I shake my head, fighting another wave of nausea. The woman's smile doesn't falter, but something in her eyes dims. "I, ah . . ." She clears her throat and tries again. "I help you dress," she says, moving toward what I now realize is a closet door.

Dress? For what? Although I'd take any kind of clothes over being half-naked and freezing. The thought dies as she emerges, holding something that makes my blood run cold and my heart stutter in my chest.

A wedding dress.

It's beautiful, an ivory confection of satin and tulle, tiny rhinestones catching the light like teardrops. In another life, I might have gasped in awe. Now, all I can do is stare in horror as the pieces start to fall into place.

Dante's words from what feels like a lifetime ago echo in my head, a cruel mockery:

He also told me to back off because you were his daughter and that you were promised to someone else.

I'd brushed off his concern at the time, too caught up in the whirlwind of emotions he stirred in me.

Oh God. This is really happening. I'm meant to be married. Tonight.

Dread hits me like an icy wave. I lunge for the fruit bowl on the table, barely registering the woman's startled exclamation as I empty the contents of my stomach—what little there is—right onto the grapes and raspberries.

As I retch, tears streaming down my face, one thought burns through the panic and confusion in my mind: I have to get out of here. Somehow.

The small-boned woman is at my side in an instant, her touch surprisingly gentle as she supports me. She guides me to a chair, then fetches a glass of water from the table. I eye it warily, paranoia and thirst warring within me. My parched throat wins out. I take small sips, the cool liquid soothing my raw throat but doing nothing to calm the storm raging inside me.

"Thank you," I manage, my voice hoarse and unfamiliar to my own ears. "What's your name?"

"Mezhen," she replies, her smile, a mirror to the conflict I feel. "I help you dress now?"

Fighting another bout of nausea, I stare at the wedding dress, wrapping my arms around myself. The cold is seeping into my bones, my teeth chattering audibly.

"I'm not wearing that rubbish." I stand and walk past Mezhen to the closet, throwing open the door to get my own clothes, stopping in my tracks when I find it's completely empty. Not even a single sock is in there. Nothing except what the woman is holding.

Suddenly, I get it. This is why they took my clothes, why the room is so frigid. I'm being left with no choice but to put on that dress.

Fury, so intense that it's almost blinding, fills me.

Fucking bastards.

With trembling hands, I reach for the gown. Mezhen helps me into it, her movements quick but not unkind. The long-sleeved material warms my skin, and the weight of the skirt is oddly grounding. I catch a glimpse of myself in a nearby mirror and have to look away. The woman staring back at me is a stranger—pale, wide-eyed, and draped in finery like a lamb dressed for slaughter.

"Mezhen," I say, fighting to keep my voice steady, "where are we?"

She shakes her head, eyes downcast. "Not to say."

My heart sinks further. "Who am I . . . who am I supposed to marry?"

Again, that sad shake of the head. "Not to say."

Frustration and fury clench my fists, and I open my mouth, ready to demand answers, when the door swings open.

Benjamin O'Shea strides in, and my breath seizes in my chest. "Daddy?"

This is what I've been wanting for so long—a confrontation, a chance to demand answers. But as I take in his flat hazel eyes, the red mop of his receding hair, I find I have nothing to say to this lying piece of shit. The man I once idolized, the father I thought I knew, is a stranger wearing familiar skin.

"Well," he says in Gaelic, his gaze raking over me with a coldness that chills me to the bone, "don't you look lovely for a dead woman."

"How did you find me?" The words tumble out, a child's question from a woman who should know better.

Benjamin faces Mezhen and jerks his head toward the door, and for a second, I wonder what the point is; I doubt she understands Gaelic.

Mezhen immediately slips out of the room, eyes glinting with an unnamed emotion. I know she's a servant, but I'm sure the circumstances of her employment are darker than meets the eye.

"I was hoping you'd have a more serious question for me, considering you have very little time to meet your groom." His casual tone, as if we're discussing the weather and not my forced marriage, makes me sick to my stomach.

"How on earth can you even think this is okay? How could you do this?"

"Again, wrong questions." His dismissal ignites a fire in my chest.

"If you think kidnapping me," I spit, the venom in my voice surprising even me, "and decking me up in some fucked up wedding dress is going to make me willingly marry some cunt and play your sick games, you've got the wrong fucking pawn.

He grunts. "Your time with the Italians has generally improved your manners, hasn't it?"

His sarcasm cuts deep, reminding me of happier times when his teasing was affectionate, not cruel.

"Why?" I demand, my voice shaking with rage.

"Finally, a good question. Now, if only you'd done as you were told and moved back into the house. If only you'd stuck within the boundaries I gave you. This wouldn't happen."

"What? You're doing this because I moved out of the house?"

"No, you. You are going to have to do this because, like your mother, you can't stop panting after some Italian vermin. They played their tricks and forced us to start an unfinishable war."

He shakes his head in disgust. "And to think that you were supposed to marry a good, honorable man from a respectable family. Now I'll need you to clean up your own mess and pay for an army large enough to wipe out those vermin once and for all. You're marrying the leader of the Shadow Gang."

His words are like many knives, cutting deep into me, but I refuse to give him the satisfaction of seeing me unraveling. I say with as much sarcasm as I can muster. "Oh, I see. This was an impromptu brokerage. You actually had another loser lined up for me. I wonder, when were you going to inform your broodmare of that match made in Mob heaven?"

His expression hardens, a mask sliding into place. "This is no joke, Adele. This is happening. And if you'd waited that day instead of running off in a childish snit, you would have heard everything you needed to."

A bitter laugh escapes me, surprising us both with its harshness. "Oh, stuff it. I now know everything you were hiding, including who my real father is."

His features contort into something ugly and terrifying. "Who is he?"

I can't believe he doesn't know. The thought is so absurd that I laugh. "You mean your sister had an affair with your enemy for more than five years, and you never found out who it was? I'm almost embarrassed for you. The Italians would have figured it out within days."

"Oh, we know it's Vito Vitelli. Naomi was a sneaky little bitch, but she wasn't half as smart as she thought she was." The casual cruelty in his voice hurts, but I steel myself against the feeling.

He continues, his mouth twisting, "Which also means that the scum you were whoring yourself with back in college is your half-brother."

I see disgust written all over his face, and something in me breaks. "Yes. Well, as you failed to mention that crucial detail to me, guess what, Benjamin? I've been doing a lot more than whoring, and I'm now pregnant with his child."

The silence that follows is thick and overwhelming. His eyebrows fly up, shock stamped on his rapidly paling face. Whether it is from hearing his first name again or the news of my pregnancy, I can't tell. And there's something else in his face. An unmistakable terror.

In an instant, he's across the room, his index finger held up against my lips. "You'd do well to keep your mouth shut," he hisses, "otherwise you will not leave here with your tongue. And if you dare mention your connection with the Italians to your new husband and his people they won't hesitate to cut that bastard out of you."

I jerk my head away from his finger, my heart pounding as I realize that Benjamin is afraid of something going wrong with this arrangement.

Just who the hell is this asshole bartering me to?

He steps back and continues in a cold, detached tone. "In any case, the situation is easily remedied. Tonight, you only have to do one thing. Spread your legs. Which shouldn't be too hard for you, considering. Tomorrow, I'll take you back to Boston where you will get rid of . . ." He trails off, glaring at my belly, "your problem."

All I can do is stare at him. And here I was, thinking nothing could ever shock or horrify me.

"And, oh. Your new husband will not be returning for you. He has a few bullets with his name on them, courtesy of his very own brothers. That should help you get through tonight."

His words sink in slowly, like poison seeping through my veins. This is really happening. I'm not just playing some sick dress-up game or trying to ward off the cold. I'm going to be forced to marry another man and sleep with him tonight.

The world tilts. My vision blurs, the edges of my sight darkening as my hands begin to tremble. My ears are ringing with the need to flee. My breath comes out in short, ragged gasps, and my legs feel like cooked noodles, threatening to buckle beneath me with every second. It's like standing alone on the deck of a ship in a terrible storm with nothing to hold on to.

Unhelpfully, my mind decides it's time to show me flashes of my immediate future—a faceless man's hands groping me, forcing me—and bile rises in my throat.

Breathe, Addy. Just breathe.

I try to suck in a breath, but I can't. The walls are closing in. My chest tightens, ribs straining under the constricting pressure of doom. And then Dante's voice pierces through the fog, the same words he says every time he's trapped me under him.

Don't panic. You drown faster when you do.

I cling to them, and I force myself to take a breath—then another—until the room steadies and the tightness in my chest begins to ease.

I focus on the air filling my lungs, the way it cools the fire in my veins. Slowly, my vision clears, the dizziness recedes, and my hands stop shaking.

As if sensing that I'm on the verge of losing it, Benjamin switches his tone to the warm comforting one I remember from childhood—the same one he'd use to talk me down the ledge of panic before another surgery. It should be soothing, if only his next words didn't completely shatter me.

"Look. You have no choice but to pay the upfront cost: An exchange of blood vows and one full night with you. But I promise, Adele, tonight will be the last time you ever lay eyes on him."

My eyelids fall closed as a calm settles over me. This is the closure I need. I was nothing but a pawn, an asset to the Mob, and a willing captive. And now, a legal tender to purchase an army.

I was never a daughter to Benjamin O'Shea. No real father would do this to his daughter. My father is Orlando De Luca, a ruthless mafia

Capo and a drug lord. And I would take him over this sadistic, lying piece of shit in front of me.

When I open my eyes, they're as cold and hard as the gun I wish I had right now. "Alright. Can I at least know more about the man I'll be marrying besides him being the top gun of some gang?"

A cruel, almost proud smile twists Benjamin's lips. He thinks I've got my shit together and ready to play ball. His mocking tone returns. "All in good time, Adele. You'll have plenty of time to meet him. You'll be spending the whole night with him, after all."

Suddenly, I let out a carefully controlled sob. My eyes, however, remain dry as a bone. The sobs continue, increasing in volume until my entire body is shaking with them.

He stands there, hesitating, watching me like a science project gone wrong. I think a part of him wants to do what he did in the past; take me in his arms and tell me it'll be okay. But the masks are off now, and he doesn't need to hide what an absolute joke of a father he is.

I cradle my lower belly as I think of Dante again. Fierce, dominant, protective Dante. Will he even realize that I'm gone? Will anyone? I'm sure Aydin could spin a tale for everyone to explain my disappearance. I can only pray it's not too late.

One thing is clear, though: I'd rather die than marry this son of a bitch.

When he continues to gawk like a stunned fish, I spit, "How about you get out so I can have a moment to myself before I'm sold off?"

Benjamin shakes his head and huffs, "As long as you remember the stakes." Then he leaves without another word. As if I'm the one being unreasonable.

The moment the door clicks shut, I straighten up, and my sobs cut off abruptly.

I don't know where the cameras are, but I need anything that could be a weapon. My gaze lands on the food table, and suddenly, I'm ravenous. As I approach, my eyes lock on a wooden spoon. There's nothing else on the table. No fork, no knife, no glassware.

Still feigning tears, I reach for a spoon and yogurt. It's not much, but the spoon is surprisingly sturdy. Better than nothing. As I eat, my mind races with possibilities, my thumb brushing over the rounded end of the spoon, making a mental note to find a way to sharpen it.

I have no illusions about escaping before the ceremony. But after? During the "wedding night"?

That's when I'll make my move. That's when I'll fight.

CHAPTER FORTY

Dante

As the door closes behind Nico, I take a deep breath and say to Sal, "Call the smug son of a bitch."

Sal fishes out a sleek black digital device, scrolls down, then starts typing a secure communication code onto the laptop.

Like a nomad, Cade's location changes every few weeks, but he never fails to update his sister, who invariably passes the information to Sal.

Within seconds, the line crackles to life, and I hear the gravelly voice of the man I despise almost as much as I need right now.

"Hey, Sparrow," he calls Sophie's road name, an unusual warmth seeping into his voice.

"It's er . . . Dante," I say through gritted teeth.

Cade's tone instantly drops a thousand degrees colder when he demands, "Is Sophie okay?"

"Sophie's fine," I reply. "But I need—"

"Then we're done here, *Dumber*." Cade cuts me off, ready to hang up.

"Wait, Quinn." I clench my fist and swallow my pride, knowing what's at stake. "I need your help finding two women."

Silence greets me for what feels like a full minute, and then Cade drawls, "So, you've lost a couple of your imported pleasure slaves. What the fuck do you want me to do about that, besides lock you up?"

I take a calming breath and then force the words out. "You know better, Quinn. You know we don't deal with flesh—"

"Which is the only reason you're all still breathing—"

"Those women have been kidnapped, you fucking sanctimonious prick!"

Another interminable pause, during which it sounds like he opened a bag of chips and ate half of it. I feel my right eyelid starting to twitch.

"Still not my problem." Cade snaps, munching.

I bite back a curse and take another breath. I knew getting Cade on board would be difficult, but I didn't expect it to feel like swallowing glass shards.

"Quinn, they're not just anyone. Addy is my woman, and Kira, her friend, is like a sister to me."

"Could be your grandma and your day-old baby, and I still wouldn't give a fuck."

God, I hate this guy. Give me hot coals to walk barefoot on any day. Not him.

In desperation, I play my last card. "Listen. Addy's pregnant with Sophie's nephew—or niece. And I have cause to believe she's being forced into a marriage tonight. And Kira, who was taken as leverage . . ." I pause, feeling like a heel for playing the sympathy card, but the only language the bastard understands is vulnerability. "Kira . . . she's registered blind."

A longer silence. When he speaks again, his voice has lost its lazy drawl. "Explain. Now."

I take a deep breath, knowing I'm about to reveal more than I'd like to this prick. "Addy is actually Benjamin O'Shea's daughter—"

"Who is now dead, so spin me another tale—"

My patience finally snapping, I growl, "If only you'd shut the fuck up and listen, Quinn, you'd learn she's not dead—"

"*Dumber,* I'm two fucking seconds away from hanging up—" Cade snaps back.

Sal shoulders me away and interjects. "Mr. Quinn, this is Salvatore."

"Oh, look who we have here," Cade's voice drips with sarcasm. "It's our Harvard felon!"

Sal doesn't rise to his bait. "Addy O'Shea is alive. We faked her death to keep her safe. The Mob is moving in, which wouldn't usually be a problem, but they need a mercenary army to face us. Addy has been sold to the Philly Shadow Gang in exchange for an army. Kira was used to get Addy and probably is of no use to them anymore. There's a chance Kira could be . . . discarded or enslaved once they've got their alliance done and dusted. Please help us."

My head whirls to Sal, the urge to deck him beating down on me. I mouth, "Please help us? Are you insane?"

Sal only shrugs, apparently not caring about having to grovel.

Doesn't he realize Cade Quinn was caught the moment I mentioned Sophie's nephew or niece? The man would do anything for his sister. He's just enjoying giving me shit.

After another long pause, Cade mutters, "You felons sure know how to fuck shit up royally, don't you?"

"Look, can you help or not?" I snap.

"I can. But only because Sal begged. Fuck, that was hot, Salvatore." I can practically hear the leer in his voice.

Jesus Christ. The guy is disgusting. Adopted brother or not, I just don't see how he and Sophie can be siblings.

I manage to remain silent. Still, Cade makes me wait. Just when I'm about to hurl the laptop at the wall, he speaks, his voice taking on a crisp note. "I'll need access to your systems and everything you know. And thirty minutes."

"Done," I say without hesitation. "Whatever you need, Sherlock."

"Good. And tell *Dumb* that when this is over, if he steps one toe out of the line I've drawn him, his ass rots in a maximum security prison. That goes for you, too, *Dumber*. Are we clear?"

"Crystal." I snap, relief and gratitude warring with my natural distaste for the man.

The line cuts off again, and I mutter, *"Dumbest."*

Waiting for another thirty minutes feels like an eternity when Addy's life is on the line, but I know Cade Quinn, and as much as it galls me to admit it, he's our best shot at extracting her quickly and safely.

I use the tense half hour to brief the men who've reported at Nico's orders, preparing for every possible scenario. Sal paces the room, his usual calm demeanor cracking under the weight of worry.

Orlando, learning of his daughter's kidnap, insists on joining us despite my initial reservations. His eyes burn with a father's determination, and I recognize the same desperation I feel.

When the secure line buzzes from the screen again, I dive for the keyboard, immediately realizing for the first time when I glance at the coordinates that the guy is outside the country.

"Talk to me," I bark.

"Calm the fuck down." Cade's sardonic voice crackles through. "1420 Callowhill Street, Philadelphia. It's a brownstone, heavily fortified. Security systems are top-notch, thankfully, which means I can fuck it up faster. Basement is where the action is. Some drunken orgy. Wedding reception Shadow Gang style, I reckon."

Clenching my fist, I suppress the urge to put it through the wall. I hate to admit it, but the bastard's reach is impressive. All the way from Havana, he's managed to pinpoint Kira and Addy's location in a matter of minutes.

"So, what are we walking into?" I ask.

"Half a dozen armed on the perimeter. I can give you a clear path to the property. But I hope you know I can't control their weapons, *Dumber*. You'll need to aim and shoot."

"Understood," I say, this time not biting. "Anything else, Sherlock?"

"Only that if you end up wasting my time and fail to get those women out in one piece, I'll be really pissed off."

He disconnects, but this time I don't have time to wonder what the guy's problem is beyond the adrenaline pumping in my veins. In a matter of minutes, we have a location, we have intel, and almost unbelievably, we have Cade Quinn on our side.

I turn to the extraction team, a group of eight men, including Sal and Orlando. "Gear up. We leave in ten."

The next few minutes are a blur of activity. Weapons are checked and loaded. Kevlar vests are donned. Comms are tested. Usually, I'd be itching for my AirPods, but right now, I want to revel in my fury. First, I need to get Addy safe.

Then I'll unleash hell on Philadelphia.

The jet touches down in exactly one hour with a jolt that matches the urgency pulsing through me. As we disembark, I relish the cold crisp night air and the faint stench of the nearby Delaware River. The city lights twinkle in the distance, oblivious to the storm brewing.

An armored Klassen Sprinter waits on the tarmac, and we pile in silently, each man's face a mask of determination. The van seats twelve comfortably, but with just nine of us—myself, Sal, Orlando, and six of our most trusted soldiers—the extra space only amplifies the tension hanging in the air.

As we pull away from the airfield, Cade's voice crackles through our earpieces. "Welcome to the City of Brotherly Love, assholes."

I grit my teeth, resisting the urge to rip out the comm. "Just give us a tested route, Quinn."

"What's the matter, *Dumber?* Too anxious for a witty comeback? Addy will be fine—if you don't fuck up." Despite his mocking tone, I can hear the rapid clack of his keyboard in the background. While reassuring me that he's finding me answers, the sound begins to wind me up after it carries on for a full minute.

"The route, Quinn," I snap. "Before I decide to find my own way."

He snorts. "As if you could find your own ass with both hands and a map. His tone turns serious. "Take I-95 North, then exit onto Callowhill Street. Your destination is halfway down the block."

I relay the directions to our driver as Cade continues. "You'll have a five-minute window once I disable their security systems."

"Copy that," I respond, then turn to the team. "Addy and Kira are the priority. Everything else is secondary. Sal and I go in and get the girls.

Orlando, you too. After they're out, the floor is all yours, *ragazzi*. And you'd better dance like it's open fucking season."

Sal nods, his usually jovial face set in hard lines. Orlando casually slips a toothpick into his mouth, but I can see his knuckles are white on his weapon, and a father's fury is radiating off him in waves.

As we near Callowhill Street, I feel the familiar pre-mission calm settling over me. The world narrows down to the objective: get in, get the girls, get out.

Everything else fades away.

CHAPTER FORTY-ONE

Adele

I managed to turn the blunt end of the spoon handle into a deeper oval, not quite the pointy edge I was hoping for, but at least it didn't splinter or break. It's now tucked securely into the side of my bra, reminding me that anything can be a weapon. For the first time in as long as I can remember, I'm grateful for my double Ds.

The spoon may be insignificant, but it's the anchor holding me together right now.

By the time Mezhen returns with a tattooed, barrel-chested guard, I'm ready—resolved to face whatever fate awaits me without flinching. I've survived worse odds.

"Is it time?" I grit out.

They both look somewhat nonplussed. I imagine the goon expected to have to drag me out.

"Yes," Mezhen says, watching me curiously as I leave the room.

"He's . . ." Mezhen starts, wringing her hands, and I look back at her. She hesitates as if searching for words. "He's waiting. For you."

There's no malice in her eyes, and yet there's a hint of something dark. Something that looks a lot like envy, but I can't be sure. Suddenly, I want to know her story. I have a feeling she might have arrived in the country under conditions similar to Aydin's, yet Mezhen might as well still be in shackles for all the freedom she appears to have.

Is she a . . . slave?

And why I'm suddenly so concerned about another woman's predicament when I might be facing a worse fate is beyond me. Without another glance at Mezhen, I follow the guard out.

And find Benjamin pacing the red-carpeted hallway.

"There you are!" He comes to me and takes my elbow, which makes me flinch.

"I see no point in pretending now, so you can take that filthy hand off me." I snap and start to walk as fast as my billowy skirt will allow.

He sighs with exaggerated patience and catches up to me. "Trust me. When you meet your husband, you'll be glad I held your hand."

I stumble, throwing my arms out. Benjamin smoothly catches me and steadies me on my feet.

I'll be glad he held my hand?

If Benjamin meant to scare me, he just succeeded because my bladder suddenly lurches, even though I've just been to the bathroom.

Although the answer couldn't be clearer if it were written in neon lights across his forehead, I'm still unable to stop myself from asking him. "Was it ever real . . . Did you ever even love me?"

He replies blandly as the guard nudges us to move down the hallway. "You are my daughter, Adele. Of course, I love you. You just don't realize how much danger you're in with those Italians."

I shake my head, trying a last-ditch effort to make him understand. "Have you for once considered that I might actually want to be with those Italians?"

"They killed your mother. They're still trying to kill you."

"They're my family!" I say, my voice getting more frantic as we near the end of the hallway. "They never tried to kill me. They found the real killer and have been protecting me."

"Is that the bullshit they fed you?" He scoffs, as we reach a tall oak door.

"That's the truth. They're the only reason I'm alive right now. So, you see, you can still stop the war. You don't have to do this. They'll come after every single one of you if you sell me off to this guy."

"Oh, I'm not worried about retaliation since they won't exist after tonight." He pushes the door and holds it open for me to enter.

Oh shit. Here we go.

***

We enter a long room reeking of stale cigarette smoke. Thick white columns carved with intricate designs rise from the floor to the ceiling and bracket the aisle. Recessed lighting casts a bluish glow across the space.

I notice the glaring lack of windows, which makes me wonder if we are in a basement. The walls are draped in rich white silk wallpaper, subtly patterned with delicate motifs that catch the light. The floors are polished concrete, buffed to a mirror sheen. A ventilation system hums quietly, barely managing to disperse the heavy smoke.

If I hadn't grown accustomed to the Vitelli brand of luxury, I might have been slightly impressed with this attempt at underground opulence.

The room is bare, except for the painted white wooden altar at the end of the narrow aisle between the pillars. The altar sits on a raised dais, its edges and posts adorned with red roses.

Somehow the sight of those roses, like drops of blood in the otherwise white room, seems so out of place. It sends icy fingers of fear tracing down my back.

Benjamin's hand forces me into the room when I hesitate on the threshold. This time I let him. I'm too busy craning my neck to see the person at the other end of the aisle.

But there's no groom waiting for me. The altar stands empty.

What I do see behind the last giant pillar at the very end of the aisle nearly makes my heart stop. Standing there, next to a stone-faced guard is Kira, her unseeing eyes wide with fear.

The pieces snap into place—Benjamin must have used her to get to Aydin and then me. A wave of guilt and fear washes over me, making my knees weak. Kira's here because of me, in danger because of me.

But when I see what she's wearing, hysterical laughter bubbles up in my throat, much to Benjamin's chagrin. The dress is an abomination—a sickly green and brown thing that looks like it was dragged through a swamp. It's ill-fitting and made of a material that's clearly driving Kira mad. As if on cue, she scratches her arms furiously.

Looks like I wasn't the only one left half-naked and freezing with no choice but to put on a revolting dress.

My snicker echoes in the room, and Kira's head snaps up.

"Addy? Is that you? Oh my God! They're smarter than I gave them credit for! I swear, when I talked, I didn't think they'd actually be able to break you out of the Fortress. I'm so sorry—"

Her words cut off as the beefy man beside her shoves a gun against her temple, a nudge for her to be quiet.

"Asshole," Kira hisses.

My laughter dies instantly, replaced by a cold dread settling in my stomach. Seeing Kira in danger because of me makes the reality of our situation hit home with brutal force.

And then the doors open. I whip my head around, my pulse a staccato rhythm in my ears.

A paunchy priest enters first, followed by a man who seems to have crawled out of someone's nightmare. He stalks down the aisle, leisurely, trailing far behind the priest, his gaze locked onto mine with sniper-like precision. Finally, he reaches me, planting himself directly in front of me.

Is the universe playing a cosmic joke on me?

He's tall. Almost as tall as Dante, but that's where the similarities end. He's wearing a suit with the shirt half unbuttoned to reveal heavy gold necklaces. His lean, sinewy chest is covered in tattoos that creep up his neck and onto half his face. One entire eyeball is tattooed black. Stringy black hair is braided at his nape, and his thin lips part in a sinister smile to reveal chipped and missing teeth.

A violent shudder runs through me, and I have to force myself not to run from the room.

"Who's there, Addy?" Kira asks, her nose wrinkling. "They reek of tobacco and garlic."

I can't speak, too horrified by what I'm seeing.

"Shut up," her captor growls, shoving the barrel of the gun harder against her temple.

"Oww! In case you haven't noticed, jerk, I can't see. I need people to make sounds or talk to me."

A part of me admires Kira for taking this remarkably well, but then again, it's Kira. I'm not really surprised. I draw more strength from that and force myself to stay calm.

The man before me speaks, his raspy voice just as repulsive as his appearance. "Your daughter's gonna fit in nicely here, Ben O'Shea. Such a sweet little thing."

Benjamin nods tightly and steps away.

He says to me. "Listen, little dove, the name's Sean Hall. But around here, you call me your King."

Sean Hall? I think, barely suppressing a snort even as my stomach turns. It is such a mundane, normal name for a man who looks like he clawed his way out of a back alley fight club.

He doesn't look or sound like a Sean Hall. He looks like a Krull the Destroyer or Gorlock the Defiler. Something that matches his grotesque appearance and the malevolence oozing from his every pore. Sean Hall sounds like he should be selling insurance, not leading a gang of criminals.

Kira makes a sound that's a cross between a shocked gasp and a disgusted gag.

My sentiments exactly, I think, fighting to keep my expression perfect: *Terrified but not repulsed. Reluctant but not resistant.*

I remind myself of those very first mindset lessons with Dante. I thought they were boring and useless, and had been all too eager to move on to the juicy part of trying out the lethal moves. But now I see how Sean's initial impression of me could make or break my plan.

He must not see me as a threat.

I square my shoulders and give him a tremulous smile, hoping it doesn't come off as a grimace of disgust. He smiles back at me, and I want to gag.

He reaches out to finger a lock of my hair. "Look at all that red. That perfect soft skin just begging for my marks. Little dove, I can't wait to fill up every damn hole you got."

I'm sorry, I can't do this. It's going to be too hard to pretend I'm not picturing all the delightful ways I'd like to kill this monster.

Kira's horrified gasp breaks the ensuing silence, but Sean, apparently, isn't done trying to make us vomit, because he says, "You're welcome to stay and watch me fuck your daughter, Ben. See that your down payment is well received."

"That will not be necessary," Benjamin mutters, a hard glint in his otherwise impassive face.

Sean shrugs, laughing—a grating, terrible sound. "Your call. Offer still stands." Now, he faces the priest, who looks bored. Or stoned? I'm not sure which. "Let's get this shit over and done with."

The ceremony starts in a blur. I repeat strange vows that sound more like an initiation chant, spurred on by the gun aimed at Kira's head. As the priest finishes, Sean produces a wicked-looking knife, its blade gleaming in the harsh light.

"Now, we seal our union in blood," Sean growls, his black eye glinting with malicious glee.

He grabs my hand roughly, slicing a deep cut across my thumb. I bite back a cry of pain as he does the same to his own. Then, with a grip like iron, he presses our bleeding thumbs together.

"Blood of my blood," he intones, his voice thick with anticipation. "Bound in life, bound in death."

Before I can react, he brings my bleeding thumb to his mouth, his tongue darting out to lick the wound. I fight the urge to recoil as he savors the taste, a low groan escaping him.

"Sweet," he murmurs, his eyes locked on mine. "Just like I knew you'd be, little dove."

Then, with deliberate slowness, he pushes his own bloody thumb into my mouth. The metallic taste makes me gag, but I force myself to remain still.

"There," Sean leers, his fetid breath hot on my face. "Now you've got a taste of your king. Very soon, you'll be choking on a lot more than that."

The vulgarity of his words, the sight of my blood on his teeth, and the feeling of his blood on my tongue make my stomach roil. He pulls away, trailing his bleeding thumb across my lips down my chin, the side of my neck, and my arm, leaving a crimson stain on my white dress.

I know that this is only the beginning of the horrors to come.

CHAPTER FORTY-TWO

Adele

The "wedding reception" is held in a cavernous hall that stinks of stale cigar smoke and beer. Steel chandeliers hang from the vaulted ceiling, their lights harsh and unforgiving, highlighting the half-drunk, leering faces of the attendees.

They're all men. Hard eyes glint beneath furrowed brows, tattoos snake across their skin, and metals glint from ears, noses, and lips. Their suits hang awkwardly on muscled frames as if borrowed from smaller, softer men for this rare occasion. But it's their faces that chill me to the bone. Scars crisscross weathered skin—some faded with time, others angry and fresh—that tell of unspeakable violence and brutality.

Half-naked girls flit between the rows of guests, getting roughly groped, some dragged onto laps, and a few bent over tables. Still, they continue to serve. They don't seem repulsed, nor do they resist. They're simply . . . resigned.

I sit beside Sean at the head table, perched on an uncomfortable gilt chair. The crystals and stones in my dress catch the light, and every little movement and each breath is a reminder that I'm trapped in this nightmare.

The last three hours have purged me of any lingering wide-eyed innocence.

I'm now Mrs. Sean Hall of the Shadow gang. Wife to a depraved savage who can't wait to get into my holes. I pinch myself again, hoping this has all been a bad dream.

But no. I don't wake up. My husband's hand still rests heavily on my thigh, his fingers digging into the flesh just above my knee.

The table before us is laden with untouched food—roast beef bleeding onto fine china, lobster tails curling in their shells, caviar glistening atop delicate blinis. The sight of it all turns my stomach.

Sean leans in close, his breath hot and sour against my ear. "Smile, little dove. This is our wedding reception."

"Yes," I force my lips into what I hope passes for a smile.

"Yes, what?" he rasps, his fingers tightening on my thigh. I resist the urge to squirm away, acutely aware of the wooden spoon hidden in my bra which now seems about as useful as a piece of wool against the monstrosity that is Sean Hall.

But I have to try.

Adam's Apple, Brachial Plexus, Eyes, Jugular, Balls. I silently chant then swallow hard, willing my voice not to shake. "Yes . . . my King."

He grins, revealing his chipped front tooth. "That's a good little dove. You're a quick learner."

Oh, you have no fucking idea.

As I scan the room, my eyes searching desperately for Kira, worry gnaws at my insides. She's disappeared since Sean and I exchanged vows.

Sean's voice suddenly rises above the din of clinking glasses and murmured conversations.

"Tomorrow, we link up with our Boston boys and take out those Chicago rats for good. What kinda dumbass name is 'The Outfit' anyway?" He throws up air quotes. "They deserve to be wiped off the fucking map for the shit they pulled. Killing children while in bed? That just ain't right no matter how you slice it."

A chorus of agreement rises from the surrounding tables. I'm numb enough to school my features into a mask of indifference, but I want to laugh at the thought of this gang taking on the Outfit. They might win in a drunken brawl. But in an all-out war? They stand about as much chance as a snowman in a sauna.

I catch sight of Benjamin at the far end of the room. He's sitting next to a lean, graying man with deep grooves along his forehead and bracketing his mouth. I recognize him as one of Benjamin's long-term clients from my childhood. Benjamin's head is slightly inclined toward him, a gesture of deference I've rarely seen.

There's something striking about this man. He exudes a polished, authoritative air, reminiscent of . . . Nico.

Is he the Irish Mob Boss?

My mind races. Why would he choose to align with this suicide squad here? Does he even comprehend the magnitude of what he's up against? That the Fortress alone houses enough weapons to annihilate an entire state? That they command billions in both legal and illegal funds, with tentacles reaching into the police force, FBI, and political spheres?

A serving girl arrives bearing a tray of champagne flutes. The bubbles catch the light, reminding me of happier times—of lounging by the pool with Dante, his laughter echoing off the water. The memory triggers a physical ache in my chest.

I reach for a glass, desperate for anything to dull the edge of this nightmare, not caring that I might puke. But Sean waves off the servant.

"No alcohol for my little dove," he announces loudly into the room, his eyes gleaming with malice. "She needs to know what a real man feels like. You'll want to feel my cock for weeks, dove, until I come back for you."

A ripple of laughter moves through the nearby guests. I feel my cheeks burn anew with humiliation and anger. From across the room, I catch Benjamin's eye. Even he looks ill and regretful. After all, he was my father for eighteen years. No man wants to see his daughter with an animal.

Adam's Apple, Brachial Plexus, Eyes, Jugular, Balls.

As the night wears on, I find myself thinking of Dante, of Nico and Sal and Enzo—father of six, and the rest of their soldiers. Compared to this lot, they're like royalty. The contrast is stark and painful.

I continue to play the naïve, dutiful wife, averting my gaze and smiling shyly whenever Sean looks my way while my mind races with possibilities. I know I will kill him tonight. Somehow.

He'll underestimate me; I'm small, and I walk with a limp. He'll not expect any aggression. Benjamin is right under his roof, waiting to take the army he paid for back to Boston. And probably most importantly, Sean is half-drunk and horny. The hand on my thigh is trembling slightly, and his erection is disgustingly obvious. His reflexes are very likely shot.

No, the problem isn't killing him. It's surviving after I do. I've worked out hundreds of scenarios and there isn't one where I don't end up dead by morning.

Eventually, Sean stands, his chair scraping loudly against the floor, making me jump. He pulls me up roughly by my arm, his fingers digging into my flesh, and I relish the pain, letting it harden my resolve.

"Time to retire with my dove," he announces to the room, eliciting a chorus of lewd cheers and whistles.

As we make our way out of the hall, I catch one last glimpse of Benjamin. His face is a mask of regret, but he doesn't move to intervene. The man I once called father turns away, abandoning me to my fate.

Adam's Apple, Brachial Plexus, Eyes, Jugular, Balls. Please give me a fucking chance.

The walk to the bedroom is a blur of dimly lit corridors and the sound of Sean's heavy breathing. When we finally reach the room, he shoves me inside, slamming the door behind us. A massive four-poster bed dominates the space. Heavy curtains block out any moonlight, leaving us in the artificial glow of ornate lamps.

Without being told, I begin to strip.

"Oh, little dove," he licks his lips, his black eye gleaming like a dark gem. "So well trained. I can smell your fear, y'know. Eager and scared. Are you wet?"

"I—I . . ." I make myself stutter.

"Are you?" He barks.

"I'm not . . . sure, My King," I whisper.

He grabs his crotch. "We'll find out, won't we? Get on with it."

The spoon feels like a dead weight against the side of my breast. As long as I take off my own clothes, we're good. I make the disrobing a show, each movement deliberate and slow.

By the time I've shed the heavy dress and I'm down to my dusky pink, lacy plunge bra and thong, I want to break down and cry. I wore them for Dante this morning. I grit my teeth, reaching behind me to undo the clasp of my bra, holding the cup against my breasts to keep the spoon from slipping out.

Carefully, I slide the bra away from my body and place it on the bed, my heart hammering. But it seems I needn't have bothered. From the glazed look in Sean's eyes—well, the normal one that's still visible in the dim light—I could have stuffed an armored tank in my cleavage and he wouldn't notice.

"Lie down," he commands, his voice thick with desire.

I nod, heaving a sigh of relief that he's had enough of the striptease, and I make myself get on the bed, facing down on the silk white bedspread so I can discreetly slide my bra under the pillows.

"On your back," he barks.

I roll over.

He comes closer, his eyes roving over me as he sheds his clothes. I keep my focus on the intricate patterns on the ceiling. I know I should look—I might catch something useful, a weakness, a tattoo—but I'm barely holding my body and mind together.

And then he falls on me.

Splinters of panic lodge in my brain as Sean's weight crushes me into the mattress, his breath hot and unwelcome on my face. My fight-or-flight response kicks in, but I force it down, along with the urge to curl up and disappear. Instead, I make my body go pliant, my mind recalibrating as I stare at his neck, waiting for the perfect moment.

Thank God my arms are still free. He didn't tie me up.

Sean's hands start to paw at me, rough and demanding. Unable to take any more without puking, I strike.

Quick as a snake, I bring the heel of my hand up, smashing it into his Adam's apple. The impact jolts up my arm, and I grit my teeth against the pain.

Sean instantly rears back, wheezing, both hands flying to his throat.

"You—" he tries to speak, but barely any sound comes out. A spark of hope flares in me. I think it worked. I crushed his windpipe—or at least bruised it.

But the wooden spoon hidden under the pillow suddenly seems woefully inadequate against the fury radiating from Sean. It's too late to go back to playing the shy, compliant wife. My cover is blown.

I reach under the pillow, but Sean is faster than I anticipated. Despite the alcohol dulling his reflexes, the instincts honed by years of violence still prevail. His hand clamps around my wrist, twisting until pain shoots up my arm.

"What's that?" he snarls, his face contorting with rage. "Trying to play the hero, are we?" He yanks away the pillow, blinks in surprise then starts to cackle like a madman when he sees it.

He wrenches my arm until I cry out, convinced my wrist is broken. "You wanna come at me with what?" He picks it up and shoves it under my nose. "A spoon? A fucking wooden spoon!"

He lets the spoon fall uselessly to the bed beside us. "You know, for a moment, I thought you might be different. I was going to treat you like a real queen. But it looks like you want to be used like a slut."

No, no, no. This wasn't how it was supposed to go. Panic rises in my throat.

Sean's hand closes around my throat, cutting off my air. "By the time I'm done with you, my dove," he hisses, "you'll never be able to look at a spoon without screaming."

Black spots dance at the edges of my vision as I gasp for breath. My free hand claws at his face, nails digging into his cheek and raking down viciously until I feel his skin peel under my fingernails. He jerks back and rolls off me with a loud curse, and I suck in desperate breaths.

When he wipes at his cheeks and sees his hands coming away bloody, he grabs me by the hair and growls into my face, his eyes pools of blue murder. "Oh, I'll so enjoy breaking the fight out of you."

Shit. My scalp is on fire, and I'm no closer to being free. All I've done is make him angrier.

Think, Addy, think. What can you do?

My eyes dart around the room, searching desperately for something, anything, I can use. That's when I see it—the heavy crystal ashtray on his nightstand. But how do I get from here to there?

I steel myself, knowing what I have to do. It's going to hurt, but it's my only chance. I hack my throat and spit into his eye, desperately wishing it were acid. Wishing it were something sharp, something that could do more damage than just piss him off and earn me a beating.

As Sean pulls back his fist, I brace myself. The backhand blow lands with explosive force, pain blooming across my cheek. But I use the momentum, letting it roll me off the bed. I hit the floor hard and pain shoots through my hip. The spoon clatters beside me, and I dive for it, feeling the hard edge dig into my throbbing thumb.

My hip spasms and stiffens, flaring up at the worst possible moment, but I grit my teeth and force myself to move. I just need to reach that ashtray.

Before I can scramble to my feet, Sean grabs my hair again and jerks me back into him. I feel him behind me, my back plastered to his naked chest, the foot-long height difference between us only adding to the intimidation. He yanks my hair so hard I cry out, and he laughs—a cruel, unmistakable excitement in the sound.

He bends down, licks the shell of my ear, and growls, "That's it, little dove. Sing for me. You all fight and resist, but in the end, you will surrender—writhing in a puddle of your tears, drool, and piss, begging for more of the cleansing pain." He twists his fist again, and as much as I hate it, hate him for the way he's getting off on my pain, I cry out again.

"You're just like all the others. Only fit to be used and broken." His other fist joins in, making me wince in pain.

"Are you going to beg, or do you want to play some more?" he breathes into my ear.

"Please," I yell. "Please."

He only twists harder.

I can't take it anymore. Driven by pure adrenaline and self-preservation, I swing high and back with all my might. This time, he's not fast enough to untangle his hands from my thick, curly hair and stop my swinging arm. It connects with a satisfying squelch.

Sean's howl of pain is unlike any sound I've heard from a human before. He reels back, his hands falling away from my hair. And then he's whimpering like a wounded dog. I'm almost too terrified to turn and see what I've done to him.

But I turn. And promptly retch onto the floor.

Blood streams down his face, and the bowl of the spoon is protruding from his black eye. The handle is lodged squarely in his eyeball. He rocks in agony, one trembling hand hovering over his injured eye, the other flailing wildly, fingers opening and closing reflexively as if desperate to grab hold of me.

My whole body trembles as adrenaline courses through me. What the fuck have I just done? I want to sob because it's far from fucking over. He's lost an eye, but that blow won't kill him. If this man gets his hands on me, I'm a dead woman.

Either I end this now, or he snaps my neck.

I try to dart around him toward the ashtray, but Sean lunges for me. My fingers brush the handle just as his hand closes around my neck and jerks me backward with such force that my legs give out and I crash to the floor.

His body follows me down. "My eye! You fucking evil bitch, I'll kill you! I'll pluck out your eyes and feed them to you!"

Instantly, he's on top of me, his good eye wild with tears of pain and rage, while the black one weeps rivulets of blood down the length of the jutting spoon, dropping onto me. His hand finds my throat, fingers digging in.

"Did the Irish put you up to this?" I nod, and he squeezes harder. "I'll kill them. I'll kill them all."

It's like déjà vu—the feeling of being choked, fighting for air. But this time, we're not sparring. This time, it's not a measured punishment delivered by a man who knows my limits. This is an enraged beast who won't stop until I stop breathing.

"Who fucking sent you?" he spits at me. I grab his unrelenting hand, nails scratching his wrist, but he only tightens his grip.

Shit.

My lungs burn with the need to breathe, and my face starts to tingle. I slam the ashtray on the floor, shattering it. I hoped the action would distract him, but instead, he squeezes harder. I blindly reach for a shard, welcoming the way it slices into the flesh of my palm.

It's probably useless to penetrate his skin, let alone stab through his chest, but I have to try something. My darkening vision zeroes in on the soft spot just below his dangling, stretched earlobe.

"Dante . . ." I sputter over and over as my instincts take over. Sean pauses, then bends his head to hear me, allowing me to drag in a breath before he tightens his grip again.

"I said give me a fucking name," he wheezes.

I repeat Dante's name, but it only comes out as a muffled sound.

The moment Sean leans in closer, I swing my arm up and jab the shard into the angle of his jaw, driving it in with all my might and then some.

There's a sickening pop, followed by pain like I've never felt before, exploding in my shoulder. I scream with the first breath that rushes into my lungs, oblivious to the warm, coppery blood spraying over me like a macabre shower.

Sean's eyes widen in shock, his hands flying to his throat. Blood bubbles from his mouth as he tries to speak.

I roll him off me, scrambling back until I hit the wall. I watch in horror as he thrashes on the floor, gurgling and choking on his own blood. It feels like an eternity before he finally goes still.

The silence that follows is oppressive. I sit there, shaking, covered in sweat and blood—mine and Sean's. My cheek throbs, my shoulder feels like someone took a mallet to it, my hip aches, and every breath hurts. But I'm alive.

Slowly, I take it all in. Sean's dying body is inches from mine, his remaining eye staring blankly at the ceiling. With a choked sob, I push myself to my feet, cradling my throbbing arm.

Shaking violently, I stumble to the bathroom, desperately searching for a way out. There are none—no windows here either, no vents big enough to crawl through. Just gleaming marble and chrome fixtures that seem to mock me. Even if there were windows, I wouldn't be able to climb out with my injured arm hanging at an awkward angle.

As the reality of what's happened—what I've done—crashes over me, I crumple to the floor, sobs wracking my body. Blood—thick, sticky, and drying in rusty patches—coats my skin.

I've done it. I've killed a man. My husband. Brutally. And now what?

"Dante," I whisper into the empty room. "Where are you?"

But there's no answer. Just the sound of my own beating heart counting down the moments until someone comes to check on the bride and groom. Until my fragile safety shatters, and I have to fight again—or die.

I close my eyes, trying to summon Dante's face, his strength. I've survived this far, but I don't know how to survive what comes next.

CHAPTER FORTY-THREE

Adele

I stumble back to the bedroom, every step a reminder of the fight for my life. Collapsing at the foot of the bed, I find myself unable to tear my eyes from Sean's motionless body. What if he's just stunned? My breath catches with each imagined twitch.

Cradling my throbbing shoulder, I shift into a position that dulls the pain from excruciating to merely agonizing. But it's not just my shoulder—every inch of my body screams in protest.

My training never covered killing a perp only to end up trapped in a basement with his corpse. So I wait. And pray. For death. For a miracle. For an oblivion that never comes because suddenly, there is a soft knock on the door.

"My King, are you okay?" A woman's voice floats through the other side. "I heard . . . something."

Mezhen.

Had she been standing right outside the door all this time?

The knock continues for a full five minutes, by which time I can hear her heart-wrenching sobs. It's as if she knows he's dead. "Please . . . Sean," she whimpers. "Please be okay."

Fucking hell. Shouldn't she be jumping for joy? Stockholm much?

I'm dimly aware that might not be the most relevant thought considering I'm about to be found out, but I can't exactly focus on anything else.

With my good arm, I reach for the scrap of lace caught under Sean's massive body and pull it free. I'm not about to make my execution more exciting by having my tits out. I slip on the blood-soaked bra, pulling it over my injured arm first, then the other. After managing only one clasp, I give up.

And Mezhen is still sobbing like her heart is breaking.

Shit. I may have just killed the man she loves. But I have no other choice. I can sit here and get killed. Or do something and get killed.

I move to the door. "Mezhen?" I call out tentatively.

"Is . . . Is h–he . . . ?" She trails off.

"He's sleeping," I say quickly. "But I'm . . . hurt. He hurt me. I'm ah, bleeding. Can you help me?"

"Liar," she spits.

Yep, she was pressed to the door the whole time.

"I swear. I just need . . . like a tampon, please." I have no idea what I'll do once I open the door and let her in, but both of us in here has to be better than her out there bawling her eyes out and alerting the guards.

After about a minute she finally says, "I go get one for you."

"Thank you," I sigh, then slide down the wall in relief.

Not even five minutes later, the banging starts. Shit. I guess Mezhen didn't buy the tampon story. I close my eyes, resigned to my fate. A few more seconds of banging, followed by loud pops and splintering wood, and then half a dozen pale-faced men pour into the room, including Benjamin.

There are shouts, groans, and colorful swearing before rough, cruel hands haul me up by my hair, jostling my injured arm. This time, I retreat into myself, letting the heightened emotions of the moment roll off my back without hitting home.

I vaguely register Benjamin and me being dragged down the hallway Sean and I came through what feels like a lifetime ago. Then we're forced up two flights of stairs.

"Do you realize what the hell you've done, Adele?" Benjamin screams at me in Gaelic. The abject horror on his face is unlike anything I've seen before. He's pale, sweating bullets, and his entire body trembles. He looks like a man facing death, and I realize this is likely the end for him.

For both of us, actually.

I shrug with my good arm, my teeth chattering against the sudden chill that envelops me. "Stopped the war?"

His shoulders sag as if resigned to his fate. "You fucking Italians are traitors. All of you," he mutters, profound regret in his tone.

A stupid, pointless pride wells up in me at his final acknowledgment of who I am.

Then we're shoved into a large lounge filled with more men. The first thing I notice is the wall of windows. The second is the man in the middle of the room. He looks exactly like Sean, except that he's bald. He's got the black eye thing going too.

And there's a gun in his hand and a bottle of vodka in the other,

A couple of beefy men lay Sean's naked body at his feet. I hadn't even realized they'd carried him up from the basement. Suddenly, I'm glad I made the effort to put on a bra. Lopsided as it is, it's better than nothing. If these savages couldn't be bothered to cover up their gang leader, I doubt they'd offer any courtesy to the traitor who mutilated him.

The Sean look-alike spits a glob of phlegm onto the floor. "Killed by a weak-ass and fucking lame woman," he sneers, his eyes roving over me with so much animosity that I take an involuntary step back, only to be roughly shoved forward by the goon behind me, my hair yanked tight enough to twist my neck.

"I warned my brother not to trust these Irishmen." He gestures with his gun toward Benjamin.

And right in front of me, Benjamin is forced to his knees.

Immediately, he starts to babble. "I swear I had no idea. The Italians got to her. She just told me now she's working with them—"

"Is she not your daughter?" He takes several gulps of his vodka right out of the bottle.

"She is. But you must understand that she has been brainwashed to side with the Italians. She betrayed me."

"So, you brought us a traitor."

"I can fix this. Give me a chance to. I could—"

Benjamin doesn't finish.

He doesn't finish because a single shot rings out from Sean's brother's gun.

A warm mist of blood splatters on my hair, the side of my face, and my neck.

And then the man who had been my father for eighteen years crumples to the floor.

I look down, my jaw slack with horror to see the clean shot to his temple. The sight yanks me out of my numb trance, and I start to scream.

"Oh, you'll scream alright, bitch." He snarls. "You will scream, broken and begging to die. And I will not let you."

For the first time since waking up in that sterile room, it becomes crystal clear to me that I'm truly in way over my head.

There is a fate much worse than death.

It's hell.

CHAPTER FORTY-FOUR

Dante

The van slows to a stop a block away from our target. Through the tinted windows, I can see the brownstone—an innocuous-looking building that holds my whole world captive. My heart rate picks up, a steady rhythm of Addy, Addy, Addy.

I glance at the men around me—Sal, Orlando, and the six soldiers hand-picked for this mission. Their faces are set in grim resolve, mirroring my own. We've been through countless operations together, but none quite as personal as this.

The thought of the woman I love in their hands makes my blood boil. But I force the rage down, channeling it into cold, calculated focus. She needs me sharp, and sane, not blinded by fury.

"Thirty seconds," Cade's voice crackles through our earpieces.

"Copy that." I take a deep breath, centering myself, and then I say to the men, "They're in the basement. The plan is to slip in unnoticed once security is disabled."

It feels surreal, trusting someone with not only zero loyalties to the Outfit but an outright enemy. Out of the corner of my eye, I catch Sal, who looks totally composed, except for the finger slowly tapping on his knee. Orlando's eyes are flat and cold as he nibbles furiously on his toothpick.

Yep, all three of us are barely keeping it together. It occurs to me that because of our overwhelming personal stakes, Sal, Orlando, and I should probably not be the ones sent on this mission. We should have gone to Boston and let Nico and his own team deal with Philly. Yet wild horses couldn't drag any of us away from here tonight.

Cade's voice comes on again. "Ten seconds." He counts down and then says, "You're clear for five minutes. Security's down."

We sprint toward the building, pausing to aim and take down the guards.

Just as we reach the front steps, a commotion erupts from inside. The sound of breaking glass, followed by gunshots, shatters the night's silence.

"What the fuck?" Cade's voice crackles in my ear. "Something's going down in there. There are heat signatures all over the place. Activity is now in the front room, not the basement."

"What?" I hiss.

Just then, there's another gunshot, followed by a bloodcurdling scream.

Everyone freezes.

That's Addy. I can pick out her voice in a crowd full of people.

Something snaps inside me, and I bark, "Change of plans. Forget slipping in unnoticed. Speed is the priority now. We crash the party."

My men nod tersely and instantly take formation to attack head-on.

"No, wait, Vitelli. Do not engage yet." Cade's voice comes on, this time like an unpleasant screeching in my brain. I'd almost forgotten the guy was there. Must be the sudden rush of adrenaline bathing my brain.

"I'll take it from here, Quinn. I don't need a road map anymore."

"Are you kidding me? Dumber, if you fuck up my mission—"

"Your mission?" I echo. I swear whatever this guy smokes must be top-notch.

"Surely, you know crashing in could spook those savages into killing the girls. I was under the impression that you needed those women alive—"

And Addy is still screaming.

I've heard enough. "I get the picture, Quinn. You can fuck off now. Thank you."

He goes silent for a beat, then scoffs in disbelief. "You're welcome, asshole." And the line goes dead.

Cade's exit feels like a tight knot has just been loosened in my gut. While I appreciate the man's help, when shit really hits the fan, like it no doubt has right now, going by my woman's anguished screams, which are loud enough to hear from fifty yards away, I am incapable of following anything else apart from my instincts. "We crash in," I tell my men, who all nod curtly. "Now!"

We reach the building, all pretense of stealth abandoned. Sal, Orlando, and I head for the main entrance while the rest surround the place.

As we near the main entrance, I steel myself for what we might find inside.

"Addy, please be fucking okay," I grit out a silent prayer, allowing myself one moment of vulnerability before the soldier in me takes over.

The door gives at the slightest twist of the knob, and I can almost hear the collective sigh of relief from Sal and Orlando. Our weapons at the ready and eye shields pulled on, we move in as a unit.

Thankfully, the hallway is short and unlit.

We hover at the end of the hallway, just shy of stepping into the expansive living room. The first thing I notice is that the opposite wall is almost completely taken up by tall windows, and that the heavy curtains are open. I'm sure the six men currently surrounding the property must be marveling at our good fortune.

"Evening, gentlemen," I drawl as we enter the room fully to face dozens of eyes snapping up to their unexpected visitors. Everything slows as I take in the scene before me.

It's beyond anything I could have imagined. The large airy room looks like a grotesque battlefield. Broken glass is scattered on the floor, and the metallic stench of blood assaults our senses.

"Dante . . ."

The room fades into insignificance when I hear her choked sigh of relief even before I see her.

The feeling that the sound of my name on her lips evokes is indescribable: A compulsion to save her, to protect her with everything inside of me.

In a split second, I take in the threats to her safety.

Addy stands surrounded by at least a dozen men, a vision of desperation. She's dressed only in blood-soaked underwear, her pale skin a stark contrast to the crimson that covers nearly every inch of her. My heart lurches painfully, but then my brain catches up to the fact that there's way too much blood for it to be entirely hers.

Her hair, matted with gore, is wound tightly in the fist of a snarling goon, her lip is split and bleeding, and the ball of her right shoulder hangs somewhat lower. I clench my jaw tight against the overwhelming rage that explodes through me at the sight of that dislocated shoulder. The compulsion to brutally tear apart whoever pulled that shoulder from its socket swells like a beast inside me.

The only thread of reason pulling me from the brink is the look on her face. Her eyes are dark with pain but also something else. Defiance. She's hurt but unbroken.

And then I glance at the floor. It's littered with three bodies. One of them, I realize with shock, is Benjamin O'Shea, his pale eyes staring sightlessly at the ceiling.

But it's the body closest to Addy that both sends shockwaves through me and makes my heart swell with a sick, demented pride. The killing blow is unmistakable. It is the handiwork of a cornered and desperate prey.

Sean Hall lies sprawled on the marble floor, a spoon protruding grotesquely from his eye and a piece of glass from his neck.

"What the actual fuck?" Sal whispers beside me, his voice a mixture of shock and awe.

And then, the moment of stunned silence shatters as one of the gang members screams, "Bloody Italians!" and raises a gun. I don't even think—my body moves on pure instinct. My Glock barks twice, and the man crumples to the floor.

And just like that, all hell breaks loose. The few seconds of hesitation, the element of our surprise entry, is over, and the rest of the men, as if just waking up from slumber, pull out their weapons and fire at us. But the dim hallway presents an excellent barrier. They are four times as many as we are, but we have the advantage of cover.

The one holding Addy ducks behind a chair, roughly pushing her to the floor while the rest boldly advance toward us.

Suddenly, two windows on the far wall explode with a deafening shatter.

The men are yet again taken by surprise. Acting on pure reflex, they drop into crouches. That split second is all the time we need to drop another four or five of them.

Two canisters burst through the broken windows and arc through the air, landing with metallic clangs. Instantly, a pungent gas begins to fill the room. My men and I are prepared, protective glasses shielding our eyes, but within seconds the gang members start to cough and stumble through their tearing eyes.

Gunshots echo through the hall as we drop more of the men. I fight my way to the couch Addy and the goon are hiding behind, taking down anyone who dares to get in my path. From the corner of my eye, I see Sal moving with deadly precision, covering my advance.

Where the hell is Kira anyway?

I don't remember seeing her. I look around the room again, seeing no sign of her. By the time my gaze swings back to the couch, the goon is rising and dragging Addy with him. A wicked-looking knife glints at her throat, the blade digging into her skin.

"Blood for blood," he snarls.

The maniacal look in his red, watering eyes tells me he's not looking to strike a bargain. He knows he's going to die; he just wants to die butchering his enemy. Fuck.

Time slows as I swing my gun to him, knowing I won't be fast enough.

Suddenly, the goon folds, the knife clattering loudly. I whirl to see Orlando who was positioned at the perfect angle and out of sight of the goon. Relief floods me as Orlando gives me a quick nod before turning to engage another threat.

Finally, I reach Addy. She's coughing violently, her puffy eyes red and streaming from the tear gas. She can barely see, but she still tries to defend herself as I approach.

"Hey, hey, I've got you, it's me," I murmur into her hair. "I've got you, *amore mio.*"

She collapses against me, her body shaking. I hold her tight with one arm, my other hand keeping my weapon ready. Her skin is covered with dried blood and sweat, and she's trembling from adrenaline and fear, but she's alive. She's alive and in my arms.

"Let's get you out of here," I murmur against her temple.

Addy stiffens. "Wait, Kira. Please, she's . . . I don't know where she is . . ."

I glance up to see Sal already taking the door to the left. "Sal will find her, *tesoro.*"

Addy nods, then hugs me tighter with one arm while her other arm just hangs limply. She buries her face in my neck, her tears soaking my Kevlar as she murmurs against me, peppering my skin with soft kisses and telling me how glad she is that I'm okay.

I walk us out of the house into the chilly night air, unable to believe that even while shaken and hurt, and with her teeth chattering from the cold, she is still more concerned about Kira and me. I wish like hell I'd worn a suit I could put on her.

Orlando appears at my side, his eyes scanning Addy with concern. "She alright?"

"She will be," I say, my voice hard. "Sal's in the basement getting Kira out. Cover him."

He nods, although I can see he badly wants to stay with Addy.

"Capo." He spins on his heels and disappears back into the house, weapon drawn, while I, for the second time tonight, pray.

I pray for Sal's sake that Kira is okay.

CHAPTER FORTY-FIVE

Adele

I cling to Dante with my good arm, burying my face in the crook of his neck. His familiar scent—a mix of sandalwood and musk—washes over me, grounding me in this moment. My entire body trembles, a cocktail of adrenaline, relief, and overwhelming joy coursing through my veins.

"Oh my God, it was horrible in there. I just wanted you. Kept praying you would come. I love you," I murmur against his skin, my lips brushing his pulse point. "So much. Are you sure you're okay?"

"I'm good, baby." He rumbles.

I continue nibbling on his skin. "Well, I love you so much. Marry me, Dante, right now."

I can't stop the words from tumbling out, my filter completely obliterated by the night's events. My nails dig into the fabric of his shirt, desperate to get closer, to meld myself to him entirely. I pepper his neck with kisses, tasting the salt of his skin, and feeling the steady thrum of his heartbeat against my lips.

Dante's arms tighten around me, one hand cradling the back of my head while the other supports my weight. Despite the chaos around us, his touch is gentle, careful of my injured shoulder. I feel the rumble of his chuckle more than I hear it.

"Amore mio," his chuckle vibrates against my chest, a soothing balm to my frayed nerves. "And you've not even been dosed up yet. I can only imagine what you'll be like once the drugs kick in."

I pull back slightly, meeting his gray eyes. The tenderness I see there, mixed with a fierce protectiveness, makes my heart stutter. "I'm not delirious, Dante," I insist, although I recognize the manic edge to my own voice. "I mean every word."

Dante's eyes search mine. "Okay," he says simply.

"Okay as in you don't think I'm delirious, or okay, we'll get married?"

Before Dante can respond, a familiar snarky voice cuts through my love-drunk haze.

"Addy. Will you please stop embarrassing me?"

I whip my head around quickly, wincing as the movement jars my injured shoulder. And then I see her in Sal's arms, still wearing that hideous green and brown dress that makes her look like a swamp monster's bride.

"Kira!" I shriek, relief flooding through me and overriding my snarky response. "Oh my God, Kira, you're okay! Where were you? I was so worried."

"I was busy reciting every spell known to man to magically castrate that absolute scum of the earth you were chanting some demonic wedding vows to," Kira spits. "Like, what the actual fuck, Addy? Disturbingly sickening does not even begin to cover it."

"I know." Kira hates Sean this much and she didn't even get to see the monster.

Sal whispers something in her ear, and I see Kira's jaw fall open as her eyebrows almost hit her hairline. I think I know what Sal might have said. "You've got to be shitting me! Addy! You killed him?"

"Trust me, Kira, you'd have done no less."

"And I was sitting in a dark room waiting to be rescued while you were being all badass Black Widow. Like, how are you even *that* woman?"

"I dunno," I smile. "Might have something to do with the company I'm keeping these days."

I look up at Dante, watching the expressions playing on his face as he gestures wordlessly to one of his men. My finger traces over the bold slash of his eyebrows, down the side of his face and his sharp jaw covered in stubble. I push a lock of hair that's escaped from his bun behind his ear, then trace the shell of it down to the small steel ring in his pierced earlobe.

"God, you're so fucking hot," I murmur.

"Uggggh, cringe. Can it stop already?" Kira grumbles, while still clinging to Sal like a baby koala. Her arms and legs are tightly wrapped around him, although I'm pretty sure she can walk.

I can't help the small giggle that escapes me. "Dante, am I being cringey?"

His lips quirk up in that devastating half-smile that never fails to make my insides melt. "Not at all, *tesoro*. I'm obsessed with you, too."

The world narrows down to just us as he leans in, his lips brushing mine in a kiss that's equal parts tender and possessive. For a moment, I forget about the blood coating my skin, the ache in my shoulder, the horrors of the night. There's only Dante, his solid presence anchoring me in the storm.

Dante breaks the kiss, then rests his forehead against mine for a moment before he pulls away and murmurs, "Let's get you away from here."

When we reach the van, Dante gently sets me on my feet, keeping one arm around my waist to steady me. The cool night air hits me, and I shiver, a reminder of how little I'm wearing. He removes his tactical vest then reaches behind him, fisting his T-shirt and pulling it over his head.

I watch, mesmerized, as he rips apart the shirt and then he's making it into some kind of sling for my arm. Heat radiates off his bare torso and suddenly I can't wait to be pressed close to him again, drowning in his fragrant warmth . . .

Just as he's tying off the makeshift sling, a tall figure approaches us from the periphery of my vision.

I tense instinctively, my fingers digging into Dante's biceps.

"It's okay, baby." Dante gently uncurls my fingers from his arm.

The man who steps into view is older, with graying hair and a weathered face that speaks of years of hard living. His light eyes—I can't quite make out the color in the dim light—are fixed on me with an intensity that makes me want to squirm. There's something familiar about the set of his jaw.

He takes off his suit jacket and offers it to me, his voice gruff but oddly gentle as he asks, "If I may?"

I glance at Dante, uncertain. He gives a slight nod then takes a step away.

Taking that as reassurance, I allow the older man to drape his coat over my shoulders. The garment's warmth envelops me immediately, carrying the scent of gunpowder and mint, but it's the man's touch that truly captures my attention. His hands tremble slightly as he adjusts the coat, lingering just a fraction longer than necessary.

As he steps back, I catch another glimpse of his face. His eyes are surprisingly glassy. He turns abruptly and leaves, his shoulders shaking slightly as he walks away.

I look up at Dante, a suspicion forming in my mind. "Is that . . .?" I ask, my voice hushed.

Dante nods, his eyes following the retreating figure. "Yes. That's your father."

The words hit me hard. My father. The man I've wondered about my entire life, now just feet away from me.

"He's . . . um, very sweet," I manage to say, though the word feels inadequate.

Dante's chuckle is low and warm as he helps me into the bench seat, then follows me in. "He's very dangerous."

"How?" I ask, curiosity piqued. The emotional whirlwind of the night leaves me craving comfort, and I find myself leaning into Dante's warmth.

Noticing my restlessness, Dante gently pulls me onto his lap, then reaches into a compartment and retrieves a dark brown bottle.

"Here," Dante says, offering me the bottle. "Take some of this."

I eye the container warily. "What is it?"

His fingers brush mine as he hands me the bottle, sending a familiar tingle up my arm despite my exhaustion. "Liquid morphine. Just something to help you sleep until I can sort out your shoulder."

I take the bottle from him, our fingers lingering together for a moment longer than necessary. The liquid inside is sweet, almost cloyingly so, as it slides down my throat. Almost immediately, I feel a heaviness settling over me.

"How is he dangerous?" I ask again, fighting the pull of sleep.

"Orlando De Luca?"

I nod.

"He's the only man Nico fears."

The name registers, and for the first time, another piece of the puzzle clicks into place. "De Luca. Isn't he your ex-girlfriend's, er, ex-fiancée's father?"

Dante's arm tightens around me, his voice taking on an edge. "Alina is not my ex-anything. And you may want to stop calling her that, seeing as she's going to be my sister-in-law very soon."

It takes me a moment to process this information through the growing haze of the morphine. "Oh," I say finally. "So you're on board with the idea. I thought you said I was delirious."

"You're not delirious. Just in shock." Dante murmurs against my neck, his voice a low rumble that I feel more than hear in the confined space of the van. "Speaking of shock . . ." he pauses, and I know he's weighing his next words. "Benjamin O'Shea."

I inhale sharply, and the scent of leather and Dante fills my nostrils. For a moment, I'm back in that room, watching Benjamin crumple to the floor.

"He was shot right in front of me," I say, my voice sounding distant to my own ears.

Dante's hand finds mine, his thumb tracing soothing circles on my skin. "How do you feel about it?"

I consider the question, probing at the emptiness inside me. "Numb. Shocked. Terrified," I admit finally. "I suppose it'll hit me in a few days. But right now . . ."

I trail off, searching for the right words while Dante patiently waits. He's almost unnaturally still. Dante isn't accustomed to waiting for people to find their words. Yet he remains motionless, softly stroking my hand.

Finally, I say, "Right now, he's just the man who sold me to a hideously vile monster in exchange for an army."

As I speak, I feel a coldness settling in my chest. It's not grief, not yet. Just a hollow acknowledgment of the truth that eluded me for years.

Dante nods slowly, his steely eyes studying my face, and I wonder what he sees there.

"Are you okay though?" he asks softly. His free hand comes up to trace the ball of my injured shoulder, and I lean into his touch, craving more. "Is there anything else I should know about?"

"Anything else like?" I ask, a bit puzzled by his tone.

Dante's voice takes on a dangerous edge, reminding me of the ruthless man beneath the gentle exterior. "Like if I need to paint the streets of Philadelphia with blood?"

His words send a shiver down my spine, a mix of fear and something else I'm not ready to name.

I understand his unspoken question and I feel a flood of relief because Dante would do exactly that if Sean Hall had really hurt me. I meet his gaze steadily. "I'm okay. I mean we fought and I kicked his ass. Eventually. Only, I threw out my shoulder stabbing him from an awkward angle."

Silence.

"Okay, No, he didn't rape me," I admit.

Dante releases a pent-up breath.

"But there were . . . other women there. They're not just house staff."

"He traffics women on the side." Dante watches me for a bit then declares, "I'll see that they're all set free when we return for a thorough cleanup."

I think I know what Dante means by cleaning up. "Really?"

He sighs dramatically. "Well, you started a war when you drew first blood and killed their leader. There's bound to be sympathizers crawling out of the woodwork, so I'm going to have to finish it, aren't I?"

I raise my still trembling hand up between us, considering the weight of what I've done. "I can't believe I did that to Sean. I suppose I should blame you, Dante. You're the one who taught me how to kill."

He flashes me a grin. "Oh, I take complete ownership of both the crime and the criminal. But, tell me, how did it feel?" he asks, his voice dropping to a whisper. "In the moment?"

Again. I know exactly what he's asking me. The memory of the moment Sean's hand fell, twitching in surrender as the light left his good eye. I should be suppressing a shudder of shame and revulsion. But I'm not. And I've never been able to hide my true feelings from Dante, so I don't bother trying.

"Powerful," I whisper back. "Heady."

Dante's lips curve into a small smile of understanding. Pride even. How did I not see through Aydin's lies? Dante might not relish the gory side of his life, but he owns it unapologetically.

"What?" I ask, curiosity momentarily overriding my exhaustion when he continues to stare at me with that cryptic smile.

"I see you, Adele." He murmurs, "I've always seen you."

"And?" I prompt.

"You wouldn't last one therapy session with Sophie, either."

I laugh. "Well, we'll never know, will we? She's stopped taking family clients, thanks to the likes of you," I smirk.

Soon, the sedative takes hold, and I surrender to its warm, fuzzy embrace. As I drift off, I dream of a gray-eyed beast dragging me from beneath a table and into the sunset.

CHAPTER FORTY-SIX

Adele

Two weeks later, we're seated in one of the smaller dining rooms in the Vitelli Fortress. Crystal light dances off polished silverware, casting a warm glow over the faces of my newfound family. Vito and Antonella sit at one end of the table, with Kira beside them, engaged in what seems to be a friendly argument. Nico and Sophie occupy the other end, completing our intimate gathering. This is exactly what I needed after everything that's happened.

Dante's hand slides over mine under the table, his finger lingering on the large-cut ruby and diamond ring nestled there. "Relax, *amore*," he murmurs.

I try to steady my nerves, but my eyes dart to the clock for the hundredth time. "He's late," I mutter.

"Orlando wouldn't miss this for the world. He's probably as nervous as you are."

Despite the unsolved puzzle of who wants me dead, Dante and I can no longer stand to be apart. After we got back from Philly, Dante took me straight to his beach house, where we've been cocooned ever since.

It's been the best two weeks of my life, recovering from my shoulder injury and enjoying life with Dante. We can't keep our hands off each other, but what surprises me more is how much we can't stop talking. Back in college, it was I who did most of the talking while he listened. Now, he speaks to me like a partner—someone he trusts.

My mind drifts back to yesterday morning. I'd woken up to find the ring on my finger, while Dante had been sitting in the chair opposite the bed, waiting for me to wake up—to discover it—and tell him how I felt about it.

And I did. In so many ways.

It was Vito and Antonella who finally coaxed us out for this family dinner and a formal engagement celebration. Feeling ready to meet my real father, I'd asked Vito to invite Orlando too.

"The last time Orlando saw me, Dante, I'd just killed my husband and was covered in his blood," I say, the memory still as fresh as if it happened yesterday.

"*Tesoro,*" Dante murmurs, his lips brushing my ear. "Your father worships the ground you walk on. First, for existing, and second, for surviving against every odd. You really are your father's daughter."

His words trigger a pang of grief, reminding me of my former dad. Benjamin O'Shea's lifeless face flashes through my mind. He hurt and betrayed me beyond words, but he was still my father for eighteen years. Watching him get shot right in front of me is something I'll never forget.

I shake myself out of these thoughts, focusing instead on Dante's warm presence beside me. "I thought that was your thing."

"What's my thing?"

"Worshipping me," I whisper. Too late. The moment the words leave my mouth and I feel him tense beside me, I realize what I just did. Dante is almost never not turned on around me, but I've just pushed a particular button of his.

Proving me right, his hand inches higher on my thigh, his voice dropping an octave. "Oh, that? I'm so fucked, I'm actually starting to think I've been placed under a spell."

"What spell?" I murmur innocently, deliberately. I want to get burned.

Dante looks up to answer a question from Vito, then bends to my ear. "Since you're completely clueless, why don't I just demonstrate for better understanding?" His fingers reach the juncture of my thighs, his index finger tracing the seam of my labia.

"Dante!" I hiss, heat flooding my cheeks as I swat his arm.

"Stay still, De Luca."

I love the way he's been calling me by my surname the last couple of weeks. Every single time he does it, it feels like another anchor holding me firm in my identity.

"Dante. We have . . . company."

"This old lot? You think they'll stop me from making you come?"

"You wouldn't dare," I challenge.

His response is to move the crotch of my panties aside, and I instantly feel the cool air hit my wet folds.

"Dante," I warn, maintaining the smile on my face for everyone while my heart starts to race.

"Wrong word." His palm rests against my straining clit, not moving, not stroking—just there, driving me insane with every second that passes.

My hand tightens on my fork. 'Red Wine', and everything stops. But do I use the safe word? Of course not. The need to orgasm right here, in front of all these people, claws at me.

What the hell is wrong with me? Why do I find this so fucking hot?

Still, he waits, finger poised at my entrance.

I glance around the table to see if anyone has any idea what's happening. What's about to happen. Nico sits at the head of the table, eating one-handed and somewhat clumsily with his right hand because his dominant hand is at the back of Sophie's neck, subtly massaging. She's almost eight months along, and the twins could make an appearance any time now.

Vito sits at the foot of the table with Antonella and Kira flanking him. They're still arguing over something, most likely her refusal to move back to Chicago. It's been a sore spot, with Vito wanting Kira closer to home for her safety, and Kira insisting on maintaining her anonymity and distance from the family.

Although Aydin has been fired and banned from the mansion, she and Kira are grateful. At first, I thought that was harsh, but after Dante explained the usual consequences of what she'd done, I realized how generous they'd been.

The memory of that conversation floods back to me, momentarily distracting me from Dante's teasing touch. *"Sangue dentro, sangue fuori, tesoro,"* he'd said. "The blood vows we take are irrevocable. You're trusted without question, but the price of betrayal is blood. Aydin was sworn to protect, with her life if necessary, and she broke those vows because she didn't trust that we'd have her back and save her daughter."

I'd been shocked by his vehemence but also endeared by the steely determination behind his words. If ever there was a moral code among criminals. "I thought only fighting men could take such vows?"

Dante had only smiled. "What would be the fun in that?"

"Does that mean I could be required to do it too at some point?"

"You've already taken those vows." He'd then placed my hand on his heart while his rested on my lower belly, and something had clenched deep inside me. I realized he was telling the truth. Something had shifted in the last two months since the night Pietro died, and I knew I'd lay down my life—and take others'—to protect not just Dante but Nico, Sophie, Vito, and Antonella. My family.

Dante's wicked finger teases my entrance, bringing me back to the table. "What do you say?" he asks lazily.

I steal a glance at him, sucking my lower lip between my teeth. Taking a steadying breath, I spread my legs wider then grab my glass, ready to hide my reactions behind it.

"Do it," I whisper, then take a casual sip of my water.

And promptly choke on it the moment Dante plunges a long finger inside me, drawing a concerned glance from Nico and Sophie.

"I'm okay," I sputter, nodding repeatedly like a marionette on strings.

Dante curves his finger inside me, his palm sliding against my clit, and I bite my lip to suppress a moan. He carries on conversing with Nico and Sophie while my vision grows more and more blurry. Every second, every stroke feels like I'm being inched closer to the edge of a cliff.

He's not even jostling the tablecloth, he's fingering me that slowly. But perhaps because he's that good at it, or because of how wrong it is, I'm so close to coming, he might as well have me bent over the table and pounding me into a screaming mess.

Dante presses firmly against my G-spot and I go rigid, feeling my pleasure start to crest.

Oh, fuck. I choke back a moan as my legs start to tremble. This was such a bad idea. I'll never live this engagement dinner orgasm down. I shove a forkful of creamed broccoli into my mouth and moan loudly around it. "Ah, it tastes . . . Oh my God . . . it's so fucking good."

"I know, right?" Sophie gushes, while Nico only snorts. I suspect he already knows, not that I have any more working brain neurons to care at this point.

Just as my fist connects with the table and the first ripples of orgasm gather into a riptide, I hear the crunch of gravel outside, saving me from needing to explain my meltdown.

"Yes! Yes! He's here!" I shout, bouncing in my seat like a jack-in-the-box. Everyone stares in puzzlement at my sudden outburst.

I swallow, jerking my thumb over my shoulder. "There's um . . . a car. Tires," I add inanely.

Dante chuckles. "It sounds like Orlando's arrived. Addy has been looking forward to meeting him. She's very excited as you can tell," he says to the room while I try to calm my roaring pulse.

"Come on, Addy, let's go." Dante's eyes meet mine, glinting with mischief. "Let's go greet your Daddy."

I take a deep breath, steeling myself against the lingering twitches of lust as he withdraws his finger from me.

Dante stands, offering me his hand. I straighten my skater dress, hoping I don't look as flushed as I feel.

As we turn away from the table, I whisper, "We're never doing that again."

"Sure."

"I mean it."

"Uh-huh," Dante grunts, leading me out of the room.

Pleasure recedes, giving way to anxiety the closer we get to the door. And then we're there. I hesitate, a wave of unease washing over me. This is it. The moment I've both dreaded and longed for. What if he's disappointed in getting to know me? What if I am?

Dante pulls me close and murmurs against my temple. "Remember, Addy, no matter what Orlando says or does, two things will never change. First, you're strong, incredible, and beautiful. And second, you're mine. Forever."

I raise my arms and lace my fingers at his nape, ignoring the slight twinge in my healing right shoulder. "I love you, Dante," I whisper, the words carrying all the gratitude and affection I feel.

He takes my mouth in a quick kiss, then pulls the door open.

Orlando De Luca steps into the hallway, and the air seems to thicken as he enters, with Bianca in tow. He's dressed in a tailored charcoal suit that accentuates his broad shoulders, a crisp white shirt underneath. His salt-and-pepper hair is neatly combed back, and a gold watch glints on his wrist. Bianca, elegant in a navy blue dress, stands slightly behind him.

I feel Dante's reassuring hand on the small of my back as we greet them. Orlando's eyes instantly lock onto mine, a storm of emotions swirling in their depths. For a moment, neither of us moves.

"Adele," Orlando breathes, breaking the silence. His voice is rough with emotion.

"Orlando," I reply, surprised by the steadiness in my own voice. "I'm glad you could make it."

He takes a hesitant step forward, then another, until he's standing right in front of me. There's an eternity where we both just stand and stare at each other. It's insane, but there's something so vaguely familiar about the set of his jaw, about the port wine stain on the side of his neck, barely visible around his tattoos. It plays at the edge of my mind, yet I can't work out the details. I only know that I know this man on a profound level.

"Figlia mia," he breaks the silence, his voice thick with unshed tears. *"La mia forte, bellissima figlia."*

I don't need to understand Italian to know that what he just said to me is the heartfelt declaration I never heard in the last eighteen years. Ms. Ida came close once or twice, but never quite like this.

I catch sight of Bianca beside us, her face pale as she shuffles uncomfortably, her expression pinched.

Dante smoothly steps in, extending his hand to her. "Bianca, it's good to see you again. Thank you for coming."

Dante leads the way to the dining room. The tension at the table spikes as we take our seats, momentarily broken by the waiting staff serving the new arrivals and Antonella pulling them into the ongoing small talk, toasts, and clinking glasses.

The stilted conversation eventually dies down, giving way to the relentless tension. By now, everyone has noticed that Orlando hasn't eaten a bite of food. Instead, his gaze is fixed on me with an intensity that's both touching and unnerving.

I'm starting to question the wisdom of inviting him to this engagement dinner when finally, unable to contain himself any longer, Orlando blurts out, "You look so much like her."

"Naomi?" I ask, my heartbeat becoming like clanging gongs in my ears.

At the mention of my mother, Orlando's composure cracks. A tear slips down his cheek, and he doesn't bother to wipe it away. "So much like Naomi."

Just when I think I'm about to start blubbering, Dante's voice booms, drawing everyone's attention. "Let's give Addy and Orlando some time to talk privately, shall we?"

Like kids in a classroom when the recess bell rings, everyone clears out of the room. Everyone except Bianca, that is. She doesn't move a muscle, leaning back in her chair as if settling in for a long wait.

Dante makes to stand, but I tighten my hand over his thigh. "Stay?"

"Baby, I'll be in the next room." He cocks his head toward the adjoining room, a door with a glass panel in the top half of it.

Knowing he'll be close and watching gives me the layer of comfort I need, so I nod.

Dante presses a lingering kiss to my temple then stands. "Shall we go, Bianca?" he says in a tone that brooks no argument, then goes round the table to help her out of her seat.

Bianca's head snaps up, her eyes flickering between Orlando and me. "I thought—"

"Give me a minute, Bi," Orlando interrupts her, his voice like cold steel, his eyes never leaving my face.

For a moment, I see a flash of . . . something in her eyes. Pain? Annoyance? It's gone before I can fully decipher it. Still, her jaw clenches as if ready to argue, as though she wants to hear the story too.

As I continue to study her face, I realize she looks more than just annoyed—she looks shaken.

Could it be that she didn't know about me? That she wasn't aware of her husband's affair with Naomi Ritter all this time?

If that's the case, she's taking this remarkably well.

Bianca hesitates for a moment longer, then stands and takes Dante's arm. "Of course," she says, her voice carefully controlled. "I'll be in the garden if you need anything."

As Dante and Bianca leave the room, I feel a momentary panic. Dante's presence has been my anchor since this whole ordeal began, and now I'm alone with a man who is both a stranger and my father.

I hear the door close with a soft click, and silence falls over the room. Orlando leans forward, elbows on his knees, hands clasped tightly together. He takes a deep breath, as if steeling himself.

"Your mother," he begins, his voice rough with emotion, "was the most beautiful woman I'd ever seen. Not just physically, though she was stunning. Her soul . . . it shone through her eyes."

I lean in, hungry for every detail. "How did you meet?"

A small, sad smile plays on Orlando's lips. "Naomi was running from her past, just like I was running from my future. She came to Chicago and started going by the name Ritter. She rented a small shop in my part of town—Brackendown Street—and turned it into a bookstore. Then she rented the apartment on top of the store and lived there. She opened early and closed late. She didn't make a lot of money, but she didn't seem to care. She loved books.

At first, I watched her from afar. Every day for a whole year, I had a ritual. I had to get a glimpse of her. It was easy because she was always there. And then it wasn't enough anymore."

He pauses, lost in the memory. "One night, I went in disguised. The moment our eyes met . . . it was like being struck by lightning. I knew, in that instant, that I was in love with her."

"What happened?" I prompt softly when he falls silent.

Orlando's eyes refocus on me, and the love and pain I see there make my heart ache. "I confessed who I was that very night. And to my surprise, she admitted who she really was too. We were in impossible situations, both of us. But we couldn't stay away from each other."

He runs a hand through his hair, a gesture so familiar it startles me. I do the same thing when I'm stressed or emotional.

"We loved in secret," he continues. "It was hard, and I didn't get to see her as often as I wanted. But our connection . . . it never faded. We'd meet out of the country once a month, steal a few days together. Back in Chicago, we pretended we didn't know each other existed."

I nod, trying to imagine the strain of such a relationship. "And then . . .?"

Orlando's face crumples, the weight of his past bearing down on him. "I made a choice that will haunt me for as long as I live. I had to choose between love and survival. I chose survival."

"Bianca?" I state, the name slipping from my lips before I can stop it.

He nods, his voice heavy with regret. "You think that as a man in this world, you can handle anything, survive anything. I saw Vito as weak for choosing love. I resented him for it. I thought he wasn't fit to lead and that the Outfit would collapse if we didn't take the Rinaldi deal." He shakes his head, pain etched into the lines of his face. "How blind and stupid I was."

Fresh tears sting my eyes. "You couldn't have known." Dante told me Orlando grew up homeless on the streets, without love or a family. He wouldn't have fully understood what he was giving up.

"It wasn't even a year before I slumped into depression. I couldn't function—at home or at work. People were dying because of me. I knew I had to go back to Naomi. It was hard for her to let me back in, but I fought for us. And then unexpectedly . . . she got pregnant."

He pauses, his voice trembling with emotion. "I thought I understood everything about love, about wanting to protect someone, about giving everything to them. And then I saw all eight pounds of you, red-haired, red-faced, and screaming at the top of your lungs. And it was that lightning bolt all over again."

His words wash over me and tears blur my vision as a knot tightens in my chest.

He reaches out, hesitates, then gently takes my hand. "The last time I saw you both was on your fifth birthday. We were in Hawaii. You were so happy, building sandcastles on the beach."

I have a vague memory of warm sand, blue water, and laughter. Was that Hawaii? Was that my last day with both my parents?

"When I heard you and Naomi had been killed," Orlando's voice breaks, "it completely destroyed me. And then the war began. Those Irish bastards were crying out for blood—my blood."

He takes a shuddering breath. "It wasn't until two years ago, when Benjamin O'Shea came to negotiate peace that we realized you were alive. I wanted to reach out, to meet you, but . . ."

"But what?" I ask, my voice barely a whisper.

Orlando's eyes meet mine. "But you were his hostage. The moment he revealed you were alive, you became his willing hostage, and attempting to extract you could be seen as a hostile move. You could've been hurt or used as a pawn. So I bided my time and waited."

I sit back, overwhelmed by the flood of information, the weight of eighteen years of secrets and longing.

"Is that why someone tried to kill me at the club?" I ask, the question trembling on my lips. "Because they thought you were trying to take me back?"

Orlando shrugs heavily. "That could be one of the many reasons. But whoever was behind that bomb knows who you really are. The weight of that remains a dark cloud over us. We have no clue who sent the Novaks after you."

He pauses, his expression shifting from concern to deep regret. His voice drops to an agonized whisper. "I'm so sorry, Adele. I know I made mistakes, and it may be too late, but I want you to know . . . I've loved you every single day of your life. You and your mother . . . you were everything to me."

His words hang in the air, raw and vulnerable. Despite the crushing weight of the past, there's a small spark of warmth that begins to grow within me, knowing that I was never forgotten. Never unloved.

"Did Bianca know?" I ask, the question burning in the back of my mind.

Orlando shakes his head. "Not until recently."

Eighteen years of being in the dark, married to a man who was desperately in love with someone else. I feel a pang of sympathy for Bianca. On the other side of the coin, there's a woman who must need some closure too.

There's so much to process, so many emotions swirling inside me. But as I look at Orlando, I feel an undeniable pull, a connection that transcends the years of separation. This is my father.

"Orlando," I begin hesitantly, "is . . . is Adele my real name?"

Orlando takes a deep breath, his eyes never leaving mine. There's a moment of heavy silence before he slowly shakes his head. "No, *cara mia*. Your name is Valentina. Valentina De Luca."

The words hang in the air between us, heavy with revelation. The weight of his words finally hits me, and I feel the room spin slightly. I stand abruptly, turning my back to Orlando as tears begin to fall.

Valentina. Not Adele.

Dear God. As if I needed final proof that everything I thought I knew about myself has been a carefully crafted facade.

I hear Orlando shift behind me, and after a moment, I feel his hesitant hand on my back. The gentle touch breaks something inside me. I turn and, surprising us both, throw my arms around him.

Orlando stiffens for a split second before his arms wrap around me, holding me tight. His body shakes with sobs that match my own. The embrace feels right in a way hugging Benjamin O'Shea never did.

It's Val . . . not Addy.

The name resonates within me, filling a void I never knew existed.

As we hold each other, years of longing and loss pouring out in our tears, I feel a sense of homecoming.

And for the first time in my life, I know exactly who I am.

CHAPTER FORTY-SEVEN

Dante

I pull into the driveway of my beachfront home, relishing the grounding weight of Addy's hand on my thigh. I used to think I was the one who couldn't keep my hands off her if she was within two feet of me, but now I'm not so sure which of us is guiltier. As I kill the engine, I catch her stifling a yawn.

"Tired?" I ask, reaching over to tuck a stray curl behind her ear.

She leans into my touch, her eyes closing briefly. "Mm, just full. I ate my body weight in pasta. And dessert," she adds meaningfully.

I chuckle, remembering how she'd practically moaned over her linguine alle vongole, and then struggled to stifle her moans at said dessert. "You certainly indulged."

"It was . . . torture." A flare of heat burns in her green eyes no doubt remembering her silent orgasm.

"I enjoyed watching you," I say.

"I bet you did." Addy chuckles, and I can't help the shit-eating grin on my face as we make our way inside, silently making it a point to do it again—and soon.

Addy immediately kicks off her flats as soon as we cross the threshold. I watch her walk barefoot across the hardwood floors, the short red dress she'd worn swishing around her thighs. Even after all this time, the sight of her in our home, so at ease, so . . . mine, does things to me.

"You're staring," she calls over her shoulder, a smile in her voice.

"Can you blame me?" I move to join her by the windows overlooking the shore. The last rays of sunlight dance across the water, and I wrap my arms around her from behind, resting my chin on her shoulder.

She leans back into me, her body fitting perfectly against mine. "Do you really have to go to Philly tomorrow?"

I sigh, tightening my hold on her. "You know I do, *amore*. The leftovers and stragglers have gathered again. It's time to put them away for good."

"But does it have to be you?" She persists, turning in my arms to face me. "You have more than twenty soldiers under you, not to mention Capos. Why do you always do the heavy lifting?"

I cup her face in my hands, my thumbs tracing her cheekbones. "You lead from the front, *tesoro*. That's how it's done."

Addy groans, but I can see the understanding in her eyes. "Besides," I add, my voice dropping lower, "this is personal. You were married to him."

It doesn't get more fucking personal than that.

"Sean Hall is dead, baby," Addy points out gently.

As if I need a reminder.

The mention of Hall's name makes something twist in my gut. The image of Addy, my woman, saying vows to that motherfucker . . . it makes me see red. Those are words I want her to say to me, and only me. Vows I want to hear from her perfect, pouty lips more than anything in this world.

Yeah, I'm jealous. Sue me.

Addy must sense the shift in my mood because she rises on her tiptoes to press a soft kiss to my lips. "Hey," she murmurs, "I'm here. With you. Always."

I'm about to show her just how much I appreciate that fact when the crunch of tires on gravel catches my attention. Headlights sweep across the room as a car pulls up outside.

"Are we expecting company?" Addy asks, peering around me.

I shake my head, already reaching for the gun I keep in the entryway drawer. "Stay here," I tell her, moving toward the door.

But as I take a look outside, I relax. It's only Nico's Lambo.

What the hell is he doing here without calling first?

I open the front door as Nico steps out of his car, the cool evening air rushing in. His face is unreadable, which immediately puts me on edge. Something's up.

"Fratello," I greet him, stepping aside to let him in. The familiar bergamot scent of his cologne mingles with the crisp breeze. "To what do we owe the pleasure?"

Nico's eyes scan the room methodically, a habit ingrained from years of cautious living. His gaze lands on Addy, who's hovering uncertainly by the windows, her silhouette framed by the last rays of the setting sun.

"Addy," he sends her a warm smile, his usual stern demeanor softening slightly. "You look well."

Addy's hand instinctively moves to her barely visible baby bump. "Thanks, Nico. How's Sophie?"

"Exhausted, cranky, and beautiful as ever," Nico replies with a fond chuckle, his eyes crinkling at the corners. Then, as if remembering why he's here, his expression sobers. He turns back to me. "We need to talk."

Addy starts to move toward the stairs, her bare feet silent on the hardwood floor. "I'll give you two some privacy—"

"No, it's alright," Nico interrupts, surprising both of us. His eyes flick to mine, seeking confirmation. I give him a slight nod, curiosity piqued. "Stay, please."

I watch as Addy's eyes widen slightly, a small smile tugging at her lips. She's pleased, I realize. Pleased to be included, to be trusted. It warms something in my chest to see it, to witness Nico's acceptance of Addy into our inner circle.

We move to the living room, the soft lights casting a warm glow over the space. Addy and I settle on the couch, her head resting comfortably on my shoulder. Nico takes the armchair across from us, half-reclining.

The room settles into a momentary silence, broken only by the distant lapping of waves against the shore. I absently trace the solitaire ruby of Addy's ring, grounding myself in its familiarity.

"It's been a while since you came here, Nico," I comment, trying to gauge his mood.

My mind wanders to the contrasts in our living situations. Nico's main home, a penthouse in the heart of Chicago, is a marvel of luxury—sleek lines and modern amenities—while I prefer the endless open space of the beach.

Nico's lips quirk in a humorless smile. "Too long," he agrees, his eyes briefly scanning the room again. "It's a little . . . quiet here though."

I know he's commenting on the absence of background music, loud or otherwise. "The waves are loud enough," I say, "And so is Addy."

Addy elbows my side in mock outrage, and I send her a wink, but she seems to miss my meaning. Nico, on the other hand, catches it. A soft look enters his eyes and he smiles at her.

"Good to hear, *fratellino*," he says, then his gaze shifts to Addy again. "How are the wedding preparations coming along?"

I grind my teeth, forcing myself to stay seated. What the hell is on Nico's mind?

Addy answers with a polite smile. "Um. It's going really well. The wedding planner is just as great as Sophie advertised."

"So," I say, cutting through the ensuing silence before Nico can ask another pointless question, "you mind cutting the crap? What's brought you here?"

I feel Addy tense beside me, but I give her hand a reassuring squeeze.

"Dante," Nico begins, "no one is going to Philly tomorrow after all."

I furrow my brow, leaning forward slightly. "Why not?"

Nico takes a deep breath, his shoulders rising and falling with the motion. "Because three buildings collapsed in Philly earlier today. They happened to be places housing a number of Shadow gang stragglers and sympathizers. It's being chalked up to some bullshit about poor structure and inappropriate load."

He pauses, letting the information sink in while my mind races with the implications.

Three buildings don't just collapse. This was deliberate, calculated. There's another player involved here. It couldn't be the Mob retaliating for Benjamin O'Shea's death—Nico wiped them out the same night I got Addy out of Philly.

"Most were killed," Nico continues, his voice low and grave. "Including, unfortunately, our inside man. Which means, for the next few hours, we have no intel apart from the bullshit the media feeds us. One of which is that no hostages were found."

I hear Addy's sharp intake of breath beside me. Her hand finds mine, squeezing tightly. I return the pressure, my thumb tracing soothing circles on her skin. My own heart races with anger.

"Who did it?" I ask, though I have a sinking feeling I already know the answer.

The silence stretches, and then Nico's eyes meet mine, a muscle ticking in his jaw. "I wondered the same thing, *fratellino,* until Quinn called me over to the docks half an hour ago. Said he had a special package for Sophie."

"Quinn?" I frown, caught off guard by the unexpected development. "I thought he was roasting his ass off in Havana. What's he doing here?"

"Apparently not," Nico grates. "He showed up in a luxury prison of a truck, with a friend of his who looks just as batshit crazy."

Nico leans forward, his forearms resting on his knees. "Dante, the psycho had sixteen women in the back of the truck. Cold, scared, barely speaking English. And unhurt."

The weight of his words hangs in the air. Sixteen women. Victims of the Shadow gang, no doubt. My mind whirls with the implications. We're no saints, but trafficking? That's a line we don't cross. And now, thanks to Quinn's intervention, we're entangled in this mess.

Telling Cade about the Shadow gang was like dangling meat in front of a predator.

Addy's grip on my hand tightens. "Oh my God," she breathes, "Sophie's brother went and rescued all those women from the Shadow gang?"

Nico nods grimly.

"So, why didn't he just let them go? Why bring them to you?" I ask.

"Because they're badly shaken and have nowhere to go. Most of them actually want to go back, if you can believe it."

I can, if they're anything like Mezhen, the woman Addy met while she was trapped there. I lean back, my mind racing. Cade Quinn decimating the Shadow gang? It doesn't add up. "Since when are we and Quinn on the same team?"

Nico scoffs, running a hand through his hair. "We're so fucking not. He's just a demented meddler and show-off, that's what he is."

I can't help but smirk. "I take it you didn't say thank you?"

"Hell no," Nico growls, his expression darkening further at my amusement. "What I desperately wanted to say was a giant 'Fuck off'."

"But you didn't?" Addy breathes.

He glances at Addy. "No, I didn't. I couldn't."

Addy lets out a breath, her face lighting up in relief. "Thank you so much, Nico." The warmth in her voice makes me want to roll my eyes.

The fucker gets my woman's eternal gratitude just for not telling some schmuck to take a hike?

"You're welcome." Nico smiles back, then sighs. "I don't suppose you'll pitch in an explanation to my wife as to why I couldn't say no to sixteen former sex slaves taking up residence in her favorite house? In a way that doesn't end with me sleeping on the couch for the foreseeable future, that is."

"Sounds like fun," Addy chuckles, her eyes twinkling.

I snort. "If you weren't too busy grinding your teeth, Nico, you might've asked Quinn for a manual on 'How to Look After Trafficked Women 101.' But it's still not too late to have a chat with him, let him walk you through the home installation."

Nico sneers. "He's a fucking caveman. The man probably thinks 'chatting' means discussing the most efficient way to disembowel someone."

"Which would be excellent information for our Associates. Hate him as much as you want. Quinn's not entirely bad company," I quip, earning myself a glare from Nico.

I catch Addy's brow furrow in confusion, her green eyes clouding with questions. Leaning in close, I whisper, my lips brushing her ear, "Associates are men who aren't made yet."

Her mouth forms a silent "Oh," understanding dawning on her face. She bites her lower lip, thinking, then suggests in a hesitant but hopeful voice, "What about them staying in one of your hotels? Like the Marston?"

I glance at Nico, letting him field this one. He shakes his head, his expression grim. "Not discreet or safe enough," he says simply, his feet tapping a restless rhythm on the floor.

Addy straightens from me to face Nico fully. "How about if you bought a place and kept them there?" she asks.

I stifle a laugh as Nico subtly pales.

"Baby," I explain gently, placing a hand on her knee, "we don't keep women." The satin smoothness of her skin calls to me, and I can't help but stroke my fingers across the strip of skin between her knee and the hem of her red dress.

Addy's eyebrows knit again as she looks between Nico and me. "But what does Cade expect you to do with these broken women?"

"He said he brought them for his sister," Nico says blandly. "To fix, or something."

"And what if Sophie doesn't want them?" Addy presses, leaning forward slightly.

Nico pauses, running a hand over the stubble on his chin. "Well, then I guess I'm stuck." Then he looks up and pins Addy with an intense gaze. "Unless you'd like to take them? Dante said you connected with a few of the women."

Addy's eyes widen, and she stiffens beside me. After a moment of stunned silence, she sputters, "Connected?" She whirls to face me.

I shrug, remembering how I'd sung Addy's praises to Nico and Sal. "You can read people, baby. Well, except for the times you choose not to." Like Benjamin O'Shea. Like me, during those three months after we first met at Loyola.

Her cheeks flush a rosy pink as she struggles to form a response. "I don't know what you mean," she hedges.

"Precisely my point," I smile.

The tension in the room breaks, and we all laugh—a welcome release from the heaviness of our conversation.

As our laughter subsides, I look at Nico, a knowing smile playing on my lips. "Now I know why you came." My arm tightens around Addy, and she leans into me.

"We could do some fishing on the pier too, if it would make you feel like I came here for you," Nico retorts.

"Fuck off." I pause briefly. "Now, back to your unexpected guests," I continue, as if the message hasn't been received loud and clear by the relevant party. "You could make them paid employees . . ."

As Nico and I trade increasingly ridiculous suggestions for dealing with the situation, I feel Addy shaking with silent laughter beside me. But when I look down at her, I notice the mirth doesn't quite reach her eyes.

Her brow is slightly furrowed, and she's biting her bottom lip—a telltale sign she's deep in thought. She knows she's just been offered her first assignment as a working member of the Outfit, should she choose to accept it. I can almost see the weight of responsibility settling on her shoulders, and a mix of pride and concern washes over me. Is she ready to get involved?

The rest of the evening passes in a blur of conversation and planning, but Addy's thoughtful expression stays with me.

***

Later that night, with the soft moonlight filtering through the curtains and the distant sound of waves lapping at the shore creating a soothing backdrop, I pull Addy's naked back flush against me and press a kiss to her temple.

"*Tesoro*. I can still hear the gears turning in your head. It wasn't an order or even a suggestion. In case you wondered, it was a cry for help."

"I get that. I just felt . . . you know . . . honored? That Nico thought I could even do this. And he didn't have to ask me. His wife is a therapist, and she's excellent at handling people. Contrary to what he said, I know Sophie would agree to take them on. So would many of the other Capos' wives."

She suddenly turns to face me, her green eyes searching mine in the dim light, narrowing with suspicion as she asks in a small voice, "Dante, did you ask Nico to be . . . you know, nicer to me?"

Dante chuckles. "I didn't need to. I keep telling you, Nico is nice, Addy. It's just hard to see it under all that scowling and bristling."

"I see. Meanwhile, you're the exact opposite," Addy points out.

"Oh really?" I smile, tracing the curve of her cheek with my fingertips. "Meaning?"

"Meaning I'm crazy about you."

"Good answer." I pull her closer, pressing a soft kiss to her temple. After a moment of comfortable silence, I add, "You'll figure this out. You always do."

As I lay here, feeling the calming rhythm of Addy's breathing, inhaling the sweet vanilla scent of her hair, I'm struck by how surreal this all is. Nico and I, in my living room, casually discussing gang wars and trafficked women with Addy like it was just another Tuesday night.

Well then.

Welcome to your fucking world, Valentina De Luca.

CHAPTER FORTY-EIGHT

Adele

It's been two weeks since Nico's unexpected visit, and I've spent every single morning like this—awake and watching Dante sleep while my mind races with plans and possibilities.

My gaze follows the steady rise and fall of his chest and the way his dark hair fans out on the pillow. He's kept it long since middle school because he and Nico could pass for twins. It was his way of asserting his individuality, I suppose.

I trace the lines of his face with my eyes—the strong jaw, the straight nose, and the eyelashes I might seriously consider killing for. But that's where the sophistication ends. He's one of the most dangerous men alive. Because he breeds and nurtures danger.

I think of Sal, who Dante trained, becoming not just a made man, but a Capo, at twenty-four.

And me. What on earth is he turning me into?

Nothing that wasn't already inside you.

Even in sleep, there's an intensity about him that takes my breath away. His mind never truly rests, always working, always planning the next move. It's part of what makes him who he is—brilliant, unpredictable, and utterly captivating.

As if sensing my gaze, Dante's eyes flutter open. His gray irises are soft with sleep, but there's also a glint of something primal. "See something you want to fuck, *tesoro?*"

His words hit me like a bolt, sending a wave of heat straight to my core. Even after all this time, his sudden intensity can catch me off guard, leaving me breathless and aching.

"Jesus, Dante," I manage to croak out. "Do you ever turn off?"

"I used to," he murmurs, his voice husky with sleep. "But that was before you broke the switch."

I can't help but smile at that. My fingers, of their own volition, start to trace his more rugged features—the intricate tattoos on his chest, some cleverly placed to hide his scars. I run my fingers down the wicked-looking veins that snake along his bulging biceps and forearm. Then I'm feeling the hard calluses on his palms and knuckles.

"You are so beautiful." I murmur.

Dante's grin widens as he pulls me closer. He drags up the hem of his t-shirt, my preferred sleep and lounge wear, then cups my lower belly with his large hand, his fingertips playing with the short curls on my mons.

"I think you might be biased," he teases, tugging lightly on the hair. "I did just buy your dream house yesterday, after all."

My heart skips a beat, and I gasp, both from his touch and the reminder of yesterday's surprise. "My God, Dante. I still can't believe you did that!"

Since Nico offered me the job I've been frantically searching for places large enough to comfortably house dozens of people, a pit stop for struggling women until they can get their lives back on track.

"For two weeks, Dante, I kept showing you all those listings, and you didn't spare them a glance."

"I glanced," he says, nibbling a path across my jaw.

"Yeah, for all of a millisecond, and all you had to say was 'Huh'," I mimic his baritone. "Then it was always back to Tommy Martelli's family business. I didn't even think you heard any of what I was saying."

His fingers continue their maddening caress. "I'm always paying attention, Addy. Even when it doesn't seem like it."

Despite the heat building inside me, I can't help but shake my head in wonder. "That's the thing, though. Your mind . . . it blows me away."

Dante laughs outright at this. "My mind? Are you sure about that?"

"Not the dark, twisty, and torture-y parts, thank you very much. I mean the way your brain works. How you can juggle so many problems at once and hyperfocus on tasks. It's . . . fascinating. Can be annoying sometimes, but mostly, it's . . . intriguing."

His expression softens, a rare vulnerability flickering in his eyes. "You're talking about my ADHD?"

I nod. "It's not a disorder. Not for you, Dante."

He's quiet for a moment, considering. "Growing up, it was hard to cope with a mind that worked a little differently. I was generally a nightmare."

I link my fingers with his. "Yet you've managed to turn what others might see as a weakness into your greatest strength. At the risk of sounding like a complete simp, I think you're pretty awesome."

Dante pulls me closer, pressing a kiss to my temple. "I fucking love you, too."

We lay in comfortable silence for a while, but my mind wanders, as it has for the past couple of weeks. Mezhen and the rest have such gory stories to tell and I just wish I could help them heal.

As the weight of their experiences presses on me, an icy chill runs through me despite Dante's warmth. I can't help but think what would have happened had Dante not shown up exactly when he did that night.

I might have killed Sean Hall, but the consequences of that would have been unspeakable. Without doubt I would have been way worse off than these women.

This realization only strengthens my resolve to help these women who didn't have someone to save them. To see that they reclaim their lives and their power back. Maybe, in a way, I'm also reclaiming a part of myself that was almost lost.

"Sophie's going to have the babies soon," I murmur, trying to distract myself from darker thoughts.

"Mmm," Dante agrees, his voice rumbling in his chest. "Any day now."

"I've been thinking about Mezhen and the others."

Dante shifts, propping himself up on one elbow. His eyes, now fully alert, study my face intently. "You're always thinking about them."

"I know, *cara*."

"*Carissimo,*" he corrects gently, a hint of amusement in his voice.

"*Carissimo,*" I repeat, melting again at the way he rolls his r's. "I'm such a slow learner."

His lips quirk up in a smirk. "Oh, I don't know about that. You seemed to pick up *'più forte'* and *'non fermarti'* pretty quickly last night."

I feel my cheeks heat up, but I can't help the laugh that escapes me. "Dante! I'm trying to have a serious conversation here."

He grins, unrepentant, but says, "Alright, alright. Talk to me. What is it about those women that worries you?"

I sigh. "To be honest, I'm not sure how we'll cope without Sophie when she's busy with the twins."

His brows furrow. "But she can still help now, can't she?"

"She sure can. But the problem is, those women aren't ready for any sort of psychological help. All we're doing now is letting them get used to being free. Some of them can't speak English. A few simply won't speak at all. And Mezhen still wants to go back."

Dante nods, his expression growing serious. "That's so messed up. Are you worried that when they're finally ready for Sophie, she won't be able to take them on?"

"Exactly. And I don't have the tools to help. Even if I did, sixteen women . . . I'm just thinking—"

"You need to employ professional help," Dante interjects, already knowing what I'm about to say.

"Yeah." I agree. "And not just mental help. They need doctors, legal advice, employment. Some need more education to get a job. One of them just found out she's pregnant. It's a lot for me as one person to deal with—"

"But not for a charity," Dante interjects again.

I roll my eyes. "Dante freaking Vitelli. Are you going to let me speak, or would you like to carry on reading my mind?"

I always want to kiss and strangle him when he does this. I know it's because he processes information so fast it's as if he can't wait for the rest of us to catch up.

Dante's eyes light up as he pinches his fingers together and mimics a zipping motion across his lips. "Go on, *tesoro*."

Shit. Now I want to stop talking altogether and do something else. But I make myself carry on. I take a deep breath, forcing myself to concentrate on the women and their needs.

"Anyway, yes, I was thinking of starting a charity. We'd employ all the professionals needed to give them the tools to reclaim their lives."

"I think that's doable. And funding won't be an issue."

My smile widens as excitement builds. "Okay, well, maybe in a few years I'd want to be more hands-off and scale it into a foundation. But for now, just a charity will do."

"What do you want to call it?"

I hesitate. "I thought it could be called Power. Because that's what we want to give them back, right? Their power, their agency."

"True." Dante nods, his eyes focused intently on me.

"And, ah, also because Potenza means power, right?"

Dante's lids fall closed for a few moments. When he opens them, his eyes are stormy, but his voice is steady. "Yeah, it does. *Grazie, tesoro.*"

He reaches out to stroke the scar on my hip. Sensations burst from under his fingers, flooding me with endorphins. He knows just how, when, and where to touch me.

I bite my lip and suppress a moan. Then, ignoring my body's protest, I place my hand over his to stop the stroking.

We should talk about this.

"Dante?"

"Addy?"

"Why haven't you spoken about Pietro Potenza since . . . that night?"

I didn't want to bring it up initially because a self-loathing part of me was afraid he'd blame me. And then as I fell more in love with him, I just wanted him to feel comfortable enough to talk about it.

Dante raises his scarred knuckles. "But I do. Every day. And I already told you, I'm not sorry."

I huff out a humorless laugh. "Three words, babe. Now that's what I call succinct." I turn his hand over, musing.

Clearly, he feels more than just 'not sorry' if he's still talking to the punching bag. And he cried that night for fuck's sake.

As if reading my mind, he places a finger under my chin and his eyes bore into mine. "Listen. Losing Pietro hurt. It probably always will. But he died protecting my entire world. You. Pietro was the most loyal soldier. And the truest friend there ever was. So I'm not sorry. I'm grateful. And, for the record, I've hit the gym every day since I was thirteen."

God, how does he do that?

A few words, and he says exactly what I need to hear. Still, he gives me space to be my dramatic self, lets me process things my way, but he's always there, solid as a rock. It's both infuriating and perfect all at once.

I grumble. "I'm pretty sure that was still under fifty words, but okay, I get it. Just know I'm going to need at least half a million words before I'm even halfway done processing all this."

A small smile tugs at Dante's lips. "Sure. And I'm here for it whenever you need. Take your time."

"Ugh. Stop doing that!"

"What?" He murmurs.

"Making me love you more. It's sickening enough as it is."

"I know. We're both done for in that area." His hand resumes stroking my thigh, but he shifts gears slightly. "Now, Aydin Sibel would be a massive help in setting up the Power Foundation. You should call her."

My brows shoot up. "Aydin? But isn't she banned from . . . I thought she'd be . . . I dunno . . . shot, if she got within fifty feet of me or something." I say, still unsure of how to navigate the rules of mafia blacklists.

Dante chuckles, his touch growing more possessive. "Not if you don't want her to be. She just can't have personal access to any member of this family. But you can hire her on a professional level if you want. She does need another job, after all."

"Okay," I nod. "I suppose after being on a billionaire's payroll for decades, a nine-to-five wouldn't quite cut it."

"Uh-uh." Dante shakes his head, then buries his face in my neck.

The idea of the Power Foundation takes root in my mind. It feels right, like the next step in this new life I've embraced—a way to turn the darkness and pain of the past into strength, hope, and love. I think this could really work.

Dante suddenly flips me onto my belly, his hands gliding over my back and ass. His touch ignites sparks along my skin, and thoughts of the Power Foundation scatter from my head like a flock of startled birds. I can't say I'm surprised, though—he's been raring to fuck since the moment he opened his eyes.

He gathers my hair away from my nape, nibbling on the skin there before slipping a hand under me, sliding upwards until he's cupping my breast. I moan into the pillow as he starts to play with my tight nipple. His nibbles turn into hard sucks, then bites, as he simultaneously pinches my nipple harder.

"Dante!" I cry, squirming against him. "Please."

"Please, what?" He switches his attention to my other breast, his hips pinning me to the bed.

I roll my eyes. "Fuck me, duh."

Nestled between my ass cheeks, his cock jerks, and I can't help grinding against his hard length.

"Fuck you where?"

"Oh Lord, here we go." I groan. When Dante gets like this, it means we could be here all morning while he edges me to within an inch of my life. "Dante . . ."

He sniggers. "Well, can you not be a little more specific? What would you like to go where?"

"What is this, a gourmet order? Just make me come all over you!"

"Really!" He stops everything he's doing, then drops his voice to that low, dangerous register that never fails to make my pussy clench with need. "Well, since you're so sassy-mouthed and bushy-tailed this morning, there's this neat little trick I'd like to teach you . . ."

I hear the bedside drawer open, and my breath catches. What new toy has he added to our collection now?

"Close your eyes," he commands.

I comply, my heart pounding with anticipation. I feel something cool and smooth touch my lips.

Suddenly, Dante's phone vibrates on the nightstand, the harsh buzz shattering the moment. He lets out a string of colorful curses, and I groan, burying my face in the pillow. Of course, Dante can't not answer his phone, even if the world were ending. Especially if the world were ending.

Dante sighs, his warm breath tickling my ear as he reaches for the phone. "Text," he mutters.

I peek at him from under my lashes as he reads, watching his brow furrow slightly.

"It's your father. He's picking me up in ten."

I turn to face Dante fully and my gaze immediately snags on the ball gag dangling from his hand and the butt plug on the pillow.

Oh my. A hot flush of disappointment washes over me, quickly chased by anxiety when Dante says, "He wants to go over security protocols for the wedding."

"Again?"

We still don't know who wants me dead. The thought sends an icy shiver down my spine. Moving from the Fortress to this slightly less secure (but still heavily guarded) beach house was one thing. But a wedding with hundreds of guests? That's like painting a giant bullseye on my back and screaming, "Come and get me!"

Dante, being Dante, has maintained his cool about the whole thing, but Orlando . . . well, that's another story.

"Orlando is, um . . . freaking out, isn't he?" I ask holding back a small smile.

Dante's lips quirk into a half-smile. "He's losing his shit a little bit, yeah. Or maybe he just wants an excuse to see you. So why don't you get dressed and give him one of your goo-goo smiles? He's much less prickly when you do that."

I can't help but laugh, the sound breaking some of the tension in the room. "He's nothing but sweet."

"He is not the least bit sweet. He's just crazy about you. No less than you deserve, but, yeah, he's not sweet." Dante gets out of bed, and my gaze runs over his sculpted body. Then he's pulling me up too.

Dante leans in close, his lips brushing my ear. "FYI. We're moving this party to the beach when I return," he growls. "I plan to get you filthy tonight."

CHAPTER FORTY-NINE

Adele

WEDDING DAY

The heavy scent of roses mingles with the crisp notes of perfume, filling the air of the bridal suite. Sunlight streams through the tall windows of the De Luca mansion's chapel, casting a warm glow on the polished wood floors and illuminating motes of dust that dance in the air.

I stand before a full-length mirror, barely recognizing the woman staring back at me. My fingers, slightly trembling, trace the intricate lace of my sleeve, feeling each delicate bump and swirl. The corseted bodice hugs my curves tightly, almost restrictively, before giving way to cascades of white silk that rustle against the floor with each subtle movement.

My eyes are drawn to my face, transformed by the artistry of makeup. The weight of the intricate updo pulls slightly at my scalp, and I watch as a few rebellious red tendrils fall around my face, softening the look.

"I'll have to hand your stunning, gorgeous self over to the rest of the girls," Antonella says, a vision in sparkly midnight blue herself.

"They're dying to catch a glimpse of you before Orlando whisks you to the altar. And I need to go preen a little as the mother of the groom."

Before she can turn to leave, I catch her hand. "Mama V," I start, my voice thick with emotion, "thank you. For raising Dante. For letting me love him."

Antonella's eyes soften, a tender smile gracing her lips. She cups my face gently, "Oh, *cara*, it's only ever been you. Those two years apart, my son wasn't really living. You brought my son back to life."

Her words wash over me, the sweetest thing I've ever heard. Tears prick at my eyes, and I blink rapidly to keep them from falling.

With a final gentle squeeze of my hand and a soft rustle of fabric, Antonella leaves, the click of the door echoing in the suddenly quiet room.

I adjust my veil, becoming aware of the sounds filtering in from outside—the low rumble of car engines, the muffled voices of the security detail. It's a stark reminder of the world beyond this room, a world where danger still lurks.

A flutter of excitement runs through me, but there's also an undercurrent of worry. The past six weeks with Dante have been a blissful bubble, but the uncomfortable fact still hangs in the air—Owen Novak died before he could talk. Someone is still out there, waiting, watching.

It's the same reason why Orlando's protective instincts have been in overdrive this past week. Just this morning he insisted on beefing up the perimeter again, not caring that it pushed the ceremony back by a couple of hours.

A small smile tugs at my lips as I think of my father's dedication. In the short time since discovering my true parentage, we've grown remarkably close. I still catch Dante bristling whenever De Luca drops by the house with flowers or gifts, which seems to be happening with increasing frequency. The man is not used to sharing me with an overenthusiastic daddy.

A gentle knock at the door breaks through my thoughts. "Come in," I call.

The door opens, bringing with it a rush of cooler air from the hallway. Sophie enters first, resplendent in a floor-length gown of powder blue. The empire waist accommodates her pregnant belly beautifully, the chiffon fabric flowing gracefully as she moves.

Kira follows, her steps light and graceful in a halter-neck dress of the same light blue. The silk hugs her curves before flaring out at the knee, a subtle mermaid style that suits her perfectly.

Finally, Bianca enters, her heels clicking decisively on the hardwood floor. Her dress, also in blue, features a one-shoulder design with intricate beading that catches the light with every movement.

"Oh, Addy, you look absolutely unreal," Sophie gushes, her voice thick with emotion. Her fingers, cool and gentle, adjust my veil, the gossamer-thin fabric settling around my shoulders like a cloud.

Kira hums in agreement, her hazel eyes shining as she reaches out to finger the intricate lace of my sleeve.

Bianca moves around me, her experienced hands making final adjustments to my dress. Her touch is sure and motherly as she smooths out invisible wrinkles. If there's anyone I'm most grateful to, it's her. She's had to give up so much to accommodate me. Here I am, the daughter she never asked for, about to marry the man she wanted for her own daughter.

I catch her eye in the mirror, returning her smile with a grateful one of my own.

Finally satisfied that I look perfect, Bianca pushes a black case into my hand. "Orlando wanted to give this to you himself, but I don't think he trusts himself not to break down. He says it was the last gift he bought . . ." she hesitates, swallowing hard, "Naomi. One he never got to give her before she died."

I take the box and open it with trembling hands, and that's when the tears, hot and salty, start to fall.

There is a collective gasp in the room. I hear Sophie softly whispering to Kira, telling her what's got them spellbound.

A pair of diamond and sapphire teardrop earrings nestle in the rich black suede lining. A name engraved inside the case: Naomi. And then a folded note, the ink of the scrawl not completely dry.

Here is something borrowed and something blue. An old flame that refuses to die and a new one to burn for all time. All my love, Orlando.

A sob escapes me.

"Ah ah ah." Bianca's curt command and her single finger held up somehow repress the dam of tears about to burst through me. She dabs at the corners of my eyes, then clasps the earrings on me while I try hard to hold in the sobs. This is the closest I've ever felt to my mother.

I want nothing more than to share the moment with Dante.

"I can't believe Orlando kept it all this while," Sophie whispers in disbelief as she dabs at her own eyes.

As they continue to fuss over me, my fingers find the teardrop earrings nestled against my neck as I just stare at the mirror. Orlando says I look just like her. I close my eyes and imagine if she was here today. What would she think of me? Of Dante? A pang of longing shoots through my chest, as grief threatens to overwhelm me.

"Adele?" Bianca's voice cuts through the fog of my thoughts. "Are you alright, dear? You look a little pale."

I blink, realizing that at some point I've sat down heavily on the arm of the nearby chaise longue. The other women have paused in their ministrations, their faces now etched with concern. Bianca's hand rests gently on my shoulder, a warm, comforting weight.

"I'm fine," I manage, forcing a smile that feels brittle on my lips. "Just a bit overwhelmed, I think."

The room suddenly feels too small, too warm. The floral scent that earlier seemed pleasant now is starting to choke me. I take a deep breath, trying to center myself, but the corset restricts my movement, adding to my discomfort.

"I just want Dante," I blurt out.

Bianca's face softens with understanding, the lines around her eyes crinkling. "Oh, you'll have him in no time, *cara*. Orlando will take you to the altar in another . . ." She checks her watch. "Ten or fifteen minutes. What I do think you need right now is a moment to yourself," she announces, her tone gentle but firm.

"Come along, ladies. Let's give Adele some space to breathe and take it all in. The ceremony is almost starting anyway. We should go take our places."

Relief washes over me at her words. As much as I appreciate their support, the solitude suddenly seems like a lifeline.

Sophie squeezes my shoulder before waddling toward the door, one hand on her swollen belly.

Kira follows, the smart cane she carries to unfamiliar places tapping softly on the plush carpet. "You make the most beautiful bride, Addy," she says, her eyes somehow finding mine unerringly. "I don't need eyes to know that."

I glance at the mirror again, and I have to agree with her.

I nod, forgetting for a moment that she can't see the gesture. "Thank you," I murmur. "And you look amazing too."

Kira has no idea how she looks in her blue maid of honor dress, her glossy dark hair cascading down her back, adorned with fresh baby's breath. Friends or not, Sal had better be showing her every single day how beautiful she is inside and out.

They file out, offering reassuring smiles and gentle touches, but Bianca lingers at the door. "I'll get you something to drink, *cara*," she says, her voice soothing. "To calm your nerves."

I smile and nod, grateful for her thoughtfulness.

As the door clicks shut behind her, the sudden silence feels almost crushing. I let out a long, shaky breath, the sound unnaturally loud in the empty room. Slowly, I stand, the layers of my dress settling around me with a soft swish.

I move to the window, drawn by the need for air, for space. Outside, the manicured gardens of the De Luca estate stretch out before me, a sea of green punctuated by bursts of colorful blooms. Security guards in full tactical vests dot the landscape, stark against the lush backdrop, a reminder that even on this joyful day, danger still lurks at the edges of our world.

I press my forehead against the cool glass, closing my eyes. In a few minutes, I'll be Mrs. Vitelli, wife of Dante, fully entrenched in a world I'm coming to embrace. A world of power and danger, of loyalty and betrayal. And a love that transcends time.

Oh Mama. I finger the earrings again, fighting tears.

The sound of the door opening again makes me turn. Bianca enters, an open bottle of champagne and two crystal flutes in her hands, and I groan inwardly.

Orlando obviously didn't tell Bianca I'm pregnant. Those two are practically strangers living in the same house for the amount of communication that happens between them.

"Now," Bianca says, her smile warm and motherly as she approaches, "let's have a little toast to endless love and new beginnings, shall we?"

Another pang of guilt hits me for how well Bianca is taking this whole situation. I represent everything wrong in her marriage: a product of an affair her husband had with a woman he's still in love with even after two decades. And wants to toast to that? I'm not sure if I'm spooked by or admire the effort she's no doubt making to put on a brave front when her heart must be breaking inside.

"Bianca, I'm sorry." The words catch in my throat.

Her brows furrow, the champagne flutes clinking softly as she sets them down. "For what?"

"For this." Meeting her dark gaze, I gesture at the earrings.

Instantly she gets it. An indefinable emotion swirls in her eyes, and I catch the sheen of tears in them before they harden again.

"It's okay." She chuckles wryly, the sound coming off wrong. "Well, it's not okay, of course. It's never been okay. But an apology is a nice start to taking ownership for the unforgivable."

"I agree," I say, glad that she's taking the chance to admit how she truly feels.

Bianca takes a deep breath, her shoulders rising and falling visibly. "I never got an apology from Orlando. Not once. He still doesn't regret having an affair. He'd do it a thousand times over."

"Why do you think he doesn't regret it?" I ask, leaning against the dresser for support.

"Because he married me when the Don wouldn't. An alliance with the powerful Rinaldis raised the Outfit's position to the top of the mafia food chain. And of course established Orlando as the most powerful Capo." Her voice turns bitter. "Although he conveniently forgot the 'forsaking all others' part of the vows he made to me. I was simply a means to an end."

I see why Orlando holds so much power with the Vitellis. Vito owes him. "When did you find out about the affair?"

Bianca's gaze drifts to the window, her reflection superimposed on the garden view. "For ten years, I had no clue. He was distant and cold, but I chalked it up to him being hardened by his life. Besides, I was still heartbroken from having to see Vito slobber over that . . . spineless woman."

My eyes widen in surprise at her description of Antonella, but I don't dare stop her, needing to hear the rest.

She releases the tie back, draws the curtains closed, and slowly walks back. "I've loved Vito for as long as I can remember. And finally, I caught his eye. For a while, he wanted me too. And then three months to our wedding, he changed his mind. Did you know that?"

I nod, the weight of her words settling heavily on me. Dante mentioned that to me, but hearing it from her hits different.

Bianca continues, her fingers now drumming a restless rhythm on the dresser. "Anyway, would you believe it was you who gave Orlando's affair away?"

"What, me? How?" I ask, startled.

She pulls up a stool and sits, leaning against the dresser. "For ten years, Orlando and your mother were extremely discreet. They never met up in Chicago. Instead, he whisked his favorite family away on exotic vacations once a month."

Her voice drops so low I have to strain to hear her. "One day, after Orlando returned from one of his monthly 'assignments' abroad, I found something hidden among his weapons: A list made by a little girl called Valentina about all the things she wanted from her daddy for her fifth birthday. Alina had just turned five and she wasn't even asked to make one."

"I'm so sorry," I say but she waves off my apology with an impatient hand, as if she doesn't want to be interrupted.

"Anyway I had him followed closely. It turned out Bianca Rinaldi, heiress of the great Rinaldi family of New York, was to find myself as second best to a man not even fit to lick my father's boots. Upstaged by some Plain Jane and her spoiled brat." Her lips curl into a sneer. "Of course, she turned out to be a Mob princess but that's neither here nor there.

I shut my lids, trying and failing to imagine how much it must have hurt Bianca. It's hard to hear her talk about my parents and me in that way. But I can't help but feel her pain. What such a proud woman had to put up with.

"Anyway. Here we go." Bianca pours the champagne and pushes mine toward me. The scent of the bubbly beverage reaches me, crisp and inviting. But I dare not. Even if I tried it, the champagne would come back up messily in minutes. She pushes mine toward me and raises her glass in a toast. I clink hers with mine but keep cradling the flute, waiting for her to leave so I can get rid of it.

She drinks deeply from hers and cocks her head at me. "Go on, *cara*."

I force a smile. "I think I'll pass on the champagne. My stomach is a bit unsettled. Nerves, you see."

"Nonsense," she insists, her voice honey-sweet. "A sip is exactly what you need to settle your nerves. It's tradition, after all."

She picks up my flute and presses it into my hand, the crystal cool against my palm. I stare at the golden liquid, watching the bubbles rise in a steady stream.

"I really can't," I take a breath and tell her. "You see, I'm pregnant."

"Pregnant?" she repeats, her tone suddenly icy. "Interesting." The change in her voice makes me look up, and that's when I see it. The shift in her demeanor is so abrupt, so complete, that for a moment I wonder if I'm imagining things. The warmth in her eyes has been replaced by a cold, hard glint. Her smile, once motherly, now seems more like a predator baring its teeth.

She calmly moves to the door and turns the lock with a soft click.

CHAPTER FIFTY

Adele

The click echoes in the silent room, chilling me to the bone. The champagne flute in my hand suddenly feels like a dead weight.

"I'm afraid I have to insist," she turns back to me, and the look on her face makes my blood run cold. Gone is any pretense of warmth or maternal affection. In its place is a mask of pure, unadulterated hatred.

"Bianca?" I ask, my voice barely above a whisper. "What's going on?"

"What's going on, my dear Valentina," she says, her voice dripping with venom, "is that I'm finishing what the Novaks spectacularly failed at."

My heart thuds so hard I can feel it in my throat. I put the champagne glass down and brace myself against the edge of the dresser.

"I don't understand," I say, but I do. In fact, my mind is reeling from how much I understand. The champagne is poisoned. Or my flute. Whichever it is, if I drink a drop of this accursed champagne, it'll be the last thing I do.

Bianca laughs, a harsh, mirthless sound that sends a chill down my spine. "Of course you do. You Irish sluts never change. You just waltz in and take what isn't yours, not ever considering who gets hurt in the process."

As she speaks, her hand disappears into her purse. When it reemerges, my breath catches in my throat. The light glints off the barrel of a small pistol, now pointed directly at me.

"Now," Bianca says, her voice eerily calm, "I'll give you one last choice. Drink the champagne, or we do this the messy way. Either way, you won't be walking down that aisle today."

I pick up the champagne flute, watching as it trembles in my hand, the golden liquid sloshing dangerously close to the rim. My mind desperately searches for a way out of this nightmare. But as I look into Bianca's cold, determined eyes, one thought echoes loudly in my head:

I'm trapped.

"Why?" I manage to croak out, my throat dry. "Why are you doing this?"

Bianca shakes her head in disappointment. "Why? You home-wrecking little gutter slut. When you apologized just now, I thought you understood why neither of you deserved to live. I thought you were ready to pay true penance."

Her grip tightens on the gun, knuckles whitening. "I thought you both died. The stupid fucks fought over that fact for the next ten years. And watching how the grief tortured Orlando was the sweetest form of revenge."

She's sick. Bianca is fucking deranged.

She takes a step closer, and I instinctively back up, the voluminous skirts of my wedding dress trapping me.

Bianca snarls. "But imagine my rage when, two years ago, I found out you not only refused to die, but you were fucking a Vitelli."

My mind reels, struggling to process this flood of information. I stare at the gun in Bianca's hand, its barrel a black hole threatening to swallow my future.

"To add insult to injury," she spits, "Orlando changed his will when he found out you were alive. He gave you everything, the cold, selfish bastard. He loved a dead woman's child more than his own family."

The gun in her hand trembles slightly, but her aim doesn't waver. "You've taken too much from me. From Alina. Her father's love. Her inheritance. The man she loves."

My mind reels, trying to process the depth of her scheming. Bianca's voice drops to a near whisper, laden with bitterness. "Especially since the man kept pining for you with his fascination with women who looked like you. I knew it was a matter of time until he came after you and brought you back here."

She takes a step closer, her eyes gleaming with a manic light. "So I was ready for you to step into Chicago. To kill you and violate the treaty with the Irish. Then I'd get Orlando to rebel against the Outfit. Nico wouldn't survive the war. The captain never leaves his sinking ship after all. But Dante would survive."

The enormity of her plan hits me like a physical blow. This goes beyond personal vengeance; she was willing to tear apart entire families, to ignite an all-out war, all for her twisted sense of justice.

"It would work out in the end," Bianca continues, a note of pride creeping into her voice. "Dante would become Don and all too eager to marry Alina to get the fractured empire back together. With you dead, there'd be no one to turn to for comfort except his wife. And she'd be more than ready to make it all better. I had it all worked out, you see."

I stare at her, horror and disbelief warring within me. "You're insane," I whisper.

Bianca's face suddenly contorts with rage. "Insane? I'm the only one who sees clearly! Men are so fucking weak and stupid. Vito. Orlando. Even my brothers who were supposed to do one thing for me, failed. They told me Emil Novak was the best. And then they said it was Owen. Liars. The lot of them."

She raises the gun higher, her finger tightening on the trigger. In that moment, I realize that this woman, consumed by hatred, won't stop until one of us is dead. The champagne flute in my hand suddenly feels woefully inadequate.

"So," Bianca says, her voice suddenly calm, almost conversational, "there's nothing left to say. Except that you have ten seconds to choose.

A bullet in your heart, or a more graceful way." She gestures to the champagne glass with her free hand.

Time seems to slow. I look at the bubbling champagne, knowing it's laced with poison. I look at the gun, steady in Bianca's grip. I think of Dante, waiting for me at the altar. Of the child growing inside me.

In that moment, a strange calm washes over me even as a bitter laugh bubbles up in my throat. I've survived six bullets, a bomb blast, a kidnapping, and a forced marriage. To die now, forced to drink poison like some tragic Shakespearean heroine, seems absurdly anticlimactic.

With a sudden burst of energy, I smash the champagne flute against the nearby dresser. The crystal shatters, poisoned wine spilling across the polished wood, leaving me clutching the jagged stem. It's not much of a weapon, but I've killed a man with less. Of course, that man was drunk and didn't have a gun trained on me with unwavering precision.

"Neither, actually," I spit out, surprising myself with the venom in my voice. "I'd prefer the idea of fucking the man your daughter loves for the rest of my long, happy life. I'd also love to bear your husband's grandchildren, to inherit everything he owns, and to become a Vitelli—a feat you never managed."

Rage contorts Bianca's features, her carefully maintained facade crumbling to reveal the monster beneath. "Why you little . . ." She cocks the gun with an ominous click, and I know I have only seconds left to act.

My eyes dart to the champagne bottle still sitting on the silver tray. It's a better weapon, and it's within reach, but can I grab it and swing before Bianca pulls the trigger? The odds aren't in my favor, but it's the only chance I have.

Bianca follows my gaze, a mocking smile twisting her lips. "Go ahead," she taunts, her voice dripping with derision. "Please. Give me a good reason to paint these walls with your brains."

Time seems to slow. I can hear my heart pounding in my ears, feel each bead of sweat trickling down my back.

This is it. I have two choices.

Lunge for the bottle and possibly die.

Or remain as a still target and surely die.

And so with my choices spelled out for me, I lunge for the champagne bottle, my muscles coiling and releasing like a spring.

The gun goes off with a thunderous crack that makes me freeze. I wait to collapse to the floor. All I felt was a searing heat in my left arm. The realization that she missed my chest sends a rush of adrenaline through me, dulling the pain.

My right hand closes around the bottle, and I use my weight to swing hard. Another explosion rings out but this misses me by a mile. Her aim is shot as she raises her arm to defend herself against the heavy champagne bottle.

It connects with the gun in Bianca's outstretched arm and shatters with a satisfying shower of champagne and glass.

She screams, and the gun clatters to the floor. I'm not sure if it's being doused in poisoned wine or that one of the glass shards has embedded itself in her wrist that's driving her panicked reaction, but I'm not done yet. I bring the bottle down again and the jagged ends connect with her bare shoulder.

Blood sprays in a crimson arc, splattering across the floor and my once-pristine white dress.

Bianca stumbles back, still screaming as blood runs from cuts on her shoulder and arm. Her eyes are wild with pain and fury, her chest heaving with each ragged breath.

"Maybe you shouldn't do things yourself then, princess, since you obviously skipped shooting classes." I taunt.

"You fucking bitch!" she snarls, lunging for the fallen gun. But I kick it away, ignoring the burning pain in my arm with every movement. That I can move my hand and arm as a unit tells me it's likely a flesh wound.

The gun skitters across the floor, disappearing under a heavy dresser.

Bianca's gaze darts between me and the dresser. I can see the calculation in her eyes, her body tensing as she weighs her options. She's wondering if she can reach the gun before I can stop her.

"Don't," I warn, brandishing the broken bottle. Blood drips steadily from my arm, staining my white dress crimson.

She laughs, a harsh, bitter sound. "Or what? You'll kill me? You don't have it in you."

Her words ignite a fire in my chest, and the corner of my mouth lifts in a cold smile. "I've killed a man with less, and I loved it. Imagine what I'd enjoy doing to you."

Bianca's eyes widen slightly, her body stiffening as she perhaps finally realizes I could kill her. But then her face hardens, jaw clenching. "You're just like your mother," she spits. "A homewrecker. A slut. A thief. You deserve to die painfully, riddled in bullets, just like she did."

Her cruel words plow into me, and before I can recover, she makes her move, diving for the dresser.

I react on instinct, my body moving before my mind can catch up. I tackle her, both of us crashing to the floor. The bottle falls from my hand and shatters. As we grapple, rolling across the carpet, it's nearly impossible to breathe in my corset, much less fight, and my injured arm screams in pain, but I ignore it, focusing on keeping Bianca away from the gun.

She claws at my face, nails raking across my cheek, and I retaliate by driving my knee into her stomach. She wheezes, momentarily stunned, her body going slack beneath me.

I take advantage of her distraction, scrambling toward the dresser, but my movements are slow, restricted by the tight corset and the overly full skirt. If only I could get the gun first.

Bianca recovers quickly, grabbing my dress. I kick back, feeling my heel connect with something soft. She grunts in pain, and her grip instantly loosens.

Just as my fingers brush the cool metal of the gun, Bianca grabs a fistful of my coiffed hair, yanking my head back.

Pain explodes across my scalp, but I don't let go of the gun, somehow more pissed with her ruining my hair than when she shot me.

Bianca throws herself on me, struggling to reach my outstretched right hand as both of us fight for control of the weapon. It goes off again, the bullet embedding itself in the ceiling. Plaster rains down on us as we continue to wrestle.

Suddenly, the doorknob starts to jiggle. Someone has heard us. Relief floods me just as the door crashes open. Orlando fills the doorway, gun drawn, his face paling in horror as he takes in the scene before him.

"Adele!" he cries, moving toward me.

In that split second of distraction, Bianca wrenches the gun from my grasp. She staggers to her knees, her bloodied hand trembling as she aims the gun at my chest. Sweat, champagne, and blood drip from her wrist and shoulder, and her eyes are wild with rage.

"Don't you fucking move," she snarls, her voice shaking.

Orlando freezes, his eyes flicking between Bianca and me, no doubt trying to figure out how to defuse the situation.

"Bi," he says softly, raising his hands in a placating gesture, his gun dangling loosely from his thumb, "please put the gun down. Let's talk about this."

Bianca laughs, a high, unhinged sound. "Talk? There's nothing to talk about. Your precious daughter needs to die. Just like her whore of a mother. It's like I always say: when you want something done right, you do it yourself."

For a heartbeat, nothing happens. Then I see something shift in Orlando's eyes—a flicker of resolve, a darkness.

The moment shatters as Dante appears at the door, his gun aimed steadily at Bianca. His voice, a low, cold, and deadly rumble, cuts through the tension like a knife. "Drop the weapon, Bianca. You have two seconds."

My breath catches. I can't tell whether I'm more relieved or terrified, but a single thought pounds through my mind—please, God, don't let this be the last time I hear that voice.

A strange chill appears to settle over Orlando, and he shrugs as if in resignation. "It's okay, Dante. Bi is right. There's really nothing to talk about."

My heart twists painfully at Orlando's words, and even Bianca seems surprised to have her husband's backing to shoot me.

And then Bianca's eyes dart back to me. Her grip on the gun wavers, appearing to be weighing her options, but in the next split second, Dante's gun fires.

The shot rings out, and Bianca's scream pierces the air as the gun is shot out of her hand. Blood pours from her now-maimed fingers, the weapon clattering uselessly to the floor.

I watch in stunned silence, the scene playing out in slow motion. Dante's done this before—shot the phone right out of someone's ear, with the same unnerving precision. But this is different. This time, it's Bianca, and her distress is palpable. She clutches her bloody hand to her chest, her face contorted in pain and disbelief.

For a split second, I allow myself to relax. Dante's absolute control, always a step ahead, and right now I could kiss him for saving my life right after I figure out what the hell went wrong with my father.

But when I look at Orlando, I see something strange. He's looking at Dante, and his gun is raised, his expression unreadable. There's a tension in his body that wasn't there before, something cold and calculating in his eyes that makes my stomach churn with unease.

"Dante?" I glance at Dante, but he hasn't lowered his weapon either. His gaze is locked on Orlando, and there's a split second where something passes between them, as if they're communicating silently.

Orlando's eyes twitch, and he shakes his head, and Dante's widen in alarm. Orlando swings his gun to Bianca, his movements deliberate and calm.

"Orlando!" Dante barks, but it's too late.

Orlando fires.

The first bullet slams into Bianca's chest, and she crumples to the floor. The second follows almost immediately, and this time, there's no scream—just a sickening thud as her body jerks under the impact.

Dante's reaction is immediate. He takes a step toward Orlando and levels his gun at his temple, his eyes blazing with fury. No words are needed.

Orlando slowly lowers his gun, his expression a mix of grim satisfaction and a strange calmness. He raises his hands in surrender, his weapon once again dangling from his thumb.

Dante's eyes stay locked on Orlando, his finger still on the trigger, his whole body taut with tension. I can see the struggle in him, the war between his loyalty to family and his instinct to protect.

Orlando steps back, moving toward the wall, his hands still raised. "I'm done," he says quietly, then holsters his gun.

I'm still staring at my father, my mind reeling, when Dante is suddenly beside me, crouching down and gathering me into his arms.

"Christ! Addy. Fuck." His entire body is shaking as he examines me. I see his sharp intake of breath when he sees my bleeding arm—I haven't even seen it myself—but I'm guessing it's not looking pretty.

"I'm okay. I'm okay, Dante." I reassure him, raising my right arm to cup his face as he pulls off his tie.

"You're so fucking not. For fuck's sake, how many bullets do you have to take before it's enough for a fucking lifetime?"

"Hopefully the last," I smile, but Dante doesn't share my humor. Then I wince when he wraps the tie around my arm with trembling fingers, ignoring my protests that it's not even bleeding anymore.

As if just remembering the other disaster in the room—that a Capo has killed his own wife—Dante turns back to Orlando. "Tell me that's not what it looked like."

Orlando raises his head, eyes cold and resolute. "Yep. It's exactly what it looked like," he says simply and turns back to the wall.

When Orlando doesn't say more, I add, "It was she and her brothers. They hired the Novaks."

Dante nods gravely, already piecing it together. I think he may have got it during their weird eye contact earlier. He helps me to my feet, his movements gentle but his body vibrates with tension still.

The room quickly fills with Capos, their faces knit with confusion and alarm. Nico shoulders his way through, his eyes darting from Bianca's lifeless body to Orlando's eerie calmness.

"De Luca," he barks, "what is the meaning of—"

"That?" Orlando interrupts, his voice bitter and filled with decades of regret. "That was an eighteen-year blind spot. That was who started the decade-long war. Along with her brothers. Right under my fucking nose."

Nico's usual composure fractures slightly as he runs a hand through his hair, leaving it uncharacteristically disheveled. "Christ," he mutters, shaking his head. "Rinaldis. How did we miss this?"

Orlando pushes away from the wall, shoulders slumped with regret. "I lived with her for two decades and I missed it." Regret, pain, and a fierce protectiveness war across his features.

"Adele," he starts, his voice rough with emotion, "I am so sorry . . ."

And the weight of it all suddenly hits me. My lids fall closed, and I'm surprised to feel tears slipping down my cheeks. It feels like every single one of my scars is throbbing along with my pounding headache. I nod, suddenly overwhelmed with it all. "I need air."

Dante understands immediately. He guides me to a nearby window, opening it to let in a rush of cool air. His hand rubs soothing circles on my back as I breathe deeply, trying to center myself.

"It's over," he murmurs, his breath warm against my ear. "You're finally safe."

I lean into him, drawing strength from his solid presence. "I know," I whisper back. "It's just—"

Suddenly I remember something. "Oh my God, Dante, the champagne," I say, "Bianca poisoned it. She may have poisoned more."

Shock ripples through the assembled men, and Nico's face is the hardest I've seen it yet. He looks like a storm that's about to erupt.

"Bar the gates," he commands as he yanks off his tie. "Not a single Rinaldi, no soul from New York, in fact, leaves this mansion in their bodies."

As chaos erupts around us, Dante's arms tighten around me protectively. "Let me take you home. We'll get you cleaned up."

"I don't want to go," I blurt out. "Not yet." My cheeks burn as every eye in the small room swings to me.

How can I say I still want to get married right here and now? In my father's house, covered in blood while justice is being served right outside the door.

But I don't need to. Because Dante's eyes find mine, a silent question in their depths.

Hell yes, I'm still up for becoming your wife today. A little gore isn't going to stop me.

I see the moment he gets it. He never fails to get it, this man.

"*Tesoro,*" Dante whispers, one word heavy with meaning.

I manage a small smile, covering his still shaking hands with mine. "What?" I whisper, "I'm learning from the best."

***

An hour later, Dante and I stand face-to-face in De Luca's library. The room, with its walls of leather-bound books and the lingering scent of aged paper, seems a fitting place for this moment. It feels right to be marrying the man who pulled me out of the mire when I didn't realize I was drowning. The man who showed me who I really am, in this unconventional setting.

His eyes, steely and intense, never leave mine as we exchange our vows.

I'm acutely aware of the state of my dress. Once pristine, it is now painted with the fury of a woman scorned. Stained with the blood of my mother's killer, the woman who left scars on me. There's a poetic justice to it, a deep satisfaction that I'm not quite ready to examine.

As we speak the words that bind us together, I know without a doubt that this is where I'm meant to be. With this man, in this world, for better or worse.

"I do," I respond to the priest's prompt.

Then Dante's hand cups my face, his touch gentle despite the strength in his hands from years of hard living. As his lips meet mine, I feel the last pieces of my old life fall away.

I am Adele Valentina Vitelli. Wife, mother, survivor.

And I will defend my right to be her with violence and blood.

EPILOGUE

Adele

ONE YEAR LATER

The Bentley's engine purrs into silence as we pull up to the Fortress. Gilded by the setting sun, Dante's profile captivates me – the tantalizing groove in his cheeks a testament to his reluctant joy.

I slide my hand up his thigh. "Happy birthday, *carissimo*."

Dante's gray eyes meet mine, swirling with heat. "I still can't believe you arranged this," he murmurs, gesturing to the mansion.

It had taken weeks of cajoling to get Dante to agree to a joint celebration with the twins, and even longer to plan a party that could satisfy both toddlers and hardened mafiosos. My husband, ever the selfless one, would move mountains to surprise me or orchestrate a getaway for Nico and Sophie, but rarely spares a thought for his own happiness.

"You're forever putting everyone else first," I say, my fingernails tracing patterns on his expensive wool suit pants. "Me, Luca," – I nod toward our sleeping six-month-old in the backseat – "Nico, the whole fucking Outfit. Let us do this for you, baby."

Dante covers my hand with his, his thumb drawing circles on my skin. "You're all I want."

"You don't want much, do you?"

"Not when you've brought me the entire universe. *Grazie, tesoro.*"

I lean in, my lips brushing his ear. "Well, there's a reason the universe decided to share your birthday with the twins. It's telling us to pull that service stick out of your ass and enjoy being loved on."

His breath hitches. In an instant, his hand tangles in my hair, pulling me into a kiss that's all heat and hunger. I melt into him, my body responding with a familiar ache. Even now, Dante ignites a fire in me with a single look.

"If you wanted that stick out of my ass," he growls against my lips, "you should have just asked. I'd be happy to put it somewhere else."

A laugh bubbles up in my throat, equal parts arousal and amusement. "Promises, promises," I tease.

We lose ourselves in the moment, hands roaming, breaths mingling. I playfully nibble his bottom lip – a move guaranteed to drive him wild. Dante groans, dragging me across the console onto his lap. The kiss turns decadent. I repeat the move, and he tears his mouth away, sliding his thumb across my lower lip.

"Such a bad girl," he whispers.

"What? I'm just giving you a birthday kiss," I purr, catching his thumb between my lips.

In the backseat, Luca sleeps on, blissfully unaware of his parents' indiscretions. It's a rare moment of uninterrupted intimacy, and we're both reluctant to let it end.

Dante's voice grows husky with unmistakable desire. "Did you want to give me a party or a present?"

"Both. But you'll have to wait until after the first to unwrap the second."

"Fuck that." He slides the seat all the way back. "Get on your knees. Now."

I laugh. "Not a chance, perv. Not when Luca is two feet away."

"Sleeping like a rock. Do it."

His rough command sends a jolt of arousal through me. But before I can contemplate obeying, a sharp rap on the window shatters our bubble. Antonella stands outside, her expression a mix of amusement and exasperation. "If you two are quite finished," she calls through the glass, "your guests are waiting."

Dante groans, resting his forehead against mine. "Saved by the bell."

"Yeah right. I wasn't going to do that!" I try to scramble off his lap, but he holds me fast, chuckling.

"Hell yes, you were, Addy. You were literally salivating."

"You're disgusting, you know that?"

"Disgustingly accurate," he deadpans, and we both burst into laughter.

Antonella raps again. "Anytime this year, kids."

We unlock the doors and pour out of the car, and I straighten my teal curve-hugging maxi dress.

Antonella immediately reaches into the back and lifts Luca from his car seat. Jarred from his nap, he blinks owlishly, his dark hair falling into his eyes. Then recognition dawns, and his round face splits into a gummy smile. His green eyes—so like mine—sparkle as a string of delighted squeals escapes him.

"There's my precious *bambino!*" Antonella coos, scooping him up with practiced ease. Luca immediately makes a grab for her diamond earrings, his taste in jewelry apparently as expensive as his father's taste in cars.

Dante's hand finds the small of my back as we follow Antonella into the house. The aroma of grilling meat and freshly baked bread mingles with the scent of flowers. Music drifts from the garden, a melodic backdrop to the cheerful chatter and laughter.

"No climbing on the—*accidenti!* Antonio! Put that down now! Tommy, don't eat that!" Enzo, looking like he's gone ten rounds with a tornado, is in hot pursuit of his six identical toddlers. The two-year-old terrors giggle maniacally as they duck and weave around priceless antiques, their father always a step behind and a curse word ahead.

Suddenly, one of the boys spots Dante. "Uncle Dante!" he shrieks, and like a well-oiled machine, all six toddlers screech to a halt and turn toward us. It's eerily reminiscent of how Dante's men snap to attention when he enters a room.

Dante grins, crouching down with open arms. "Come here, you little monsters!"

In a flash, the boys are upon him like a swarm of very small, very sticky locusts. Dante is suddenly buried under a pile of giggling toddlers. It's a sight that makes my ovaries do a little dance, even as my brain screams 'not yet' in horror.

"Alright, troops," Dante announces in his best Don voice, somewhat undermined by the child hanging off his neck like a demented koala. "Let's move this party to the garden. I hear there's ice cream out there."

A chorus of excited squeals erupts as Dante marches toward the garden, his giggling entourage in tow.

Enzo watches with relief, running a hand through his disheveled hair. He offers me a weary smile. "I swear those boys listen to him more than they do to me."

I laugh, patting Enzo's shoulder sympathetically. "Don't worry, I'm sure that'll change . . . in about sixteen years. Or whenever they decide to stage their first coup."

Enzo groans good-naturedly, and we share a chuckle that's equal parts amusement and existential dread. As we follow the parade of mayhem out to the garden, I see that the event planners have brought to life exactly what Sophie and I wanted for the twins' first birthday and Dante's thirty-second: one part Sesame Street, one part 'The Godfather', and all parts utterly amazing.

I find Sophie in the kitchen, her dark hair swept up in an elegant updo that makes her look even more radiant than usual. She's in the middle of what looks like a delicate negotiation with the curly-haired twins, Aldo and Celia, trying to get them to eat their vegetables. The elaborate birthday cake on the counter seems to be both the carrot and the stick in this particular battle.

"Just a few more bites, sweethearts," Sophie coaxes, her voice a mix of sweetness and determination that I've come to admire. "Then you can have cake, I promise."

I sidle up next to her, grinning at the scene. "How's it going, Supermom? Need me to play good cop or bad cop?"

Sophie's eyes light up when she sees me. "Addy! Thank God you're here. I was starting to wonder if Dante had whisked you off for some 'private celebrating'."

We share a laugh, both of us all too familiar with Dante's tendency—and let's face it, mine also—to misbehave in public. "And speaking of missing in action," she continues, "what's this about Kira not coming? I was looking forward to having her spin something perfect for our dual theme."

"Triple theme," I correct, "if you count the mommies' corner. But yeah, Kira got a last-minute gig in Fiji. She was invited to some reality TV dating show to 'treat the couples to a good time'."

As if on cue, the music changes to something upbeat.

"She would have had to fly for that," Sophie muses, and I can see her connecting the dots.

"Yes, she had to. She was going to have to break the fear at some point. But I don't think she's by herself."

"No, it would seem not." Sophie's smile widens, and I can tell she's thinking the same thing I am. "It just so happens that Sal has conveniently taken a week's leave of absence."

We share a look that speaks volumes. Everyone and their blind grandmother can see the attraction between Kira and Sal. Despite Kira's initial giddiness over him, she's now playing it cool, insisting that they're "just friends".

I sigh, hoping that whatever is truly going on between those two isn't too complicated. Knowing Kira, we'd be lucky if we find out they're dating before the wedding invitations arrive.

Just then, Nico sweeps into the kitchen, exuding his usual mix of suave confidence and fatherly warmth. I watch as he plants kisses on Sophie and the twins before turning to me with open arms. I step into his hug, grateful for how close we've become.

Once I got beyond his Don persona, I realized Dante is right about him. They are polar opposites yet also the same. Nico has Dante's warmth and humor on the inside, while Dante embodies all of Nico's ruthless intensity once you scratch his playful surface. It's a complexity I'm still unraveling.

"Addy," Nico says, holding me at arm's length, his hands gently gripping my arms. "Thank you for doing this for Dante. He never takes the time to enjoy the spotlight—it's like trying to get George to take a bath."

I chuckle. George is even fatter now, what with the twins' habit of feeding him the bits of veggies they don't want. Sophie has had to keep him on a strict meal plan.

"I know, Dante is always too busy looking out for everyone else."

"True, but so are you, too, Addy," Nico points out. "You're just like him."

A flush of pride warms my cheeks at the comparison. Being likened to Dante feels like a high compliment. I duck my head, trying to hide my pleased smile.

"Speaking of," Nico continues, his eyes twinkling as if he caught my reaction, "you might want to head outside. There's about twenty Power Rangers there, and a few have been asking for you." He nods toward the garden.

"Twenty!" Sophie and I exclaim in unison, sharing a look of 'what the hell?'

"Give or take," Nico shrugs. "I thought you wanted them here?"

"I did, but I only mentioned the party in passing to a couple of them, not really expecting so many to turn up." The Power Foundation, now affectionately called 'Power Rangers' by Dante and the rest of the men, now supports close to fifty women.

This turnout is unexpected but heartening.

I scan the crowd, taking in the 'Power Rangers' mingling with the guests. Each face tells a story of survival. My gaze lingers on the petite brunette in a fuchsia dress, chatting with a few moms. She throws her head back and laughs at what one of them is saying.

"Can you believe Mezhen? Out in the open and mingling," I murmur to Sophie, nodding toward the petite brunette.

Sophie follows my gaze, her eyes widening slightly. "I'm so proud of how much progress she's made in one year."

Mezhen not only had a severe case of Stockholm syndrome, but she also suffered from mild agoraphobia. But she was determined to get better and continues pushing herself daily. Her progress is a testament to the Power Foundation's work.

Nico's voice pulls me from my reverie. "Those women adore you, Addy. They'd go to war for you." His eyes light up, and I'm instantly wary of his next words.

"Actually, speaking of loyal soldiers—" Nico begins, a new idea clearly forming.

Sophie gives him a playful shove. "No thank you, Don Vitelli. Leave Addy's women alone. She's not running a paramilitary organization here."

Nico laughs, scooping up the twins with ease. As he heads out, he calls over his shoulder, "Well, we don't think you're fully 'empowered' until you know how to break a man's arm in three places."

Sophie rolls her eyes, but as we head into the garden the wheels start to turn in my head.

It's not such a terrible idea, actually.

The party spreads over the massive grounds in three groups, each about fifty yards apart and with its own decor. The groups are close enough for convenience, but also far enough to pretend we're not all part of the same circus. The event planner was well worth every penny spent.

Nearest to the house is the children's party, a wild jumble of color and noise. Tables laden with treats dot the area. A "pirate" entertainer, who I'm pretty sure is actually one of Dante's enforcers in a costume, is captivating the rugrats with magic tricks.

Nearby, a giant piñata in the shape of a treasure chest dangles enticingly as blindfolded children flail at it with more enthusiasm than accuracy. A small soft play area sits to the side, more to the speed for toddlers like Aldo and Celia to roll around in.

By the tranquil lakeside, the men's gathering provides a stark contrast. Chicago's most lethal—and arguably most attractive—men surround Dante, sipping cocktails and exchanging good-natured barbs in rapid-fire Italian. Their voices carry across the water, and I find myself unconsciously translating snippets of their conversation, pleased at my growing grasp of the language.

It's the least I can do, considering how many languages Dante juggles. In our world, 'hello' in a certain language can mean anything from a warm welcome to a deadly warning, depending on who's saying it and where their loyalties lie.

My gaze lingers on the group of men. Mafiosos aren't supposed to be this appealing, really. Their sculpted, tattooed bodies are barely concealed by expertly tailored suits—a necessity to hide their holsters. Not that their kids haven't seen those guns before, but discretion is always desired in public. So instead of casual wear, it's Armani and Brioni for these men.

I notice the guards strategically placed around the perimeter and the subtle hum of drones in the air. Paranoia, thy name is The Outfit. But I get it, their most precious possessions are here. Letting their guard down completely would be unthinkable.

Finally, I turn my attention to the "normal" party. Wait staff weave through the crowd like ninjas, refilling drinks and offering hors d'oeuvres. The Power Rangers engage in animated conversation, mostly with each other and some of the parents not occupied with child-minding duties.

I can't help noticing some of them casting longing glances toward the lakeside gathering. Old habits die hard, I suppose. Those women have tasted danger; I doubt they'll ever be satisfied with ordinary men again.

Just then, Sophie joins me, following my gaze and noting the same thing.

"I wonder how long it'll take them to sidle toward the lakeside?" Sophie remarks.

I nod, unsure it was a good idea to put them in sighting distance of those hot-as-hell red flags. "PTSD much?"

Sophie follows my gaze and shakes her head. "Not PTSD, Addy. Just plain ol' temptation calling. Good thing kids are here. Otherwise, we could be hosting the prelude to an orgy."

I snort. "Not that it could ever stop them. Hello, cell phone and locked doors."

Sophie's phone rings, slicing through our conversation. She answers with an uncharacteristic eye roll that makes me wonder who is at the other end.

"Yeah, just come in," she says with exaggerated patience. "I promise there are no bioweapons with your name on it."

Sophie pauses to listen, then her expression morphs into one of exasperated fondness. "Cade, you do realize this is a kids' party, don't you? You're going to have to smile at a lot more people than just me and the twins. Lucky for you, it's also Dante's birthday. So I suggest you put out the fire on your breath, and try not to scare the children. We're in the garden."

She hangs up with a theatrical sigh. "Gotta love him."

My eyebrows shoot up. "Cade Quinn is here? I thought he hates Nico."

Sophie snorts. "He hates everyone. Well, except kids, and women—when they're in trouble. Not so sure about when they're not."

I feel a spark of curiosity. I've heard so much about this enigmatic brother of Sophie's, the man who indirectly propelled me toward my new career. My mind races with questions, but before I can ask any of them, the atmosphere shifts.

As if summoned by our gossip, a man appears at the large patio leading to the house. He scans the crowd for approximately half a second before making a beeline for us, moving through the sea of guests like Moses with a hangover. I watch, fascinated, as people instinctively step out of his way, their conversations faltering mid-sentence.

Holy shit. And I thought Nico looked dangerous. Cade Quinn is a fucking natural disaster in human form.

The first thing that strikes me is his raw, untamed beauty—and I use that term loosely, like calling a hurricane 'breezy'. Dark blonde hair that's just shy of 'I've been electrocuted' and more tattoos than skin. His simple T-shirt, leather jacket, and jeans ensemble screams 'I could kill you with my pinky, but I'd rather not get blood on my boots'. He holds two large stuffed animals.

As he approaches, I can't help but notice how his movements are both fluid and predatory. It's like watching a panther stalk through a cocktail party.

He reaches us, and while his face remains stoic, something in his eyes softens imperceptibly when he looks at Sophie.

Sophie throws an arm around him in a bone-crushing hug. "Missed you, Cade!"

Cade simply drops a kiss on her head, endures the hug for a couple more seconds then gently disengages.

"Are you okay, Sparrow?" he asks Sophie, his voice like gravel being crushed by a steamroller. The concern in his tone contrasts sharply with his intimidating presence.

I notice one of the teddies is wearing a black eyepatch, a red bandanna, and what looks like a leather cut. The other looks to be in a police uniform.

"Of course I'm alright." Sophie retorts, her chin jutting slightly. "Why wouldn't I be?"

Cade's lips twitch. "Oh, I don't know. Maybe because you're surrounded by a bunch of overgrown tigers?"

Sophie smirks. "Says the bad-tempered T-Rex. Anyway, here's Addy." She turns to me. "Addy is Dante's wife, and she runs that charity I told you about. Addy, my big brother, Cade."

Cade's gaze swings to me, and I beam at him. "Hello, Cade."

His eyes, a shade of green I've never seen before, meet mine briefly before scanning the area, then comes back to rest on mine.

When he says nothing, I continue. "I feel like I know you already, but yeah, thanks again for . . . you know, your help with the Shadow gang situation. And getting the women out."

At the mention of Shadow gang, the ghost of a smile flickers across Cade's face, gone so fast I almost think I imagined it. He gives a short nod, his fingers tapping once against his leg.

Seconds tick by, stretching into what feels like minutes. I resist the urge to fidget under his gaze. His look isn't lustful or hostile—it's assessing, like he's piecing together a puzzle.

Sophie eventually pokes him in the side, breaking the tension. "Use your words, Cade," she mutters.

He grunts, "Right, Addy. You're welcome."

His tone is neutral but not cold. It's direct and lacking in social niceties, but I find myself unbothered by it. There's something refreshing about his straightforward manner.

And then to my surprise, Mezhen sidles up to us, her face redder than a fire truck at a chili cook-off. "Hi, it's Special Agent Quinn, isn't it?" she squeaks. Her English has improved a lot, but it still carries the lilt of her native accent.

Cade's gaze flicks to her briefly before looking away. "At your service," he says, his tone unchanged. If he recognizes her, he gives no indication. I realize with a start that this is just who he is—uninterested in, or perhaps incapable of, the social niceties most of us take for granted.

Sophie, ever the tactful hostess, smoothly cuts in. "Oh, Mezhen, exactly the person I wanted to catch. Can you help me tear the twins away from their toy war so they can meet their uncle?" I can see the disappointment on Mezhen's face as Sophie leads her away.

Once we're alone, I face Cade again, and I already know he'll be perfectly comfortable standing there, silent until Sophie gets back. But if there's something I've learned from Dante, it's how effective poking the bear can be.

So I take a breath and say. "I hated Sean, you know—Sean Hall. My husband for, I don't know, all of two hours. He was the head of the Shadow gang."

Cade just continues to look at me.

"But of course, you know who Sean was. Anyway, in those few hours of marriage, I found out what pure hatred tasted like. And now, I love Dante more than I thought possible to love a person."

Cade's bored expression morphs into one of mild nausea. Gratified by his reaction, I press on. "But here's the kicker," I lean in slightly as if sharing a secret, "Hate feels so much better than love. Hate is a furnace that warms you from the inside while you plot your revenge. Love? Love's a mindfuck that turns you into a drooling idiot."

I notice a slight narrowing of the eyes, and a twitch at the corner of his mouth. He's listening, really listening.

"Your point?" Cade finally asks, his tone neutral but his body language more engaged than I've seen it since he arrived.

I glance pointedly at the teddy bears in his hand, the sight of the custom-made soft toys in his big tattooed hands striking me anew. "You hate Nico Vitelli. And yet," I nod toward where he is standing with the rest of the men by the lake, "there he is living and breathing free air, not even close to seeing the inside of a prison cell. And here you are, with two well-thought-out presents for his kids."

The corner of his mouth quirks up and he tilts his head, regarding me with newfound interest. "Missing your old job, Valentina?"

I don't even bother asking how he knows my real name. The man probably knows what I had for breakfast three Tuesdays ago. Instead, I meet his gaze squarely, a smirk playing on my lips. "Nah. I've just gotten better at profiling criminals."

And then, the impossible happens. Cade throws his head back and laughs—a real, genuine laugh that sounds like it's being torn from his very soul. The sound is startling in its richness and depth, completely at odds with his earlier demeanor. It's like watching a statue come to life.

Sophie returns with the twins, her eyes wide with shock as she takes in the scene. Dante also materializes beside me, tension rolling off him. I can practically see the wheels turning in his head as he tries to make sense of what he's witnessing.

Cade, still chuckling, drops the teddies and scoops up the twins, who are already squealing, their chubby limbs kicking in excitement.

As Cade lets the twins pull on his necklace and hair and everything else they can reach, Dante leans in to whisper, his breath warm against my ear, "What the fuck just happened?"

I shrug, still a bit shell-shocked myself. "No clue. We were just talking." But even as I whisper it, I realize it's not entirely true.

Dante turns to Cade with a smile that looks more like a baring of fangs. "Quinn. Didn't think you'd show."

"Chicago's finest all in one place? Couldn't resist." The sarcasm in his voice is thick enough to cut with a knife, but I sense there's no real venom behind it. Or maybe that's just my naïve desire to have everyone get along.

As Cade abruptly turns away, presumably to play with the twins in peace, he tosses a "thanks" to Dante. The casual way he says it like he's thanking Dante for passing the salt, catches my attention.

Dante's eyebrows furrow, voicing the confusion we're all feeling. "For what?"

Without turning, he says, "The Shadow gang was never on my radar. But they proved very useful in the end."

And with that cryptic bombshell, he heads for the kids section. As I watch him walk away, I know he's a man who operates outside the norms of society, dangerous and unpredictable, yet capable of incredible acts of heroism. Like all the other men in my life.

I turn to Dante, "Well," I say, a grin spreading across my face, "that was interesting."

"Fucking weirdo," Dante mutters.

I clear my throat pointedly, and Dante has the grace to look sorry, and then he pulls Sophie into an apologetic hug.

"Bella," he huffs, "you know your brother."

"I know you too," Sophie replies, then she turns to me. "By the way, what did you say that got Cade laughing?"

I admit, "I think it was because I called him a criminal."

"I can see why Cade would love that." Sophie chuckles, shaking her head. "You do know he's an FBI agent, right?"

I shrug, and Sophie's laughter grows. "Yeah." *I also know he's a criminal.*

Dante pulls me close, his breath hot against my ear. "You disarming our arch-enemy in two minutes flat. Do you have any idea how sexy that is?"

I laugh, trying to play it cool despite the fire igniting in my core. "I was just playing host."

"And you're just my wife," Dante deadpans, his hands roaming possessively over my hips. "Maybe we should sic you on him permanently. To manage all negotiations relating to Cade Quinn and the FBI, since he and Nico can't string a single civil sentence between themselves."

"Why does he hate Nico so much anyway?"

Dante looks at me like it should be obvious. "Nico is Cade's worst nightmare, and he married his baby sister here. I don't think that ever gets forgiven."

We all share a laugh, but I can't help adding, "Actually, I think what he can't admit is how much he likes us."

Dante grunts, clearly uninterested in discussing Cade further. His hands tighten on my waist. "Can you come to your old room? I need to show you something real quick."

Sophie rolls her eyes and leaves us with an exasperated huff, and I whirl on Dante in mock outrage. "Dante! You can't just disappear from your own party!"

"It will only take a few minutes."

"Not a chance."

His eyes only darken with desire. "You, me, a house full of guests and a soundproofed room? It'll be a fucking warzone, *tesoro*. Not at all sure it's a chance you should be passing up."

The temptation is almost overwhelming. I bite my lip as I consider it. The responsible part of me knows we should stay, mingle, and be the perfect hosts. But the other part, the part that's been setting me on fire since I met this dangerous, irresistible man, is screaming to throw caution to the wind.

I lean in close, my lips brushing his ear. "I'll consider it . . . but only if you behave yourself for the rest of the party."

I hear Dante's sharp intake of breath. "Be there in ten minutes. Naked on the bed with your legs spread."

He saunters away, heading for the toddlers section. I watch as he tosses a squealing Luca in the air, laughing as if he's without a care in the world. As if he hasn't just torched my self-control and seized my breath. As if in exactly ten minutes, he won't be showing me again why I trust him with my body and soul.

I can't help but marvel at the turn my life has taken. From a shy woman desperately searching for clues to the puzzle that my life was. To a bold Mafia princess, a wife, and a mentor.

As I head toward the house to do as I'm told, I realize that whatever comes next, whatever challenges we face, one thing for certain: life with Dante Vitelli is never going to be boring.

And honestly? I wouldn't have it any other way.

THE END

Thanks for reading!
If you enjoyed this book, please consider leaving a review on Amazon

Read Nico's story here The Don's Deadly Games

Pre-Order Cade's story here The Outlaw's Savage Revenge

Acknowledgements

want to say thank you to my absolute rock of a man, Shawn, and to Muskaan Khan and Thea Santiago.

You guys rock

THE END

Thanks for reading!
If you enjoyed this book, please consider leaving a review on Amazon

Read Nico's story here The Don's Deadly Games

Pre-Order Cade's story here The Outlaw's Savage Revenge

Also by Judy Hale

TWISTED SAVIORS

The Don's Deadly Games

The Outlaw's Savage Revenge

NEW YORK BILLIONAIRES

Wanted By The Billionaire

Hello Billionaire Beast

The Nanny's Bossy Billionaire

The Damaged Billionaire's Obsession

The Playboy Billionaire's Fake Marriage

L.A FORBIDDEN MEN

Craving Dr. Silver Fox

Craving Professor Grump

KINGS AND SINNERS

Forged In Sin (Novella)

As you can probably tell, there are many more characters begging for their own stories. And yes, every single one of them will be told.

To ensure you are kept up to date about my newest releases, sign up for my newsletter

Acknowledgements

I want to say thank you to my absolute rock of a man, Shawn, and to Muskaan Khan and Thea Santiago.

You guys rock